A-Level Mathematics

A Comprehensive and Supportive Companion to the Unified Curriculum

WORKED SOLUTIONS

$$P(A|B) = \frac{P(A \cap B)}{P(B)}$$

$\sin(x)$

$2ab \leq a^2 + b^2$

$+ \dfrac{f(x_2)}{2} + \ldots + \dfrac{f(x_N)}{2}$

$\dfrac{d\sin(x)}{dx} = \cos(x)$

$\sin^2\left(\dfrac{\pi}{24}\right)$

Year 1

Editors/Authors:
Dr. Tom Bennison;
Dr. Edward Hall.

Contributing Authors:
Rob Beckett;
Katie Binks;
Kieran Fitness;
Dr. Jenny Gladstone;
Dr. David Marles;
Stuart Price;
Matilde Warden;
Dr. Tom Wicks.

©2017 Tarquin Publications and the Authors
Book: ISBN 978 1 911093 36 7
EBook: ISBN 978 1 911093 41 1

Printed in the UK
All rights reserved.

Tarquin Publications
Suite 74, 17 Holywell Hill
St Albans
AL1 1DT
UK
www.tarquingroup.com

Contents

1. Worked Solutions - Chapters 2 to 6 5
2. Worked Solutions - Chapters 7 to 11 105
3. Worked Solutions - Chapters 12 to 16 176
4. Worked Solutions - Chapters 17 to 21 267
5. Worked Solutions - Chapters 22 to 27 298
6. Worked Solutions - Chapters 28 to 31 351

1. Worked Solutions - Chapters 2 to 6

Worked Solutions — Exercise 2.1

Q1. (a)
$$2^3 \times 2^5 = 2^{3+5}$$
$$= 2^8$$

(b)
$$275^0 = 1$$

(c)
$$49^{\frac{1}{2}} = \sqrt{49}$$
$$= 7$$

(d)
$$8^{-2} = \frac{1}{8^2}$$
$$= \frac{1}{64}$$

(e)
$$25^{-\frac{1}{2}} = \frac{1}{25^{\frac{1}{2}}}$$
$$= \frac{1}{\sqrt{25}}$$

(f)
$$32^{\frac{4}{5}} = \left(32^{\frac{1}{5}}\right)^4$$
$$= \left(\sqrt[5]{32}\right)^4$$
$$= 2^4$$
$$= 16$$

(g)
$$\left(\frac{625}{81}\right)^{\frac{3}{4}} = \left(\left(\frac{625}{81}\right)^{\frac{1}{4}}\right)^3$$
$$= \left(\frac{\sqrt[4]{625}}{\sqrt[4]{81}}\right)^3$$
$$= \left(\frac{5}{3}\right)^3$$
$$= \frac{125}{27}$$

(h)
$$36^{1.5} = 36^{\frac{3}{2}}$$
$$= \left(\sqrt{36}\right)^3$$
$$= 6^3$$
$$= 216$$

(i)
$$\left(\frac{4}{9}\right)^{-2} = \frac{1}{\left(\frac{4}{9}\right)^2}$$
$$= \frac{1}{\frac{4^2}{9^2}}$$
$$= \frac{1}{\frac{16}{81}}$$
$$= \frac{81}{16}$$

(j)
$$\left(\frac{32}{243}\right)^{-\frac{3}{5}} = \frac{1}{\left(\frac{32}{243}\right)^{\frac{3}{5}}}$$
$$= \frac{1}{\left(\left(\frac{32}{243}\right)^{\frac{1}{5}}\right)^3}$$
$$= \frac{1}{\left(\frac{\sqrt[5]{32}}{\sqrt[5]{243}}\right)^3}$$
$$= \frac{1}{\left(\frac{2}{3}\right)^3}$$
$$= \frac{1}{\frac{8}{27}}$$
$$= \frac{27}{8}$$

Q2. (a)
$$x^3 \times x^5 = x^{3+5}$$
$$= x^8$$

(b)
$$(2y)^4 \times 3y^2 = 16y^4 \times 3y^2$$
$$= 48y^6$$

(c)
$$20x^8 \div 30x^2 = \frac{20x^8}{30x^2}$$
$$= \frac{2}{3}x^{8-2}$$
$$= \frac{2}{3}x^6$$

(d)
$$\frac{12xy^3 \times 3x^5}{2x^2 y} = \frac{36x^{1+6}y^3}{2x^2 y}$$
$$= \frac{36x^6 y^3}{2x^2 y}$$
$$= 18x^{6-2}y^{3-1}$$
$$= 18x^4 y^2$$

(e)
$$\left(\frac{2}{x^2}\right)^{-2} = \frac{1}{\left(\frac{2}{x^2}\right)^2}$$
$$= \frac{1}{\frac{4}{x^4}}$$
$$= \frac{x^4}{4}$$

(f)
$$(7x^2y^{-1})^{-2} = \frac{1}{(7x^2y^{-1})^2}$$
$$= \frac{1}{49x^4y^{-2}}$$
$$= \frac{y^2}{49x^4}$$

(g)
$$\frac{1}{x^{-3}} = x^3$$

(h)
$$(8x^6)^{\frac{1}{3}} \times 2x^{\frac{1}{2}} = (2x^2) \times 2x^{\frac{1}{2}}$$
$$= 4x^{2+\frac{1}{2}}$$
$$= 4x^{\frac{5}{2}}$$

(i)
$$\sqrt{x} \times \sqrt[4]{x} = x^{\frac{1}{2}} \times x^{\frac{1}{4}}$$
$$= x^{\frac{2}{4}} \times x^{\frac{1}{4}}$$
$$= x^{\frac{3}{4}}$$

(j)
$$\frac{\sqrt[3]{x} \times x^2}{\sqrt{x}} = \frac{x^{\frac{1}{3}+2}}{x^{\frac{1}{2}}}$$
$$= \frac{x^{\frac{7}{3}}}{x^{\frac{1}{2}}}$$
$$= x^{\frac{11}{6}}$$

Q3. (a)

$$7^x = \frac{1}{49}$$
$$\Rightarrow 7^x = \frac{1}{7^2}$$
$$\Rightarrow 7^x = 7^{-2}$$
$$\Rightarrow x = -2$$

(b)

$$3^x \times 27^{x-1} = 243$$
$$\Rightarrow 3^x \times (3^3)^{x-1} = 3^5$$
$$\Rightarrow 3^x \times 3^{3x-3} = 3^5$$
$$\Rightarrow 3^{4x-3} = 3^5$$
$$\Rightarrow 4x - 3 = 5$$
$$\Rightarrow 4x = 8$$
$$\Rightarrow x = 2$$

(c)

$$5^{2x} = 125^{1-3x}$$
$$\Rightarrow 5^{2x} = 5^{3(1-3x)}$$
$$\Rightarrow 2x = 3(1 - 3x)$$
$$\Rightarrow 2x = 3 - 9x$$
$$\Rightarrow 11x = 3$$
$$\Rightarrow x = \frac{3}{11}$$

(d)

$$9^{2x+1} = 27^{5-x}$$
$$\Rightarrow 3^{2(2x+1)} = 3^{3(5-x)}$$
$$\Rightarrow 2(2x+1) = 3(5-x)$$
$$\Rightarrow 4x + 2 = 15 - 3x$$
$$\Rightarrow 7x = 13$$
$$\Rightarrow x = \frac{13}{7}$$

(e)
$$16 - 8^{x-4} = 0$$
$$\Rightarrow 2^4 = 2^{3(x-4)}$$
$$\Rightarrow 4 = 3(x-4)$$
$$\Rightarrow 4 = 3x - 12$$
$$\Rightarrow 16 = 3x$$
$$\Rightarrow x = \frac{16}{3}$$

(f)
$$\left(\frac{1}{4}\right)^{x+2} = \sqrt[3]{8}$$
$$\Rightarrow \left(2^{-2}\right)^{x+2} = \sqrt[3]{2^3}$$
$$\Rightarrow 2^{-2(x+2)} = 2$$
$$\Rightarrow -2(x+2) = 1$$
$$\Rightarrow -2x - 4 = 1$$
$$\Rightarrow -2x = 5$$
$$\Rightarrow x = -\frac{5}{2}$$

(g)
$$\frac{2^{3x+1}}{4^{2-x}} = \frac{8^{2x}}{16}$$
$$\Rightarrow \frac{2^{3x+1}}{(2^2)^{2-x}} = \frac{(2^3)^{2x}}{2^4}$$
$$\Rightarrow \frac{2^{3x+1}}{2^{4-2x}} = \frac{2^{6x}}{2^4}$$
$$\Rightarrow 2^{(3x+1)-(4-2x)} = 2^{6x-4}$$
$$\Rightarrow 2^{5x-3} = 2^{6x-4}$$
$$\Rightarrow 5x - 3 = 6x - 4$$
$$\Rightarrow x = 1$$

Worked Solutions — Exercise 2.2

Q1. (a) $\sqrt{5} \times \sqrt{5} = \sqrt{25} = 5$
(b) $\sqrt{8} \times \sqrt{2} = \sqrt{16} = 4$
(c) $2\sqrt{7} \times 3\sqrt{7} = 6\sqrt{49} = 42$
(d) $\sqrt{12} \times \sqrt{3} = \sqrt{36} = 6$
(e) $\frac{\sqrt{30}}{\sqrt{5}} = \sqrt{6}$
(f) $\frac{\sqrt{24}}{\sqrt{3}} = \sqrt{8} = \sqrt{4 \times 2} = 2\sqrt{2}$

(g) $\frac{\sqrt{180}}{\sqrt{5}} = \sqrt{36} = 6$

(h) $\frac{\sqrt{5}}{\sqrt{20}} = \sqrt{\frac{1}{4}} = \frac{1}{2}$

Q2. (a) $\sqrt{18} = \sqrt{9 \times 2} = 3\sqrt{2}$

(b) $\sqrt{120} = \sqrt{4 \times 30} = 2\sqrt{30}$

(c) $\sqrt{72} = \sqrt{36 \times 2} = 6\sqrt{2}$

(d) $\sqrt{24} = \sqrt{4 \times 6} = 2\sqrt{6}$

(e) $\sqrt{20} + \sqrt{5} = 2\sqrt{5} + \sqrt{5} = 3\sqrt{5}$

(f) $\sqrt{12} + \sqrt{12} = 2\sqrt{3} + 2\sqrt{3} = 4\sqrt{3}$

(g) $\sqrt{8} + \sqrt{50} = 2\sqrt{2} + 5\sqrt{2} = 7\sqrt{2}$

(h) $3\sqrt{27} + \sqrt{48} = 9\sqrt{3} + 4\sqrt{3} = 13\sqrt{3}$

Q3. (a) $(2+\sqrt{3})(2-\sqrt{3}) = 4 - 2\sqrt{3} + 2\sqrt{3} - 3 = 1$

(b) $(1-2\sqrt{5})^2 = 1 - 2\sqrt{5} - 2\sqrt{5} + 4 \times 5 = 21 - 4\sqrt{5}$

(c) $(2\sqrt{2}+\sqrt{3})(3\sqrt{2}+2\sqrt{3}) = 6 \times 2 + 4\sqrt{6} + 3\sqrt{6} + 2 \times 3 = 18 + 7\sqrt{6}$

(d) $(\sqrt{3}+\sqrt{5})(\sqrt{3}+\sqrt{7}) = 3 + \sqrt{3}\sqrt{7} + \sqrt{5}\sqrt{3} + \sqrt{5}\sqrt{7} = 3 + \sqrt{21} + \sqrt{15} + \sqrt{35}$

Q4. (a) $\frac{1}{\sqrt{7}} = \frac{1}{\sqrt{7}} \times \frac{\sqrt{7}}{\sqrt{7}} = \frac{\sqrt{7}}{7}$

(b) $\frac{20}{\sqrt{5}} = \frac{20}{\sqrt{5}} \times \frac{\sqrt{5}}{\sqrt{5}} = \frac{20\sqrt{5}}{5} = 4\sqrt{5}$

(c) $\frac{\sqrt{7}}{\sqrt{2}} = \frac{\sqrt{7}}{\sqrt{2}} \times \frac{\sqrt{2}}{\sqrt{2}} = \frac{\sqrt{14}}{2}$

(d) $\frac{3\sqrt{10}}{2\sqrt{15}} = \frac{3\sqrt{10}}{2\sqrt{15}} \times \frac{\sqrt{15}}{\sqrt{15}} = \frac{3\sqrt{150}}{30} = \frac{15\sqrt{6}}{30} = \frac{\sqrt{6}}{2}$

(e) $\frac{1}{4+\sqrt{2}} = \frac{1}{4+\sqrt{2}} \times \frac{4-\sqrt{2}}{4-\sqrt{2}}$

$= \frac{4-\sqrt{2}}{16 - \sqrt{2} + \sqrt{2} - 2}$

$= \frac{4-\sqrt{2}}{14}.$

(f) $\frac{12}{\sqrt{5}-1} = \frac{12}{\sqrt{5}-1} \times \frac{\sqrt{5}+1}{\sqrt{5}+1}$

$= \frac{12(\sqrt{5}+1)}{5 + \sqrt{5} - \sqrt{5} - 1}$

$= \frac{12(\sqrt{5}+1)}{4}$

$= 3\sqrt{5} + 3.$

(g) $\frac{2+\sqrt{2}}{\sqrt{2}-2} = \frac{2+\sqrt{2}}{\sqrt{2}-2} \times \frac{\sqrt{2}+2}{\sqrt{2}+2}$

$= \frac{4 + 2\sqrt{2} + 2\sqrt{2} + 2}{2 + 2\sqrt{2} - 2\sqrt{2} - 4}$

$= \frac{6 + 4\sqrt{2}}{-2}$

$= -3 - 2\sqrt{2}.$

(h) $\dfrac{5+2\sqrt{3}}{4-\sqrt{3}} = \dfrac{5+2\sqrt{3}}{4-\sqrt{3}} \times \dfrac{4+\sqrt{3}}{4+\sqrt{3}}$

$= \dfrac{20+5\sqrt{3}+8\sqrt{3}+6}{16+4\sqrt{3}-4\sqrt{3}-3}$

$= \dfrac{26+13\sqrt{3}}{13}$

$= 2+\sqrt{3}.$

Worked Solutions — Exercise 3.1

Q1. (a) $\overrightarrow{AB} = \overrightarrow{AO} + \overrightarrow{OB} = -\mathbf{a} + \mathbf{b} = \mathbf{b} - \mathbf{a}.$

(b) $\overrightarrow{BA} = -\overrightarrow{AB} = -(\mathbf{b} - \mathbf{a}) = \mathbf{a} - \mathbf{b}.$ Alternatively, we can complete the full calculation from the diagram: $\overrightarrow{BA} = \overrightarrow{BO} + \overrightarrow{OB} = -\mathbf{b} + \mathbf{a} = \mathbf{a} - \mathbf{b}.$

(c) $\overrightarrow{BC} = \overrightarrow{BO} + \overrightarrow{OB} = -\mathbf{b} + \mathbf{c} = \mathbf{c} - \mathbf{b}.$

(d) $\overrightarrow{AC} = \overrightarrow{AO} + \overrightarrow{OC} = -\mathbf{a} + \mathbf{c} = \mathbf{c} - \mathbf{a}.$ Note that we could also have constructed a different path, e.g. $\overrightarrow{AC} = \overrightarrow{AB} + \overrightarrow{BC} = (\mathbf{b} - \mathbf{a}) + (\mathbf{c} - \mathbf{b}) = \mathbf{c} - \mathbf{a}$, which is identical in terms of $\mathbf{a}$, $\mathbf{b}$ and $\mathbf{c}$.

Q2. Since M is the midpoint of AB, we have

$$\overrightarrow{OM} = \overrightarrow{OA} + \tfrac{1}{2}\overrightarrow{AB}.$$

We know that $\overrightarrow{OA} = \mathbf{a}$, but we need to express $\overrightarrow{AB}$ in terms of $\mathbf{a}$ and $\mathbf{b}$.

$$\overrightarrow{AB} = \overrightarrow{AO} + \overrightarrow{OB} = -\mathbf{a} + \mathbf{b} = \mathbf{b} - \mathbf{a}.$$

Hence,

$$\overrightarrow{OM} = \mathbf{a} + \tfrac{1}{2}(\mathbf{b} - \mathbf{a}) = \tfrac{1}{2}(\mathbf{a} + \mathbf{b}).$$

Q3. (a) The complete force diagram with the resultant force **R** is shown below. We have also used the fact that parallel vectors are equal to complete the right-angled triangle with hypotenuse **R**.

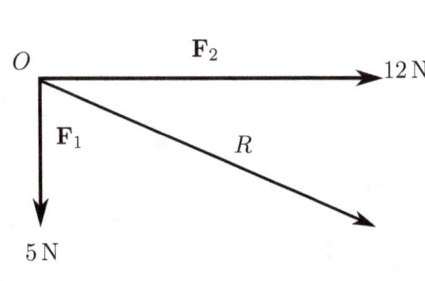

(b) The magnitude of the force **R** is equivalent to its geometric length, R in the diagram. Using Pythagoras for the right-angled triangle with perpendicular sides of length 5 and 12, we obtain
$$R = \sqrt{(5\,\text{N})^2 + (12\,\text{N})^2} = 13\,\text{N}.$$

(c) The angle θ between **R** and $\mathbf{F}_2$ is given by
$$\theta = \arctan\left(\frac{5}{12}\right) \approx 0.395\,\text{radians}.$$

Q4. To answer this question, first sketch the vectors described in the question.

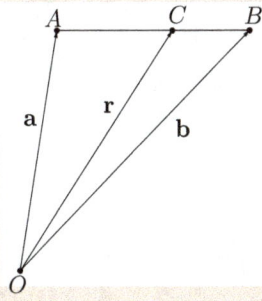

Let the position vector of C be **r**. Then
$$\overrightarrow{AC} = \frac{4}{5}\overrightarrow{AB}, \quad \text{where } \overrightarrow{AB} = \mathbf{b} - \mathbf{a}.$$

Hence,
$$\mathbf{r} = \mathbf{a} + \frac{4}{5}(\mathbf{b} - \mathbf{a}) = \frac{1}{5}\mathbf{a} + \frac{4}{5}\mathbf{b}.$$

Q5. Consider the sketch of the vectors **a** and **b** described in the question below.

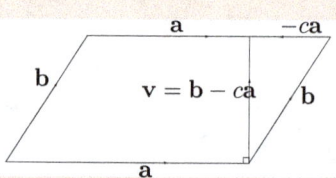

We construct $\mathbf{v} = \mathbf{b} - c\mathbf{a}$ by choosing c such that $v\mathbf{v}$ is perpendicular to $\mathbf{a}$. The diagram shows that $\mathbf{v}$ is the vector in the direction of the perpendicular height of the parallelogram and that the length of $\mathbf{v}$, $|\mathbf{v}|$, is the perpendicular height of the parallelogram.

Q6. First, sketch the triangle ABC, marking the midpoints P and Q of AB and AC respectively.

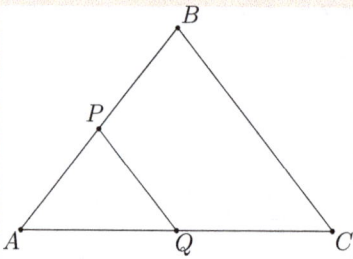

Let $\mathbf{a}$, $\mathbf{b}$, $\mathbf{c}$, $\mathbf{p}$ and $\mathbf{q}$ be the position vectors of A, B, C, P and Q respectively. Then

$$\mathbf{p} = \frac{1}{2}(\mathbf{b} - \mathbf{a}), \text{ and } \mathbf{q} = \frac{1}{2}(\mathbf{c} - \mathbf{a}).$$

Then the vector $\overrightarrow{PQ}$ is given by

$$\overrightarrow{PQ} = \mathbf{q} - \mathbf{p} = \frac{1}{2}(\mathbf{c} - \mathbf{a} - \mathbf{b} + \mathbf{a}) = \frac{1}{2}(\mathbf{c} - \mathbf{b}).$$

The vector $\overrightarrow{BC} = \mathbf{c} - \mathbf{b}$, and therefore

$$\overrightarrow{PQ} = \frac{1}{2}\overrightarrow{BC}.$$

Hence, PQ is parallel to BC and the length of PQ is half the length of BC.

Q7. If $\alpha\mathbf{a} + \beta\mathbf{b} = \mathbf{0}$, then

$$\alpha\mathbf{a} = -\beta\mathbf{b}.$$

If $\mathbf{a}$ and $\mathbf{b}$ are nonzero vectors that are not parallel, then the only way to satisfy this equation is $\alpha = \beta = 0$.

Worked Solutions — Exercise 3.2

Q1. (a) $(1,1)$, $\begin{pmatrix} 1 \\ 1 \end{pmatrix}$. (b) $(2,0)$, $\begin{pmatrix} 2 \\ 0 \end{pmatrix}$. (c) $(0,-3)$, $\begin{pmatrix} 0 \\ -3 \end{pmatrix}$.

(d) $(3,2)$, $\begin{pmatrix} 3 \\ 2 \end{pmatrix}$. (e) $(-4,1)$, $\begin{pmatrix} -4 \\ 1 \end{pmatrix}$. (f) $\left(\frac{1}{2}, -\frac{3}{2}\right)$, $\begin{pmatrix} 1/2 \\ -3/2 \end{pmatrix}$.

Q2. (a) $|\mathbf{a}| = \sqrt{3^2 + 4^2} = \sqrt{25} = 5$. Then $\hat{\mathbf{a}} = \frac{3}{5}\mathbf{i} + \frac{4}{5}\mathbf{j}$.

(b) $|\mathbf{a}| = \sqrt{1^2 + (-2)^2} = \sqrt{5}$. Then $\hat{\mathbf{a}} = \frac{1}{\sqrt{5}}(1,-2)$.

(c) $|\mathbf{a}| = \sqrt{(-2)^2 + 4^2} = \sqrt{20} = 2\sqrt{5}$. Then $\hat{\mathbf{a}} = \frac{1}{2\sqrt{5}}\begin{pmatrix} -2 \\ 4 \end{pmatrix} = \frac{1}{\sqrt{5}}\begin{pmatrix} -1 \\ 2 \end{pmatrix}$.

(d) $|\mathbf{a}| = \sqrt{(-1)^2 + 1^2} = \sqrt{2}$. Then $\hat{\mathbf{a}} = \frac{1}{\sqrt{2}}(-1,1)$.

Q3. (a) $\overrightarrow{AB} = \mathbf{b} - \mathbf{a} = (0,1) - (1,1) = (-1,0)$. $|\overrightarrow{AB}| = \sqrt{(-1)^2 + 0^2} = 1$.

(b) $\overrightarrow{AB} = (1,-2) - (3,2) = (-2,-4)$. $|\overrightarrow{AB}| = \sqrt{(-2)^2 + (-4)^2} = \sqrt{20} = 2\sqrt{5}$.

(c) $\overrightarrow{AB} = (4,0) - (0,4) = (4,-4)$. $|\overrightarrow{AB}| = \sqrt{4^2 + (-4)^2} = \sqrt{32} = 4\sqrt{2}$.

(d) $\overrightarrow{AB} = (-2,3) - (5,4) = (-7,-1)$. $|\overrightarrow{AB}| = \sqrt{(-7)^2 + (-1)^2} = \sqrt{50} = 5\sqrt{2}$.

Q4. (a) $|\mathbf{a}| = \sqrt{3^2 + 4^2} = 5$, so $\hat{\mathbf{a}} = \frac{1}{5}(3,4)$. The desired vector is $9\hat{\mathbf{a}} = \frac{9}{5}(3,4)$.

(b) $|\mathbf{a}| = \sqrt{1^2 + (-2)^2} = \sqrt{5}$, so $\hat{\mathbf{a}} = \frac{1}{\sqrt{5}}(1,-2)$. The desired vector is $3\hat{\mathbf{a}} = \frac{3}{\sqrt{5}}(1,-2)$.

(c) $|\mathbf{a}| = \sqrt{(-4)^2 + 2^2} = \sqrt{20} = 2\sqrt{5}$, so $\hat{\mathbf{a}} = \frac{1}{2\sqrt{5}}(-4,2) = \frac{1}{\sqrt{5}}(-2,1)$. The desired vector is $\frac{1}{3}\hat{\mathbf{a}} = \frac{1}{3\sqrt{5}}(-2,1)$.

(d) $|\mathbf{a}| = \sqrt{2^2 + 2^2} = \sqrt{8} = 2\sqrt{2}$, so $\hat{\mathbf{a}} = \frac{1}{2\sqrt{2}}(2,2) = \frac{1}{\sqrt{2}}(1,1)$. The desired vector is $\sqrt{2}\hat{\mathbf{a}} = \frac{\sqrt{2}}{\sqrt{2}}(1,1) = (1,1)$.

Worked Solutions — Exercise 4.1

Q1. (a)   i. We use Formula 4.1 to calculate the distance $|AB|$.

$$|AB| = \sqrt{(x_B - x_A)^2 + (y_B - y_A)^2}$$
$$= \sqrt{(4-2)^2 + (4-2)^2}$$
$$= \sqrt{2^2 + 2^2}$$
$$= \sqrt{4 + 4}$$
$$= \sqrt{8}$$
$$= 2\sqrt{2}.$$

ii. Letting m represent the gradient of the line segment joining point A to point B and using Definition 4.1 we have,

$$m = \frac{y_B - y_A}{x_B - x_A}$$
$$= \frac{4-2}{4-2}$$
$$= \frac{2}{2}$$
$$= 1.$$

iii. We use Formula 4.2 to calculate the midpoint. Letting C represent this point, the x-coordinate of C is,

$$x_C = \frac{x_A + x_B}{2}$$
$$= \frac{2+4}{2}$$
$$= \frac{6}{2}$$
$$= 3.$$

Similarly, the y-coordinate is given by,

$$y_C = \frac{y_A + y_B}{2}$$
$$= \frac{2+4}{2}$$
$$= \frac{6}{2}$$
$$= 3.$$

Hence, the midpoint of AB is the following,

$$C = (3, 3).$$

(b) i. We use Formula 4.1 to calculate the distance $|AB|$.

$$\begin{aligned} |AB| &= \sqrt{(x_B - x_A)^2 + (y_B - y_A)^2} \\ &= \sqrt{(11-8)^2 + (2-5)^2} \\ &= \sqrt{3^2 + (-3)^2} \\ &= \sqrt{9+9} \\ &= \sqrt{18} \\ &= 3\sqrt{2}. \end{aligned}$$

ii. Letting m represent the gradient of the line segment joining point A to point B and using Definition 4.1 we have,

$$\begin{aligned} m &= \frac{y_B - y_A}{x_B - x_A} \\ &= \frac{2-5}{11-8} \\ &= \frac{-3}{3} \\ &= -1. \end{aligned}$$

iii. We use Formula 4.2 to calculate the midpoint. Letting C represent this point, the x-coordinate of C is,

$$\begin{aligned} x_C &= \frac{x_A + x_B}{2} \\ &= \frac{8+11}{2} \\ &= \frac{19}{2}. \end{aligned}$$

Similarly, the y-coordinate is given by,

$$\begin{aligned} y_C &= \frac{y_A + y_B}{2} \\ &= \frac{2+5}{2} \\ &= \frac{7}{2}. \end{aligned}$$

Hence, the midpoint of AB is the following,

$$C = \left(\frac{19}{2}, \frac{7}{2}\right).$$

(c) i. We use Formula 4.1 to calculate the distance $|AB|$.

$$|AB| = \sqrt{(x_B - x_A)^2 + (y_B - y_A)^2}$$
$$= \sqrt{(6-6)^2 + (3-(-3))^2}$$
$$= \sqrt{0^2 + 6^2}$$
$$= \sqrt{36}$$
$$= 6.$$

ii. Since point B is vertically above point A (*i.e.* their x-coordinates are the same, the gradient of the straight line segment AB is undefined.

iii. We use Formula 4.2 to calculate the midpoint. Letting C represent this point, the x-coordinate of C is,

$$x_C = \frac{x_A + x_B}{2}$$
$$= \frac{6+6}{2}$$
$$= \frac{12}{2}$$
$$= 6$$

Similarly, the y-coordinate is given by,

$$y_C = \frac{y_A + y_B}{2}$$
$$= \frac{(-3)+3}{2}$$
$$= \frac{0}{2}$$
$$= 0$$

Hence, the midpoint of AB is the following,

$$C = (6, 0).$$

(d) i. We use Formula 4.1 to calculate the distance $|AB|$.

$$|AB| = \sqrt{(x_B - x_A)^2 + (y_B - y_A)^2}$$
$$= \sqrt{(2-12)^2 + (5-7)^2}$$
$$= \sqrt{(-10)^2 + (-2)^2}$$
$$= \sqrt{100 + 4}$$
$$= \sqrt{104}$$
$$= 2\sqrt{26}.$$

ii. Letting m represent the gradient of the line segment joining point A to

point B and using Definition 4.1 we have,

$$m = \frac{y_B - y_A}{x_B - x_A}$$
$$= \frac{5 - 7}{2 - 12}$$
$$= \frac{-2}{-10}$$
$$= \frac{2}{10}$$
$$= \frac{1}{5}.$$

iii. We use Formula 4.2 to calculate the midpoint. Letting C represent this point, the x-coordinate of C is,

$$x_C = \frac{x_A + x_B}{2}$$
$$= \frac{12 + 2}{2}$$
$$= \frac{14}{2}$$
$$= 7.$$

Similarly, the y-coordinate is given by,

$$y_C = \frac{y_A + y_B}{2}$$
$$= \frac{7 + 5}{2}$$
$$= \frac{12}{2}$$
$$= 6.$$

Hence, the midpoint of AB is the following,

$$C = (7, 6).$$

(e) i. We use Formula 4.1 to calculate the distance $|AB|$.

$$|AB| = \sqrt{(x_B - x_A)^2 + (y_B - y_A)^2}$$
$$= \sqrt{(3 - (-3))^2 + ((-3) - 6)^2}$$
$$= \sqrt{6^2 + (-9)^2}$$
$$= \sqrt{36 + 81}$$
$$= \sqrt{117}$$
$$= 3\sqrt{13}.$$

ii. Letting m represent the gradient of the line segment joining point A to

point B and using Definition 4.1 we have,

$$m = \frac{y_B - y_A}{x_B - x_A}$$
$$= \frac{-3 - 6}{3 - (-3)}$$
$$= \frac{-9}{6}$$
$$= \frac{-3}{2}.$$

iii. We use Formula 4.2 to calculate the midpoint. Letting C represent this point, the x-coordinate of C is,

$$x_C = \frac{x_A + x_B}{2}$$
$$= \frac{(-3) + 3}{2}$$
$$= \frac{0}{2}$$
$$= 0.$$

Similarly, the y-coordinate is given by,

$$y_C = \frac{y_A + y_B}{2}$$
$$= \frac{6 + (-3)}{2}$$
$$= \frac{3}{2}.$$

Hence, the midpoint of AB is the following,

$$C = \left(0, \frac{3}{2}\right).$$

(f) i. We use Formula 4.1 to calculate the distance $|AB|$.

$$|AB| = \sqrt{(x_B - x_A)^2 + (y_B - y_A)^2}$$
$$= \sqrt{(15 - 11)^2 + (6 - (-2))^2}$$
$$= \sqrt{4^2 + 8^2}$$
$$= \sqrt{16 + 64}$$
$$= \sqrt{80}$$
$$= 4\sqrt{5}.$$

ii. Letting m represent the gradient of the line segment joining point A to

point B and using Definition 4.1 we have,

$$m = \frac{y_B - y_A}{x_B - x_A}$$
$$= \frac{6 - (-2)}{15 - 11}$$
$$= \frac{8}{4}$$
$$= 2.$$

iii. We use Formula 4.2 to calculate the midpoint. Letting C represent this point, the x-coordinate of C is,

$$x_C = \frac{x_A + x_B}{2}$$
$$= \frac{11 + 15}{2}$$
$$= \frac{26}{2}$$
$$= 13.$$

Similarly, the y-coordinate is given by,

$$y_C = \frac{y_A + y_B}{2}$$
$$= \frac{(-2) + 6}{2}$$
$$= \frac{4}{2}$$
$$= 2.$$

Hence, the midpoint of AB is the following,

$$C = (13, 2).$$

(g) i. We use Formula 4.1 to calculate the distance $|AB|$.

$$|AB| = \sqrt{(x_B - x_A)^2 + (y_B - y_A)^2}$$
$$= \sqrt{((-1) - 3)^2 + ((5 - 8)^2}$$
$$= \sqrt{(-4)^2 + (-3)^2}$$
$$= \sqrt{16 + 9}$$
$$= \sqrt{25}$$
$$= 5.$$

ii. Letting m represent the gradient of the line segment joining point A to

point B and using Definition 4.1 we have,

$$m = \frac{y_B - y_A}{x_B - x_A}$$
$$= \frac{5 - 8}{(-1) - 3}$$
$$= \frac{-3}{-4}$$
$$= \frac{3}{4}.$$

iii. We use Formula 4.2 to calculate the midpoint. Letting C represent this point, the x-coordinate of C is,

$$x_C = \frac{x_A + x_B}{2}$$
$$= \frac{3 + (-1)}{2}$$
$$= \frac{-2}{2}$$
$$= -1.$$

Similarly, the y-coordinate is given by,

$$y_C = \frac{y_A + y_B}{2}$$
$$= \frac{8 + 5}{2}$$
$$= \frac{13}{2}.$$

Hence, the midpoint of AB is the following,

$$C = \left(-1, \frac{13}{2}\right).$$

(h) i. We use Formula 4.1 to calculate the distance $|AB|$.

$$m = \frac{y_B - y_A}{x_B - x_A}$$
$$= \sqrt{(1 - (-2))^2 + ((-1) - 2)^2}$$
$$= \sqrt{3^2 + (-3)^2}$$
$$= \sqrt{9 + 9}$$
$$= \sqrt{18}$$
$$= 3\sqrt{2}.$$

ii. Letting m represent the gradient of the line segment joining point A to

point B and using Definition 4.1 we have,

$$m = \frac{y_B - y_A}{x_B - x_A}$$
$$= \frac{(-1) - 2}{1 - (-2)}$$
$$= \frac{-3}{3}$$
$$= -1$$

iii. We use Formula 4.2 to calculate the midpoint. Letting C represent this point, the x-coordinate of C is,

$$x_C = \frac{x_A + x_B}{2}$$
$$= \frac{(-2) + 1}{2}$$
$$= \frac{-1}{2}.$$

Similarly, the y-coordinate is given by,

$$y_C = \frac{y_A + y_B}{2}$$
$$= \frac{2 + (-1)}{2}$$
$$= \frac{1}{2}.$$

Hence, the midpoint of AB is the following,

$$C = \left(-\frac{1}{2}, \frac{1}{2}\right).$$

Q2. (a) For the distance between $A(a, a)$ and $B(2a, 2a)$, we use Formula 4.1.

$$|AB| = \sqrt{(x_B - x_A)^2 + (y_B - y_A)^2}$$
$$= \sqrt{(2a - a)^2 + (2a - a)^2}$$
$$= \sqrt{a^2 + a^2}$$
$$= \sqrt{2a^2}$$
$$= \sqrt{2}a.$$

Using definition 4.1 to calculate the gradient between the two points, letting the two points be $A(a,a)$ and $B(2a,2a)$,

$$\begin{aligned} m &= \frac{y_B - y_A}{x_B - x_A} \\ &= \frac{2a-a}{2a-a} \\ &= \frac{a}{a} \\ &= 1. \end{aligned}$$

(b) For the distance between $A(a,a)$ and $B(2a,2a)$, we use Formula 4.1.

$$\begin{aligned} |AB| &= \sqrt{(x_B - x_A)^2 + (y_B - y_A)^2} \\ &= \sqrt{(0-10a)^2 + (5a-0)^2} \\ &= \sqrt{(-10a)^2 + (5a)^2} \\ &= \sqrt{100a^2 + 25a^2} \\ &= \sqrt{125}a \\ &= 5\sqrt{5}a. \end{aligned}$$

Using definition 4.1 to calculate the gradient between the two points, letting the two points be $A(10a,0)$ and $B(0,5a)$,

$$\begin{aligned} m &= \frac{y_B - y_A}{x_B - x_A} \\ &= \frac{5a-0}{0-10a} \\ &= \frac{5a}{-10a} \\ &= -\frac{1}{2}. \end{aligned}$$

(c) For the distance between $A(a,a)$ and $B(2a,2a)$, we use Formula 4.1.

$$\begin{aligned} |AB| &= \sqrt{(x_B - x_A)^2 + (y_B - y_A)^2} \\ &= \sqrt{(8t-4t)^2 + (2t^2-t^2)^2} \\ &= \sqrt{(4t)^2 + (t^2)^2} \\ &= \sqrt{16t^2 + t^4} \\ &= \sqrt{t^2(16+t^2)}. \end{aligned}$$

Using definition 4.1 to calculate the gradient between the two points, letting the two points be $A(4t, t^2)$ and $B(8t, 2t^2)$,

$$m = \frac{y_B - y_A}{x_B - x_A}$$
$$= \frac{2t^2 - t^2}{8t - 4t}$$
$$= \frac{t^2}{4t}$$
$$= \frac{t}{4}.$$

Q3. We use Definition 4.1 to find the value of p. Since the gradient is $\frac{4}{5}$, we have

$$\frac{4}{5} = \frac{y_B - y_A}{x_B - x_A},$$
$$\Rightarrow \frac{4}{5} = \frac{p-1}{6-1},$$
$$\Rightarrow \frac{4}{5} = \frac{p-1}{5},$$
$$\Rightarrow 4 = p - 1,$$
$$\Rightarrow p = 4 + 1,$$
$$= 5.$$

Q4. We use Definition 4.1 to find the value of z. Since the gradient is -1, we have

$$-1 = \frac{y_B - y_A}{x_B - x_A},$$
$$\Rightarrow -1 = \frac{-3 - 3}{z - 5},$$
$$\Rightarrow -1 = \frac{-6}{z - 5},$$
$$\Rightarrow -z + 5 = -6,$$
$$\Rightarrow z = 5 + 6,$$
$$= 11.$$

Q5. To show that the three points, $A(-2, 8)$, $B(4, 4)$ and $C(13, -2)$ are collinear it suffices to show that the gradients of the line segments AB and BC are equal (since the x coordinates of A, B and C form an increasing sequence).
Let m_1 be the gradient of the line segment AB, then by Definition 4.1,

$$m_1 = \frac{y_B - y_A}{x_B - x_A}$$
$$= \frac{4 - 8}{4 - (-2)}$$
$$= \frac{-4}{6}$$
$$= \frac{-2}{3}.$$

Let m_2 be the gradient of the line segment BC, then by Definition 4.1,

$$m_2 = \frac{y_C - y_B}{x_C - x_B}$$
$$= \frac{-2 - (4)}{13 - 4}$$
$$= \frac{-6}{9}$$
$$= \frac{-2}{3}.$$

Since $m_1 = m_2$ the points A, B and C are collinear and can be joined by a straight line.

Q6. We calculate the midpoint, E, of AB using Formula 4.2.

$$(x_E, y_E) = \left(\frac{x_A + x_B}{2}, \frac{y_A + y_B}{2}\right)$$
$$= \left(\frac{8 + 14}{2}, \frac{2 + 6}{2}\right)$$
$$= \left(\frac{22}{2}, \frac{8}{2}\right)$$
$$= (11, 4).$$

Similarly, we calculate the midpoint, F, of CD using Formula 4.2.

$$(x_F, y_F) = \left(\frac{x_C + x_D}{2}, \frac{y_C + y_D}{2}\right)$$
$$= \left(\frac{7 + 15}{2}, \frac{5 + 3}{2}\right)$$
$$= \left(\frac{22}{2}, \frac{8}{2}\right)$$
$$= (11, 4).$$

Since the x-coordinates of E and F, and the y-coordinates of E and F are equal, the midpoints coincide.

Q7. Denoting the midpoint of AB by the point $C(x_C, y_C)$, we can find the values of x_B and y_B using Formula 4.2.

$$(x_C, y_C) = \left(\frac{x_A + x_B}{2}, \frac{y_A + y_B}{2}\right),$$
$$\Rightarrow \left(\frac{13}{2}, 5\right) = \left(\frac{1 + x_B}{2}, \frac{3 + y_B}{2}\right).$$

Considering the x-coordinate only,
$$\frac{13}{2} = \frac{1+x_B}{2},$$
$$\Rightarrow \quad 13 = 1 + x_B,$$
$$\Rightarrow \quad x_B = 13 - 1,$$
$$\Rightarrow \quad x_B = 12.$$

Now, considering the y-coordinate only,
$$5 = \frac{3+y_B}{2},$$
$$\Rightarrow \quad 10 = 3 + y_B,$$
$$\Rightarrow \quad y_B = 10 - 3,$$
$$\Rightarrow \quad y_B = 7.$$

Hence, the point B has coordinates $B(12, 7)$.

Q8. We can find the values of y_A and x_B using Formula 4.2.
$$(x_C, y_C) = \left(\frac{x_A + x_B}{2}, \frac{y_A + y_B}{2}\right),$$
$$\Rightarrow \quad \left(\frac{13}{2}, -\frac{5}{2}\right) = \left(\frac{1+x_B}{2}, \frac{y_A + (-4)}{2}\right),$$
$$= \left(\frac{1+x_B}{2}, \frac{y_A - 4}{2}\right).$$

Considering the x-coordinate only,
$$\frac{13}{2} = \frac{1+x_B}{2},$$
$$\Rightarrow \quad 13 = 1 + x_B,$$
$$\Rightarrow \quad x_B = 13 - 1,$$
$$\Rightarrow \quad x_B = 12.$$

Now, considering the y-coordinate only,
$$-\frac{5}{2} = \frac{y_A - 4}{2},$$
$$\Rightarrow \quad -5 = y_A - 4,$$
$$\Rightarrow \quad y_A = -5 + 4,$$
$$\Rightarrow \quad y_B = -1.$$

Hence, $y_A = -1$ and $x_B = 12$.

Q9. We consider 15 possible line segments: AB, AC, AD, AE, AF, BC, BD, BE, BF, CD, CE, CF, DE, DF and EF. To find the gradients of each of these we use Definition 4.1.

- **Line Segment** AB
  Let m_1 be the gradient of the line segment AB, then,
  $$m_1 = \frac{y_B - y_A}{x_B - x_A}$$
  $$= \frac{7 - 4}{9 - 3}$$
  $$= \frac{3}{6}$$
  $$= \frac{1}{2}$$

- **Line Segment** AC
  Let m_2 be the gradient of the line segment AC, then,
  $$m_2 = \frac{y_C - y_A}{x_C - x_A}$$
  $$= \frac{1 - 4}{3 - 3}$$
  $$= \frac{-3}{0}$$

  Hence the gradient of AC is undefined.

- **Line Segment** AD
  Let m_3 be the gradient of the line segment AD, then,
  $$m_3 = \frac{y_D - y_A}{x_D - x_A}$$
  $$= \frac{6 - 4}{3 - 3}$$
  $$= \frac{-3}{0}$$

  Hence the gradient of AD is undefined.

- **Line Segment** AE
  Let m_4 be the gradient of the line segment AC, then,
  $$m_4 = \frac{y_E - y_A}{x_E - x_A}$$
  $$= \frac{3 - 4}{7 - 3}$$
  $$= \frac{-1}{4}$$
  $$= -\frac{1}{4}.$$

- **Line Segment** AF

Let m_5 be the gradient of the line segment AC, then,

$$m_5 = \frac{y_F - y_A}{x_F - x_A}$$
$$= \frac{-3 - 4}{10 - 3}$$
$$= \frac{-7}{7}$$
$$= -1.$$

- **Line Segment** BC

Let m_6 be the gradient of the line segment BC, then,

$$m_6 = \frac{y_C - y_B}{x_C - x_B}$$
$$= \frac{1 - 7}{3 - 9}$$
$$= \frac{-6}{-6}$$
$$= 1.$$

- **Line Segment** BD

Let m_7 be the gradient of the line segment BD, then,

$$m_7 = \frac{y_D - y_B}{x_D - x_B}$$
$$= \frac{6 - 7}{3 - 9}$$
$$= \frac{-1}{-6}$$
$$= \frac{1}{6}.$$

- **Line Segment** BE

Let m_8 be the gradient of the line segment BE, then,

$$m_8 = \frac{y_E - y_B}{x_E - x_B}$$
$$= \frac{3 - 7}{7 - 9}$$
$$= \frac{-4}{-2}$$
$$= 2.$$

- **Line Segment** BF

Let m_9 be the gradient of the line segment BF, then,

$$\begin{aligned} m_9 &= \frac{y_F - y_B}{x_F - x_B} \\ &= \frac{-3 - 7}{10 - 9} \\ &= \frac{-10}{1} \\ &= -10. \end{aligned}$$

- **Line Segment** CD

  Let m_{10} be the gradient of the line segment CD, then,

  $$\begin{aligned} m_{10} &= \frac{y_D - y_C}{x_D - x_C} \\ &= \frac{6 - 1}{3 - 3} \\ &= \frac{5}{0}. \end{aligned}$$

  Hence the gradient of CD is undefined.

- **Line Segment** CE

  Let m_{11} be the gradient of the line segment CE, then,

  $$\begin{aligned} m_{11} &= \frac{y_E - y_C}{x_E - x_C} \\ &= \frac{3 - 1}{7 - 3} \\ &= \frac{2}{4} \\ &= \frac{1}{2}. \end{aligned}$$

- **Line Segment** CF

  Let m_{12} be the gradient of the line segment CF, then,

  $$\begin{aligned} m_{12} &= \frac{y_F - y_C}{x_F - x_C} \\ &= \frac{-3 - 1}{10 - 3} \\ &= \frac{-4}{7} \\ &= -\frac{4}{7}. \end{aligned}$$

- **Line Segment** DE

Let m_{13} be the gradient of the line segment DE, then,

$$\begin{aligned} m_{13} &= \frac{y_E - y_D}{x_E - x_D} \\ &= \frac{3 - 6}{7 - 3} \\ &= \frac{-3}{4} \\ &= -\frac{3}{4}. \end{aligned}$$

- **Line Segment** DF

  Let m_{14} be the gradient of the line segment DF, then,

  $$\begin{aligned} m_{14} &= \frac{y_F - y_D}{x_F - x_D} \\ &= \frac{-3 - 6}{10 - 3} \\ &= \frac{-9}{7} \\ &= -\frac{9}{7}. \end{aligned}$$

- **Line Segment** EF

  Let m_{15} be the gradient of the line segment EF, then,

  $$\begin{aligned} m_{15} &= \frac{y_F - y_E}{x_F - x_E} \\ &= \frac{-3 - 3}{10 - 7} \\ &= \frac{-6}{3} \\ &= -2. \end{aligned}$$

Putting these values for the gradients of all the line segments in a table make it easier to spot parallel and perpendicular pairs of line segments.

Line segment	Gradient	Value of Gradient
AB	m_1	$\frac{1}{2}$
AC	m_2	Undefined
AD	m_3	Undefined
AE	m_4	$-\frac{1}{4}$
AF	m_5	-1
BC	m_6	1
BD	m_7	$\frac{1}{6}$
BE	m_8	2
BF	m_9	-10
CD	m_{10}	Undefined
CE	m_{11}	$\frac{1}{2}$
CF	m_{12}	$-\frac{4}{7}$
DE	m_{13}	$-\frac{3}{4}$
DF	m_{14}	$-\frac{9}{7}$
EF	m_{15}	-2

Line segments AC, AD and CD are all parallel to each other as they are vertical lines. Line segments AB and CE are parallel. Line segment BC is perpendicular to AF. Line Segment AB is perpendicular to EF. Line segment CE is perpendicular to EF.

Worked Solutions — Exercise 4.2

Q1. (a) Since $y = 2x - 2$ is in the form $y = mx + c$, where m is the gradient and c is the y-intercept we can see that the gradient, in this case, is 2.

(b) Since $y = 6$ is in the form $y = mx + c$, where m is the gradient and c is the y-intercept we can see that the gradient, in this case, is 0.

(c) Since $y = -4x + 1$ is in the form $y = mx + c$, where m is the gradient and c is the y-intercept we can see that the gradient, in this case, is -4.

(d) We first rearrange $-y = 2x - 4$ into the form $y = mx + c$.

$$-y = 2x - 4,$$
$$\Rightarrow \quad y = -2x + 4.$$

From this we see that the gradient, in this case, is -2.

(e) Since $y = -4x + 1$ is in the form $y = mx + c$, where m is the gradient and c is the y-intercept we can see that the gradient, in this case, is $\frac{1}{3}$.

(f) We first rearrange $2x + 3y - 12 = 0$ into the form $y = mx + c$.

$$2x + 3y - 12 = 0,$$
$$\Rightarrow \quad 3y = -2x + 12,$$
$$\Rightarrow \quad y = -\frac{2}{3}x + 4.$$

From this we see that the gradient, in this case, is $-\frac{2}{3}$.

(g) We first rearrange $9x - 3y + 2 = 0$ into the form $y = mx + c$.

$$9x - 3y + 2 = 0,$$
$$\Rightarrow -3y = -9x - 2,$$
$$\Rightarrow y = 3x + \frac{2}{3}.$$

From this we see that the gradient, in this case, is 3.

(h) We first rearrange $6y + 4 = 13x$ into the form $y = mx + c$.

$$6y + 4 = 13x,$$
$$\Rightarrow 6y = 13x - 4,$$
$$\Rightarrow y = \frac{13}{6}x - \frac{2}{3}.$$

From this we see that the gradient, in this case, is $\frac{13}{6}$.

Q2. (a) We rearrange into the form $ax + by + c = 0$.

$$y = 3x - 2,$$
$$\Rightarrow y - 3x + 2 = 0,$$
$$\Rightarrow -3x + y + 2 = 0.$$

This is of the required form with $a = -3$, $b = 1$ and $c = 2$. Equivalently we could have $3x - y - 2 = 0$ with $a = 3$, $b = -1$ and $c = -2$.

(b) We rearrange into the form $ax + by + c = 0$.

$$y = \frac{1}{2}x - 6,$$
$$\Rightarrow y - \frac{1}{2}x + 6 = 0,$$
$$\Rightarrow -x + 2y + 12 = 0.$$

This is of the required form with $a = -1$, $b = 2$ and $c = 12$.

(c) We rearrange into the form $ax + by + c = 0$.

$$y = -3x - 7,$$
$$\Rightarrow y + 3x + 7 = 0,$$
$$\Rightarrow 3x + y + 7 = 0.$$

This is of the required form with $a = 3$, $b = 1$ and $c = 7$.

(d) We rearrange into the form $ax + by + c = 0$.
$$y = \frac{1}{3}x + \frac{5}{4},$$
$$\Rightarrow \quad y - \frac{1}{3}x - \frac{5}{4} = 0,$$
$$\Rightarrow \quad 3y - x - \frac{15}{4} = 0,$$
$$\Rightarrow \quad 12y - 4x - 15 = 0,$$
$$\Rightarrow \quad -4x + 12y - 15 = 0.$$

This is of the required form with $a = -4$, $b = 12$ and $c = -15$.

Q3. To find the equation of the line parallel to $l_1 : x + 2y + 3 = 0$ we first need to find the gradient of l_1. Rearranging,
$$x + 2y + 3 = 0,$$
$$\Rightarrow \quad 2y = -x - 3,$$
$$\Rightarrow \quad y = -\frac{1}{2}x - \frac{3}{2}.$$

Hence, the gradient of $l_1 = -\frac{1}{2}$. Since we seek the equation of the line parallel to l_1 that passes through the point $(-2, 5)$ we use the $y = mx + c$ form of the equation of a straight line:
$$y = mx + c,$$
$$\Rightarrow \quad 5 = -\frac{1}{2} \times (-2) + c,$$
$$\Rightarrow \quad = 5 + \frac{1}{2} \times (-2),$$
$$\Rightarrow \quad = 5 + (-1),$$
$$\Rightarrow \quad = 4.$$

Hence, the equation of the line we seek is $y = -\frac{1}{2}x + 4$.

Q4. **Method 1:**

As the line crosses the y-axis at $(0, 7)$ and the x-axis at $(12, 0)$ we have two points that the line passes through which we can use to find the gradient. Let m be the gradient of the line, then,
$$m = \frac{0 - 7}{12 - 0}$$
$$= \frac{-7}{12}$$
$$= -\frac{7}{12}.$$

Using the form $y = mc + c$ with the point $(0, 7)$,

$$y = mx + c,$$
$$\Rightarrow 7 = -\frac{7}{12} \times 0 + c,$$
$$\Rightarrow c = 7.$$

Hence, the equation of the line is $y = -\frac{7}{12}x + 7$, this can be rearranged in the following way.

$$y = -\frac{7}{12}x + 7,$$
$$\Rightarrow 12y = -7x + 84,$$
$$\Rightarrow -7x - 12y + 84 = 0.$$

Method 2: Using Formula 4.7 we can find the equation of a line given two points. In this case, the two points are $A(0, 7)$ and $B(12, 0)$.

$$\frac{y-7}{0-7} = \frac{x-0}{12-0},$$
$$\Rightarrow \frac{y-7}{-7} = \frac{x}{12},$$
$$\Rightarrow 12(y-7) = -7x,$$
$$\Rightarrow 12y - 84 = -7x,$$
$$\Rightarrow 0 = -7x - 12y + 84.$$

Q5. To find the area of the triangle we find where the line $l_1 : 3x + 2y - 18$ crosses the x- and y-axes.

The line crosses the x-axis when $y = 0$, hence,

$$3x + 2 \times 0 - 18 = 0,$$
$$\Rightarrow 3x = 18,$$
$$\Rightarrow x = 6.$$

And so, the line crosses the x-axis at the point $(6, 0)$.
The line crosses the y-axis when $x = 0$, hence,

$$3 \times 0 + 2y - 18 = 0,$$
$$\Rightarrow 2y = 18,$$
$$\Rightarrow y = 9.$$

And so, the line crosses the x-axis at the point $(0, 9)$.
The triangle, therefore, has vertices $A(0, 0)$, $B(6, 0)$ and $C(0, 9)$ and we can find

the area in the following way,

$$\text{Area} = \frac{1}{2}|AB||AC|$$
$$= \frac{1}{2} \times 6$$
$$= \frac{54}{2}$$
$$= 27.$$

Q6. Substituting the x and y values from the point $(1, 9)$ into the equation $y = mx + 5$ we find

$$y = mx + 5,$$
$$\Rightarrow \quad 9 = m \times 1 + 5,$$
$$\Rightarrow \quad m = 9 - 5,$$
$$= 4.$$

Hence the gradient is $m = 4$.

Q7. To find a and b we need two equations which can be solved simultaneously. We can find one equation by substituting the values of the x- and y-coordinates of the given point into the equation of the line $ax + by - 4 = 0$.

$$ax + by - 4 = 0,$$
$$\Rightarrow \quad a \times 0 + b \times 2 - 4 = 0,$$
$$\Rightarrow \quad 2b = 4,$$
$$\Rightarrow \quad b = 2.$$

Rearranging $ax + 2y - 4 = 0$ into the form $y = mx + c$,

$$ax + 2y - 4 = 0,$$
$$\Rightarrow \quad 2y = -ax + 4,$$
$$\Rightarrow \quad y = -\frac{a}{2} + 2.$$

Since we know the gradient is $\frac{1}{2}$ we have that $a = -1$.
Hence, $a = -1$, $b = 2$.

Q8. (a) Using Formula 4.4 we find the y-intercept, c, of the line with gradient $m = 2$ which passes through the point $A(0, 0)$.

$$y = mx + c,$$
$$\Rightarrow \quad 0 = 2 \times 0 + c,$$
$$\Rightarrow \quad c = 0.$$

Hence, the equation of the line with gradient $m = 2$ which passes through the point $A(0, 0)$ is,

$$y = 2x.$$

(b) Using Formula 4.4 we find the y-intercept, c, of the line with gradient $m = 3$ which passes through the point $A(3, 2)$.

$$y = mx + c,$$
$$\Rightarrow \quad 2 = 3 \times 3 + c,$$
$$\Rightarrow \quad 2 = 9 + c,$$
$$\Rightarrow \quad c = 2 - 9$$
$$= -7$$

Hence, the equation of the line with gradient $m = 3$ which passes through the point $A(3, 2)$ is,

$$y = 3x - 7.$$

(c) Using Formula 4.4 we find the y-intercept, c, of the line with gradient $m = -1$ which passes through the point $A(1, 4)$.

$$y = mx + c,$$
$$\Rightarrow \quad 4 = (-1) \times 1 + c,$$
$$\Rightarrow \quad 4 = -1 + c,$$
$$\Rightarrow \quad c = 4 + 1$$
$$= 5$$

Hence, the equation of the line with gradient $m = -1$ which passes through the point $A(1, 4)$ is,

$$y = -x + 5.$$

(d) Using Formula 4.4 we find the y-intercept, c, of the line with gradient $m = -2$ which passes through the point $A(-3, 7)$.

$$y = mx + c,$$
$$\Rightarrow \quad 7 = (-2) \times (-3) + c,$$
$$\Rightarrow \quad 7 = 6 + c,$$
$$\Rightarrow \quad c = 7 - 6$$
$$= 1$$

Hence, the equation of the line with gradient $m = -2$ which passes through the point $A(-3, 7)$ is,

$$y = -2x + 1.$$

(e) Using Formula 4.4 we find the y-intercept, c, of the line with gradient $m = \frac{3}{2}$

which passes through the point $A(4,12)$.

$$y = mx + c,$$
$$\Rightarrow \quad 12 = \frac{3}{2} \times 4 + c,$$
$$\Rightarrow \quad 12 = 6 + c,$$
$$\Rightarrow \quad c = 12 - 6$$
$$= 6$$

Hence, the equation of the line with gradient $m = \frac{3}{2}$ which passes through the point $A(4,12)$ is,

$$y = \frac{3}{2}x + 6$$

(f) Using Formula 4.4 we find the y-intercept, c, of the line with gradient $m = -\frac{2}{3}$ which passes through the point $A\left(5, -\frac{25}{3}\right)$.

$$y = mx + c,$$
$$\Rightarrow \quad -\frac{25}{3} = -\frac{2}{3} \times 5 + c,$$
$$\Rightarrow \quad -\frac{25}{3} = -\frac{10}{3} + c,$$
$$\Rightarrow \quad c = -\frac{25}{3} + \frac{10}{3}$$
$$= -5$$

Hence, the equation of the line with gradient $m = -\frac{2}{3}$ which passes through the point $A\left(5, -\frac{25}{3}\right)$ is,

$$y = -\frac{2}{3}x - 5$$

(g) Using Formula 4.4 we find the y-intercept, c, of the line with gradient $m = 6$ which passes through the point $A(2, 25)$.

$$y = mx + c,$$
$$\Rightarrow \quad 25 = 6 \times 2 + c,$$
$$\Rightarrow \quad 25 = 12 + c,$$
$$\Rightarrow \quad c = 25 - 12$$
$$= 13$$

Hence, the equation of the line with gradient $m = 6$ which passes through the point $A(2, 25)$ is,

$$y = 6x + 13$$

(h) Using Formula 4.4 we find the y-intercept, c, of the line with gradient $m = -\frac{2}{13}$ which passes through the point $A\left(3, \frac{1}{2}\right)$.

$$y = mx + c,$$
$$\Rightarrow \quad \frac{1}{2} = -\frac{2}{13} \times 3 + c,$$
$$\Rightarrow \quad \frac{1}{2} = -\frac{6}{13} + c,$$
$$\Rightarrow \quad c = \frac{1}{2} + \frac{6}{13}$$
$$= \frac{13}{26} + \frac{12}{26}$$
$$= \frac{25}{26}$$

Hence, the equation of the line with gradient $m = -\frac{2}{13}$ which passes through the point $A\left(3, \frac{1}{2}\right)$ is,

$$y = -\frac{2}{13}x + \frac{25}{26}$$

Q9. We wish to find the equation of the line which passes through the point $(2a, 4a)$ and has gradient $\frac{5}{2}$. Since any straight line is of the form $y = mx + c$, where m is the gradient and c is the y-intercept, as we know that the point with x-coordinate $2a$ and y-coordinate $4a$ lies on the line we can use Formula 4.4.

$$y = mx + c,$$
$$\Rightarrow \quad 4a = \frac{5}{2} \times 2a + c,$$
$$\Rightarrow \quad 4a = 5a + c,$$
$$\Rightarrow \quad c = 4a - 5a$$
$$= -a$$

Hence, the equation of the line with gradient $m = \frac{5}{2}$ which passes through the point $A(2a, 4a)$ is,

$$y = \frac{5}{2}x - a$$

Q10. We present two methods for each of these questions.
  (a) **Method 1:** Given the two points $A(-1, 1)$ and $B(2, 4)$ we first find the gradient, which we denote m, of the line which passes through both of these points.

Using Definition 4.1,
$$m = \frac{y_B - y_A}{x_B - x_A}$$
$$= \frac{4 - 1}{2 - (-1)}$$
$$= \frac{3}{3}$$
$$= 1.$$

Using this gradient and point A, we find the y-intercept, c, appearing in the equation of the line $y = mx + c$:

$$y = mx + c,$$
$$\Rightarrow \quad 1 = 1 \times (-1) + c,$$
$$\Rightarrow \quad 1 = -1 + c,$$
$$\Rightarrow \quad c = 1 + 1$$
$$= 2$$

Hence, the equation of the line is $y = x + 2$, or equivalently $-x + y - 2 = 0$.

Method 2: Here, we use Formula 4.7 with the two points $A(-1, 1)$ and $B(2, 4)$.

$$\frac{y - y_A}{y_B - y_A} = \frac{x - x_A}{x_B - x_A},$$
$$\Rightarrow \quad \frac{y - 1}{4 - 1} = \frac{x - (-1)}{2 - (-1)},$$
$$\Rightarrow \quad \frac{y - 1}{3} = \frac{x + 1}{3},$$
$$\Rightarrow \quad y - 1 = x + 1,$$
$$\Rightarrow \quad y = x + 2.$$

Hence, the equation of the line is $y = x + 2$, or equivalently $-x + y - 2 = 0$.

(b) **Method 1:** Given the two points $A(-1, 6)$ and $B(0, 5)$ we first find the gradient, which we denote m, of the line which passes through both of these points.

Using Definition 4.1,
$$m = \frac{y_B - y_A}{x_B - x_A}$$
$$= \frac{5 - 6}{0 - (-1)}$$
$$= \frac{-1}{1}$$
$$= -1.$$

Using this gradient and point A, we find the y-intercept, c, appearing in the equation of the line $y = mx + c$:

$$y = mx + c,$$
$$\Rightarrow \quad 6 = (-1) \times (-1) + c,$$
$$\Rightarrow \quad 6 = 1 + c,$$
$$\Rightarrow \quad c = 6 - 1$$
$$= 5$$

Hence, the equation of the line is $y = -x + 5$, or equivalently $x + y - 5 = 0$.

Method 2: Here, we use Formula 4.7 with the two points $A(-1, 6)$ and $B(0, 5)$.

$$\frac{y - y_A}{y_B - y_A} = \frac{x - x_A}{x_B - x_A},$$
$$\Rightarrow \quad \frac{y - 6}{5 - 6} = \frac{x - (-1)}{0 - (-1)},$$
$$\Rightarrow \quad \frac{y - 6}{-1} = \frac{x + 1}{1},$$
$$\Rightarrow \quad y - 6 = -x - 1,$$
$$\Rightarrow \quad y = -x + 5.$$

Hence, the equation of the line is $y = -x + 5$, or equivalently $x + y - 5 = 0$.

(c) **Method 1:** Given the two points $A(3, 1)$ and $B(9, 9)$ we first find the gradient, which we denote m, of the line which passes through both of these points.
Using Definition 4.1,

$$m = \frac{y_B - y_A}{x_B - x_A}$$
$$= \frac{9 - 1}{9 - 3}$$
$$= \frac{8}{6}$$
$$= \frac{4}{3}.$$

Using this gradient and point A, we find the y-intercept, c, appearing in the equation of the line $y = mx + c$:

$$y = mx + c,$$
$$\Rightarrow \quad 1 = \frac{4}{3} \times 3 + c,$$
$$\Rightarrow \quad 1 = 4 + c,$$
$$\Rightarrow \quad c = 1 - 4$$
$$= -3$$

Hence, the equation of the line is $y = \frac{4}{3}x - 3$, or equivalently $-4x + 3y + 9 = 0$.

Method 2: Here, we use Formula 4.7 with the two points $A(3, 1)$ and $B(9, 9)$.

$$\frac{y - y_A}{y_B - y_A} = \frac{x - x_A}{x_B - x_A},$$
$$\Rightarrow \frac{y - 1}{9 - 1} = \frac{x - 3}{9 - 3},$$
$$\Rightarrow \frac{y - 1}{8} = \frac{x - 3}{6},$$
$$\Rightarrow 6(y - 1) = 8(x - 3),$$
$$\Rightarrow 6y - 6 = 8x - 24,$$
$$\Rightarrow -8x + 6y + 18 = 0,$$
$$\Rightarrow -4x + 3y + 9 = 0.$$

Hence, the equation of the line is $-4x + 3y + 9 = 0$, or equivalently $y = \frac{4}{3}x - 3$.

(d) **Method 1:** Given the two points $A(2, 8)$ and $B(7, 7)$ we first find the gradient, which we denote m, of the line which passes through both of these points.
Using Definition 4.1,

$$m = \frac{y_B - y_A}{x_B - x_A}$$
$$= \frac{7 - 8}{7 - 2}$$
$$= \frac{-1}{5}$$
$$= -\frac{1}{5}.$$

Using this gradient and point A, we find the y-intercept, c, appearing in the equation of the line $y = mx + c$:

$$y = mx + c,$$
$$\Rightarrow 8 = -\frac{1}{5} \times 2 + c,$$
$$\Rightarrow 8 = -\frac{2}{5} + c,$$
$$\Rightarrow c = 8 + \frac{2}{5}$$
$$= \frac{42}{5}$$

Hence, the equation of the line is $y = -\frac{1}{5}x + \frac{42}{5}$, or equivalently $x + 5y - 42 = 0$.

Method 2: Here, we use Formula 4.7 with the two points $A(2,8)$ and $B(7,7)$.

$$\frac{y - y_A}{y_B - y_A} = \frac{x - x_A}{x_B - x_A},$$

$$\Rightarrow \frac{y - 8}{7 - 8} = \frac{x - 2}{7 - 2)},$$

$$\Rightarrow \frac{y - 8}{-1} = \frac{x - 2}{5},$$

$$\Rightarrow 5(y - 8) = -1(x - 2),$$

$$\Rightarrow 5y - 40 = -x + 2,$$

$$\Rightarrow x + 5y - 40 - 2 = 0,$$

$$\Rightarrow x + 5y - 42 = 0.$$

Hence, the equation of the line is $-x + 5y - 42 = 0$, or equivalently $y = -\frac{1}{5}x + \frac{42}{5}$.

(e) **Method 1:** Given the two points $A(2,1)$ and $B(5,8)$ we first find the gradient, which we denote m, of the line which passes through both of these points.

Using Definition 4.1,

$$m = \frac{y_B - y_A}{x_B - x_A}$$
$$= \frac{8 - 1}{5 - 2}$$
$$= \frac{7}{3}$$

Using this gradient and point A, we find the y-intercept, c, appearing in the equation of the line $y = mx + c$:

$$y = mx + c,$$
$$\Rightarrow 1 = \frac{7}{3} \times 2 + c,$$
$$\Rightarrow 1 = \frac{14}{3} + c,$$
$$\Rightarrow c = 1 - \frac{14}{3}$$
$$= -\frac{11}{3}$$

Hence, the equation of the line is $y = \frac{7}{3}x - \frac{14}{3}$, or equivalently $-7x + 3y + 11 = 0$.

Method 2: Here, we use Formula 4.7 with the two points $A(2,1)$ and $B(5,8)$.

$$\frac{y - y_A}{y_B - y_A} = \frac{x - x_A}{x_B - x_A},$$

$$\Rightarrow \quad \frac{y - 1}{8 - 1} = \frac{x - 2}{5 - 2)},$$

$$\Rightarrow \quad \frac{y - 1}{7} = \frac{x - 2}{3},$$

$$\Rightarrow \quad 3(y - 1) = 7(x - 2),$$

$$\Rightarrow \quad 3y - 3 = 7x - 14,$$

$$\Rightarrow \quad -7x + 3y - 3 + 14 = 0,$$

$$\Rightarrow \quad -7x + 3y + 11 = 0.$$

Hence, the equation of the line is $-7x + 3y + 11 = 0$, or equivalently $y = \frac{7}{3}x - \frac{14}{3}$.

(f) **Method 1:** Given the two points $A(-5, 9)$ and $B(1, 4)$ we first find the gradient, which we denote m, of the line which passes through both of these points.

Using Definition 4.1,

$$m = \frac{y_B - y_A}{x_B - x_A}$$
$$= \frac{4 - 9}{1 - (-5)}$$
$$= \frac{-5}{6}$$
$$= -\frac{5}{6}$$

Using this gradient and point A, we find the y-intercept, c, appearing in the equation of the line $y = mx + c$:

$$y = mx + c,$$
$$\Rightarrow \quad 9 = -\frac{5}{6} \times (-5) + c,$$
$$\Rightarrow \quad 9 = \frac{25}{6} + c,$$
$$\Rightarrow \quad c = 9 - \frac{25}{6}$$
$$= \frac{29}{6}$$

Hence, the equation of the line is $y = -\frac{5}{6}x + \frac{29}{6}$, or equivalently $5x + 6y - 29 = 0$.

Method 2: Here, we use Formula 4.7 with the two points $A(-5, 9)$ and

$B(1, 4)$.

$$\frac{y - y_A}{y_B - y_A} = \frac{x - x_A}{x_B - x_A},$$

$\Rightarrow \quad \dfrac{y - 9}{4 - 9} = \dfrac{x - (-5)}{1 - (-5)},$

$\Rightarrow \quad \dfrac{y - 9}{-5} = \dfrac{x + 5}{6},$

$\Rightarrow \quad 6(y - 9) = -5(x + 5),$

$\Rightarrow \quad 6y - 54 = -5x - 25,$

$\Rightarrow \quad 5x + 6y - 54 + 25 = 0,$

$\Rightarrow \quad 5x + 6y - 29 = 0.$

Hence, the equation of the line is $5x + 6y - 29 = 0$, or equivalently $y = -\frac{5}{6}x + \frac{29}{6}$.

(g) **Method 1:** Given the two points $A(3, -8)$ and $B(8, -3)$ we first find the gradient, which we denote m, of the line which passes through both of these points.

Using Definition 4.1,

$$m = \frac{y_B - y_A}{x_B - x_A}$$
$$= \frac{-3 - (-8)}{8 - 3}$$
$$= \frac{5}{5}$$
$$= 1$$

Using this gradient and point A, we find the y-intercept, c, appearing in the equation of the line $y = mx + c$:

$y = mx + c,$

$\Rightarrow \quad -8 = 1 \times 3 + c,$

$\Rightarrow \quad -8 = 3 + c,$

$\Rightarrow \quad c = -8 - 3$

$\qquad = -11$

Hence, the equation of the line is $y = x - 11$, or equivalently $-x + y + 11 = 0$.

Method 2: Here, we use Formula 4.7 with the two points $A(3, -8)$ and

$B(8, -3)$.

$$\frac{y - y_A}{y_B - y_A} = \frac{x - x_A}{x_B - x_A},$$
$$\Rightarrow \quad \frac{y - (-8)}{-3 - (-8)} = \frac{x - 3}{8 - 3},$$
$$\Rightarrow \quad \frac{y + 8}{5} = \frac{x - 3}{5},$$
$$\Rightarrow \quad y + 8 = x - 3,$$
$$\Rightarrow \quad -x + y + 8 + 3 = 0,$$
$$\Rightarrow \quad -x + y + 11 = 0.$$

Hence, the equation of the line is $-x + y + 11 = 0$, or equivalently $y = x - 11$.

(h) **Method 1:** Given the two points $A(2, -5)$ and $B(15, 1)$ we first find the gradient, which we denote m, of the line which passes through both of these points.

Using Definition 4.1,

$$m = \frac{y_B - y_A}{x_B - x_A}$$
$$= \frac{1 - (-5)}{15 - 2}$$
$$= \frac{6}{13}.$$

Using this gradient and point A, we find the y-intercept, c, appearing in the equation of the line $y = mx + c$:

$$y = mx + c,$$
$$\Rightarrow \quad -5 = \frac{6}{13} \times 2 + c,$$
$$\Rightarrow \quad -5 = \frac{12}{13} + c,$$
$$\Rightarrow \quad c = -5 - \frac{12}{13}$$
$$= -\frac{77}{13}.$$

Hence, the equation of the line is $y = \frac{6}{13}x - \frac{77}{13}$, or equivalently $-6x + 13y + 77 = 0$.

Method 2: Here, we use Formula 4.7 with the two points $A(2, -5)$ and

$B(15, 1)$.

$$\frac{y - y_A}{y_B - y_A} = \frac{x - x_A}{x_B - x_A},$$

$$\Rightarrow \quad \frac{y - (-5)}{1 - (-5)} = \frac{x - 2}{15 - 2},$$

$$\Rightarrow \quad \frac{y + 5}{6} = \frac{x - 2}{13},$$

$$\Rightarrow \quad 13(y + 5) = 6(x - 2),$$

$$\Rightarrow \quad 13y + 65 = 6x - 12 \Rightarrow \quad -6x + 13y + 65 + 12 = 0,$$

$$\Rightarrow \quad -6x + 13y + 77 = 0.$$

Hence, the equation of the line is $-6x + 13y + 77 = 0$, or equivalently $y = \frac{6}{13}x - \frac{77}{13}$.

Q11. We are given that the line $l1 : 5x + 4y - 30 = 0$ meets the x-axis at the point P and that the line $l_2 : -2x - 5y + 20 = 0$ meets the y-axis at the point Q. Since we wish to find the equation of the line which passes through both P and Q we first need the coordinates of these two points.

The y-coordinate of P must be zero since P is where the line l_1 meets the x-axis; to find the x-coordinate we substitute $y = 0$ into the equation for l_1.

$$5x + 4y - 30 = 0,$$
$$\Rightarrow \quad 5x + 4 \times 0 - 30 = 0,$$
$$\Rightarrow \quad 5x = 30,$$
$$\Rightarrow \quad x = 6.$$

Hence the point P has coordinates $(6, 0)$. Similarly, to find Q we note that the x-coordinate must be zero; substituting this into the equation of the line l_2 we have,

$$-2x - 5y + 20 = 0,$$
$$\Rightarrow \quad -2 \times 0 - 5y + 20 = 0,$$
$$\Rightarrow \quad -5y = -20,$$
$$\Rightarrow \quad y = 4.$$

Hence, the point Q has coordinates $(0, 4)$.

Since we now know the coordinates of the two points we can find the equation of the line passing through them.

Method 1: Given the two points $P(6, 0)$ and $Q(0, 4)$ we first find the gradient, which we denote m, of the line which passes through both of these points.

Using Definition 4.1,

$$m = \frac{y_Q - y_P}{x_Q - x_P}$$
$$= \frac{4-0}{0-6}$$
$$= \frac{4}{-6}$$
$$= -\frac{2}{3}$$

Using this gradient and point P, we find the y-intercept, c, appearing in the equation of the line $y = mx + c$:

$$y = mx + c,$$
$$\Rightarrow \quad 0 = -\frac{2}{3} \times 6 + c,$$
$$\Rightarrow \quad 0 = -4 + c,$$
$$\Rightarrow \quad c = 0 + 4$$
$$= 4$$

Hence, the equation of the line is $y = -\frac{2}{3}x + 4$, or equivalently $-2x - 3y + 12 = 0$.

Method 2: Here, we use Formula 4.7 with the two points $P(6, 0)$ and $Q(0, 4)$.

$$\frac{y - y_P}{y_Q - y_P} = \frac{x - x_P}{x_Q - x_P},$$
$$\Rightarrow \quad \frac{y-0}{4-0} = \frac{x-6}{0-6},$$
$$\Rightarrow \quad \frac{y-0}{4} = \frac{x-6}{-6},$$
$$\Rightarrow \quad -6y = 4(x-6),$$
$$\Rightarrow \quad -6y = 4x - 24 \Rightarrow \quad -6y - 4x + 24 = 0,$$
$$\Rightarrow \quad -3y - 2x + 12 = 0.$$

Hence, the equation of the line is $-2x - 3y + 12 = 0$, or equivalently $y = -\frac{2}{3}x + 4$.

Q12. To find the point of intersection of the two lines we consider the following pair of simultaneous equations:

$$y = x + 1, \quad \text{①}$$
$$x + 2y - 14 = 0. \quad \text{②}$$

Substituting Equation ① into Equation ② and solving for x,

$$x + 2y - 14 = 0,$$
$$\Rightarrow x + 2(x+1) - 14 = 0,$$
$$\Rightarrow x + 2x + 2 - 14 = 0,$$
$$\Rightarrow 3x = 12,$$
$$\Rightarrow x = 4.$$

From Equation ①, substituting $x = 4$, we find that the y-coordinate of the point of intersection of the two lines, P, is $y = 5$. We now have two points with which to find the equation of the line passing through them.

Method 1: Given the two points $P(4,5)$ and $Q(9,7)$ we first find the gradient, which we denote m, of the line which passes through both of these points.
Using Definition 4.1,

$$m = \frac{y_Q - y_P}{x_Q - x_P}$$
$$= \frac{7 - 5}{9 - 4}$$
$$= \frac{2}{5}$$
$$= -\frac{2}{5}$$

Using this gradient and point P, we find the y-intercept, c, appearing in the equation of the line $y = mx + c$:

$$y = mx + c,$$
$$\Rightarrow 5 = \frac{2}{5} \times 4 + c,$$
$$\Rightarrow 5 = \frac{8}{5} + c,$$
$$\Rightarrow c = 5 - \frac{8}{5}$$
$$= \frac{17}{5}$$

Hence, the equation of the line is $y = \frac{2}{5}x + \frac{17}{5}$, or equivalently $2x - 5y + 17 = 0$.

Method 2: Here, we use Formula 4.7 with the two points $P(4,5)$ and $Q(9,7)$.

$$\frac{y - y_P}{y_Q - y_P} = \frac{x - x_P}{x_Q - x_P},$$

$\Rightarrow \quad \dfrac{y - 5}{7 - 5} = \dfrac{x - 4}{9 - 4},$

$\Rightarrow \quad \dfrac{y - 5}{2} = \dfrac{x - 4}{5},$

$\Rightarrow \quad 5(y - 5) = 2(x - 4),$

$\Rightarrow \quad 5y - 25 = 2x - 8 \Rightarrow \quad 0 = 2x - 5y - 8 + 25,$

$\Rightarrow \quad 0 = 2x - 5y + 17.$

Hence, the equation of the line is $2x - 5y + 17 = 0$, or equivalently $y = \frac{2}{5}x + \frac{17}{5}$.

Q13. (a) Let m_1 be the gradient of the given line, and m_2 be the gradient of the perpendicular line we wish to find the equation for. Since the given line $y = 3x - 2$ is expressed in the form $y = mx + c$, we can see that $m_1 = 3$. Equation 4.12 can then be used to find the gradient of any line that is perpendicular to this given line.

$$m_1 m_2 = -1,$$

$\Rightarrow \quad 3m_2 = -1,$

$\Rightarrow \quad m_2 = -\dfrac{1}{3}.$

As the line we wish to find passes through the point $(5, 3)$ we find the y-intercept, c, appearing in the equation of the line $y = m_2 x + c$:

$$y = m_2 x + c,$$

$\Rightarrow \quad 3 = -\dfrac{1}{3} \times 5 + c,$

$\Rightarrow \quad 3 = -\dfrac{5}{5} + c,$

$\Rightarrow \quad c = 3 + \dfrac{5}{3}$

$\quad = \dfrac{14}{3}$

Hence, the equation of the line is $y = -\frac{1}{3}x + \frac{14}{3}$, or equivalently $-x - y + 14 = 0$.

(b) Let m_1 be the gradient of the given line, and m_2 be the gradient of the perpendicular line we wish to find the equation for. Since the given line $y = \frac{5}{7}x + 4$ is expressed in the form $y = mx + c$, we can see that $m_1 = \frac{5}{7}$. Equation 4.12 can then be used to find the gradient of any line that is perpendicular to this given line.

$$m_1 m_2 = -1,$$
$$\Rightarrow \quad \frac{5}{7} m_2 = -1,$$
$$\Rightarrow \quad m_2 = -\frac{7}{5}.$$

As the line we wish to find passes through the point $(1,8)$ we find the y-intercept, c, appearing in the equation of the line $y = m_2 x + c$:

$$y = m_2 x + c,$$
$$\Rightarrow \quad 8 = -\frac{7}{5} \times 1 + c,$$
$$\Rightarrow \quad 8 = -\frac{7}{5} + c,$$
$$\Rightarrow \quad c = 8 + \frac{7}{5}$$
$$= \frac{47}{5}.$$

Hence, the equation of the line is $y = -\frac{7}{5}x + \frac{14}{3}$, or equivalently $-7x - 5y + 47 = 0$.

(c) Let m_1 be the gradient of the given line, and m_2 be the gradient of the perpendicular line we wish to find the equation for. Since the given line $3x + 8y - 7 = 0$ is not expressed in the form $y = mx + c$, we must rearrange to find the gradient m_1.

$$3x + 8y - 7 = 0,$$
$$\Rightarrow \quad 8y = -3x + 7,$$
$$\Rightarrow \quad y = -\frac{3}{8}x + \frac{7}{8}.$$

Hence, $m_1 = -\frac{3}{8}$. Equation 4.12 can then be used to find the gradient of any line that is perpendicular to this given line.

$$m_1 m_2 = -1,$$
$$\Rightarrow \quad -\frac{3}{8} m_2 = -1,$$
$$\Rightarrow \quad m_2 = \frac{8}{3}.$$

As the line we wish to find passes through the point $(5,3)$ we find the y-

intercept, c, appearing in the equation of the line $y = m_2 x + c$:

$$y = m_2 x + c,$$
$$\Rightarrow 3 = \frac{8}{3} \times 5 + c,$$
$$\Rightarrow 3 = \frac{40}{3} + c,$$
$$\Rightarrow c = 3 - \frac{40}{3}$$
$$= \frac{31}{3}$$

Hence, the equation of the line is $y = \frac{8}{3}x - \frac{31}{3}$, or equivalently $8x - 3y - 31 = 0$.

(d) Let m_1 be the gradient of the given line, and m_2 be the gradient of the perpendicular line we wish to find the equation for. Since the given line $6x - 11y + 28 = 0$ is not expressed in the form $y = mx + c$, we must rearrange to find the gradient m_1.

$$6x - 11y + 28 = 0,$$
$$\Rightarrow 11y = 6x + 28,$$
$$\Rightarrow y = \frac{6}{11}x + \frac{28}{11}.$$

Hence, $m_1 = \frac{6}{11}$. Equation 4.12 can then be used to find the gradient of any line that is perpendicular to this given line.

$$m_1 m_2 = -1,$$
$$\Rightarrow \frac{6}{11} m_2 = -1,$$
$$\Rightarrow m_2 = -\frac{11}{6}.$$

As the line we wish to find passes through the point $(8, -2)$ we find the y-intercept, c, appearing in the equation of the line $y = m_2 x + c$:

$$y = m_2 x + c,$$
$$\Rightarrow -2 = -\frac{11}{6} \times 8 + c,$$
$$\Rightarrow -2 = -\frac{44}{3} + c,$$
$$\Rightarrow c = -2 + \frac{44}{3}$$
$$= \frac{38}{3}$$

Hence, the equation of the line is $y = -\frac{11}{6}x + \frac{38}{3}$, or equivalently $11x + 6y - 76 = 0$.

Worked Solutions — Exercise 5.1

Q1. (a) Yes, as the leading term is x^2.
   (b) No, as there is no x^2 term.
   (c) Yes, as this is a quadratic in y.
   (d) Yes, since $(x+3)^2 = x^2 + 6x + 9$
   (e) Yes, since the highest order term is $5x^2$.
   (f) No, since $(2x-3)^2 - 4x^2 = 4x^2 - 12x + 9 - 4x^2 = -12x + 9$.

Worked Solutions — Exercise 5.2

Q1. The red, geen and navy blue functions are quadratic.

Worked Solutions — Exercise 5.3

Q1. (a) $x = 0$, $(0, 1)$

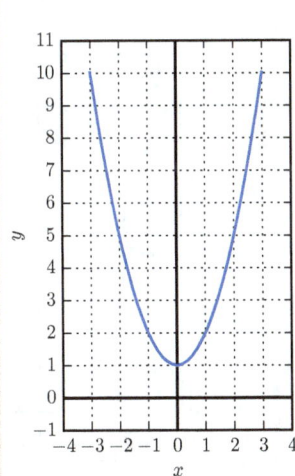

(b) $x = -1$, $(-1, -1)$

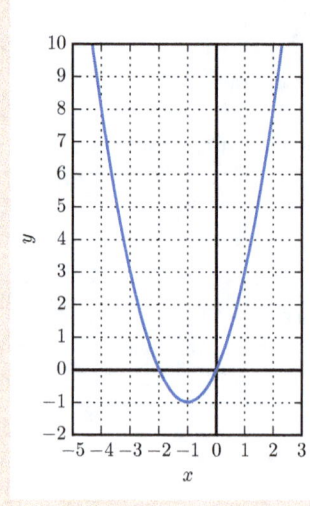

(c) $x = -1$, $(-1, 0)$

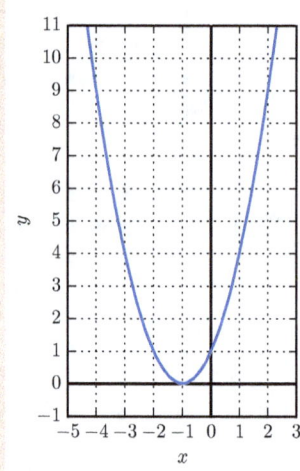

(d) $x = -1$, $(-1, 4)$

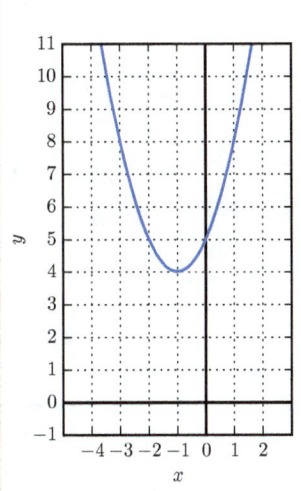

(e) $x = -2$, $(-2, 0)$

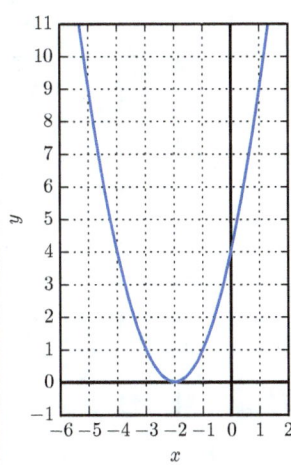

(f) $x = -2$, $(2, 11)$

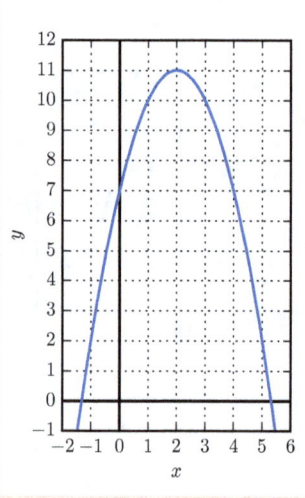

(g) $x = 2$, $(2, 0)$

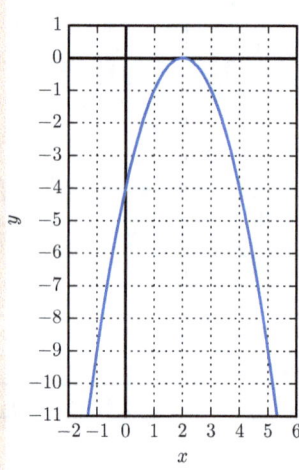

(h) $y = -1/2$, $(7/4, -1/2)$

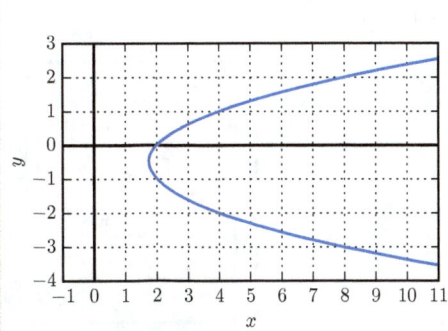

Q2. The plot below shows $f(x) = x^2 - 4x + 3$ (blue) and $f(x) = -x^2 + 4x - 3$ (green). The plot is symmetrical about the x-axis.

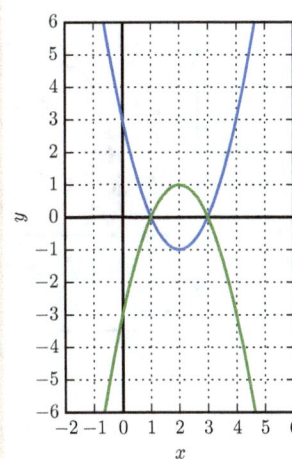

Worked Solutions — Exercise 5.4

Q1. (a) $x^2 + 4x + 4 = (x+2)^2$.

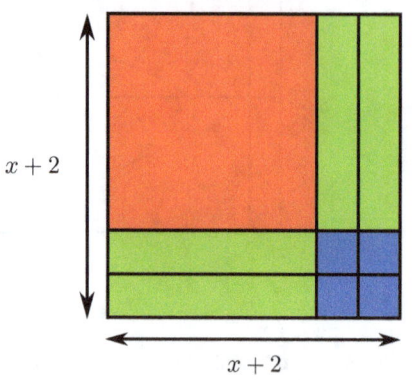

(b) $x^2 + 5x + 6 = (x+2)(x+3)$.

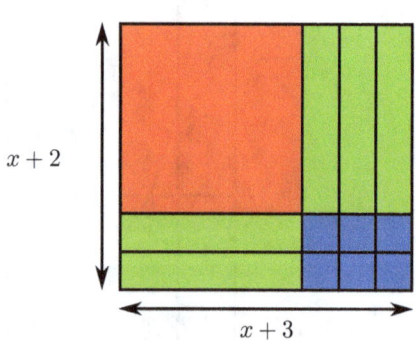

Q2. (a) Since 11 is prime, $(d,e) = (1,11)$ and the factorised form is $x^2 + 12x + 11 = (x+1)(x+11)$.

(b) Since 17 is prime, $(d,e) = (1,17)$ and the factorised form is $x^2 + 18x + 17 = (x+1)(x+17)$.

(c) Since 41 is prime, $(d,e) = (1,41)$ and the factorised form is $x^2 + 42x + 41 = (x+1)(x+41)$.

(d) Since 23 is prime, $(d,e) = (1,23)$ and the factorised form is $t^2 + 24t + 23 = (x+1)(x+23)$.

(e) Since 13 is prime, $(d,e) = (1,-13)$ and the factorised form is $x^2 - 12x - 13 = (x+1)(x-13)$.

(f) Since 23 is prime, $(d,e) = (-1,-23)$ and the factorised form is $x^2 - 24x - 23 = (x-1)(x-23)$.

Q3. (a) We find the possible values of (d,e) by considering the factors of 24: We have $(1,24)$, $(2,12)$, $(3,8)$ and $(4,6)$ as possible pairs. The only pair that sums to 25 is $(d,e) = (1,24)$. Hence, the factorised form is $y = (x+1)(x+24)$.

(b) We find the possible values of (d,e) by considering the factors of 28: We have $(1,28)$, $(2,14)$ and $(4,7)$ as possible pairs. The only pair that sums to 11 is

$(d, e) = (4, 7)$. Hence, the factorised form is $y = (x + 4)(x + 7)$.

(c) We find the possible values of (d, e) by considering the factors of 9: We have $(1, 9)$, and $(3, 3)$ as possible pairs. The only pair that sums to 6 is $(d, e) = (3, 3)$. Hence, the factorised form is $y = (x + 3)(x + 3) = (x + 3)^2$.

(d) We find the possible values of (d, e) by considering the factors of 20: We have $(1, 20)$, $(2, 10)$ and $(4, 5)$ as possible pairs. The only pair that sums to 9 is $(d, e) = (4, 5)$. Hence, the factorised form is $y = (x + 4)(x + 5)$.

(e) We find the possible values of (d, e) by considering the factors of 21: We have $(1, 21)$ and $(3, 7)$ as possible pairs. The only pair that sums to 10 is $(d, e) = (3, 7)$. Hence, the factorised form is $y = (x + 3)(x + 7)$.

(f) We find the possible values of (d, e) by considering the factors of 8: We have $(1, 8)$ and $(2, 4)$ as possible pairs. The only pair that sums to 6 is $(d, e) = (2, 4)$. Hence, the factorised form is $y = (x + 2)(x + 4)$.

(g) We find the possible values of (d, e) by considering the factors of 6, ensuring we account for all possible sign combinations: We have $(1, -6)$, $(-1, 6)$, $(2, -3)$ and $(-2, 3)$ as possible pairs. The only pair that sums to 1 is $(d, e) = (-2, 3)$. Hence, the factorised form is $y = (x - 2)(x + 3)$.

(h) We find the possible values of (d, e) by considering the factors of 35, ensuring we account for all possible sign combinations: We have $(1, -35)$, $(-35, 1)$, $(5, -7)$ and $(-5, 7)$ as possible pairs. The only pair that sums to 2 is $(d, e) = (-5, 7)$. Hence, the factorised form is $y = (x - 5)(x + 7)$.

(i) We find the possible values of (d, e) by considering the factors of 4, ensuring we account for all possible sign combinations: We have $(1, -4)$, $(-1, 4)$, $(2, -2)$ and $(-2, 2)$ as possible pairs. The only pair that sums to 3 is $(d, e) = (-1, 4)$. Hence, the factorised form is $y = (x - 1)(x + 4)$.

(j) We find the possible values of (d, e) by considering the factors of 15, ensuring we account for all possible sign combinations: We have $(1, -15)$, $(-1, 15)$, $(3, -5)$ and $(-3, 5)$ as possible pairs. The only pair that sums to -2 is $(d, e) = (3, -5)$. Hence, the factorised form is $y = (x + 3)(x - 5)$.

(k) We find the possible values of (d, e) by considering the factors of 8, ensuring we account for all possible sign combinations: We have $(1, -8)$, $(-1, 8)$, $(2, -4)$ and $(-2, 4)$ as possible pairs. The only pair that sums to 2 is $(d, e) = (-2, 4)$. Hence, the factorised form is $y = (x - 2)(x + 4)$.

(l) We find the possible values of (d, e) by considering the factors of 8, ensuring we account for all possible sign combinations: We have $(1, -8)$, $(-1, 8)$, $(2, -4)$ and $(-2, 4)$ as possible pairs. The only pair that sums to -2 is $(d, e) = (2, -4)$. Hence, the factorised form is $y = (x + 2)(x - 4)$.

(m) We find the possible values of (d, e) by considering the factors of 5, ensuring we account for all possible sign combinations: We have $(1, -5)$ and $(-1, 5)$ as possible pairs. The only pair that sums to -4 is $(d, e) = (1, -5)$. Hence, the factorised form is $y = (x + 1)(x - 5)$.

(n) We find the possible values of (d, e) by considering the factors of 12, ensuring we account for all possible sign combinations: We have $(1, -12)$, $(-1, 12)$, $(2, -6)$, $(-2, 6)$, $(3, -4)$ and $(-3, 4)$ as possible pairs. The only pair that sums to 1 is $(d, e) = (-3, 4)$. Hence, the factorised form is $y = (x - 3)(x + 4)$.

(o) We find the possible values of (d, e) by considering the factors of 8, ensuring we account for all possible sign combinations: We have $(1, 6)$, $(-1, -6)$, $(2, 3)$

and $(-2,-3)$ as possible pairs. The only pair that sums to -5 is $(d,e) = (-2,-3)$. Hence, the factorised form is $y = (x-2)(x-3)$.

(p) We find the possible values of (d,e) by considering the factors of 8, ensuring we account for all possible sign combinations: We have $(1,6)$, $(-1,-6)$, $(2,3)$ and $(-2,-3)$ as possible pairs. The only pair that sums to -7 is $(d,e) = (-1,-6)$. Hence, the factorised form is $y = (x-1)(x-6)$.

(q) We find the possible values of (d,e) by considering the factors of 24, ensuring we account for all possible sign combinations: We have $(1,24)$, $(-1,-24)$, $(2,12)$, $(-2,-12)$, $(3,8)$, $(-3,-8)$, $(4,6)$ and $(-4,-6)$ as possible pairs. The only pair that sums to -11 is $(d,e) = (-3,-8)$. Hence, the factorised form is $y = (x-3)(x-8)$.

(r) We find the possible values of (d,e) by considering the factors of 35, ensuring we account for all possible sign combinations: We have $(1,35)$, $(-1,-35)$, $(5,7)$ and $(-5,-7)$ as possible pairs. The only pair that sums to -5 is $(d,e) = (-5,-7)$. Hence, the factorised form is $y = (x-5)(x-7)$.

(s) We find the possible values of (d,e) by considering the factors of 24, ensuring we account for all possible sign combinations: We have $(1,24)$, $(-1,-24)$, $(2,12)$, $(-2,-12)$, $(3,8)$, $(-3,-8)$, $(4,6)$ and $(-4,-6)$ as possible pairs. The only pair that sums to -14 is $(d,e) = (-2,-12)$. Hence, the factorised form is $y = (x-2)(x-12)$.

(t) We find the possible values of (d,e) by considering the factors of 42, ensuring we account for all possible sign combinations: We have $(1,42)$, $(-1,-42)$, $(2,21)$, $(-2,-21)$, $(3,14)$, $(-3,-14)$, $(6,7)$ and $(-6,-7)$ as possible pairs. The only pair that sums to -13 is $(d,e) = (-6,-7)$. Hence, the factorised form is $y = (x-6)(x-7)$.

(u) We find the possible values of (d,e) by considering the factors of 42, ensuring we account for all possible sign combinations: We have $(1,-42)$, $(-1,42)$, $(2,-21)$, $(-2,21)$, $(3,-14)$, $(-3,14)$, $(6,-7)$ and $(-6,7)$ as possible pairs. The only pair that sums to -1 is $(d,e) = (6,-7)$. Hence, the factorised form is $y = (x+6)(x-7)$.

(v) We find the possible values of (d,e) by considering the factors of 21, ensuring we account for all possible sign combinations: We have $(1,-21)$, $(3,-7)$ and $(-3,7)$ as possible pairs. The only pair that sums to 4 is $(d,e) = (-3,7)$. Hence, the factorised form is $y = (x-3)(x+7)$.

Worked Solutions — Exercise 5.5

Q1. (a) $y = 2x^2 + 7x + 3 = (2x+1)(x+3)$

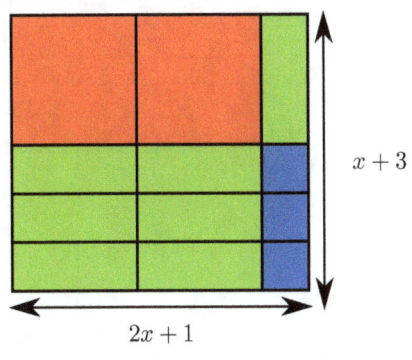

(b) $y = 3x^2 + 4x + 1 = (3x+1)(x+1)$.

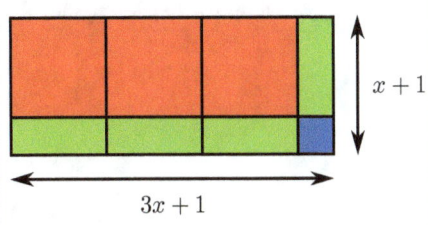

Q2. (a) Since 2 is prime, $f = 2$ and $g = 1$ and so we have,

$$2x^2 + 3x + 1 = (2x+d)(x+e).$$

Hence,

$$de = 1,$$
$$2e + d = 3.$$

Solving the above simultaneous equations we find that $d = 1$ and $e = 1$. Therefore,

$$2x^2 + 3x + 1 = (2x+1)(x+1)$$

(b) Since 2 is prime, $f = 2$ and $g = 1$ and so we have,

$$2x^2 + 5x + 3 = (2x+d)(x+e).$$

Hence,

$$de = 3,$$
$$2e + d = 5.$$

Solving the above simultaneous equations we find that $d = 3$ and $e = 1$. Therefore,
$$2x^2 + 5x + 3 = (2x+3)(x+1)$$

(c) Since 3 is prime, $f = 3$ and $g = 1$ and so we have,
$$3x^2 + 11x + 6 = (3x+d)(x+e).$$

Hence,
$$de = 6,$$
$$3e + d = 11.$$

Solving the above simultaneous equations we find that $d = 2$ and $e = 3$. Therefore,
$$3x^2 + 11x + 6 = (3x+2)(x+3)$$

(d) Since 5 is prime, $f = 5$ and $g = 1$ and so we have,
$$5x^2 + 8x + 3 = (5x+d)(x+e).$$

Hence,
$$de = 3,$$
$$5e + d = 8.$$

Solving the above simultaneous equations we find that $d = 3$ and $e = 1$. Therefore,
$$5x^2 + 8x + 3 = (5x+3)(x+1)$$

(e) Since 5 is prime, $f = 5$ and $g = 1$ and so we have,
$$5x^2 + 14x + 8 = (5x+d)(x+e).$$

Hence,
$$de = 8,$$
$$5e + d = 14.$$

Solving the above simultaneous equations we find that $d = 4$ and $e = 2$. Therefore,
$$5x^2 + 14x + 8 = (5x+4)(x+2)$$

(f) Since 7 is prime, $f = 7$ and $g = 1$ and so we have,
$$7x^2 + 20x - 33 = (7x+d)(x+e).$$

Hence,
$$de = -3,$$
$$7e + d = 20.$$

Solving the above simultaneous equations we find that $d = -1$ and $e = 3$. Therefore,
$$7x^2 + 20x - 3 = (7x - 1)(x + 3)$$

(g) Since 7 is prime, $f = 7$ and $g = 1$ and so we have,
$$7x^2 - 33x - 10 = (7x + d)(x + e).$$

Hence,
$$de = -10,$$
$$7e + d = -33.$$

Solving the above simultaneous equations we find that $d = 2$ and $e = -5$. Therefore,
$$7x^2 - 33x - 10 = (7x + 2)(x - 5)$$

(h) Since 13 is prime, $f = 13$ and $g = 1$ and so we have,
$$13x^2 - 29x + 6 = (13x + d)(x + e).$$

Hence,
$$de = 6,$$
$$7e + d = -29.$$

Solving the above simultaneous equations we find that $d = -3$ and $e = -2$. Therefore,
$$13x^2 - 29x + 6 = (13x - 3)(x - 2)$$

Q3. (a) We take $(f, g) = (2, 2)$ and consider $(2x + d)(2x + e)$. Hence,
$$de = = 4,$$
$$2e + 2d = 8.$$

Solving the above simultaneous equations we find that $e = 2$ and $d = 2$. Therefore,
$$4x^2 + 8x + 4 = (2x + 2)(2x + 2),$$
$$= (2x + 2)^2.$$

(b) First we notice that $4x^2 + 10x + 6 = 2(2x^2 + 5x + 3)$ and so we need to factorise $2x^2 + 5x + 3$. We take $(f,g) = (2,1)$ and consider $(2x+d)(x+e)$. Hence,

$$de = 3,$$
$$d + 2e = 5.$$

Solving the above simultaneous equations we find that $e = 1$ and $d = 3$. Therefore,

$$4x^2 + 10x + 6 = 2(x+1)(2x+3)$$

(c) We take $(f,g) = (2,3)$ and consider $(2x+d)(3x+e)$. Hence,

$$de = = 2,$$
$$2e + 3d = 8.$$

Solving the above simultaneous equations we find that $d = 2$ and $e = 1$. Therefore,

$$6x^2 + 8x + 2 = (2x+2)(3x+1)$$

(d) Trying $(f,g) = (2,2)$ and considering $(2x+d)(2x+e)$ we obtain the following simultaneous equations,

$$de = 3,$$
$$2d + 2e = 7.$$

This system of equations does not admit a solution, so we try $(f,g) = (1,4)$ and consider $(x+d)(4x+e)$. Hence,

$$de = = 3,$$
$$4d + e = 7.$$

Solving the above simultaneous equations we find that $d = 1$ and $e = 3$. Therefore,

$$4x^2 + 7x + 3 = (x+1)(4x+3)$$

(e) We take $(f,g) = (2,4)$ and consider $(2x+d)(4x+e)$. Hence,

$$de = = -15,$$
$$2e + 4d = -2.$$

Solving the above simultaneous equations we find that $d = -3$ and $e = 5$. Therefore,

$$8x^2 - 2x - 15 = (2x-3)(4x+5)$$

(f) Here the possible factor pairs for (f,g) are $(1,12)$, $(2,6)$ and $(3,4)$. Following the heuristic we choose $(f,g) = (3,4)$ and consider $(3x+d)(4x+e)$. Hence,

$$de == 2,$$
$$4d + 3e = -10.$$

Solving the above simultaneous equations we find that $d = -1$ and $e = -2$. Therefore,

$$12x^2 - 10x + 2 = (3x-1)(4x-2)$$

(g) Here the possible factor pairs for (f,g) are $(1,10)$ and $(2,5)$. Following the heuristic we choose $(f,g) = (2,5)$ and consider $(2x+d)(5x+e)$. Hence,

$$de == -2,$$
$$2e + 5d = -1.$$

Solving the above simultaneous equations we find that $d = -1$ and $e = 2$. Therefore,

$$10x^2 - x - 2 = (5x+2)(2x-1)$$

(h) Here the possible factor pairs for (f,g) are $(1,10)$ and $(2,5)$. Following the heuristic we choose $(f,g) = (2,5)$ and consider $(2x+d)(5x+e)$. Hence,

$$de == 6,$$
$$2e + 5d = 32.$$

The above pair of equations does not admit a solution, and so we instead take $(f,g) = (1,10)$ and consider $(x+d)(10x+e)$. This leads to the following system of equations,

$$de = 6,$$
$$10d + e = 32.$$

Solving the above simultaneous equations we find that $d = 3$ and $e = 2$. Therefore,

$$10x^2 + 32x + 6 = (10x+2)(x+3)$$

(i) Here the possible factor pairs for (f,g) are $(1,12)$, $(2,2)$ and $(3,4)$. Following the heuristic we choose $(f,g) = (3,4)$ and consider $(3x+d)(4x+e)$. Hence,

$$de == 5,$$
$$3e + 4d = 32.$$

The above pair of equations does not admit a solution, and so we instead try $(f, g) = (2, 6)$ and consider $(2x + d)(6x + e)$. This leads to the following system of equations,

$$de = 5,$$
$$6d + 2e = 32.$$

Solving the above simultaneous equations we find that $d = 5$ and $e = 1$. Therefore,

$$12x^2 + 32x + 5 = (2x + 5)(6x + 1)$$

(j) Here the possible factor pairs for (f, g) are $(1, 30), (2, 15), (3, 10)$ and $(5, 6)$. Following the heuristic we choose $(f, g) = (5, 6)$ and consider $(5x + d)(6x + e)$. Hence,

$$de = = 14,$$
$$6d + 5e = 47.$$

Solving the above simultaneous equations we find that $d = 2$ and $e = 7$. Therefore,

$$30x^2 + 47x + 14 = (5x + 2)(6x + 7)$$

Worked Solutions — Exercise 5.6

Q1. (a) $y = x^2 + 6x + 9 = (x + 3)^2$.

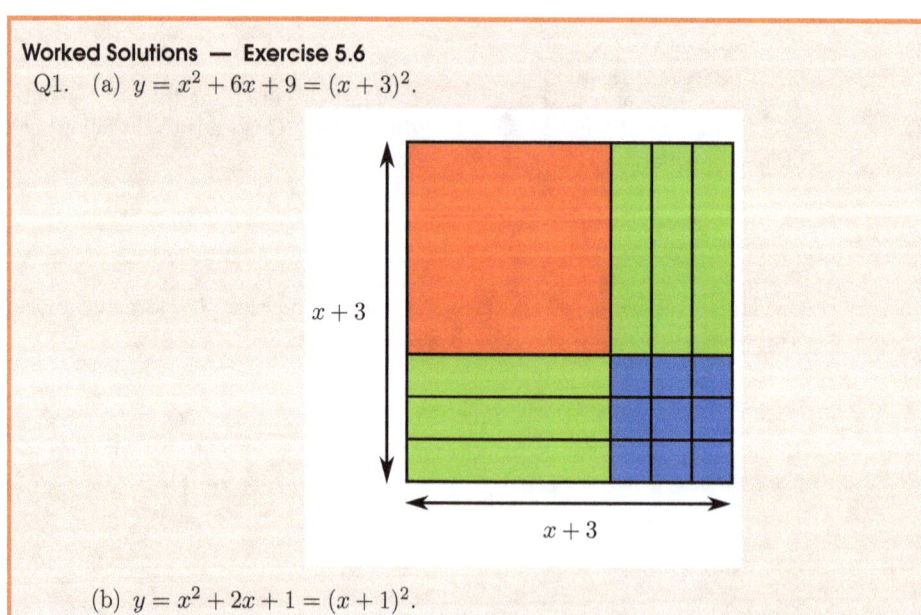

(b) $y = x^2 + 2x + 1 = (x + 1)^2$.

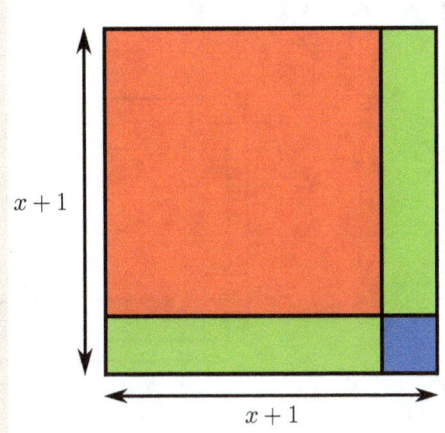

Q2. (a) We halve 4 to get 2, so we check that $(x+2)^2$ gives us the desired quadratic. It does, and so, $y = x^2 + 4x + 4 = (x+2)^2$.
 (b) We halve 14 to get 7, so we check that $(x+7)^2$ gives us the desired quadratic. It does, and so, $y = x^2 + 14x + 49 = (x+7)^2$.
 (c) We halve 16 to get 8, so we check that $(x+8)^2$ gives us the desired quadratic. It does, and so, $y = x^2 + 16x + 64 = (x+8)^2$.
 (d) We halve 6 to get 3, so we check that $(x+3)^2$ gives us the desired quadratic. It does, and so, $y = x^2 + 6x + 9 = (x+3)^2$.
 (e) We halve -2 to get -1, so we check that $(x-1)^2$ gives us the desired quadratic. It does, and so, $y = x^2 - 2x + 1 = (x-1)^2$.
 (f) We halve -10 to get -5, so we check that $(x-5)^2$ gives us the desired quadratic. It does, and so, $y = x^2 - 10x + 25 = (x-5)^2$.

Q3. (a) We halve $\frac{2}{3}$ to get $\frac{1}{3}$ and check that $\left(x+\frac{1}{3}\right)^2$ leads to the desired quadratic function. It does, and so, $y = x^2 + \frac{2}{3}x + \frac{1}{9} = \left(x+\frac{1}{3}\right)^2$.
 (b) We halve $-\frac{2}{3}$ to get $-\frac{1}{3}$ and check that $\left(x-\frac{1}{3}\right)^2$ leads to the desired quadratic function. It does, and so, $y = x^2 - \frac{2}{3}x + \frac{1}{9} = \left(x-\frac{1}{3}\right)^2$.
 (c) We halve $\frac{8}{5}$ to get $\frac{4}{5}$ and check that $\left(x+\frac{4}{5}\right)^2$ leads to the desired quadratic function. It does, and so, $y = x^2 + \frac{8}{5}x + \frac{16}{25} = \left(x+\frac{4}{5}\right)^2$.
 (d) We halve $\frac{6}{7}$ to get $\frac{3}{7}$ and check that $\left(x+\frac{3}{7}\right)^2$ leads to the desired quadratic function. It does, and so, $y = x^2 + \frac{6}{7}x + \frac{9}{49} = \left(x+\frac{3}{7}\right)^2$.
 (e) We halve $-\frac{2}{5}$ to get $-\frac{1}{5}$ and check that $\left(x-\frac{1}{5}\right)^2$ leads to the desired quadratic function. It does, and so, $y = x^2 - \frac{2}{5}x + \frac{1}{25} = \left(x-\frac{1}{5}\right)^2$.
 (f) We halve $\frac{8}{9}$ to get $\frac{4}{9}$ and check that $\left(x+\frac{4}{9}\right)^2$ leads to the desired quadratic function. It does, and so, $y = x^2 + \frac{8}{9}x + \frac{16}{81} = \left(x+\frac{4}{9}\right)^2$.

Worked Solutions — Exercise 5.7

Q1. (a) $y = x^2 + 2x + 2$.

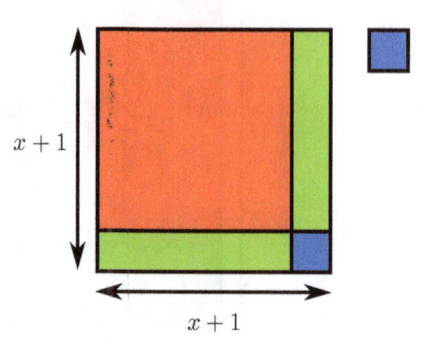

(b) $y = x^2 + 6x + 3$.

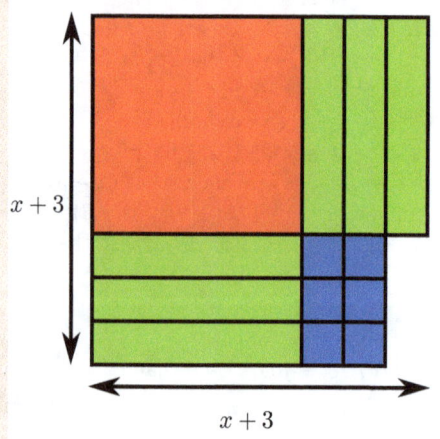

Q2. (a)
$$y = x^2 + 2x + 2$$
$$= (x+1)^2 - 1^2 + 2$$
$$= (x+1)^2 + 1.$$

(b)
$$y = x^2 + 2x + 5$$
$$= (x+1)^2 - 1^2 + 5$$
$$= (x+1)^2 + 4.$$

(c)
$$y = x^2 + 4x + 9$$
$$= (x+2)^2 - 2^2 + 9$$
$$= (x+2)^2 + 5.$$

(d)
$$y = x^2 + 6x + 11$$
$$= (x+3)^2 - 3^2 + 11$$
$$= (x+3)^2 + 2.$$

(e)
$$y = x^2 + 6x + 4$$
$$= (x+3)^2 - 3^2 + 4$$
$$= (x+3)^2 - 5.$$

(f)
$$y = x^2 + 4x - 4$$
$$= (x+2)^2 - 2^2 - 4$$
$$= (x+2)^2 - 8.$$

(g)
$$y = x^2 + 2x - 5$$
$$= (x+1)^2 - 1^2 - 5$$
$$= (x+1)^2 - 6.$$

(h)
$$y = x^2 - 4x + 9$$
$$= (x-2)^2 - (-2)^2 + 9$$
$$= (x-2)^2 + 5.$$

(i)
$$y = x^2 - 8x + 22$$
$$= (x-4)^2 - (-4)^2 + 22$$
$$= (x-4)^2 + 6.$$

(j)
$$y = x^2 - 2x + 16$$
$$= (x-1)^2 - (-1)^2 + 16$$
$$= (x-1)^2 + 15.$$

Q3. (a)
$$y = x^2 + 3x + 4$$
$$= \left(x + \frac{3}{2}\right)^2 - \frac{9}{4} + 4$$
$$= \left(x + \frac{3}{2}\right)^2 + \frac{7}{4}.$$

(b)
$$y = x^2 + 3x + 7$$
$$= \left(x + \frac{3}{2}\right)^2 - \frac{9}{4} + 7$$
$$= \left(x + \frac{3}{2}\right)^2 + \frac{19}{4}.$$

(c)
$$y = x^2 + x + 4$$
$$= \left(x + \frac{1}{2}\right)^2 - \frac{1}{4} + 4$$
$$= \left(x + \frac{1}{2}\right)^2 + \frac{15}{4}.$$

(d)
$$y = x^2 + 5x - 7$$
$$= \left(x + \frac{5}{2}\right)^2 - \frac{25}{4} - 7$$
$$= \left(x + \frac{5}{2}\right)^2 - \frac{53}{4}.$$

(e)
$$y = x^2 + 5x + 9$$
$$= \left(x + \frac{5}{2}\right)^2 - \frac{25}{4} + 9$$
$$= \left(x + \frac{5}{2}\right)^2 + \frac{11}{4}.$$

(f)
$$y = x^2 - 3x - 3$$
$$= \left(x - \frac{3}{2}\right)^2 - \frac{9}{4} - 3$$
$$= \left(x - \frac{3}{2}\right)^2 - \frac{21}{4}.$$

(g)
$$y = x^2 - 11x + 4$$
$$= \left(x - \frac{11}{2}\right)^2 - \frac{121}{4} - 3$$
$$= \left(x - \frac{11}{2}\right)^2 - \frac{105}{4}.$$

(h)
$$y = x^2 - 5x - 3$$
$$= \left(x - \frac{5}{2}\right)^2 - \frac{25}{4} - 3$$
$$= \left(x - \frac{5}{2}\right)^2 - \frac{37}{4}.$$

(i)
$$y = x^2 - x - 1$$
$$= \left(x - \frac{1}{2}\right)^2 - \frac{1}{4} - 1$$
$$= \left(x - \frac{1}{2}\right)^2 - \frac{5}{4}.$$

(j)
$$y = x^2 - 5x + 6$$
$$= \left(x - \frac{5}{2}\right)^2 - \frac{25}{4} + 6$$
$$= \left(x - \frac{5}{2}\right)^2 - \frac{1}{4}.$$

Q4. (a)
$$\begin{aligned} y &= -x^2 - 6x - 2 \\ &= -\left(x^2 + 6x\right) - 2 \\ &= -\left[(x+3)^2 - 9\right] - 2 \\ &= -(x+3)^2 + 7. \end{aligned}$$

(b)
$$\begin{aligned} y &= -x^2 + 2x + 1 \\ &= -\left(x^2 - 2x\right) + 1 \\ &= -\left[(x-1)^2 - 1\right] + 1 \\ &= -(x-1)^2 + 2. \end{aligned}$$

(c)
$$\begin{aligned} y &= -x^2 + 4x - 3 \\ &= -\left(x^2 - 4x\right) - 3 \\ &= -\left[(x-2)^2 - 4\right] - 3 \\ &= -(x-2)^2 + 1. \end{aligned}$$

(d)
$$\begin{aligned} y &= -x^2 - 8x + 4 \\ &= -\left(x^2 + 8x\right) + 4 \\ &= -\left[(x+4)^2 - 16\right] + 4 \\ &= -(x+4)^2 + 20. \end{aligned}$$

(e)
$$\begin{aligned} y &= -x^2 + 5x - 2 \\ &= -\left(x^2 - 5x\right) - 2 \\ &= -\left[\left(x - \frac{5}{2}\right)^2 - \frac{25}{4}\right] - 2 \\ &= -\left(x - \frac{5}{2}\right)^2 + \frac{17}{4}. \end{aligned}$$

(f)
$$y = -x^2 - 3x$$
$$= -\left(x^2 + 3x\right)$$
$$= -\left[\left(x + \frac{3}{2}\right)^2 - \frac{9}{4}\right]$$
$$= -\left(x + \frac{3}{2}\right)^2 + \frac{9}{4}.$$

(g)
$$y = -x^2 - 14x - 49$$
$$= -\left(x^2 + 14x\right) - 49$$
$$= -\left[(x+7)^2 - 49\right] - 49$$
$$= -(x+7)^2.$$

(h)
$$y = -x^2 + 7x - 4$$
$$= -\left(x^2 - 7x\right) - 4$$
$$= -\left[\left(x - \frac{7}{2}\right)^2 - \frac{49}{4}\right] - 4$$
$$= -\left(x - \frac{7}{2}\right)^2 + \frac{33}{4}.$$

Q5. (a)
$$y = 2x^2 + 4x + 6$$
$$= 2\left[x^2 + 2x\right] + 6$$
$$= 2\left[(x+1)^2 - 1\right] + 6$$
$$= 2(x+1)^2 + 4.$$

(b)
$$y = 2x^2 - 8x + 2$$
$$= 2\left[x^2 - 4x\right] + 2$$
$$= 2\left[(x-2)^2 - 4\right] + 2$$
$$= 2(x-2)^2 - 6.$$

(c)
$$\begin{aligned}y &= 3x^2 + 12x + 1 \\ &= 3\left[x^2 + 4x\right] + 1 \\ &= 3\left[(x+2)^2 - 4\right] + 1 \\ &= 3(x+1)^2 - 11.\end{aligned}$$

(d)
$$\begin{aligned}y &= 5x^2 - 20x - 2 \\ &= 5\left[x^2 - 4x\right] - 2 \\ &= 5\left[(x-2)^2 - 4\right] - 2 \\ &= 5(x-2)^2 - 22.\end{aligned}$$

(e)
$$\begin{aligned}y &= 2x^2 - 3x + 1 \\ &= 2\left[x^2 - \frac{3}{2}x\right] + 1 \\ &= 2\left[\left(x - \frac{3}{4}\right)^2 - \frac{9}{16}\right] + 1 \\ &= 2\left(x - \frac{3}{4}\right)^2 - \frac{1}{8}.\end{aligned}$$

(f)
$$\begin{aligned}y &= 3x^2 + 4x + 5 \\ &= 3\left[x^2 - \frac{4}{3}x\right] + 5 \\ &= 3\left[\left(x - \frac{2}{3}\right)^2 - \frac{4}{9}\right] + 5 \\ &= 3\left(x - \frac{2}{3}\right)^2 - \frac{11}{3}.\end{aligned}$$

(g)
$$\begin{aligned}y &= 7x^2 - 3x + 14 \\ &= 7\left[x^2 - \frac{3}{7}x\right] + 14 \\ &= 7\left[\left(x - \frac{3}{14}\right)^2 - \frac{9}{196}\right] + 14 \\ &= 7\left(x - \frac{3}{14}\right)^2 - \frac{383}{28}.\end{aligned}$$

(h)
$$\begin{aligned}y &= 5x^2 - 12x + 3 \\ &= 5\left[x^2 - \frac{12}{5}x\right] + 3 \\ &= 5\left[\left(x - \frac{6}{5}\right)^2 - \frac{36}{25}\right] + 3 \\ &= 5\left(x - \frac{6}{5}\right)^2 - \frac{21}{5}.\end{aligned}$$

Q6. (a) $(-1, -6)$.

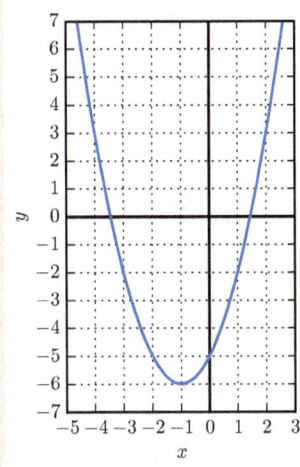

(b) $(-3, -6)$.

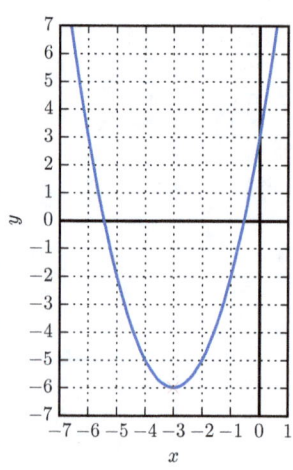

(c) $(3, 2)$.

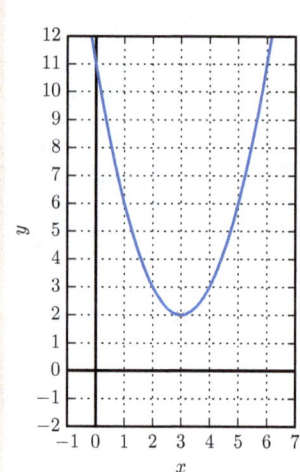

(d) $\left(\frac{1}{2}, \frac{43}{4}\right)$.

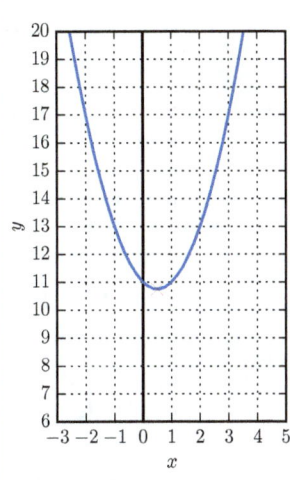

(e) $\left(\frac{3}{2}, -\frac{25}{4}\right)$.

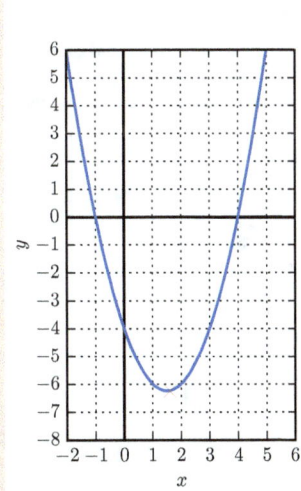

(f) $\left(\frac{1}{2}, -\frac{19}{4}\right)$.

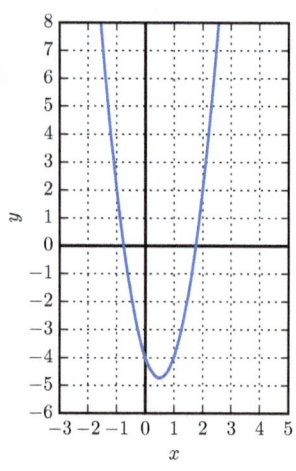

(g) $\left(-\frac{5}{8}, -\frac{441}{16}\right)$.

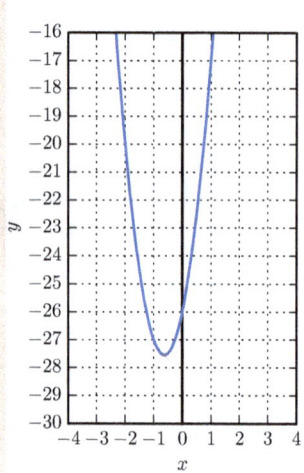

(h) $\left(\frac{1}{4}, \frac{39}{8}\right)$

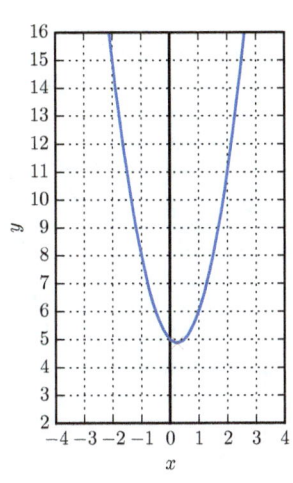

(i) $\left(\frac{7}{10}, -\frac{29}{20}\right)$

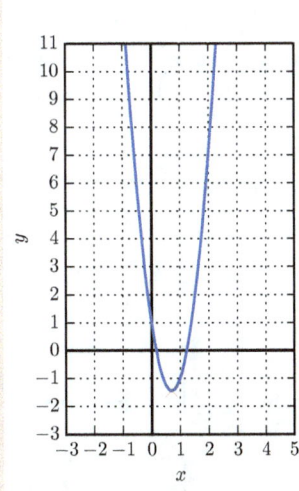

(j) $(-4, -39)$

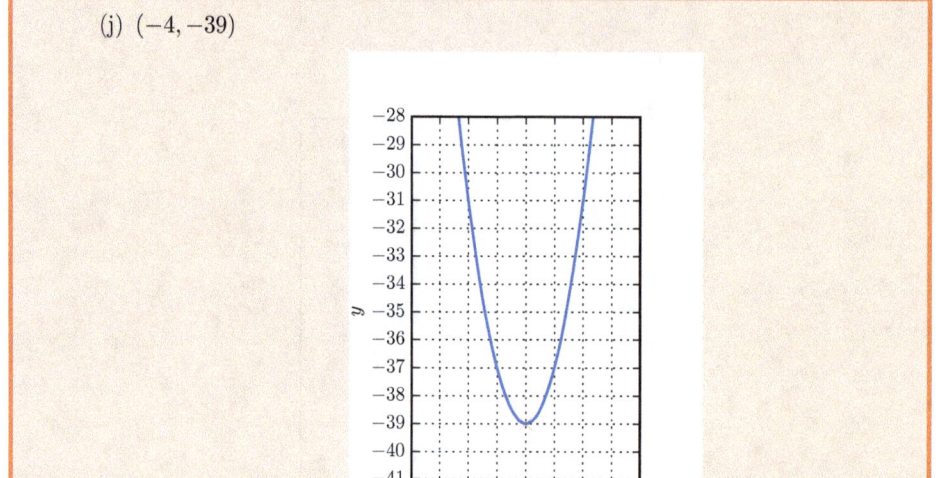

Worked Solutions — Exercise 5.8

Q1. (a) Plotting the graph as shown below we find that the solutions are approximately $x_1 \approx -0.2$ and $x_2 \approx 4.2$.

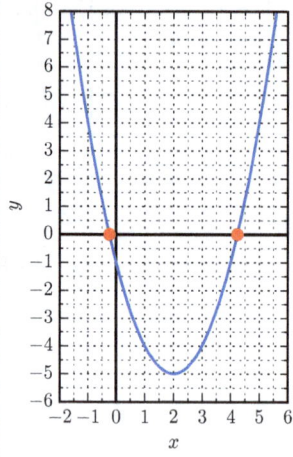

(b) Plotting the graph as shown below we find that the solutions are approximately $x_1 \approx -1.2$ and $x_2 \approx 3.2$.

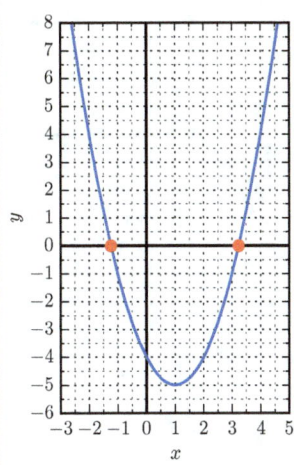

(c) Plotting the graph as shown below we find that the solutions are approximately $x_1 \approx -3.2$ and $x_2 \approx 1.2$.

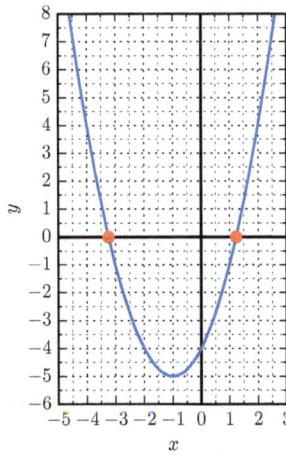

(d) Plotting the graph as shown below we find that the solutions are approximately $x_1 \approx -5.8$ and $x_2 \approx -0.2$.

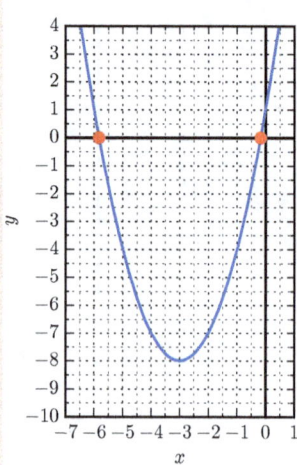

(e) Plotting the graph as shown below we find that the solutions are approximately $x_1 = -5$ and $x_2 = -1$.

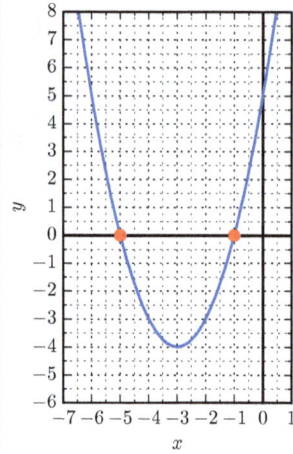

(f) Plotting the graph as shown below we find that the solutions are approximately $x_1 \approx -1.4$ and $x_2 \approx 3.4$.

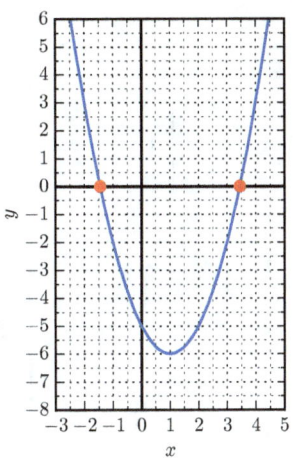

(g) Plotting the graph as shown below we find that the solutions are approximately $x_1 \approx -4.7$ and $x_2 \approx 1.7$.

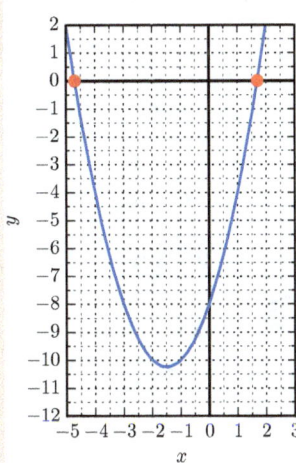

(h) Plotting the graph as shown below we find that the solutions are approximately $x_1 \approx -3.6$ and $x_2 \approx 0.6$.

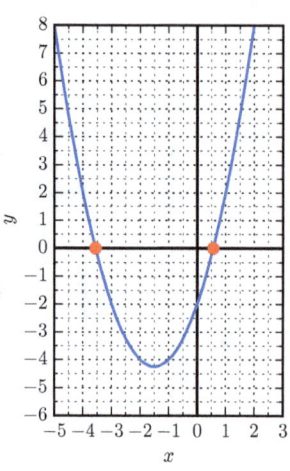

Q2. (a) Factorising the quadratic,
$$x^2 - 2x - 3 = 0$$
$$\Rightarrow \quad (x-3)(x+1) = 0.$$

From this, we have $x - 3 = 0$ or $x + 1 = 0$, and so the roots of the equation are $x = 3$ and $x = -1$.

(b) Factorising the quadratic,
$$x^2 + 11x + 28 = 0$$
$$\Rightarrow \quad (x+4)(x+7) = 0.$$

From this, we have $x + 4 = 0$ or $x + 7 = 0$, and so the roots of the equation are $x = -4$ and $x = -7$.

(c) Factorising the quadratic,
$$x^2 - x - 12 = 0$$
$$\Rightarrow \quad (x+3)(x-4) = 0.$$

From this, we have $x + 3 = 0$ or $x - 4 = 0$, and so the roots of the equation are $x = -3$ and $x = 4$.

(d) Factorising the quadratic,
$$2x^2 + 7x + 3 = 0$$
$$\Rightarrow \quad (2x+1)(x+3) = 0.$$

From this, we have $2x + 1 = 0$ or $x + 3 = 0$, and so the roots of the equation are $x = -\frac{1}{2}$ and $x = -3$.

(e) Factorising the quadratic,
$$2x^2 - x - 3 = 0$$
$$\Rightarrow \quad (2x-3)(x+1) = 0.$$

From this, we have $2x - 3 = 0$ or $x + 1 = 0$, and so the roots of the equation are $x = \frac{3}{2}$ and $x = -1$.

(f) Factorising the quadratic,
$$6x^2 - 11x + 3 = 0$$
$$\Rightarrow \quad (2x-3)(3x-1) = 0.$$

From this, we have $2x - 3 = 0$ or $3x - 1 = 0$, and so the roots of the equation are $x = \frac{3}{2}$ and $x = \frac{1}{3}$.

(g) Factorising the quadratic,
$$6x^2 + 7x - 5 = 0$$
$$\Rightarrow \quad (3x+5)(2x-1) = 0.$$

From this, we have $3x + 5 = 0$ or $2x - 1 = 0$, and so the roots of the equation are $x = -\frac{5}{3}$ and $x = \frac{1}{2}$.

(h) Factorising the quadratic,
$$12x^2 - 25x + 7 = 0$$
$$\Rightarrow \quad (4x-7)(3x-1) = 0.$$

From this, we have $4x - 7 = 0$ or $3x - 1 = 0$, and so the roots of the equation are $x = \frac{7}{4}$ and $x = \frac{1}{3}$.

Q3. (a) Completing the square, we have
$$x^2 + 4x - 1 = (x+2)^2 - 5$$

Setting this equal to zero, we can rearrange to find the roots of the quadratic.
$$(x+2)^2 - 5 = 0$$
$$\Rightarrow \quad (x+2)^2 = 5$$
$$\Rightarrow \quad x+2 = \pm\sqrt{5}$$
$$\Rightarrow \quad x = -2 \pm \sqrt{5}$$

(b) Completing the square, we have
$$x^2 - 8x + 9 = (x-4)^2 - 7$$

Setting this equal to zero, we can rearrange to find the roots of the quadratic.

$$(x-4)^2 - 7 = 0$$
$$\Rightarrow \quad (x-4)^2 = 7$$
$$\Rightarrow \quad x-4 = \pm\sqrt{7}$$
$$\Rightarrow \quad x = 4 \pm \sqrt{7}$$

(c) Completing the square, we have

$$x^2 + 8x - 4 = (x+4)^2 - 20$$

Setting this equal to zero, we can rearrange to find the roots of the quadratic.

$$(x+4)^2 - 20 = 0$$
$$\Rightarrow \quad (x+4)^2 = 20$$
$$\Rightarrow \quad x+4 = \pm\sqrt{20}$$
$$\Rightarrow \quad x = -4 \pm \sqrt{20}$$

(d) Completing the square, we have

$$x^2 + 2x - 1 = (x+1)^2 - 2$$

Setting this equal to zero, we can rearrange to find the roots of the quadratic.

$$(x+1)^2 - 2 = 0$$
$$\Rightarrow \quad (x+1)^2 = 2$$
$$\Rightarrow \quad x+1 = \pm\sqrt{2}$$
$$\Rightarrow \quad x = -1 \pm \sqrt{2}$$

(e) Completing the square, we have

$$x^2 - 3x - 3 = \left(x - \frac{3}{2}\right)^2 - \frac{21}{4}$$

Setting this equal to zero, we can rearrange to find the roots of the quadratic.

$$\left(x - \frac{3}{2}\right)^2 - \frac{21}{4} = 0$$
$$\Rightarrow \quad \left(x - \frac{3}{2}\right)^2 = \frac{21}{4}$$
$$\Rightarrow \quad x - \frac{3}{2} = \pm\sqrt{\frac{21}{4}}$$
$$\Rightarrow \quad x = \frac{3}{2} \pm \sqrt{\frac{21}{4}}$$

(f) Completing the square, we have
$$x^2 + 4x + 3 = (x+2)^2 - 1$$

Setting this equal to zero, we can rearrange to find the roots of the quadratic.

$$(x+2)^2 - 1 = 0$$
$$\Rightarrow (x+2)^2 = 1$$
$$\Rightarrow x + 2 = \pm\sqrt{1}$$
$$\Rightarrow x = -2 \pm 1$$

Hence, $x = -3$ or $x = -1$.

(g) Completing the square, we have
$$x^2 - 2x - 4 = (x-1)^2 - 5$$

Setting this equal to zero, we can rearrange to find the roots of the quadratic.

$$(x-1)^2 - 5 = 0$$
$$\Rightarrow (x-1)^2 = 5$$
$$\Rightarrow x - 1 = \pm\sqrt{5}$$
$$\Rightarrow x = 1 \pm \sqrt{5}$$

(h) Completing the square, we have
$$x^2 + 6x + 3 = (x+3)^2 - 6$$

Setting this equal to zero, we can rearrange to find the roots of the quadratic.

$$(x+3)^2 - 6 = 0$$
$$\Rightarrow (x+3)^2 = 6$$
$$\Rightarrow x + 3 = \pm\sqrt{6}$$
$$\Rightarrow x = -3 \pm \sqrt{6}$$

Q4. (a) Looking at the coefficients in the quadratic $x^2 + 3x + 1$ we note that $a = 1$, $b = 3$ and $c = 1$. Applying the quadratic formula we find that the solutions are,

$$x = \frac{-3 \pm \sqrt{3^2 - 4 \cdot 1 \cdot 1}}{2 \cdot 1}$$
$$= \frac{-3 \pm \sqrt{9 - 4}}{2}$$
$$= \frac{-3 \pm \sqrt{5}}{2}.$$

(b) Looking at the coefficients in the quadratic $x^2 + 5x - 2$ we note that $a = 1$, $b = 5$ and $c = -2$. Applying the quadratic formula we find that the solutions

are,
$$x = \frac{-5 \pm \sqrt{5^2 - 4 \cdot 1 \cdot (-2)}}{2 \cdot 1}$$
$$= \frac{-5 \pm \sqrt{25 + 8}}{2}$$
$$= \frac{-5 \pm \sqrt{33}}{2}.$$

(c) Looking at the coefficients in the quadratic $x^2 - 3x + 1$ we note that $a = 1$, $b = -3$ and $c = 1$. Applying the quadratic formula we find that the solutions are,
$$x = \frac{3 \pm \sqrt{(-3)^2 - 4 \cdot 1 \cdot 1}}{2 \cdot 1}$$
$$= \frac{3 \pm \sqrt{9 - 4}}{2}$$
$$= \frac{3 \pm \sqrt{5}}{2}.$$

(d) Looking at the coefficients in the quadratic $x^2 + 2x + 1$ we note that $a = 1$, $b = 2$ and $c = 1$. Applying the quadratic formula we find that the solutions are,
$$x = \frac{-2 \pm \sqrt{2^2 - 4 \cdot 1 \cdot 1}}{2 \cdot 1}$$
$$= \frac{-2 \pm \sqrt{4 - 4}}{2}$$
$$= \frac{-2}{2}$$
$$= -1,$$
which is a repeated root.

(e) Looking at the coefficients in the quadratic $2x^2 + 3x - 4$ we note that $a = 2$, $b = 3$ and $c = -4$. Applying the quadratic formula we find that the solutions are,
$$x = \frac{-3 \pm \sqrt{3^2 - 4 \cdot 2 \cdot (-4)}}{2 \cdot 2}$$
$$= \frac{-3 \pm \sqrt{9 + 32}}{4}$$
$$= \frac{-3 \pm \sqrt{41}}{4}.$$

(f) Looking at the coefficients in the quadratic $5x^2 + 5x - 2$ we note that $a = 5$, $b = 5$ and $c = -2$. Applying the quadratic formula we find that the solutions

are,
$$x = \frac{-5 \pm \sqrt{5^2 - 4 \cdot 5 \cdot (-2)}}{2 \cdot 5}$$
$$= \frac{-5 \pm \sqrt{25 + 40}}{10}$$
$$= \frac{-5 \pm \sqrt{65}}{10}.$$

(g) Looking at the coefficients in the quadratic $3x^2 + 8x - 4$ we note that $a = 3$, $b = 8$ and $c = -4$. Applying the quadratic formula we find that the solutions are,
$$x = \frac{-8 \pm \sqrt{8^2 - 4 \cdot 3 \cdot (-4)}}{2 \cdot 3}$$
$$= \frac{-8 \pm \sqrt{64 + 48}}{6}$$
$$= \frac{-8 \pm \sqrt{112}}{6}$$
$$= \frac{-8 \pm 4\sqrt{7}}{6}$$
$$= \frac{-4 \pm 2\sqrt{7}}{3}.$$

(h) Looking at the coefficients in the quadratic $3x^2 - 5x - 2$ we note that $a = 3$, $b = -5$ and $c = -2$. Applying the quadratic formula we find that the solutions are,
$$x = \frac{5 \pm \sqrt{(-5)^2 - 4 \cdot 3 \cdot (-2)}}{2 \cdot 3}$$
$$= \frac{5 \pm \sqrt{25 + 24}}{6}$$
$$= \frac{5 \pm \sqrt{49}}{6}$$
$$= \frac{5 \pm 7}{6}.$$

In this case the two roots are $x = -\frac{1}{3}$ and $x = 2$.

Worked Solutions — Exercise 5.9

Q1. (a)
$$\Delta = b^2 - 4ac$$
$$= 3^2 - 4 \times 1 \times (-2)$$
$$= 17$$

(b)
$$\Delta = b^2 - 4ac$$
$$= 1^2 - 4 \times 1 \times 5$$
$$= -19$$

(c)
$$\Delta = b^2 - 4ac$$
$$= 2^2 - 4 \times 2 \times (-1)$$
$$= 12$$

(d)
$$\Delta = b^2 - 4ac$$
$$= (-2)^2 - 4 \times 1 \times 6$$
$$= -20$$

(e)
$$\Delta = b^2 - 4ac$$
$$= (-2)^2 - 4 \times (-1) \times 5$$
$$= 24$$

(f)
$$\Delta = b^2 - 4ac$$
$$= (-6)^2 - 4 \times (-1)$$
$$= 40$$

(g)
$$\Delta = b^2 - 4ac$$
$$= 8^2 - 4 \times 1 \times 4$$
$$= 48$$

(h)
$$\Delta = b^2 - 4ac$$
$$= 3^2 - 4 \times 1 \times 4$$
$$= -7$$

(i)
$$\Delta = b^2 - 4ac$$
$$= 4^2 - 4 \times 2 \times 2$$
$$= 0$$

(j)
$$\Delta = b^2 - 4ac$$
$$= 2^2 - 4 \times 1 \times (-5)$$
$$= 24$$

Q2. (a)
$$\Delta = b^2 - 4ac$$
$$= 5^2 - 4 \times 1 \times 6$$
$$= 1$$

So there are two real and distinct roots.

(b)
$$\Delta = b^2 - 4ac$$
$$= 5^2 - 4 \times 1 \times 1$$
$$= 21$$

So there are two real and distinct roots.

(c)
$$\Delta = b^2 - 4ac$$
$$= 0^2 - 4 \times 1 \times 1$$
$$= -4$$

So there are no real roots.

(d)
$$\Delta = b^2 - 4ac$$
$$= 6^2 - 4 \times 3 \times 3$$
$$= 0$$

So there is one real, repeated root.

(e)
$$\Delta = b^2 - 4ac$$
$$= (-3)^2 - 4 \times 1 \times 2$$
$$= 1$$

So there are two real and distinct roots.

(f)
$$\Delta = b^2 - 4ac$$
$$= (-2)^2 - 4 \times 1 \times (-1)$$
$$= 8$$

So there are two real and distinct roots.

(g)
$$\Delta = b^2 - 4ac$$
$$= (-2)^2 - 4 \times 1 \times 8$$
$$= -28$$

So there are no real roots.

(h)
$$\Delta = b^2 - 4ac$$
$$= 10^2 - 4 \times 5 \times 5$$
$$= 0$$

So there is one real, repeated root.

Q3. Calculating the discriminant, we have
$$\Delta = b^2 - 4ac$$
$$= 16k^2 - 4 \times 2 \times (-2)$$
$$= 16k^2 + 16$$

$16k^2 + 16 > 0 \quad \forall k$ and so the quadratic equation has two real and distinct roots for all k.

Q4. Calculating the discriminant, we have
$$\Delta = b^2 - 4ac$$
$$= 3^2 - 4 \times 1 \times p$$
$$= 9 - 4p.$$

For a repeated root if $\Delta = 0$, hence,

$$9 - 4p = 0$$
$$-4p = -9$$
$$p = \frac{9}{4}$$

Q5. Calculating the discriminant, we have

$$\Delta = b^2 - 4ac$$
$$= (2k)^2 - 4 \times 1 \times (-k)$$
$$= 4k^2 + 4k.$$

For $x^2 + 2kx - k$ to have real roots the discriminant must be greater than 0. Hence,

$$4k^2 + 4k > 0$$
$$4k(k+1) > 0.$$

So, $k > 0$ or $k < -1$.

Worked Solutions — Exercise 5.10

Q1. (a) Completing the square $x^2 + 4x - 5 = (x+2)^2 - 9$. Hence, the coordinates of the roots of this quadratic are $(1,0)$ and $(-5,0)$. It has a minimum point at $(-2,-9)$ and when $x = 0$, $y = -5$.

(b) Completing the square $x^2 - 6x + 5 = (x-3)^2 - 4$. Hence, the coordinates of the roots of this quadratic are $(1,0)$ and $(5,0)$. It has a minimum point at $(3,-4)$ and when $x = 0$, $y = 5$.

(c) Completing the square $x^2 - x - 8.75 = \left(x - \frac{1}{2}\right)^2 - 9$. Hence, the coordinates of the roots of this quadratic are $\left(-\frac{5}{2}, 0\right)$ and $\left(\frac{7}{2}, 0\right)$. It has a minimum point at $\left(\frac{1}{2}, -9\right)$ and when $x = 0$, $y = -8.75$.

(d) Completing the square $-x^2 - 5x + 4 = -\left(x - \frac{5}{2}\right)^2 + \frac{41}{4}$. Hence, the coordinates of the roots of this quadratic are $\left(\frac{1}{2}\left(-5 - \sqrt{41}\right), 0\right)$ and $\left(\frac{1}{2}\left(-5 + \sqrt{41}\right), 0\right)$. It has a maximum point at $\left(-\frac{5}{2}, \frac{41}{4}\right)$ and when $x = 0$, $y = 4$.

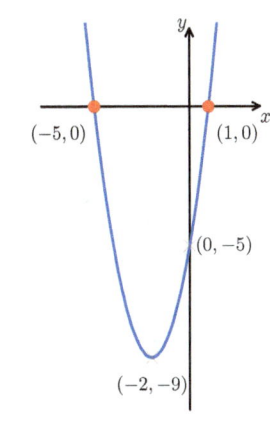

(a)

(b)

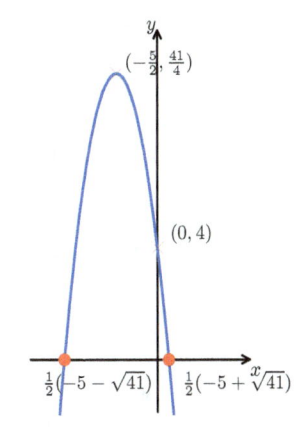

(a)

(b)

Q2. (a) Writing $y = x^2 - 2x - 3$ as $y = x(x - 2) - 3$ we see that the points $(0, -3)$ and $(2, -3)$ lie on the quadratic. The minimum lies half way between the x coordinate of these points and, therefore, has coordinates $(1, -4)$.

(b) Writing $y = -x^2 - 2x + 4$ as $y = -x(x + 2) + 4$ we see that the points $(0, 4)$ and $(-2, 4)$ lie on the quadratic. The maximum lies half way between the x coordinate of these points and, therefore, has coordinates $(-1, 5)$.

(c) Writing $y = x^2 + x - 6$ as $y = x(x + 1) - 6$ we see that the points $(0, -6)$ and $(-1, -6)$ lie on the quadratic. The maximum lies half way between the x coordinate of these points and, therefore, has coordinates $\left(-\frac{1}{2}, -\frac{25}{4}\right)$.

(d) Writing $y = x^2 - 5x + 4$ as $y = x(x-5) + 4$ we see that the points $(0, 4)$ and $(5, 4)$ lie on the quadratic. The minimum lies half way between the x coordinate of these points and, therefore, has coordinates $\left(\frac{5}{2}, -\frac{9}{4}\right)$.

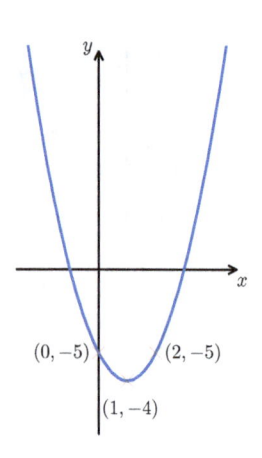

(a)

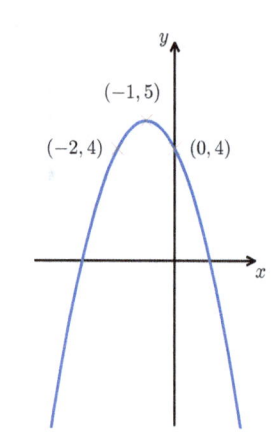

(b)

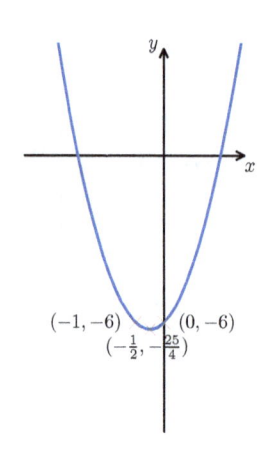

(a)

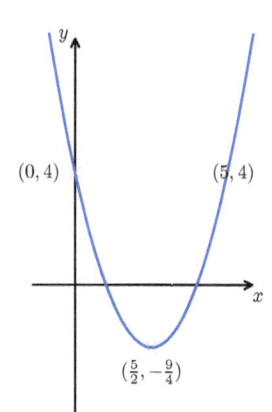

(b)

Worked Solutions — Exercise 5.11

Q1. We complete the square on both quadratics to obtain,

$$y_1 = x^2 + 8x - 2$$
$$= (x+4)^2 - 18,$$
$$y_2 = x^2 + 6x + b$$
$$= (x+3)^2 - 9 + b.$$

Comparing these two, we can form an equation to find b.

$$-9 + b = -18$$

Hence, $b = -9$.

Q2. Completing the square on y_1 we have,

$$y_1 = x^2 - 4x + 8$$
$$= (x-2)^2 + 4.$$

Hence, the minimum of this quadratic is at $(2, 4)$.
Now, completing the square on the second quadratic,

$$y_2 = x^2 - 2ax + 20$$
$$= (x-a)^2 - a^2 + 20.$$

Since they have the same minimum value,

$$-a^2 + 20 = 4$$
$$\Rightarrow \quad a^2 = 16$$
$$\Rightarrow \quad a = \pm 4$$

So, the possible quadratics which have the same minimal value are $y = x^2 - 8x + 20$ or $y = x^2 + 8x + 20$.

Q3. We can use the first two quadratics, y_1 and y_2 to determine the common difference. Completing the square on both we have the following,

$$y_1 = x^2 + 2x - 1$$
$$= (x+1)^2 - 2,$$
$$y_2 = x^2 - 2x + 1$$
$$= (x-1)^2.$$

From this, we see that y_1 and y_2 have minimal values of -2 and 0 respectively. So the common difference of the arithmetic progression is two. Now, completing the square on y_3,

$$x^2 + bx + 11 = \left(x + \frac{b}{2}\right)^2 - \frac{b^2}{4} + 11.$$

Since, the minimal value must be two (to satisfy the arithmetic progression condition),

$$-\frac{b^2}{4} + 11 = 2$$
$$\Rightarrow \qquad 9 = \frac{b^2}{4}$$
$$\Rightarrow \qquad 36 = b^2$$
$$\Rightarrow \qquad \pm 6 = b.$$

Since, the x coordinates of the minimal points form an increasing arithmetic sequence with common difference 2, the minimal point must lie on the line $x = 2$ and so b must equal -6. Hence,

$$y_3 = x^2 - 6x + 11$$

Q4. We first complete the square on the two given quadratics to obtain two vertices of the square.
For quadratic A we have,

$$x^2 - 4x + 2 = (x-2)^2 - 2,$$

which has a minimum at $a = (2, -2)$. Similarly, for Quadratic B,

$$x^2 - 12x + 38 = (x-6)^2 + 2,$$

which has a minimum at $b = (6, 2)$.
Labelling these as the first two vertices of our square anti-clockwise, the other vertices must be $c = (2, 6)$ and $d = (-2, 2)$. A quadratic with a minimum at c is given by,

$$y = (x-2)^2 + 6$$
$$= x^2 - 4x + 10.$$

Similarly, a quadratic that has a minimum at d is,

$$y = (x+2)^2 + 2$$
$$= x^2 + 4x$$

This is shown graphically in the figure below.

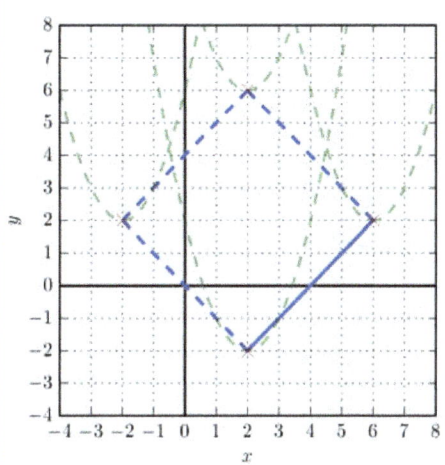

To find the area of the square, consider the side ab;

$$|ab| = \sqrt{(6-2)^2 + (2--2)^2}$$
$$= \sqrt{4^2 + 4^2}$$
$$= \sqrt{32}.$$

Hence the area is 32.

Note that choosing quadratics with minima at $(10, -2)$ and $(6, -6)$ would also solve this problem. The associated quadratics are $y = x^2 - 20x + 98$ and $y = x^2 - 12x + 30$.

Q5. To solve this question we complete the square twice. Working with the original quadratic,

$$x^2 + 4kx + 2k = (x + 2k)^2 - (2k)^2 + 2k$$
$$= (x + 2k)^2 - 4k^2 + 2k.$$

Hence, the location of the minimum point has a dependence on k for both the x coordinate and the y coordinate. We now complete the square on the y coordinate of our minimum point to find the value of k that maximises this.

$$-4k^2 + 2k = -4\left(k^2 + \frac{k}{2}\right)$$
$$= -4\left(k - \frac{1}{4}\right)^2 + \frac{1}{4}.$$

The value of k which maximises the y coordinate of the minimal point is therefore $k = \frac{1}{4}$. To find the location of the minimum in this case, consider the quadratic

$y = x^2 + 4kx + 2k$ in the case $k = \frac{1}{4}$;

$$x^2 + x + \frac{1}{2} = \left(x + \frac{1}{2}\right)^2 + \frac{1}{4},$$

which has a minimum point at $\left(-\frac{1}{2}, \frac{1}{4}\right)$.

Q6. We have to consider the following three cases,
  (a) $a^0 = 1$ for any $a \in \mathbb{R}$.
  In this case, we solve $x^2 + 7x + 12 = 0$.

$$x^2 + 7x + 12 = 0$$
$$\Rightarrow (x+3)(x+4) = 0,$$

  which has solutions $x = -3$ and $x = -4$.
  (b) $1^b = 1$ for any $b \in \mathbb{R}$.
  In this case, we solve $x^2 - 3x + 3 = 1$.

$$x^2 - 3x + 3 = 1$$
$$\Rightarrow x^2 - 3x + 2 = 0$$
$$\Rightarrow (x-2)(x-1) = 0,$$

  which has solutions $x = 2$ and $x = 1$.
  (c) $(-1)^{2b} = 1$ for any $b \in \mathbb{R}$.
  In this case, we solve $x^2 - 3x + 3 = -1$.

$$x^2 - 3x + 3 = -1$$
$$\Rightarrow x^2 - 3x + 4 = 0,$$

  which has no real solutions.

Thus, there are four values for x which solve $\left(x^2 - 3x + 2\right)^{x^2+7x+12} = 1$, namely $x = -3$, $x = -4$, $x = 2$ and $x = 1$.

Q7. (a) Since we want integer roots, we have that $(x+d)(x+e) = x^2 + \Box x + 6$. Hence, the numbers that can be placed inside $\Box$ depend on the factor pairs of 6. There are four such pairs. For $(1,6)$, $\Box = 7$, for $(-1,-6)$, $\Box = -7$, for $(3,2)$, $\Box = 5$ and for $(-3,-2)$, $\Box = -5$.
  (b) We proceed as above, but in this case 24 has more factor pairs. There are in fact eight such pairs, namely: $(\pm 1, \pm 24)$, $(\pm 2, \pm 12)$, $(\pm 3, \pm 8)$, $(\pm 4, \pm 6)$. These pairs give rise to the following 8 options for the integer coefficient of x: ± 25, ± 14, ± 11 and ± 10.
  (c) In this case we want numbers (d, e) such that $d + e = 10$, the product of d and e then gives us the value of $\Box$. If we allow $\Box$ to be negative then there are an infinite number of possible integers. If instead, we say that $\Box$ must be positive, we are considering the partitions of 10 into two integers. This leads to $\Box$ being $9, 16, 21, 24$ or 25.

Worked Solutions — Exercise 6.1

Q1. (a) We can show that $f(x) = 0$ at these values by substituting the given values into the polynomial expression.

$$f(-1) = (-1)^3 - 4 \times (-1)^2 - (-1) + 4 = -1 - 4 + 1 + 4 = 0,$$
$$f(1) = (1)^3 - 4 \times (1)^2 - 1 + 4 = 1 - 4 - 1 + 4 = 0,$$
$$f(4) = (4)^3 - 4 \times (4)^2 - 4 + 4 = 64 - 64 - 4 + 4 = 0.$$

(b) We know that the polynomial crosses the x-axis at $x = -1$, $x = 1$ and $x = 4$, and nowhere else. We can find the sign of the polynomial between these points by choosing a value and calculating $f(x)$ at that point. For example,

$$f(0) = 4 > 0,$$
$$f(2) = (2)^3 - 4(2)^2 - (2) + 4 = 8 - 16 - 2 + 4 = -6 < 0,$$

For large values of x, the highest order term, x^3 will dominate. This means that as $x \to -\infty$ the polynomial is negative. As $x \to \infty$ the polynomial is positive.

This gives us the information we need to sketch the polynomial, indicating the points where it crosses the axes.

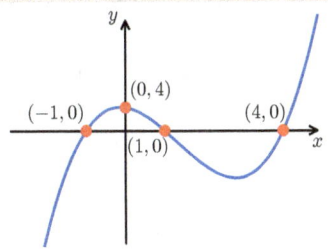

Q2. For large values of x, the expression is dominated by $-3x^5$. For large, negative values of x, this will be a large positive number. For large, positive values of x, this will be a large negative number.

Since the graph goes from positive to negative, and the polynomial expression is continuous, it must cross the x-axis at least once.

Q3. (a) Writing out the polynomial for $f(-2)$ and $f(2)$ gives us a pair of simultaneous equations.

$$f(-2) = -8 + 4a - 2b + 4 = -16,$$
$$f(2) = 8 + 4a + 2b + 4 = 0.$$

Adding these together gives us

$$8a + 8 = -16.$$

Solving this equation gives us the result $a = -3$. We can now put this back into one of the original equations.

$$8 - 12 + 2b + 4 = 0.$$

Which gives us the result $b = 0$.

(b) We can now write out the polynomial as $f(x) = x^3 - 3x^2 + 4$, and from this we can complete the table.

x	-2	-1	0	1	2	3	4
$f(x)$	-16	0	4	2	0	4	20

(c) The roots of the polynomial are at $x = -1$ and $x = 2$. We can see from the table that $f(x)$ is negative for $x < -1$ and $f(x) \geq 0$ for $x > -1$. This means that $x = 2$ must be a turning point for the polynomial, so that $f(x) > 0$ to either side of $x = 2$.

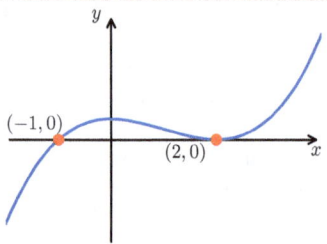

Q4. (a) The cost of the feed is proportional to the area of the lawn, but the cost of the fencing is proportional to its width. Therefore, whatever the price of the feed and the fencing, for very large lawns, the cost of the feed will eventually be larger.

(b) Let x be the width of the lawn, so that the length is $2x$. The area of the lawn is $2x^2$ and so the price of the feed is $2x^2$. The perimeter of the lawn is $6x$ and so the price of the fencing is $12x$. The total cost is $2x^2 + 12x$.

(c) The point at which the feed and the fencing cost the same is when $2x^2 = 12x$. Dividing by $2x$ gives the result $x = 6$ and so the area of the lawn is $72\,\text{m}^2$.

Worked Solutions — Exercise 6.2

Q1. (a) $(x^2 - 3 + 4x) - (7 - x^3 + 2x) = x^3 + x^2 + 2x - 10$.

(b) First we expand the brackets, then we collect the terms together.

$$\begin{aligned} x(3ax - 2x^2) + 2ax^2 - 3(x+2) &= 3ax^2 - 2x^3 + 2ax^2 - 3x - 6 \\ &= -2x^3 + 5ax^2 - 3x - 6. \end{aligned}$$

(c) $(x-2)(x+2) = x^2 - 2x + 2x - 4 = x^2 - 4$.

(d)
$$(x-2)(2x^2+3x-1)+(x-2)(x+3)$$
$$=(2x^3-4x^2+3x^2-6x-x+2)+(x^2+3x-2x-6)$$
$$=(2x^3-x^2-7x+2)+(x^2+x-6)$$
$$=2x^3-6x-4.$$

(e)
$$(2x^2-x+1)(x^2-4x-1)-x^2(2x^2+1)$$
$$=(2x^4-8x^3-2x^2-x^3+4x^2+x+x^2-4x-1)-2x^4-x^2$$
$$=(2x^4-9x^3+3x^2-3x-1)-2x^4-x^2$$
$$=-9x^3+2x^2-3x-1.$$

Q2. (a) $(x-3)(x+c)+2 = x^2+cx-3x-3c+2 = x^2+(c-3)x+(2-3c)$.
(b) Since $f(2)=1$, we have $2^2+2(c-3)+(2-3c)=-c=1$. Therefore, $c=-1$. We can now write $f(x)=x^2-4x+5$ and so $f(0)=5$.

Worked Solutions — Exercise 6.3

Q1. (a) $(2x^2+2x-12) \div (x+3) = (2x-4)$.

$$\begin{array}{r} 2x \quad -4 \\ (x+3) \overline{\smash{\big)} 2x^2 \ +2x \ -12} \\ \underline{2x^2 \ +6x } \\ -4x \ -12 \\ \underline{-4x \ -12} \\ 0 \end{array}$$

(b) $(x^3+x^2-5x+3) \div (x-1) = (x^2+2x-3)$.

$$\begin{array}{r} x^2 \ +2x \ -3 \\ (x-1) \overline{\smash{\big)} x^3 \ +x^2 \ -5x \ +3} \\ \underline{x^3 \ -x^2 } \\ 2x^2 \ -5x \\ \underline{2x^2 \ -2x } \\ -3x \ +3 \\ \underline{-3x \ +3} \\ 0 \end{array}$$

(c) $(2x^4 - x^3 - 6x^2 + 8x + 12) \div (2x + 3) = (x^3 - 2x^2 + 4)$.

$$
\begin{array}{r}
x^3 \quad -2x^2 \qquad\quad +4 \\
(2x+3)\overline{\smash{\big)}\,2x^4 \quad -x^3 \quad -6x^2 \quad +8x \quad +12} \\
\underline{2x^4 \quad +3x^3\qquad\qquad\qquad\qquad} \\
-4x^3 \quad -6x^2 \\
\underline{-4x^3 \quad -6x^2} \\
8x \quad +12 \\
\underline{8x \quad +12} \\
0
\end{array}
$$

(d) $(-2x^4 + 7x^3 - 14x^2 + 19x - 6) \div (-x + 2) = (2x^3 - 3x^2 + 8x - 3)$.

$$
\begin{array}{r}
2x^3 \quad -3x^2 \quad +8x \quad -3 \\
(-x+2)\overline{\smash{\big)}\,-2x^4 \quad +7x^3 \quad -14x^2 \quad +19x \quad -6} \\
\underline{-2x^4 \quad +4x^3\qquad\qquad\qquad\qquad} \\
3x^3 \quad -14x^2 \\
\underline{3x^3 \quad -6x^2} \\
-8x^2 \quad +19x \\
\underline{-8x^2 \quad +16x} \\
3x \quad -6 \\
\underline{3x \quad -6} \\
0
\end{array}
$$

Q2. $(x^3 + 11x^2 + 4x - 60) \div (x + 10) = (x^2 + x - 6)$.

$$
\begin{array}{r}
x^2 \quad +x \quad -6 \\
(x+10)\overline{\smash{\big)}\,+x^3 \quad +11x^2 \quad +4x \quad -60} \\
\underline{x^3 \quad +10x^2\qquad\qquad\qquad} \\
x^2 \quad +4x \\
\underline{x^2 \quad +10x} \\
-6x \quad -60 \\
\underline{-6x \quad -60} \\
0
\end{array}
$$

Factorising $(x^2 + x - 6) = (x + 3)(x - 2)$ gives us the complete factorisation $f(x) = (x + 10)(x + 3)(x - 2)$.

Q3. (a) By the remainder theorem, the remainder when $f(x)$ is divided by $(x - 1)$ is equal to $f(1) = 6 - 5 - 3 + 10 = 8$.

(b)

$$
\begin{array}{r}
6x^2 +x -2 \\
(x-1) \overline{\smash{\big)}\, 6x^3 -5x^2 -3x +10} \\
\underline{6x^3 -6x^2 } \\
x^2 -3x \\
\underline{x^2 -x } \\
-2x +10 \\
\underline{-2x +2} \\
8
\end{array}
$$

Therefore $f(x) = (x-1)(6x^2 + x - 2) + 8$.

Q4. (a) If $(x+1)$ is a factor of $f(x) = x^4 - 5x^3 + px^2 + 5x - 6$, then $f(-1) = 0$. Therefore, $1 + 5 + p - 5 - 6 = 0$ and so $p = 5$.

(b) The remainder when $f(x)$ is divided by $(x-4)$ is given by

$$f(4) = 4^4 - 5.4^3 + 5.4^2 + 5.4 - 6 = 256 - 320 + 80 + 20 - 6 = 30.$$

Q5. (a) The remainder when $f(x)$ is divided by $(x-1)$ is equal to $f(1)$. Therefore $f(1) = 2$ and, similarly, $f(-2) = -40$ and so

$$
\begin{aligned}
f(1) &= a - 1 - b + 2 = 2, \\
f(-2) &= -8a - 4 + 2b + 2 = -40.
\end{aligned}
$$

If we multiply the top line by two and add the equations, we have $-6a - 6 + 6 = -36$ and so $a = 6$. Putting this value back into either equation gives $b = 5$.

(b) The remainder when $f(x)$ is divided by $(x-3)$ is equal to $f(3) = 6.3^3 - 3^2 - 5.3 + 2 = 162 - 9 - 15 + 2 = 140$.

Q6. (a) Let $g(x) = 4x^2 - ax + 2$. When $g(x)$ is divided by $(x-1)$, the remainder is -3, therefore, $g(1) = -3$. Therefore,

$$g(1) = 4 - a + 2 = 6 - a = -3.$$

Therefore, $a = 9$.

(b) We have $g(x) = 4x^2 - 9x + 2$. We can factorise this, either by inspection or using long division, to obtain $g(x) = (x-2)(4x-1)$. Therefore, $(x-2)$ and $(x-1/4)$ are both factors of $g(x)$ and so $g(2) = 0$ and $g(1/4) = 0$.
The roots of $4x^2 - 9x + 2$ are 2 and $1/4$.

(c) Using the substitution $x = 4^t$, we have

$$f(t) = 4^{2t+1} - 9.4^t + 2 = 4x^2 - 9x + 2.$$

From the previous part of the question, we know that the roots of this polynomial are $x = 2$ and $x = \frac{1}{4}$. Solving $4^t = 2$ gives us $t = \frac{1}{2}$, and similarly solving $4^t = \frac{1}{4}$ gives us $t = -1$.
Therefore $f(t) = 0$ at $t = \frac{1}{2}$ and $t = -1$.

Q7. (a) We can expand the brackets in the expression of $f(x)$ and then collect the terms together.
$$f(x) = (x-2)(x+4k) - kx = x^2 + 4kx - 2x - 8k - kx$$
$$= x^2 + (3k-2)x - 8k.$$

(b) To complete the square, we use $p = 1 - 3k/2$. We can then calculate the value of q.
$$x^2 + (3k-2)x - 8k = \left(x - 1 + \frac{3k}{2}\right)^2 - \left(1 - \frac{3k}{2}\right)^2 - 8k$$
$$= \left(x - 1 + \frac{3k}{2}\right)^2 - \frac{9}{4}k^2 + 3k - 1 - 8k$$
$$= \left(x - 1 + \frac{3k}{2}\right)^2 - \left(\frac{9}{4}k^2 + 5k + 1\right).$$

(c) If $f(x)$ has a repeated root, then it is of the form $(x-p)^2$. That is, $q = 0$, which we can write as follows.
$$9k^2 + 20k + 4 = 0.$$

Therefore $g(x) = 9x^2 + 20x + 4$ is a polynomial with a root at k, that is, $g(k) = 0$.

(d) We know that k is a small integer, so we can calculate $g(x)$ at these values to find a factor of g. We find $g(-3) = 25$, so $(x+3)$ is not a factor of g. However, we find that $g(-2) = 0$ and so $k = -2$. Therefore $(x+2)$ is a factor of $g(x)$.
$$g(x) = 9x^2 + 20x + 4 = (x+2)(9x+2).$$

The repeated root of $f(x)$ is equal to $p = 1 - 3k/2 = 4$.

2. Worked Solutions - Chapters 7 to 11

Worked Solutions — Exercise 7.1

Q1. Expanding the left-hand side, we obtain
$$(x+y)(x-y) = x^2 - xy + xy - y^2 = x^2 - y^2.$$
Hence, we have shown directly that the left-hand side is equivalent to the right-hand side.

Q2. If $(x-p)$ is a factor of the polynomial expression $f(x)$, then there exists a polynomial expression $g(x)$ such that $f(x) = (x-p)g(x)$. Then
$$f(p) = (p-p)g(p) = (0)g(p) = 0.$$

Q3. Factorising,
$$x^3 + x^2 - 2x - 8 = (x-2)(x^2 + 3x + 4).$$
The quadratic equation $x^2 + 3x + 4 = 0$ has discriminant $b^2 - 4ac = 3^2 - 4(1)(4) = -7 < 0$, and so has no real roots. Hence, the expression $x^3 + x^2 - 2x - 8$ has only one real factor.

Q4. The quadratic $kx^2 + 2kx - 3 = 0$ has discriminant $b^2 - 4ac = 4k^2 - 4(k)(-3) = 4k(k+3)$. If the quadratic has no real roots, then k satisfies
$$4k(k+3) < 0 \Rightarrow -3 < k < 0.$$

Q5. The quadratic $kx^2 - 3x + k = 0$ has discriminant $b^2 - 4ac = (-3)^2 - 4(k)(k) = 9 - 4k^2$. If the quadratic has two distinct real roots, then k satisfies

$$9 - 4k^2 > 0 \Rightarrow -\frac{3}{2} < k < \frac{3}{2}.$$

Q6. (a) Consider the diagram below.

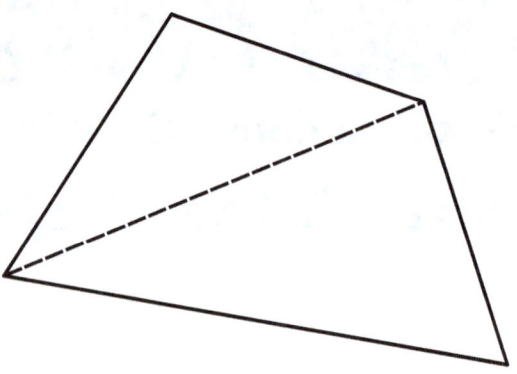

Any convex quadrilateral can be divided into two triangles. Since the interior angles of a triangle sum to $180°$, the interior angles of a convex quadrilateral sum to $2 \times 180° = 360°$.

(b) Extending the proof in part (a), any n-sided convex polygon can be divided into $n - 2$ triangles. Hence, the interior angles of an n-sided polygon sum to $180(n - 2)°$.

Q7. Completing the square,

$$x^2 - 6x + 10 = (x - 3)^2 + 1.$$

Since $(x - 3)^2 \geq 0$ for all real x, $(x - 3)^2 + 1 \geq 1$ for all real x.

Q8. The coordinates of a point where the line and circle intersect satisfies $y = mx + 2$ and $(x + 1)^2 + (y - 2)^2 = r$ simultaneously. Substituting $y = mx + 2$ into the circle equation,

$$(x + 1)^2 + (mx)^2 = r,$$
$$\Rightarrow x^2 + 2x + 1 + m^2x^2 - r = 0,$$
$$\Rightarrow (1 + m^2)x^2 + 2x + 1 - r = 0.$$

If the line and circle intersect at two distinct points, this quadratic has two distinct real roots. Hence,

$$b^2 - 4ac = 4 - 4(1 + m^2)(1 - r) > 0,$$
$$\Rightarrow 4 - 4 - 4m^2 + 4r + 4rm^2 > 0,$$
$$\Rightarrow r(1 + m^2) > m^2,$$
$$\Rightarrow r > \frac{m^2}{1 + m^2}.$$

Q9. Using symmetry, the four shaded triangles surrounding the inner square are congruent. Each of the congruent triangles has area $\frac{1}{2}ab$. The smaller and larger squares have area c^2 and $(a+b)^2$ respectively. An alternative expression for the smaller square is the area of the larger square minus the area of the four congruent triangles. Hence

$$c^2 = (a+b)^2 - 4\left(\frac{1}{2}ab\right),$$
$$= a^2 + b^2 + 2ab - 2ab,$$
$$= a^2 + b^2.$$

Hence, we have deduced Pythagoras' theorem.

Worked Solutions — Exercise 7.2

Q1. **(a)** Every square is a rhombus, but not every rhombus is a square. Hence,

$$S \text{ is a rhombus} \Leftarrow S \text{ is a square}.$$

(b) Every rhombus is a parallelogram, but not every parallelogram is a rhombus. Hence

$$X \text{ is a rhombus} \Rightarrow X \text{ is a parallelogram}.$$

(c) Since n is an integer, the compound statement "$n^2 > 8$ and $n > 0$" is equivalent to $n \geq 3$, since 3 is the least integer greater than or equal to $\sqrt{8}$. Hence,

$$n^2 > 8 \text{ and } n > 0 \Leftrightarrow n \geq 3.$$

(d) It is clear that any rational number squared is rational, since for integer p, q with $q \neq 0$,

$$\left(\frac{p}{q}\right)^2 = \frac{p^2}{q^2}.$$

However, it is false that every rational number has rational square roots. For example,

$$\left(\sqrt{2}\right)^2 = 2,$$

which is rational, but $\sqrt{2}$ is irrational. Hence,

$$x^2 \text{ is rational} \Leftarrow x \text{ is rational}.$$

Q2. **(a)** This is a valid argument. P1 and P2 can be written as

P1: Cats $\Rightarrow$ Wings,   P2: Wings $\Rightarrow$ Four legs.

Combining P1 and P2, we obtain Q. Regardless of whether P1 and P2 are true, the conclusion Q follows from P1 and P2, so the argument is valid.

(b) This is not a valid argument. The statement P1 is true for all real x and y. The inequality $x^2 + y^2 \leq 1$ describes the interior and boundary of a circle centred at the origin with radius 1. Hence, $-1 \leq x \leq 1$ in this region. Statement P2 forces $x = 1/4$.

Now, let $x = 1/4$, $y = 2$. P1 and P2 are satisfied (since P1 is a one-way implication), but Q is not satisfied. Since there is at least one counter example, the argument is invalid.

(c) This is a valid argument. P1 and P2 can be written as

$$\text{P1: } y \leq 4 \Rightarrow x \geq 3, \qquad \text{P2: } y \leq 4 \Rightarrow z^2 > x.$$

Combining P1 and P2, we obtain $y \leq 4 \Rightarrow z^2 > x \geq 3$ and so

$$y \leq 4 \Rightarrow z^2 > 3.$$

We can read this statement as "$y \leq 4$ only if $z^2 > 3$". In particular, if $z = 0 \leq 3$, then we must have $y > 4$, *i.e.* Q follows from P1 and P2.

(d) This is not a valid argument. For a counter example, take $x = 1$, $y = 6$, $z = 2$. Then P1 and P2 are satisfied, but Q is not, so Q does not follow from P1 and P2.

(e) This is not a valid argument. For a counter example, take $x = 5$, $y = 4$, $z = 6$. P1 and P2 are satisfied, but Q is not, so Q does not follow from P1 and P2.

Worked Solutions — Exercise 7.3

Q1. (a) Let $n = 7$. Then $7! = 5040 > 2187 = 3^7$, so the statement is false.
(b) Consider $30 = 2 \times 3 \times 5$, which has an odd number of distinct prime factors. Hence, the statement is false.
(c) Let $n = 1$. Then $n^2 + 2n - 2 = 1$, which is odd. Hence, the statement is false.
(d) Let $m = 0$, $c \neq 0$. The straight line $y = c$ is parallel to the x-axis and so does not intersect it. Hence, the statement is false.

Q2. (a) Since a and b are both positive integers, $a, b \geq 1$. Rearranging,

$$\frac{a}{b} + \frac{b}{a} = \frac{a^2 + b^2}{ab}.$$

Since $a, b \geq 1$, $a^2 + b^2 \geq 2$ and $ab \geq 1$. Thus,

$$\frac{a^2 + b^2}{ab} \geq 2.$$

(b) Let $a = 1$, $b = -2$. Then

$$\frac{a}{b} + \frac{b}{a} = -\frac{1}{2} - 2 = -\frac{5}{2} < 2,$$

so the statement is false when at least one of a or b is negative.

Q3. (a) If n is odd, then there exists a positive integer p such that $n = 2p - 1$. Then
$$n^2 = (2p-1)^2 = 4p^2 - 2p + 1 = 2(p^2 - p) + 1.$$
Since $p^2 - p$ is a positive integer, n^2 has the form of an odd integer, so if n is odd, n^2 is odd.

(b) If m and n are odd, there exist positive integers p and q such that $m = 2p-1$, $n = 2q - 1$. Then
$$mn = (2p-1)(2q-1) = 4pq - 2p - 2q + 1 = 2(2pq - p - q) + 1.$$
Since $2pq - p - q$ is a positive integer, mn has the form of an odd integer. Hence, if m and n are odd, mn is odd.

(c) If m and n are even, then there exist positive integers p and q such that $m = 2p$ and $n = 2q$. Then
$$mn = (2p)(2q) = 4pq = 2(2pq).$$
Since $2pq$ is a positive integer, mn has the form of an even number. Thus, if m and n are even, mn is even.

(d) If m is odd and n is even, then there exist positive integers p and q such that $m = 2p - q$ and $n = 2q$. Then
$$mn = (2p-1)2q = 4pq - 2q = 2(2pq - q).$$
Since $2pq - q$ is a positive integer, mn has the form of an even number. Hence, if m is odd and n is even, mn is even.

(e) If n is even, then there exists a positive integer p such that $n = 2p$. Then
$$7(n+4) = 7(2p+4) = 14p + 28 = 2(7p + 14).$$
Since $7p + 14$ is a positive integer, $7n + 4$ has the form of an even number. Hence, if n is even, $7n + 4$ is even.

Note that we could have used the previously proven facts that the product of an even and odd integer is even, and the sum of two even numbers is even to deduce this result.

Q4. (a) If n^2 is odd, then n is odd.
This is true. We found in Q1 that a product involving at least one even number is even. Hence, if n^2 is odd, n must be odd.

(b) If mn is odd, m and n are odd.
This is also true, with the same reasoning as in **(a)**.

(c) If mn is even, then m and n are even.
This is false. For a counter example, consider $m = 2$, $n = 3$. Then $mn = 6$ is even, but n is odd.

(d) If mn is even, then m is odd and n is even.
This is false. Consider $m = n = 2$. Then $mn = 4$ is even, but m is even.

(e) If $7n + 4$ is even, then n is even.
This is true. If $7n+4$ is even, then there exists a positive integer q such that $7n + 4 = 2p$. Then

$$7n + 4 = 2p \Rightarrow 7n = 2p - 4 = 2(p-2).$$

Since $2(p-2)$ is even, we must have $7n$ even for this equation to make sense. Since 7 is clearly odd, we conclude that n is even.

Q5. Let a and b be positive integers with $a \neq b$. Then the square of the sum of a and b is

$$(a+b)^2 = a^2 + b^2 + 2ab > a^2 + b^2,$$

so the square of the sum of a and b is greater than the sum of their squares. If $a = b$, then

$$(2a)^2 = 4a^2 > a^2 + a^2 = 2a^2,$$

so the statement is also true for $a = b$.

Q6. (a) Let m and n be two consecutive even numbers. Then there exists positive integer k such that $m = 2k$ and $n = 2(k+1)$. Then

$$n^2 - m^2 = 4(k+1)^2 - 4k^2 = 4(2k+1).$$

Hence, the statement is true.

(b) Let m and n be two consecutive odd numbers. Then there exists positive integer k such that $m = 2k - 1$, $n = 2k + 1$. Then

$$n^2 - m^2 = 4k^2 + 4k + 1 - (4k^2 - 4k + 1) = 4(2k).$$

Hence, the statement is true.

(c) Let $m = 2$, $n = 3$. Then

$$n^2 - m^2 = 9 - 4 = 5.$$

Since 5 is not a multiple of 4, the statement is false.

Q7. Let $n = 5$. Then $5! - 1 = 119 = 7 \times 17$. Hence, the statement is false.

Q8. (a) If b and c are divisible by a, then there exist positive integers p and q such that $b = ap$ and $c = aq$. Then

$$b + c = ap + aq = a(p+q),$$

so $b + c$ is also divisible by a.

(b) If b is divisible by a and c is divisible by b, then there exist positive integers p and q such that $b = ap$, $c = qb$. Then

$$c = qb = q(ap) = a(qp).$$

Since qp is an integer, c is divisible by a.

Q9. The first point to note is that $4a + 3$ is odd. Using previous results, $4a$ is even regardless of whether a is odd or even, then $4a + 3$ is odd (even + odd = odd). Hence, we need $b^2 + c^2$ to be odd for the equation to be valid. We have already proven in Q3 that if n is odd, then n^2 is odd. Similarly, if n is even, n^2 is even. Also, odd + odd = even, and even + even = even. Hence, we must have c odd and b even, say.

Thus, there exist positive integers p and q such that $c = 2p - 1$ and $b = 2q$. Then,

$$4a + 3 = b^2 + c^2 = (2p-1)^2 + (2q)^2 = 4p^2 - 4p + 1 + 4q^2 = 4(p^2 + q^2 - p) + 1.$$

The equation is inconsistent. Although both sides of the equations are odd, the left-hand side has remainder 3 when divided by 4. However, since $p^2 + q^2 - p$ is an integer, the right-hand side has remainder 1 when divided by 4. Hence, there are no integers a, b and c for which the equation holds.

Worked Solutions — Exercise 8.1

Q1. (a) $5! = 5 \times 4 \times 3 \times 2 \times 1 = 120$;
(b) $6! = 6 \times 5! = 5 \times 120 = 720$;
(c) $7! = 7 \times 6! = 7 \times 720 = 5040$;
(d)
$$\frac{7!}{5!} = \frac{7 \times 6 \times 5!}{5!}$$
$$= 7 \times 6$$
$$= 42.$$

Q2. (a)
$$\binom{5}{2} = \frac{5!}{2!(5-2)!}$$
$$= \frac{5!}{2!3!}$$
$$= \frac{5 \times 4 \times 3!}{2!3!}$$
$$= \frac{5 \times 4}{2}$$
$$= 10;$$

(b)
$$\binom{2}{1} = \frac{2!}{1!(2-1)!}$$
$$= \frac{2!}{1!1!}$$
$$= \frac{2 \times 1}{1 \times 1}$$
$$= 2;$$

(c)
$$\binom{4}{3} = \frac{4!}{3!(4-3)!}$$
$$= \frac{4!}{3!1!}$$
$$= \frac{4 \times 3!}{3!}$$
$$= 4;$$

(d)
$$\binom{7}{2} = \frac{7!}{2!(7-2)!}$$
$$= \frac{7!}{2!5!}$$
$$= \frac{7 \times 6 \times 5!}{2!5!}$$
$$= \frac{7 \times 6}{2 \times 1}$$
$$= \frac{42}{2}$$
$$= 21;$$

(e)
$$\binom{9}{4} = \frac{9!}{4!(9-4)!}$$
$$= \frac{9!}{4!5!}$$
$$= \frac{9 \times \times 8 \times 7 \times 6 \times 5!}{4!5!}$$
$$= \frac{9 \times \times 8 \times 7 \times 6}{4!}$$
$$= \frac{3024}{24}$$
$$= 126;$$

Q3. (a)
$$\binom{4}{1} = \frac{4!}{1!3!}$$
$$= \frac{4 \times 3!}{3!}$$
$$= 4;$$

(b)
$$\binom{10}{0} = \frac{10!}{0!10!}$$
$$= \frac{10!}{1 \times 10!}$$
$$= 1;$$

(c)
$$\binom{5}{3} = \frac{5!}{3!2!}$$
$$= \binom{5}{2}$$
$$= 10;$$

(d)
$$\binom{6}{3} = \frac{6!}{3!3!}$$
$$= \frac{6 \times 5 \times 4 \times 3!}{3!3!}$$
$$= \frac{6 \times 5 \times 4}{3!}$$
$$= \frac{6 \times 5 \times 4}{3 \times 2}$$
$$= 20;$$

(e)
$$\binom{n}{0} = \frac{n!}{0!n!}$$
$$= \frac{n!}{1 \times n!}$$
$$= \frac{n!}{n!}$$
$$= 1;$$

(f)
$$\binom{n}{1} = \frac{n!}{1!(n-1)!}$$
$$= \frac{n \times (n-1)!}{(n-1)!}$$
$$= n;$$

(g)
$$\binom{n}{n} = \frac{n!}{n!0!}$$
$$= \binom{n}{0}$$
$$= 1.$$

Q4. (a) In this case $n = 2$ and hence r can take values 0, 1 and 2. The entries in Pascal's triangle are therefore:
$$\binom{2}{0} \quad \binom{2}{1} \quad \binom{2}{2}$$

(b) In this case $n = 4$ and hence r can take values 0, 1, 2, 3 and 4. The entries in Pascal's triangle are therefore:
$$\binom{4}{0} \quad \binom{4}{1} \quad \binom{4}{2} \quad \binom{4}{3} \quad \binom{4}{4}.$$

Q5. (a) 43 949 268;
(b) 10 400 600;
(c) 10 737 573;
(d) 108 043 253 365 600;
(e) 29 462 227 291 176 635 718 126.

Worked Solutions — Exercise 8.2

Q1. (a) Using the binomial theorem we obtain
$$(1+x)^{11} = 1^{11}\binom{11}{0}x^0 + 1^{10}\binom{11}{1}x^1$$
$$+ 1^9\binom{11}{2}x^2 + 1^8\binom{11}{3}x^3 + \ldots$$
$$= 1 + 11x + 55x^2 + 330x^3 + \ldots.$$

(b) Using the binomial theorem we obtain

$$(1-2x)^9 = 1^9 \binom{9}{0}(-2x)^2 + 1^8 \binom{9}{1}(-2x)^1$$
$$+ 1^7 \binom{9}{2}(-2x)^2 + 1^6 \binom{9}{3}(-2x)^3 + \ldots$$
$$= 1 - 9 \cdot 2x + 36 \cdot 4x^2 - 84 \cdot 8x^3 + \ldots$$
$$= 1 - 18x + 144x^2 - 672x^3 + \ldots.$$

(c) Using the binomial theorem we obtain

$$(2+x)^5 = 2^5 \binom{5}{0}x^0 + 2^4 \binom{5}{1}x^1$$
$$+ 2^3 \binom{5}{2}x^2 + 2^2 \binom{4}{3}x^3 + \ldots$$
$$= 32 + 16 \cdot 5x + 8 \cdot 10x^2 + 4 \cdot 10x^3$$
$$= 32 + 80x + 80x^2 + 40x^3 + \ldots.$$

Q2. We use Theorem 8.4 for all of these.

(a)
$$(1-3x)^4 = \binom{4}{0} + \binom{4}{1}(-3x) + \binom{4}{2}(-3x)^2 + \binom{4}{3}(-3x)^3$$
$$+ \binom{4}{4}(-3x)^4,$$
$$= 1 - 12x + 54x^2 - 108x^3 + 81x^4.$$

(b)
$$(2-x)^5 = \binom{5}{0}(2^5) + \binom{5}{1}(2^4)(-x) + \binom{5}{2}(2^3)(-x)^2 + \binom{5}{3}(2^2)(-x)^3$$
$$+ \binom{5}{4}(2)(-x)^4 + \binom{5}{5}(-x)^5,$$
$$= 32 - 80x + 80x^2 - 40x^3 + 10x^4 - x^5.$$

(c)
$$\left(1-\frac{x}{4}\right)^4 = \binom{4}{0} + \binom{4}{1}\left(-\frac{x}{4}\right) + \binom{4}{2}\left(-\frac{x}{4}\right)^2 + \binom{4}{3}\left(-\frac{x}{4}\right)^3$$
$$+ \binom{4}{4}\left(-\frac{x}{4}\right)^4,$$
$$= 1 - x + \frac{3}{8}x^2 - \frac{1}{16}x^3 + \frac{1}{256}x^4.$$

(d)
$$\left(2+\frac{1}{x}\right)^5 = \binom{5}{0}(2^5) + \binom{5}{1}(2^4)\left(\frac{1}{x}\right) + \binom{5}{2}(2^3)\left(\frac{1}{x}\right)^2$$
$$+ \binom{5}{3}(2^2)\left(\frac{1}{x}\right)^3 + \binom{5}{4}(2)\left(\frac{1}{x}\right)^4 + \binom{5}{5}\left(\frac{1}{x}\right)^5,$$
$$= 32 + \frac{80}{x} + \frac{80}{x^2} + \frac{40}{x^3} + \frac{10}{x^4} + \frac{1}{x^5}.$$

(e)
$$(x+y)^3 = \binom{3}{0}x^3 + \binom{3}{1}x^2y + \binom{3}{2}xy^2 + \binom{3}{3}y^3,$$
$$= x^3 + 3x^2y + 3xy^2 + y^3.$$

(f)
$$(2x-y)^5 = \binom{5}{0}(2x)^5 + \binom{5}{1}(2x)^4(-y) + \binom{5}{2}(2x)^3(-y)^2$$
$$+ \binom{5}{3}(2x)^2(-y^3) + \binom{5}{4}(2x)(-y)^4 + \binom{5}{5}(-y)^5,$$
$$= 32x^5 - 80x^4y + 80x^3y^2 - 40x^3y^2 - 40x^2y^3 + 10xy^4 - y^5.$$

(g)
$$\left(x+\frac{1}{x}\right)^4 = \binom{4}{0}x^4 + \binom{4}{1}(x^3)\left(\frac{1}{x}\right) + \binom{4}{2}(x^2)\left(\frac{1}{x}\right)^2$$
$$+ \binom{4}{3}(x)\left(\frac{1}{x}\right)^3 + \binom{4}{4}\left(\frac{1}{x}\right)^4,$$
$$= x^4 + 4x^2 + 6 + \frac{4}{x^2} + \frac{1}{x^4}.$$

(h)
$$\left(x-\frac{1}{x}\right)^5 = \binom{5}{0}(x^5) + \binom{5}{1}(x^4)\left(-\frac{1}{x}\right) + \binom{5}{2}(x^3)\left(-\frac{1}{x}\right)^2$$
$$+ \binom{5}{3}(x^2)\left(-\frac{1}{x}\right)^3 + \binom{5}{4}(x)\left(-\frac{1}{x}\right)^4 + \binom{5}{5}\left(-\frac{1}{x}\right)^5,$$
$$= x^5 - 5x^3 + 10x - \frac{10}{x} + \frac{5}{x^3} - \frac{1}{x^5}.$$

Q3. As for Q1, we use Theorem 8.4.

(a)
$$(1-3x)^{12} = \binom{12}{0} + \binom{12}{1}(-3x) + \binom{12}{2}(-3x)^2 + \binom{12}{3}(-3x)^3$$
$$+ \binom{12}{4}(-3x)^4 + \ldots$$
$$= 1 - 36x + 594x^2 - 5940x^3 + 40\,095x^4 + \ldots$$

(b)
$$\left(1 + \frac{3}{2}x\right)^7 = \binom{7}{0} + \binom{7}{1}\left(\frac{3}{2}x\right) + \binom{7}{2}\left(\frac{3}{2}x\right)^2 + \binom{7}{3}\left(\frac{3}{2}x\right)^3$$
$$+ \binom{7}{4}\left(\frac{3}{2}x\right)^4 + \ldots,$$
$$= 1 + \frac{21}{2}x + \frac{189}{4}x^2 + \frac{945}{8}x^3 + \frac{2835}{16}x^4 + \ldots$$

(c)
$$(x+2y)^{15} = \binom{15}{0}x^{15} + \binom{15}{1}(x^{14})(2y) + \binom{15}{2}(x^{13})(2y)^2$$
$$+ \binom{15}{3}(x^{12})(2y)^3 + \binom{15}{4}(x^{11})(2y)^4 + \ldots$$
$$= x^{15} + 30x^{14}y + 420x^{13}y^2 + 3640x^{12}y^3 + 21\,840x^{11}y^4 + \ldots$$

(d)
$$\left(2x - \frac{2}{x}\right)^{11} = 2^{11}\left(1 - \frac{1}{x}\right)^{11},$$
$$= 2^{11}\left[\binom{11}{0}x^{11} + \binom{11}{1}(x^{10})\left(-\frac{1}{x}\right) + \binom{11}{2}(x^9)\left(-\frac{1}{x}\right)^2\right.$$
$$\left. + \binom{11}{3}(x^8)\left(-\frac{1}{x}\right)^3 + \binom{11}{4}(x^7)\left(-\frac{1}{x}\right)^4 + \ldots\right],$$
$$= 2048[x^{11} - 11x^9 + 55x^7 - 165x^5 + 330x^3 + \ldots],$$
$$= 2048x^{11} - 22\,528x^9 + 112\,640x^7 - 337\,920x^5$$
$$+ 675\,840x^3 + \ldots$$

Q4. (a) We find the first three terms of $(1+x)^4$ first:
$$(1+x)^4 = \binom{4}{0}x^0 + \binom{4}{1}x^1 + \binom{4}{2}x^2 + \ldots$$
$$= 1 + 4x + 6x^2 + \ldots.$$

Hence,
$$x^2(1+x)^4 = x^2(1 + 4x + 6x^2 + \ldots)$$
$$= x^2 + 4x^3 + 6x^4 + \ldots.$$

(b) We find the first three terms of $(2-4x)^6$ first:
$$(2-4x)^6 = 2^6 \binom{6}{0}(-4x)^0 + 2^5 \binom{6}{1}(-4x)^1 + 2^4 \binom{6}{2}(-4x)^2 + \ldots$$
$$= 64 - 4 \cdot 6 \cdot 32x + 15 \cdot 16 \cdot 16x^2 + \ldots.$$
$$= 64 - 768x + 3840x^2 + \ldots.$$

Hence,
$$x(2-4x)^6 = x(64 - 768x + 3840x^2 + \ldots)$$
$$= 64x - 768x^2 + 3840x^3 + \ldots.$$

Q5. We use Theorem 8.4 to expand with as many terms as are needed to pick out the terms which contribute to the coefficient of x^3 in each case.

(a) We just need to pick out the x^3 term in the Binomial expansion of $\left(1 - \dfrac{x}{2}\right)^8$. Namely, this is
$$\binom{8}{3}\left(-\dfrac{1}{2}\right)^3 = -7.$$

(b) First, we expand $(2+3x)^4$.
$$(2+3x)^4 = \binom{4}{0}(2^4) + \binom{4}{1}(2^3)(3x) + \binom{4}{2}(2^2)(3x)^2 + \binom{4}{3}(2)(3x)^3$$
$$+ \binom{4}{4}(3x)^4,$$
$$= 16 + 96x + 216x^2 + 216x^3 + 81x^4.$$

Thus,
$$(1+x)(2+3x)^4 = (1+x)(16 + 96x + 216x^2 + 216x^3 + 81x^4).$$

Picking out the contributions to the x^3 term,
$$(1)(216) + (1)(216) = 432.$$

(c) First, we find the necessary terms in the expansion of $\left(1-\frac{x}{5}\right)^{10}$.

$$\left(1-\frac{x}{5}\right)^{10} = \binom{10}{0} + \binom{10}{1}\left(-\frac{x}{5}\right) + \binom{10}{2}\left(-\frac{x}{5}\right)^2$$
$$+ \binom{10}{3}\left(-\frac{x}{5}\right)^3 + \ldots$$
$$= 1 - 2x + \frac{9}{5}x^2 - \frac{24}{25}x^3 + \ldots$$

Thus,

$$(2+x^2)\left(1-\frac{x}{5}\right)^{10} = (2+x^2)\left(1 - 2x + \frac{9}{5}x^2 + \frac{24}{25}x^3 + \ldots\right).$$

The contribution to the x^3 term is

$$(2)\left(\frac{24}{25}\right) + (1)(-2) = \frac{48}{25} - 2 = -\frac{2}{25}.$$

(d) First, we find the necessary terms in the expansion of $(1-x)^3$ and $(2+x)^6$ separately.

$$(1-x)^3 = 1 - 3x + 3x^2 - x^3,$$
$$(2+x)^6 = \binom{6}{0}(2^6) + \binom{6}{1}(2^5)(x) + \binom{6}{2}(2^4)(x^2) + \binom{6}{3}(2^3)(x^3) + \ldots$$
$$= 64 + 192x + 240x^2 + 160x^3 + \ldots$$

Thus,

$$(1-x)^3(2+x)^6 = (1 - 3x + 3x^2 - x^3)(64 + 192x + 240x^2 + 160x^3 + \ldots).$$

The contribution to the x^3 term is

$$(1)(160) + (-3)(240) + (3)(192) + (-1)(64) = -48.$$

Q6. (a) If we expand the first few terms of $\left(x+\frac{1}{x}\right)^{10}$, we see a pattern emerging:

$$\left(x+\frac{1}{x}\right)^{10} = \binom{10}{0}x^{10}\left(\frac{1}{x}\right)^0 + \binom{10}{1}x^9\left(\frac{1}{x}\right)^1$$
$$+ \binom{10}{2}x^8\left(\frac{1}{x}\right)^2 + \binom{10}{3}x^7\left(\frac{1}{x}\right)^3 + \ldots$$
$$= \binom{10}{0}x^{10} + \binom{10}{1}x^8$$
$$+ \binom{10}{2}x^6 + \binom{10}{3}x^4 + \ldots$$

We notice that the power of x drops by 2 for each additional term. Thus, evaluating the $\binom{10}{r}$ terms for $r = 0, \ldots, 10$ we find

$$\left(x + \frac{1}{x}\right)^{10} = x^{10} + 10x^8 + 45x^6 + 120x^4 + 210x^2 + 252$$
$$+ 210x^{-2} + 120x^{-4} + 45x^{-6} + 10x^{-8} + x^{-10}.$$

(b) We similarly expand a few terms of $\left(x - \frac{1}{x^2}\right)^{10}$:

$$\left(x - \frac{1}{x^2}\right)^{10} = \binom{10}{0}x^{10}\left(\frac{1}{x^2}\right)^0 - \binom{10}{1}x^9\left(\frac{1}{x^2}\right)^1$$
$$+ \binom{10}{2}x^8\left(\frac{1}{x^2}\right)^2 - \binom{10}{3}x^7\left(\frac{1}{x^2}\right)^3 + \ldots$$
$$= \binom{10}{0}x^{10} - \binom{10}{1}x^7$$
$$+ \binom{10}{2}x^3 - \binom{10}{3}x^1 + \ldots.$$

We see that in this case the pattern is that the power of x drops by 3 each time and the sign of the terms also alternates. Thus, evaluating the $\binom{10}{r}$ terms for $r = 0, \ldots, 10$ we find

$$\left(x - \frac{1}{x^2}\right)^{10} = x^{10} - 10x^7 + 45x^4 - 120x + 210x^{-2}$$
$$- 252x^{-5} + 210x^{-8} - 120x^{-11} + 45x^{-14}$$
$$- 10x^{-17} + x^{-20}.$$

Q7. (a) The coefficient of the x^5 term is

$$\binom{20}{5} = 15\,504.$$

(b) The coefficient of the x^4 term is

$$(-2)^4 \times \binom{12}{4} = 16 \times 495 = 7920.$$

(c) The coefficient of the x^5 term is

$$\left(\frac{3}{2}\right)^5 \times 2^3 \times \binom{8}{5} = \frac{3^5}{2^2} \times 56$$
$$= 3402.$$

(d) The coefficient of the y^3 term is

$$x^2 \times 2^3 \times \binom{5}{3} = x^2 \times 8 \times 10$$
$$= 80x^2.$$

(e) The coefficient of the x^3 terms is

$$2^3 \times \left(\frac{1}{2}y\right)^3 \times \binom{6}{3} = 8 \times \frac{y^3}{8} \times 20$$
$$= 20y^3.$$

Q8. (a) In this case r in $\binom{n}{r}$ varies from 0 to 4, hence, the expansion of $(1-2x)^n$ has the form

$$(1-2x)^n = 2^0 \binom{n}{0} - 2^1 \binom{n}{1} x + 2^2 \binom{n}{2} x^2$$
$$- 2^3 \binom{n}{3} x^3 + 2^4 \binom{n}{4} x^4 - \ldots$$
$$= 1 - 2nx + 4\binom{n}{2} x^2 - 8 \binom{n}{3} x^3 + 16 \binom{n}{4} x^4 - \ldots$$
$$= 1 - 2nx + 4\frac{n(n-1)}{2} x^2 - 8 \frac{n(n-1)(n-2)}{3 \times 2} x^3$$
$$+ 16 \frac{n(n-1)(n-2)(n-3)}{4 \times 3 \times 2} x^4 - \ldots$$
$$= 1 - 2nx + 2n(n-1)x^2$$
$$- \frac{4}{3} n(n-1)(n-2) x^3 + \frac{2}{3} n(n-1)(n-2)(n-3) x^4 - \ldots$$

(b) Again, r in $\binom{n}{r}$ varies from 0 to 4, hence, the expansion of $(2+3x)^n$ has the form

$$(2+3x)^n = 2^n \cdot 3^0 \binom{n}{0} + 2^{n-1} 3^1 \binom{n}{1} x + 2^{n-2} 3^2 \binom{n}{2} x^2$$
$$+ 2^{n-3} 3^3 \binom{n}{3} x^3 + 2^{n-4} 3^4 \binom{n}{4} x^4 + \ldots$$
$$= 2^n \cdot 3^0 + 2^{n-1} 3^1 nx + 2^{n-2} 3^2 \frac{n(n-1)}{2} x^2$$
$$+ 2^{n-3} 3^3 \frac{n(n-1)(n-2)}{3 \times 2} x^3$$
$$+ 2^{n-4} 3^4 \frac{n(n-1)(n-2)(n-3)}{4 \times 3 \times 2} x^4 + \ldots$$
$$= 2^n + 2^{n-1} \cdot 3nx + 2^{n-3} \cdot 9n(n-1)x^2$$
$$+ 2^{n-4} \cdot 9n(n-1)(n-2)x^3$$
$$+ 2^{n-7} \cdot 27n(n-1)(n-2)(n-3)x^4 + \ldots.$$

Q9. (a) We have

$$(1+\sqrt{2})^3 = 1 \cdot (\sqrt{2})^0 \binom{3}{0} + 1 \cdot (\sqrt{2})^1 \binom{3}{1}$$
$$+ 1 \cdot (\sqrt{2})^2 \cdot \binom{3}{2} + 1 \cdot (\sqrt{2})^3 \cdot \binom{3}{3}$$
$$= 1 + 3\sqrt{2} + 3 \cdot 2 + 2\sqrt{2}$$
$$= 7 + 5\sqrt{2}.$$

(b) We have

$$(2-3\sqrt{3})^4 = 2^4 \cdot (3\sqrt{3})^0 \cdot \binom{4}{0}$$
$$- 2^3 \cdot (3\sqrt{3})^1 \cdot \binom{4}{1} + 2^2 \cdot (3\sqrt{3})^2 \cdot \binom{4}{2}$$
$$- 2^1 \cdot (3\sqrt{3})^3 \cdot \binom{4}{3} + 2^0 \cdot (3\sqrt{3})^4 \cdot \binom{4}{0}$$
$$= 16 - 8 \cdot 3\sqrt{3} \cdot 4 + 4 \cdot 27 \cdot 6 - 2 \cdot 81\sqrt{3} \cdot 4 + 729$$
$$= 1393 - 744\sqrt{3}.$$

(c) We have

$$(\sqrt{2}+2\sqrt{3})^4 = (\sqrt{2})^4 \cdot (2\sqrt{3})^0 \cdot \binom{4}{0}$$
$$+ (\sqrt{2})^3 \cdot (2\sqrt{3})^1 \cdot \binom{4}{1} + (\sqrt{2})^2 \cdot (2\sqrt{3})^2 \cdot \binom{4}{2}$$
$$+ (\sqrt{2})^1 \cdot (2\sqrt{3})^3 \cdot \binom{4}{3} + (\sqrt{2})^0 \cdot (2\sqrt{3})^4 \cdot \binom{4}{0}$$
$$= 4 + 2\sqrt{2} \cdot 2\sqrt{3} \cdot 4 + 2 \cdot 12 \cdot 6 + \sqrt{2} \cdot 24\sqrt{3} \cdot 4 + 144$$
$$= 292 + 112\sqrt{2}\sqrt{3}$$
$$= 292 + 112\sqrt{6}.$$

(d) We have

$$\left(\frac{\sqrt{2}}{3}+\frac{\sqrt{3}}{2}\right)^3 = \left(\frac{\sqrt{2}}{3}\right)^3 \cdot \left(\frac{\sqrt{3}}{2}\right)^0 \cdot \binom{3}{0}$$
$$+ \left(\frac{\sqrt{2}}{3}\right)^2 \cdot \left(\frac{\sqrt{3}}{2}\right)^1 \cdot \binom{3}{1}$$
$$+ \left(\frac{\sqrt{2}}{3}\right)^1 \cdot \left(\frac{\sqrt{3}}{2}\right)^2 \cdot \binom{3}{2}$$
$$+ \left(\frac{\sqrt{2}}{3}\right)^0 \cdot \left(\frac{\sqrt{3}}{2}\right)^3 \cdot \binom{3}{0}$$
$$= \frac{2\sqrt{2}}{27} + \frac{2}{9} \cdot \frac{\sqrt{3}}{2} \cdot 3 + \frac{\sqrt{2}}{3} \cdot \frac{3}{4} \cdot 3 + \frac{3\sqrt{3}}{8}$$
$$= \frac{2}{27}\sqrt{2} + \frac{1}{3}\sqrt{3} + \frac{3}{4}\sqrt{2} + \frac{3}{8}\sqrt{3}$$
$$= \frac{89}{108}\sqrt{2} + \frac{17}{24}\sqrt{3}.$$

(e) We have

$$(1+\sqrt{6})^4 = 1 \cdot (\sqrt{6})^0 \binom{4}{0} + 1 \cdot (\sqrt{6})^1 \binom{4}{1}$$
$$+ 1 \cdot (\sqrt{6})^2 \cdot \binom{4}{2} + 1 \cdot (\sqrt{6})^3 \cdot \binom{4}{3} + 1 \cdot (\sqrt{6})^4 \cdot \binom{4}{4}$$
$$= 1 + 4\sqrt{6} + 6 \cdot 6 + 4 \cdot 6\sqrt{6} + 36$$
$$= 73 + 28\sqrt{6}.$$

Similarly, we have

$$(2-2\sqrt{3})^4 = 2^3 \cdot (2\sqrt{3})^0 \cdot \binom{3}{0}$$
$$- 2^2 \cdot (2\sqrt{3})^1 \cdot \binom{3}{1} + 2^1 \cdot (2\sqrt{3})^2 \cdot \binom{3}{2}$$
$$- 2^0 \cdot (2\sqrt{3})^3 \cdot \binom{3}{3}$$
$$= 8 - 4 \cdot 2\sqrt{3} \cdot 3 + 2 \cdot 12 \cdot 3 - 24\sqrt{3}.$$
$$= 80 - 48\sqrt{3}.$$

Hence,

$$(1+\sqrt{6})^4 + (2-2\sqrt{3})^4 = 153 + 28\sqrt{6} - 48\sqrt{3}.$$

(f) We have

$$(1-\sqrt{5})^6 = 1 \cdot (\sqrt{6})^0 \binom{6}{0} - 1 \cdot (\sqrt{5})^1 \binom{6}{1}$$
$$+ 1 \cdot (\sqrt{5})^2 \cdot \binom{6}{2} - 1 \cdot (\sqrt{5})^3 \cdot \binom{6}{3} + 1 \cdot (\sqrt{5})^4 \cdot \binom{6}{4}$$
$$- 1 \cdot (\sqrt{5})^5 \cdot \binom{6}{5} + 1 \cdot (\sqrt{5})^6 \cdot \binom{6}{6}$$
$$= 1 - \sqrt{5} \cdot 6 + 5 \cdot 15 - 5\sqrt{5} \cdot 20$$
$$+ 25 \cdot 15 - 25\sqrt{5} \cdot 6 + 125$$
$$= 576 - 256\sqrt{5}.$$

Similarly,

$$(2-3\sqrt{5})^4 = 2^4 \cdot (3\sqrt{5})^0 \cdot \binom{4}{0}$$
$$- 2^3 \cdot (3\sqrt{5})^1 \cdot \binom{4}{1} + 2^2 \cdot (3\sqrt{5})^2 \cdot \binom{4}{2}$$
$$- 2^1 \cdot (3\sqrt{5})^3 \cdot \binom{4}{3} + 2^0 \cdot (3\sqrt{5})^4 \cdot \binom{4}{0}$$
$$= 16 - 8 \cdot 3\sqrt{5} \cdot 4 + 4 \cdot 45 \cdot 6 - 2 \cdot 135\sqrt{5} \cdot 4 + 2025$$
$$= 3121 - 1176\sqrt{3}.$$

Hence,

$$(1-\sqrt{5})^6 - (2-3\sqrt{5})^4 = 576 - 256\sqrt{5} - (3121 - 1176\sqrt{3})$$
$$= -2545 + 920\sqrt{5}.$$

Q10. (a) We use the binomial theorem to expand $(1+2x)^6$ up to the x^3 term:

$$(1+2x)^6 \approx 1 + 2^1 \cdot \binom{6}{1} x$$
$$+ 2^2 \binom{6}{2} x^2 + 2^3 \binom{6}{3} x^3$$
$$= 1 + 12x + 60x^2 + 160x^3.$$

(b) If $x = 0.01$, then $1 + 2x = 1.02$, hence we let $x = 0.01$ in the expression above and find

$$1.02 \approx 1 + 0.12 + 0.006 + 0.00016$$
$$= 1.12616.$$

(c) If $x = -0.02$, then $1 + 2x = 0.96$, hence we let $x = -0.02$ in the expression from part (a) and find

$$0.96^5 \approx 1 - 0.24 + 0.024 - 0.00128$$
$$= 0.78272.$$

Q11. (a) We use the binomial theorem to expand $(3 - 4x)^5$ up to the x^3 term:

$$(3 - 4x)^5 \approx 3^5 - 3^4 \cdot 4^1 \cdot \binom{5}{1} x$$
$$+ 3^3 \cdot 4^2 \binom{5}{2} x^2 - 3^2 \cdot 4^3 \binom{5}{3} x^3$$
$$= 243 - 1620x + 4320x^2 - 5760x^3.$$

(b) If $x = 0.01$, then $3 - 4x = 2.96$, hence we let $x = 0.01$ in the expression above and find

$$2.86^5 \approx 243 - 16.2 + 0.432 - 0.00576$$
$$= 227.22624.$$

(c) If $x = -0.02$, then $3 - 4x = 3.08$, hence we let $x = -0.02$ in the expression from part (a) and find

$$3.08^5 \approx 243 + 32.4 + 1.728 + 0.04608$$
$$= 277.17408.$$

Q12. Using the binomial theorem, we find that the coefficient of the x^3 term of $(1+x)^p$ is given by $\binom{p}{3} = 10$. By looking at Pascal's triangle, we see that $\binom{5}{3} = 10$ and hence $p = 5$.

Q13. Using the binomial theorem, we find the coefficient of the x^3 term is

$$a^3 \binom{4}{3} = 108.$$

Now, $\binom{4}{3} = 4$, hence,

$$a^3 = \frac{108}{4} = 27,$$
$$\Rightarrow \quad a = 3.$$

Q14. As we are only requiring the terms up x^2 we expand $(2 + x)^5$ as follows:

$$(2 + x)^5 \approx 2^5 + 2^4 \binom{5}{1} x + 2^3 \binom{5}{2} x^2$$
$$= 32 + 80x + 80x^2.$$

We then multiply this by $(3+x)$ to obtain

$$(3+x)(32+80x+80x^2) = 96 + 240x + 240x^2$$
$$+ 32x + 80x^2 + 80x^3$$
$$= 96 + 272x + 320x^2 + (80x^3).$$

Hence, $a = 96$, $b = 272$ and $c = 320$.

Q15. There are many possible ways to answer this. One way is to use an approximation to $(4+x)^6$. Expanding only to the x^4 terms we have

$$(4+x)^2 \approx 4^6 + 4^5 \binom{6}{1} x + 4^4 \binom{6}{2} x^2$$
$$+ 4^3 \binom{6}{3} x^3 + 4^2 \binom{6}{4} x^4$$
$$= 4096 + 6144x + 3840x^2$$
$$+ 1280x^3 + 240x^4.$$

Now, if we let $x = 0.04$, we find

$$4.04^6 \approx 4096 + 245.76 + 6.144$$
$$+ 0.08192 + 0.0006144$$
$$= 4347.9864344.$$

This is a very good approximation to the true answer. The terms involving x^5 and x^6 will be smaller than 0.0006144 and hence are very small compared to the size of the answer. in fact, a calculator gives $4.04^6 = 4347.986536861697$.

Worked Solutions — Exercise 9.1

Q1. (a) Similar shape to $y = x^3$, see Figure 9.3.

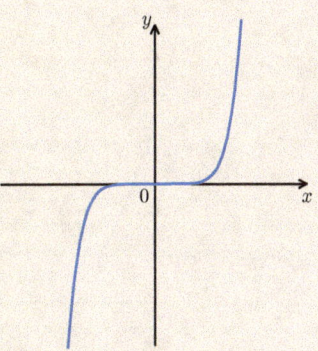

(b) Similar shape to $y = x^{\frac{1}{3}}$, see Figure 9.5.

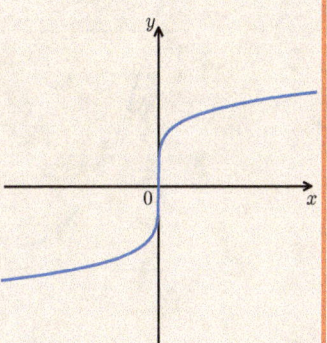

(c) The power of x is greater than 1 so the gradient will be increasing for $x > 0$. An alternative form for this curve is $y = (\sqrt[4]{x})^5$ so we can see that negative values of x do not give real numbers.

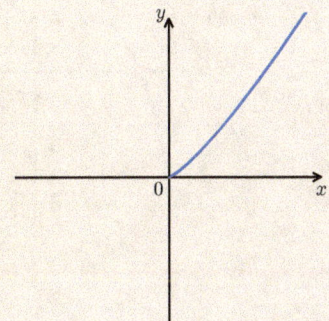

(d) $y > 0$ for $x < 0$ and $x > 3$, $y < 0$ for $0 < x < 3$. The overall shape is similar to $y = x^2$.

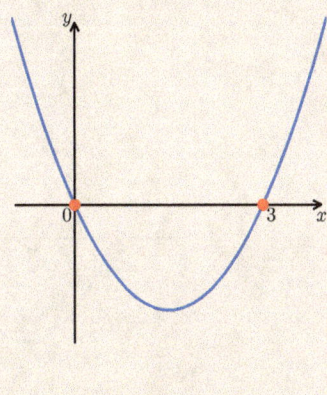

(e) $y > 0$ for $x < -7$ and $x > 2$, $y < 0$ for $-7 < x < 2$. The overall shape is similar to $y = x^2$.

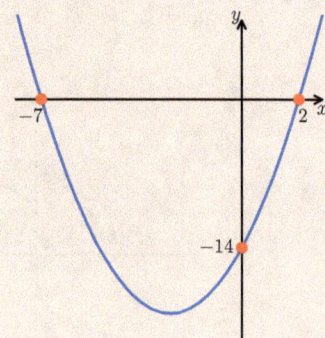

(f) $y \geq 0$ for all x. There is a repeated root at $x = -3$ so the curve touches the x-axis at that point. The overall shape is similar to $y = x^2$.

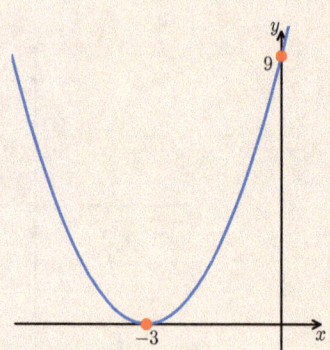

(g) $y > 0$ for $x < -4$ and $x > \frac{1}{2}$, $y < 0$ for $-4 < x < \frac{1}{2}$. The overall shape is similar to $y = x^2$.

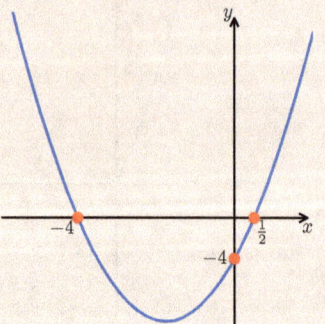

(h) $y > 0$ for $x < -2$ and $0 < x < 2$, $y < 0$ for $-2 < x < 0$ and $x > 2$. The overall shape is similar to $y = x^3$.

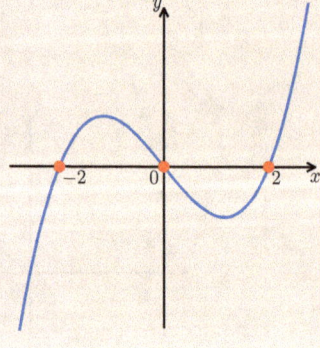

(i) $y \geq 0$ for $x \leq 1$, $y < 0$ for $x > 1$. There is a repeated root at $x = -2$ so the curve touches the x-axis at that point. The overall shape is similar to $y = x^3$.

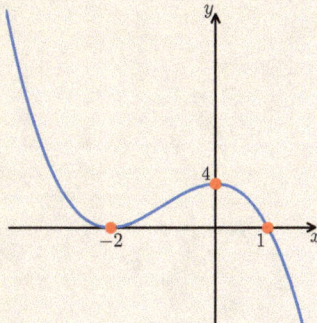

(j) $y \geq 0$ for $x \geq -3$, $y < 0$ for $x < -3$. There is a repeated root at $x = 5$ so the curve touches the x-axis at that point. The overall shape is similar to $y = x^3$.

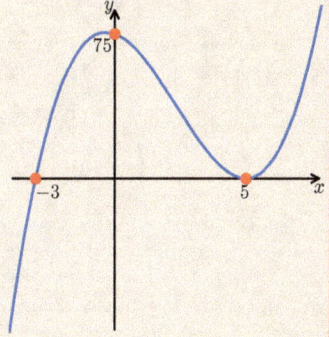

(k) $y > 0$ for $x < -3$ and $x > -1$, $y \leq 0$ for $-3 \leq x \leq -1$. There is a repeated root at $x = -2$ so the curve touches the x-axis at that point. The overall shape is similar to $y = x^4$.

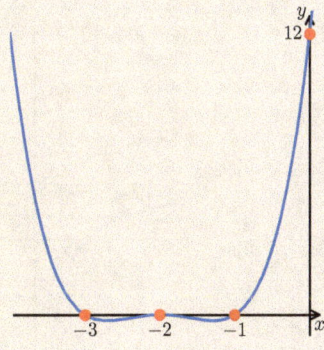

(l) $y \geq 0$ for $x \leq 0$ and $x \geq 2$, $y < 0$ for $0 < x < 2$. There is a repeated root at $x = 4$ so the curve touches the x-axis at that point. The overall shape is similar to $y = x^4$.

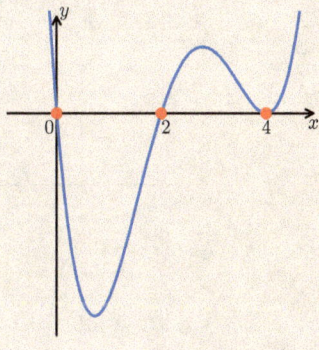

(m) $y > 0$ for $-1 < x < 1$ and $x > 2$, $y < 0$ for $x < -1$ and $1 < x < 2$. There is a repeated root at $x = 1$, which is repeated three times, so there is an inflection point at $x = 1$. The overall shape is similar to $y = x^5$.

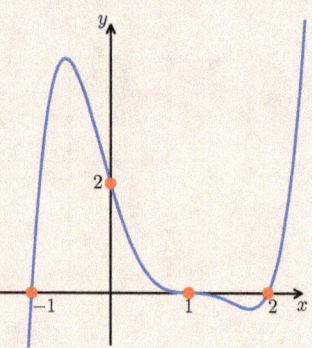

Q2. (a) Use a table of values to determine behaviour near asymptotes.

x	-100	0.999	1.001	100
y	-0.0099	-1000	1000	0.01010

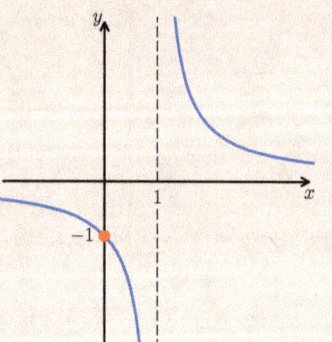

(b) Use a table of values to determine behaviour near asymptotes.

x	-100	-0.001	0.001	100
y	0.99	-999	1001	1.01

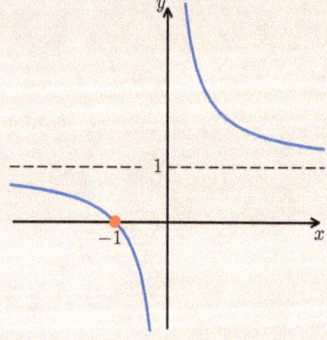

(c) Use a table of values to determine behaviour near asymptotes.

x	-100	1.999	2.001	100
y	-0.9608	3999	-4001	-1.0408

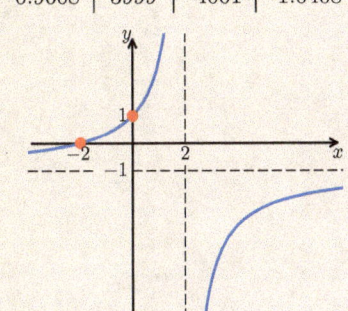

(d) Use a table of values to determine behaviour near asymptotes.

x	-100	3.99	4.01	100
y	1.0001	10001	10001	1.0001

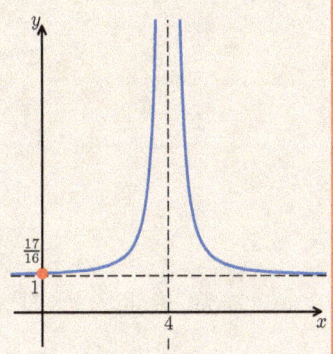

Worked Solutions — Exercise 9.2

Q1. The sketch indicates there is a single intersection between $y = \frac{2}{x^2}$ and $y = 3x + 1$, hence the equation $0 = 3x^3 + x^2 - 2$ has one real root.

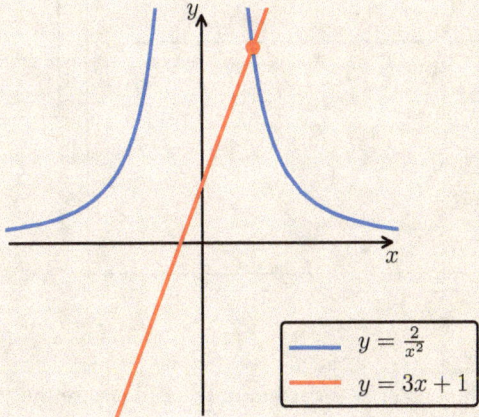

Q2. Since the gradient of the straight line is constant, varying the value of k will result in a set of parallel lines. There are two parallel straight lines which are tangent to the curve $y = \frac{1}{x+1}$.

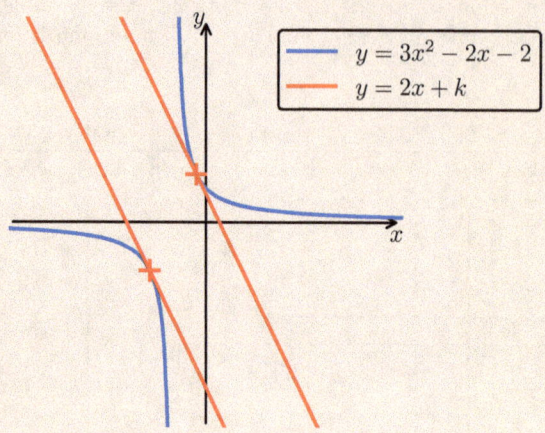

Q3. The minimum point for each curve should be calculated to help with the sketch.

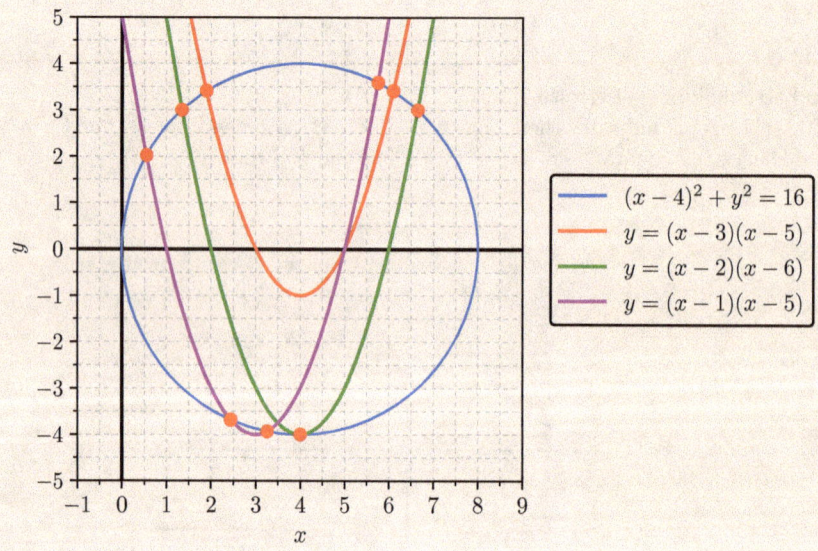

Q4. Choosing equations in factorised form helps to ensure the correct number of intersections with the hyperbola.

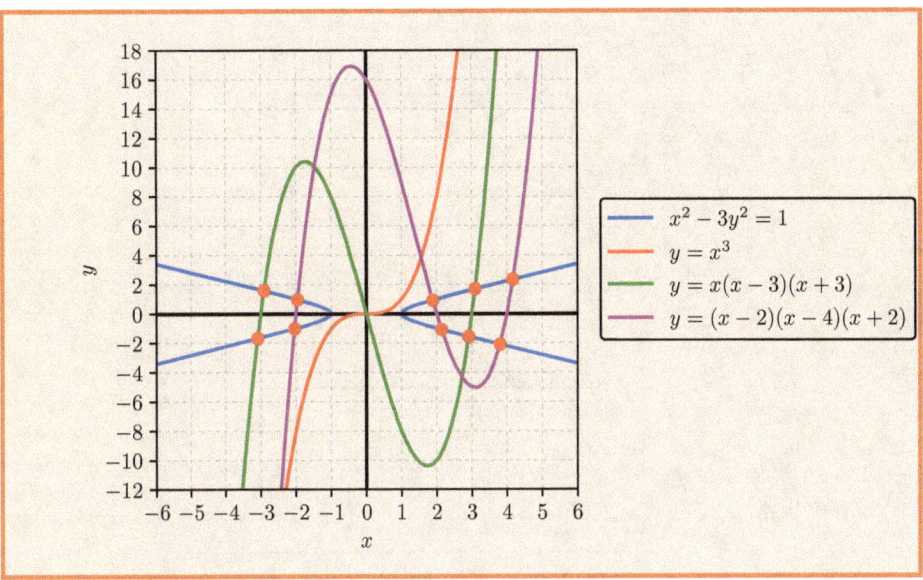

Worked Solutions — Exercise 9.3

Q1. The area of the rectangle is $A = xy$. The area is fixed such that $A = 15$. Rearranging, we get $y = \frac{15}{x}$.

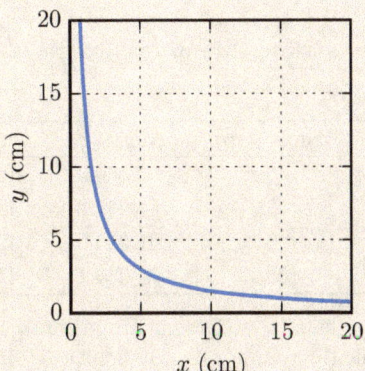

Q2. The volume of a hemisphere is $V = \frac{2}{3}\pi r^3$, hence the constant of proportionality is $\frac{2}{3}\pi$.

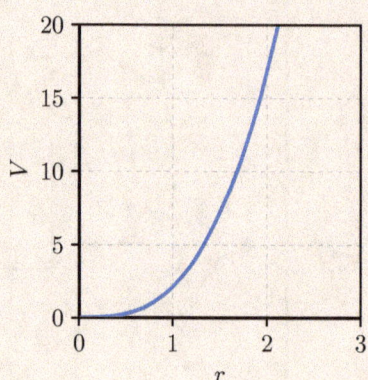

Q3. If C is proportional to F then we would expect $\frac{C}{F}$ to be constant.

Celsius (C)	Fahrenheit (F)	$\frac{C}{F}$
-40	-40	1
-20	-4	5
0	32	0
20	68	0.294
40	104	0.385

The ratio $\frac{C}{F}$ is not constant, hence Celsius is not proportional to Fahrenheit. However, there is a *linear* relationship between Celsius and Fahrenheit $F = \frac{9}{5}C + 32$.

Q4. If mass (m) is proportional to the square of the radius (r) then $m = kr^2$, hence $k = \frac{m}{r^2}$

Radius (cm)	Mass (g)	$\frac{m}{r^2}$
5	1060.3	42.41
10	4241.2	42.41
20	16 964.6	42.41
35	51 954.1	42.41

From Example 9.5 we know that mass is proportional to volume so we can write $m = \hat{k}V$. Substituting the volume of a cylinder we get $m = \hat{k}\pi \times 5 \times r^2$. Comparing to our original proportion equation we see that $k = \hat{k}\pi \times 5$ so $\hat{k} = 2.70\,\text{g/cm}^3$, which is the density of Aluminium.

Q5. If pressure is inversely proportional to volume then $P = \frac{k}{V}$.

Length (cm)	Pressure (Pa)	Volume (cm^3)	PV (N m)
9	101325	254.469	25784000
7	130275	197.920	25784000
5	182385	141.372	25784000
3	303975	84.823	25784000

The constant of proportionality is $25\,784\,000$ N m (5 s.f.).

Worked Solutions — Exercise 10.1

Q1. First, we sketch the graph of $f(x)$ using techniques seen in Chapter 9.

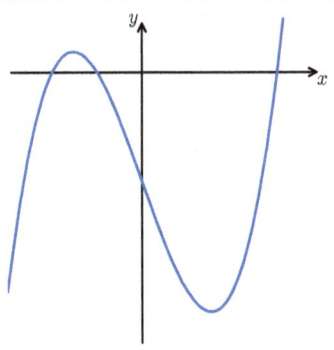

(a) The transformation defined by $f(x-4)$ is is a translation by the column vector $\begin{pmatrix} 4 \\ 0 \end{pmatrix}$, which results in the blue graph in the figure below.

(b) The transformation defined by $f(x+3)$ is a translation by the column vector $\begin{pmatrix} -3 \\ 0 \end{pmatrix}$, which results in the green graph in the figure below.

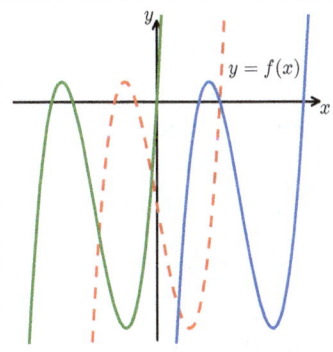

(c) The transformation defined by $f(x)+2$ is a translation by the column vector

$\begin{pmatrix} 0 \\ 2 \end{pmatrix}$, which results in the sketch below.

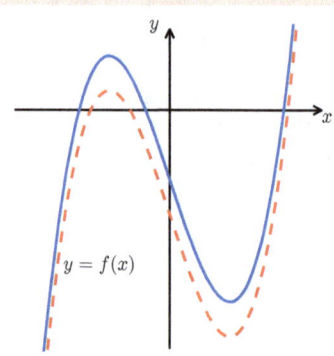

Q2. (a) A translation by the column vector $\begin{pmatrix} 0 \\ -5 \end{pmatrix}$ is a translation parallel to the y axis, therefore the transformation is defined as $f(x) - 5$. This results in the blue graph in the figure below.

(b) A translation by the column vector $\begin{pmatrix} 0 \\ 2 \end{pmatrix}$ is a translation parallel to the y axis, therefore the transformation is defined as $f(x) + 2$. This results in the green graph in the figure below.

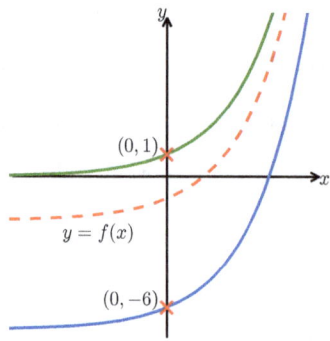

(c) A translation by the column vector $\begin{pmatrix} 3 \\ 0 \end{pmatrix}$ is a translation parallel to the y axis, therefore the transformation is defined as $f(x - 3)$. This results in the blue graph in the figure below.

(d) A translation by the column vector $\begin{pmatrix} -4 \\ 0 \end{pmatrix}$ is a translation parallel to the y axis, therefore the transformation is defined as $f(x + 4)$. This results in the green graph in the figure below.

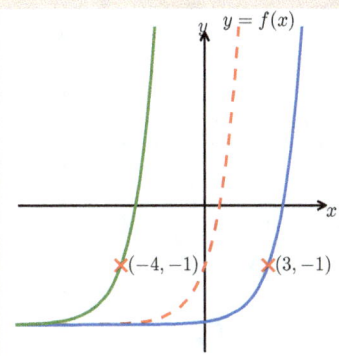

Q3. The transformation, $f(x-1)$ is a translation parallel to the x axis by one unit. The excludes (b), a translation parallel to the x by a negative quantity, and (c), a translation parallel to the y axis, from the given choices. Since we are not given any scale either (a) or (d) are reasonable suggestions. The coordinates of the new point are $(1,1)$.

Q4. (a) The graph of $f(x) = 3 - x^2$ is shown below.

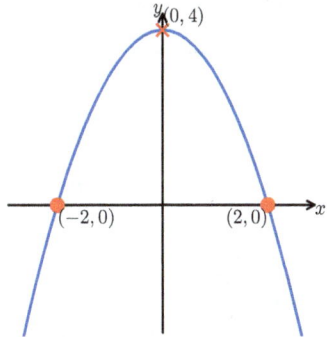

(b) A translation 3 units down is defined by $f(x) - 3$ and can be written as the column vector, $\begin{pmatrix} 0 \\ -3 \end{pmatrix}$.

(c) By translating $f(x)$ by this column vector we obtain the equation $f(x) - 3 = -x^2$. This results in the following graph.

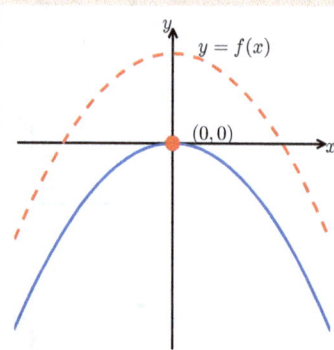

Q5. First we sketch the graph of $f(x) = -\frac{1}{x}$ using techniques from Chapter 9. This is shown below.

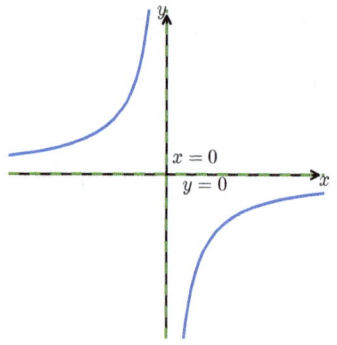

(a) The transformation defined by $f(x+3)$ results in a horizontal translation by column vector $\begin{pmatrix} -3 \\ 0 \end{pmatrix}$. This results in the asymptote moving 3 units left. The graph of $f(x+3)$ is shown below.

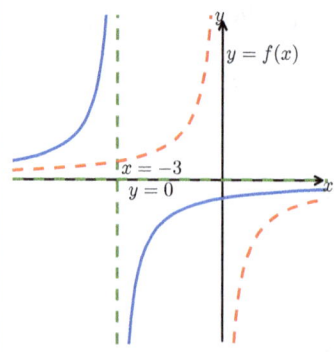

(b) The transformation defined by $f(x) - 2$ is a vertical translation by column vector $\begin{pmatrix} 0 \\ -2 \end{pmatrix}$. This does not affect the asymptote of $f(x)$ and result in the following graph.

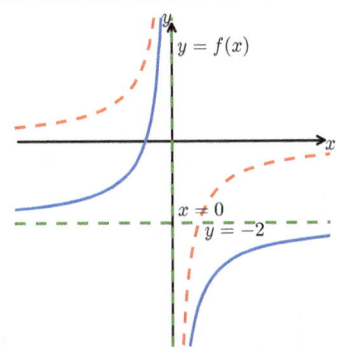

Q6. (a) The transformation defined by $f(x) + 3$ is a vertical translation by column vector $\begin{pmatrix} 0 \\ 3 \end{pmatrix}$. This results in the blue graph in the figure below.

(b) The transformation defined by $f(x-4)$ is a horizontal translation by column vector $\begin{pmatrix} 4 \\ 0 \end{pmatrix}$. This results in the green graph in the figure below.

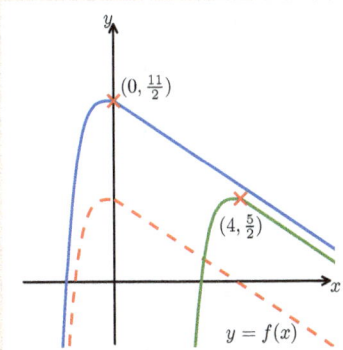

(c) The transformation defined by the column vector $\begin{pmatrix} -1 \\ -2 \end{pmatrix}$ results in the following graph.

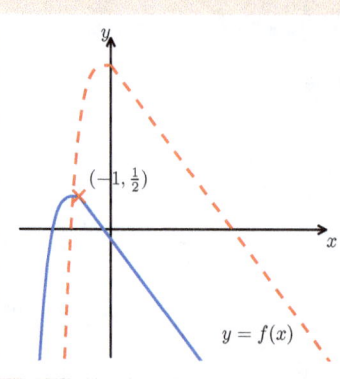

This is the graph of $f(x+1) - 2$.

Worked Solutions — Exercise 10.2

Q1. (a) The graph of $g(x)$ is clearly a reflection in the x axes, and has also been stretched by a scale factor parallel to the y axis. Therefore, from the possible choices, the correct equation for the transformation of $f(x)$ to $g(x)$ is ii - $y = -3f(x)$.

(b) Thus, the transformation which will take $g(x)$ to $f(x)$ is $= y = -\frac{1}{3}g(x)$.

Q2. First we sketch the graph of $f(x)$ using techniques from Chapter **??**.

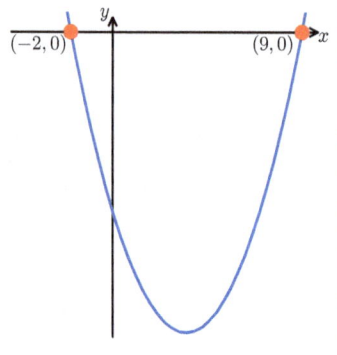

(a) The transformation defined by $2f(x)$ is a stretch parallel to the y axis by scale factor 2. Therefore the x-coordinates of intersection remain unchanged. The resulting graph is shown in blue in the figure below.

(b) The transformation defined by $\frac{1}{2}f(x)$ is a stretch parallel to the y axis by scale factor $\frac{1}{2}$. Therefore the x-coordinates of intersection remain unchanged. The resulting graph is shown in green in the figure below.

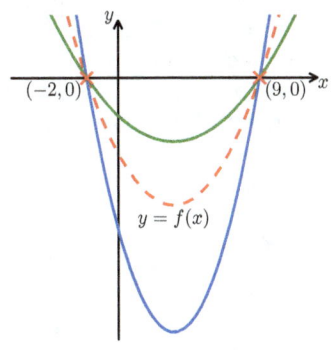

(c) The transformation defined by $f\left(\frac{1}{2}x\right)$ is a stretch parallel to the x axis by scale factor 2. Therefore the x-coordinates of intersection will have doubled. This results in the blue graph in the figure below.

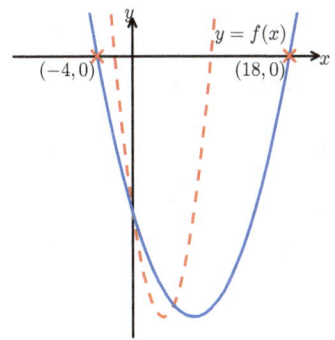

(d) The transformation defined by $f(2x)$ is a stretch parallel to the x axis by scale factor $\frac{1}{2}$. Therefore the x-coordinates of intersection will have halved. This results in the green graph in the figure below.

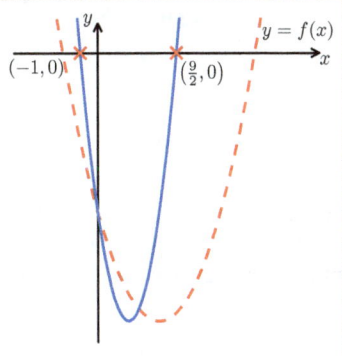

Q3. The change in the equation, $y = f(x)$, is multiplication by a scale factor of $-\frac{1}{2}$. This is equivalent to stretch parallel to the y axis by scale factor $-\frac{1}{2}$.

Q4. (a) The transformation defined by $f(4x)$ is a stretch parallel to the x axis by scale factor $\frac{1}{4}$. Therefore the x coordinates of the labelled point will have quartered in size. This results in the blue graph in the figure below.

(b) The transformation defined by $f(-2x)$ is a reflection in the y axis with scale factor $\frac{1}{2}$. The x coordinates of the given labelled point will be halved and reflected in the y axis. The resulting graph is shown in the green in the figure below.

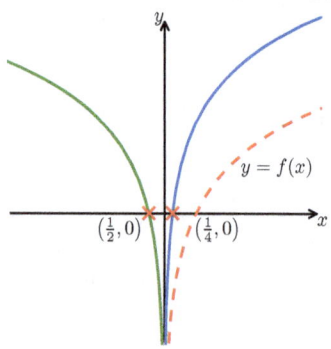

(c) The transformation defined by $3f(x)$ is a stretch parallel to the y axis by scale factor 3. The y coordinates of the labelled point will triple, though in this case since $y = 0$ the point remains unchanged. The resulting graph is shown in blue in the figure below.

(d) The transformation defined by $-f(x)$ is a reflection in the x axis with scale factor 1. The y coordinates of the given labelled point will remain unchanged. This results in the green graph in the figure below.

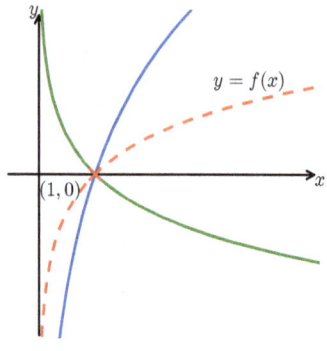

Q5. (a) A sketch vertically by scale factor -2 corresponds to the equation $y = -2f(x)$. Therefore, $y = -2(x-1)(x-2)(x-3)$.

(b) The resulting graph is shown below.

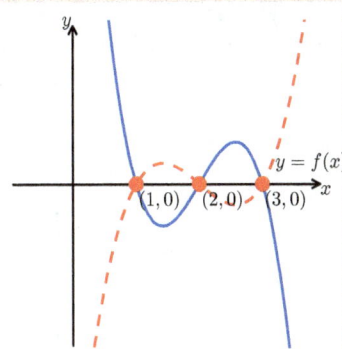

Q6. (a) The transformation defined by $f\left(\frac{1}{2}x\right)$ is a horizontal stretch by scale factor 2. Therefore the x coordinates of the labelled points will double. The resulting graph is sketched below.

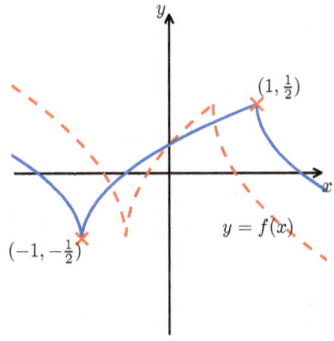

(b) The transformation defined by $2f(x)$ is a vertical stretch by scale factor 2. Therefore the y coordinates of the labelled points will double. The resulting graph is sketched below.

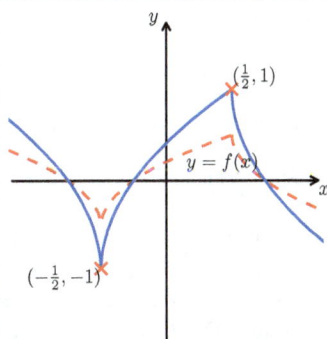

(c) The transformation defined by $-f(x)$ is a reflection in the x axis with scale factor 1. The resulting graph is sketched below.

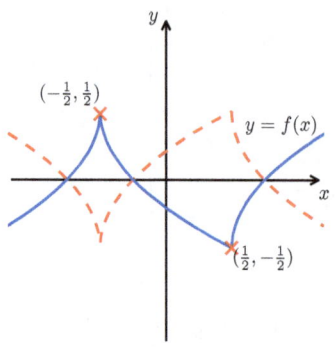

Worked Solutions — Exercise 10.3

Q1. (a) i. A stretch parallel to the y axis by a scale factor of $\frac{1}{4}$ is described by the transformation $\frac{1}{4}f(x)$.

ii. A translation parallel to the x axis by column vector $\begin{pmatrix} 4 \\ 0 \end{pmatrix}$ is described by the transformation $f(x-4)$.

iii. A reflection in the x axis is described by the transformation $-f(x)$.

iv. A translation parallel to the y axis by column vector $\begin{pmatrix} 0 \\ -3 \end{pmatrix}$ is described by the transformation $f(x) - 3$.

v. A stretch parallel to the x axis by scale factor -2 is described by the transformation $f\left(-\frac{1}{2}x\right)$.

(b) i. The transformation defined by $f(-x)$ is a reflection in the y axis.

ii. The transformation defined by $f(x-1)$ is a translation parallel to the x axis by the column vector $\begin{pmatrix} 1 \\ 0 \end{pmatrix}$.

iii. The transformation defined by $f(x) + 2$ is a translation parallel to the y axis by the column vector $\begin{pmatrix} 0 \\ 2 \end{pmatrix}$.

iv. The transformation defined by $\frac{1}{2}f(x)$ is a stretch parallel to the y axis by scale factor $\frac{1}{2}$.

v. The transformation defined by $f\left(\frac{1}{2}x\right)$ is a stretch parallel to the x axis by scale factor 2.

Q2. (a) The transformation $f(-2x)$ is a reflection in the y axis with a scale factor of $\frac{1}{2}$. This means that point B will remain unchanged, however point A will be transformed to the coordinates $\left(\frac{1}{2}, 0\right)$. The resulting graph is shown in (a).

(b) The transformation $f(x-2)$ is a translation parallel to the x axis by column vector $\begin{pmatrix} 2 \\ 0 \end{pmatrix}$. This results in both points A and B changing position, transforming to coordinates $(1, 0)$ and $(2, 1)$ respectively. This results in the graph shown in (b).

(c) The transformation $3f(x)$ is a stretch parallel to the y axis by scale factor 3. This results in the point B being transformed to the coordinates $(0, 3)$ with point A remaining unchanged. This results in the graph shown in (c).

(d) The transformations $f(x) + 1$ is a translation parallel to the y axis by column vector $\begin{pmatrix} 0 \\ 1 \end{pmatrix}$. This results in both points A and B changing position, transforming to coordinates $(-1, 1)$ and $(0, 2)$ respectively. The resulting graph is shown in (d).

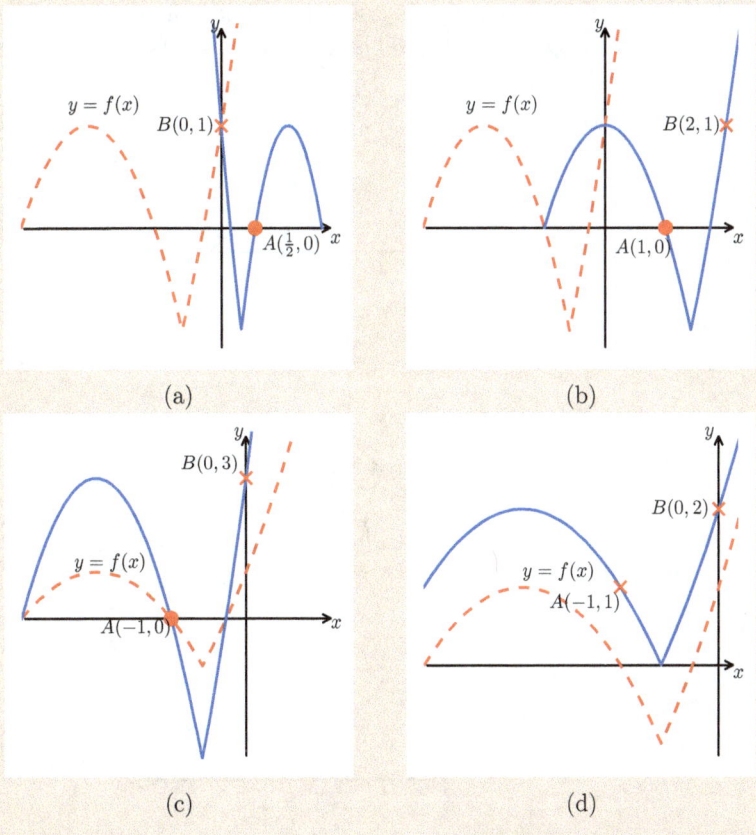

Q3. (a) The function $f(x)$ is a straight line with gradient 3 and y intercept -4. This is shown below.

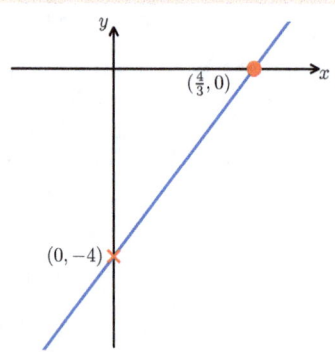

(b) A reflection in the x axis is a transformation defined as $-f(x)$. Therefore the equation of the image will be $y = -3x + 4$. This can be seen below.

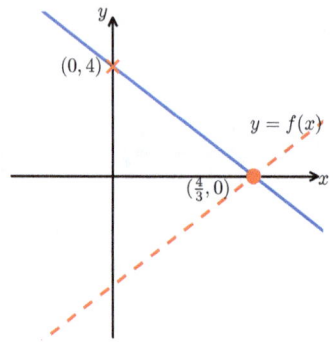

(c) The new function is translated horizontally by -2 units. So $-f(x)$ is translated by column vector $\begin{pmatrix} -2 \\ 0 \end{pmatrix}$. Therefore the equation of this new function in terms of $f(x)$ will be $-f(x+2)$.

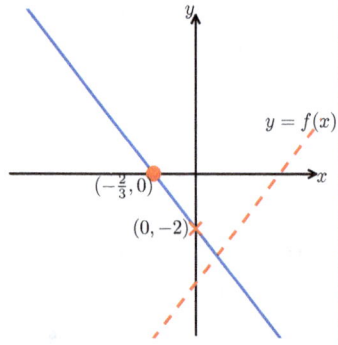

Q4. (a) The transformation defined by $f\left(\frac{1}{2}x\right)$ is a stretch parallel to the x axis by scale factor 2. Therefore all x coordinates double. So the point A will

transform to the coordinates $(6, -1)$.
(b) The equations $3y = f(x)$ indicates a transformation defined by $\frac{1}{3}f(x)$. This is a stretch parallel to the y axis by scale factor $\frac{1}{3}$. Therefore all y coordinates will be divided by 3. So the point A will transform to the coordinates $\left(3, -\frac{1}{3}\right)$.
(c) The transformation $f(x+3)$ is a translation parallel to the x axis by column vector $\begin{pmatrix} -3 \\ 0 \end{pmatrix}$. Therefore all x coordinates will be translated by -3 units. So the point A will transform to the coordinates $(0, -1)$.

Q5. (a) The transformation defined by $f(x+4)$ is a translation parallel to the x axis by column vector $\begin{pmatrix} -4 \\ 0 \end{pmatrix}$. The resulting graph is shown below.

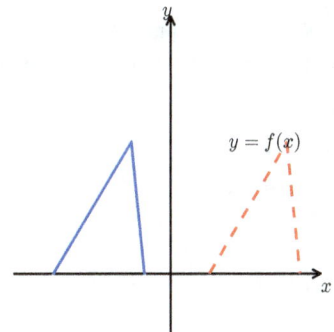

(b) The transformation $3f(x)$ is a stretch parallel to the y axis by scale factor 3. This results in the graph shown below.

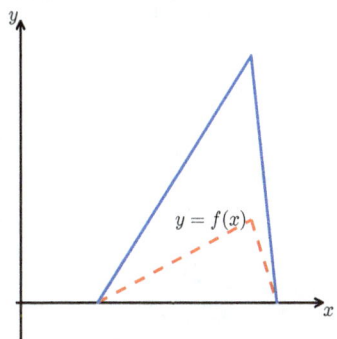

Q6. (a) In the given sketch, the y coordinates of the labelled points have both been multiplied by a scale factor of 3. This suggests a transformation of $f(x)$ defined by $3f(x)$.
(b) In the given sketch, both labelled points have be reflected in the y axis. This suggests a transformation of $f(x)$ defined by $f(-x)$.
(c) In the given sketch, the labelled points have translated 1 unit left and 1 unit

> down. This corresponds to the column vector $\begin{pmatrix} -1 \\ -1 \end{pmatrix}$. This is a combination of transformations (studied further in Year 2) and can be described as the transformation defined by $f(x+1) - 1$.

Worked Solutions — Exercise 11.1

Q1. (a) We consider

$$2x + 2y = 14, \quad ①$$
$$2x + 3y = 18. \quad ②$$

Subtracting ① from ② we find that $y = 4$. This can now be substituted into one of the original equations. If we choose to substitute into ①, then

$$2x + 2y = 14,$$
$$\Rightarrow \quad 2x + 8 = 14,$$
$$\Rightarrow \quad 2x = 6,$$
$$\Rightarrow \quad x = 3.$$

Hence, the solution pair is $(x, y) = (3, 4)$.

(b) We consider

$$3x + 4y = 21, \quad ①$$
$$7x + 4y = 10. \quad ②$$

Subtracting ② from ① we find,

$$-4x = 11,$$
$$\Rightarrow \quad x = -\frac{11}{4}.$$

This can now be substituted into one of the original equations. If we choose to substitute into ①, then

$$3x + 4y = 21,$$
$$\Rightarrow \quad -\frac{33}{4} + 4y = 21,$$
$$\Rightarrow \quad 4y = \frac{117}{4},$$
$$\Rightarrow \quad y = \frac{117}{16}.$$

Hence, the solution pair is $(x, y) = \left(-\frac{11}{4}, \frac{117}{6}\right)$.

(c) We consider
$$7x + 3y = 21, \quad \text{①}$$
$$7x + 6y = 30. \quad \text{②}$$

Subtracting ① from ② we find,
$$3y = 9,$$
$$\Rightarrow \quad y = 3.$$

This can now be substituted into one of the original equations. If we choose to substitute into ①, then
$$7x + 3y = 21,$$
$$\Rightarrow \quad 7x + 9 = 21,$$
$$\Rightarrow \quad 7x = 12,$$
$$\Rightarrow \quad x = \frac{12}{7}.$$

Hence, the solution pair is $(x, y) = \left(\frac{12}{7}, 3\right)$.

(d) We consider
$$3t + 4p = 56, \quad \text{①}$$
$$t + 4p = 32. \quad \text{②}$$

Subtracting ② from ① we find,
$$2t = 24,$$
$$\Rightarrow \quad t = 12.$$

This can now be substituted into one of the original equations. If we choose to substitute into ②, then
$$t + 4p = 32,$$
$$\Rightarrow \quad 12 + 4p = 32,$$
$$\Rightarrow \quad 4p = 20,$$
$$\Rightarrow \quad p = 5.$$

Hence, the solution pair is $(p, t) = (5, 12)$.

Q2. (a) We consider
$$2x + y = 11, \quad \text{①}$$
$$4x - y = 19. \quad \text{②}$$

Adding ① to ② we have,
$$6x = 30,$$
$$\Rightarrow \quad x = 5.$$

This can now be substituted into one of the original equations. If we choose to substitute into ①, then

$$2x + y = 11,$$
$$\Rightarrow 10 + y = 11,$$
$$\Rightarrow y = 1.$$

Hence, the solution pair is $(x, y) = (5, 1)$.

(b) We consider

$$-x + 5y = 12, \quad \text{①}$$
$$x + 3y = 20. \quad \text{②}$$

Adding ① to ② we have,

$$8y = 32,$$
$$\Rightarrow y = 4.$$

This can now be substituted into one of the original equations. If we choose to substitute into ①, then

$$-x + 5y = 12,$$
$$\Rightarrow -x + 20 = 12,$$
$$\Rightarrow -x = -8,$$
$$\Rightarrow x = 8.$$

Hence, the solution pair is $(x, y) = (8, 5)$.

(c) We consider

$$3x - 2y = 15, \quad \text{①}$$
$$5x + 2y = 22. \quad \text{②}$$

Adding ① to ② we have,

$$8x = 37,$$
$$\Rightarrow x = \frac{37}{8}.$$

This can now be substituted into one of the original equations. If we choose to substitute into ①, then

$$3x - 2y = 15,$$
$$\Rightarrow -\frac{111}{8} - 2y = 15,$$
$$\Rightarrow -2y = \frac{9}{8},$$
$$\Rightarrow y = -\frac{9}{16}.$$

Hence, the solution pair is $(x, y) = \left(\frac{37}{8}, -\frac{9}{16}\right)$.

(d) We consider

$$4x - 5y = 33, \quad ①$$
$$3x + 5y = 56. \quad ②$$

Adding ① to ② we have,

$$7x = 89,$$
$$\Rightarrow x = \frac{89}{7}.$$

This can now be substituted into one of the original equations. If we choose to substitute into ①, then

$$4x - 5y = 33,$$
$$\Rightarrow \frac{356}{7} - 5y = 33,$$
$$\Rightarrow -5y = -\frac{125}{7},$$
$$\Rightarrow y = \frac{25}{7}.$$

Hence, the solution pair is $(x, y) = \left(\frac{89}{7}, \frac{25}{7}\right)$.

Q3. (a) We consider

$$xy = 16, \quad ①$$
$$\frac{x}{y} = 4. \quad ②$$

Multiplying ① by ② we see that,

$$x^2 = 64,$$
$$\Rightarrow x = \pm 8.$$

Using ①, when $x = 8$,

$$xy = 16,$$
$$\Rightarrow 8y = 16,$$
$$\Rightarrow y = 2.$$

Similarly, when $x = -8$, $y = -2$. Hence, we have two solution pairs: $(x, y) = (8, 2)$ and $(x, y) = (-8, -2)$.

(b) We consider

$$xy = 20, \quad ①$$
$$\frac{x}{y} = 5. \quad ②$$

Multiplying ① by ② we see that,

$$x^2 = 100,$$
$$\Rightarrow x = \pm 10.$$

Using ①, when $x = 8$,

$$xy = 20,$$
$$\Rightarrow 10y = 20,$$
$$\Rightarrow y = 2.$$

Similarly, when $x = -10$, $y = -2$. Hence, we have two solution pairs: $(x, y) = (10, 2)$ and $(x, y) = (-10, -2)$.

(c) We consider

$$2xy = 30, \quad ①$$
$$\frac{x}{y} = 8. \quad ②$$

Multiplying ① by ② we see that,

$$2x^2 = 240,$$
$$\Rightarrow x^2 = 120$$
$$\Rightarrow x = \pm\sqrt{120},$$
$$\Rightarrow x = \pm 2\sqrt{30}.$$

Using ①, when $x = 2\sqrt{30}$,

$$2xy = 30,$$
$$\Rightarrow 4\sqrt{30}y = 30,$$
$$\Rightarrow y = \frac{\sqrt{30}}{4}.$$

Similarly, when $x = -2\sqrt{30}$, $y = -\frac{\sqrt{30}}{4}$. Hence, we have two solution pairs: $(x, y) = \left(2\sqrt{30}, \frac{\sqrt{30}}{4}\right)$ and $(x, y) = \left(-2\sqrt{30}, -\frac{\sqrt{30}}{4}\right)$.

(d) We consider

$$xy = \frac{10}{4} \quad ①$$
$$\frac{x}{y} = 4. \quad ②$$

Multiplying ① by ② we see that,

$$x^2 = 10,$$
$$\Rightarrow x = \pm\sqrt{10},$$

Using ①, when $x = \sqrt{10}$,

$$xy = \frac{10}{4},$$
$$\Rightarrow \quad \sqrt{10}y = 10,$$
$$\Rightarrow \quad y = \frac{\sqrt{10}}{4}.$$

Similarly, when $x = -\sqrt{10}$, $y = -\frac{\sqrt{10}}{4}$. Hence, we have two solution pairs: $(x,y) = \left(\sqrt{10}, \frac{\sqrt{10}}{4}\right)$ and $(x,y) = \left(-\sqrt{10}, -\frac{\sqrt{10}}{4}\right)$.

Q4. (a) We consider

$$xy^2 = 12 \quad ①$$
$$xy^4 = 48. \quad ②$$

Dividing ② by ①,

$$y^2 = 4,$$
$$\Rightarrow \quad y = \pm 2.$$

When $y = 2$, we use ① to obtain,

$$xy^2 = 12,$$
$$\Rightarrow \quad 4x = 12,$$
$$\Rightarrow \quad x = 3.$$

Similarly, when $y = -2$ we have $x = 3$. Hence, the two solution pairs are $(x,y) = (3,2)$ and $(x,y) = (3,-2)$.

(b) We consider

$$xy^2 = 45 \quad ①$$
$$xy^4 = 405. \quad ②$$

Dividing ② by ①,

$$y^2 = 9,$$
$$\Rightarrow \quad y = \pm 3.$$

When $y = 3$, we use ① to obtain,

$$xy^2 = 45,$$
$$\Rightarrow \quad 9x = 45,$$
$$\Rightarrow \quad x = 5.$$

Similarly, when $y = -3$ we have $x = 5$. Hence, the two solution pairs are $(x,y) = (5,3)$ and $(x,y) = (5,-3)$.

(c) We consider
$$xy^2 = 12 \quad \text{①}$$
$$xy^4 = 54. \quad \text{②}$$

Dividing ② by ①,
$$y^2 = \frac{9}{2},$$
$$\Rightarrow y = \pm\frac{3}{\sqrt{2}}.$$

When $y = \frac{3}{\sqrt{2}}$, we use ① to obtain,
$$xy^2 = 12,$$
$$\Rightarrow \frac{9}{2}x = 12,$$
$$\Rightarrow x = \frac{24}{9},$$
$$\Rightarrow x = \frac{8}{3}.$$

Similarly, when $y = -\frac{3}{\sqrt{2}}$ we have $x = \frac{8}{3}$. Hence, the two solution pairs are $(x, y) = (\frac{8}{3}, \frac{3}{\sqrt{2}})$ and $(x, y) = (\frac{8}{3}, -\frac{3}{\sqrt{2}})$.

(d) We consider
$$y^3 x = 8 \quad \text{①}$$
$$y^5 x = 32. \quad \text{②}$$

Dividing ② by ①,
$$y^2 = 4,$$
$$\Rightarrow y = \pm 2.$$

When $y = 2$, we use ① to obtain,
$$y^3 x = 8,$$
$$\Rightarrow 8x = 8,$$
$$\Rightarrow x = 1.$$

Similarly, when $y = -2$ we have $x = -1$. Hence, the two solution pairs are $(x, y) = (-1, -2)$ and $(x, y) = (1, 2)$.

Q5. (a) We consider
$$x + 2y = 8, \quad \text{①}$$
$$3x + 3y = 18. \quad \text{②}$$

Multiplying ① by three, we obtain

$$3x + 6y = 24, \quad ③$$

Subtracting ③ from ② we find,

$$-3y = -6,$$
$$\Rightarrow \quad y = 2.$$

We now use ① to find the value of x when $y = 2$.

$$x + 2y = 8,$$
$$\Rightarrow \quad x + 4 = 8,$$
$$\Rightarrow \quad x = 4.$$

Therefore, the solution pair is $(x, y) = (4, 2)$.

(b) We consider

$$3p - q = 12, \quad ①$$
$$4p + 3q = 29. \quad ②$$

Multiplying ① by three, we obtain

$$9p - 3q = 36, \quad ③$$

Adding ③ to ② we find,

$$13p = 65,$$
$$\Rightarrow \quad p = 5.$$

We now use ① to find the value of q when $p = 5$.

$$3p - q = 12,$$
$$\Rightarrow \quad 15 - q = 12,$$
$$\Rightarrow \quad -q = -3,$$
$$\Rightarrow \quad q = 3.$$

Therefore, the solution pair is $(p, q) = (5, 3)$.

(c) We consider

$$4x + 2y = 21, \quad ①$$
$$5x - y = 18. \quad ②$$

Multiplying ② by two, we obtain

$$10x - 2y = 36, \quad ③$$

Adding ③ to ① we find,

$$14x = 57,$$
$$\Rightarrow \quad x = \frac{57}{14}.$$

We now use ① to find the value of y when $x = \frac{57}{14}$.

$$4x + 2y = 21,$$
$$\Rightarrow \quad \frac{114}{7} + 2y = 21,$$
$$\Rightarrow \quad 2y = \frac{33}{7},$$
$$\Rightarrow \quad y = \frac{33}{14}.$$

Therefore, the solution pair is $(x, y) = \left(\frac{57}{14}, \frac{33}{14}\right)$.

(d) We consider

$$7x - 2y = 47, \quad ①$$
$$8x + y = 68. \quad ②$$

Multiplying ② by two, we obtain

$$16x + 2y = 136, \quad ③$$

Adding ① and ③ we find,

$$23x = 183,$$
$$\Rightarrow \quad x = \frac{183}{23}.$$

We now use ① to find the value of y when $x = \frac{183}{23}$.

$$7x - 2y = 47,$$
$$\Rightarrow \quad \frac{1281}{23} - 2y = 47,$$
$$\Rightarrow \quad -2y = -\frac{200}{23},$$
$$\Rightarrow \quad y = \frac{100}{23}.$$

Therefore, the solution pair is $(x, y) = \left(\frac{183}{23}, \frac{100}{23}\right)$.

Q6. From the information in the question we can form a pair of simultaneous equations which can be solved to find the cost of the two items. Let b denote a brake calliper and c denote a cable, then we have the following pair of simultaneous equations to solve.

$$b + c = 30, \quad ①$$
$$b = 3c. \quad ②$$

Substituting ② into ① we see that,

$$b + c = 30,$$
$$\Rightarrow \quad 4c = 30,$$
$$\Rightarrow \quad c = 7.50.$$

Using ② with $c = 7.50$ gives $b = 22.50$.

We conclude that a brake cable costs £7.50 and a brake calliper £22.50.

Q7. (a) We consider the following equations,

$$y = x, \quad ①$$
$$x^2 + y^2 = 9. \quad ②$$

Substituting ① into ② we have that,

$$x^2 + y^2 = 9,$$
$$\Rightarrow \quad x^2 + x^2 = 9,$$
$$\Rightarrow \quad 2x^2 = 9,$$
$$\Rightarrow \quad x^2 = \frac{9}{2},$$
$$\Rightarrow \quad x = \pm \frac{3}{\sqrt{2}}.$$

From ① we can find y when $x = \frac{3}{\sqrt{2}}$.

$$y = x,$$
$$\Rightarrow \quad y = \frac{3}{\sqrt{2}}.$$

Similarly, for $x = -\frac{3}{\sqrt{2}}$ we obtain $y = -\frac{3}{\sqrt{2}}$.

Hence, the straight line intersects the circle at two points, namely $(x,y) = \left(\frac{3}{\sqrt{2}}, \frac{3}{\sqrt{2}}\right)$ and $(x,y) = \left(-\frac{3}{\sqrt{2}}, -\frac{3}{\sqrt{2}}\right)$.

(b) We consider the following equations,

$$y = 3x + 2, \quad ①$$
$$x^2 + y^2 = 16. \quad ②$$

Substituting ① into ② we have that,

$$x^2 + y^2 = 16,$$
$$\Rightarrow \quad x^2 + (3x + 2)^2 = 16,$$
$$\Rightarrow \quad x^2 + 9x^2 + 12x + 4 = 16,$$
$$\Rightarrow \quad 10x^2 + 12x - 12 = 0.$$

Using the quadratic formula we find possible values for x.

$$x = \frac{-12 \pm \sqrt{12^2 - 4 \times 10 \times (-12)}}{2 \times 10},$$
$$= \frac{-12 \pm \sqrt{144 + 480}}{20},$$
$$= \frac{-12 \pm \sqrt{624}}{20},$$
$$= \frac{-12 \pm 4\sqrt{39}}{20},$$
$$= \frac{-3 \pm \sqrt{39}}{5}.$$

From ① we can find y when $x = \frac{-3+\sqrt{39}}{5}$.

$$y = 3x + 2,$$
$$\Rightarrow y = \frac{1 + 3\sqrt{39}}{5}.$$

Similarly, for $x = \frac{-3-\sqrt{39}}{5}$ we obtain $y = \frac{1-3\sqrt{39}}{5}$.

Hence, the straight line intersects the circle at two points, namely $(x,y) = \left(\frac{-3+\sqrt{39}}{5}, \frac{1+3\sqrt{39}}{5}\right)$ and $(x,y) = \left(\frac{-3-\sqrt{39}}{5}, \frac{-3-\sqrt{39}}{5}\right)$.

(c) We consider the following equations,

$$y = x + 1, \quad ①$$
$$x^2 + y^2 = 9. \quad ②$$

Substituting ① into ② we have that,

$$x^2 + y^2 = 16,$$
$$\Rightarrow x^2 + (x+1)^2 = 9,$$
$$\Rightarrow x^2 + x^2 + 2x + 1 = 9,$$
$$\Rightarrow 2x^2 + 2x - 8 = 0.$$

Using the quadratic formula we find possible values for x.

$$x = \frac{-2 \pm \sqrt{2^2 - 4 \times 2 \times (-8)}}{2 \times 2},$$
$$= \frac{-2 \pm \sqrt{4 + 64}}{4},$$
$$= \frac{-2 \pm \sqrt{68}}{4},$$
$$= \frac{-2 \pm 2\sqrt{17}}{4},$$
$$= \frac{-1 \pm \sqrt{17}}{2}.$$

From ① we can find y when $x = \frac{-1+\sqrt{17}}{2}$.

$$y = x + 1,$$
$$\Rightarrow y = \frac{1+\sqrt{17}}{2}.$$

Similarly, for $x = \frac{-1-\sqrt{17}}{2}$ we obtain $y = \frac{1-\sqrt{17}}{2}$.

Hence, the straight line intersects the circle at two points, namely $(x,y) = \left(\frac{-1+\sqrt{17}}{2}, \frac{1+\sqrt{17}}{2}\right)$ and $(x,y) = \left(\frac{-1-\sqrt{17}}{2}, \frac{1-\sqrt{17}}{2}\right)$.

(d) We consider the following equations,

$$x^2 + y^2 = 4, \quad \text{①}$$
$$y = x - 1. \quad \text{②}$$

Substituting ② into ① we have that,

$$x^2 + y^2 = 4,$$
$$\Rightarrow x^2 + (x-1)^2 = 4,$$
$$\Rightarrow x^2 + x^2 - 2x + 1 = 4,$$
$$\Rightarrow 2x^2 - 2x - 3 = 0.$$

Using the quadratic formula we find possible values for x.

$$x = \frac{2 \pm \sqrt{(-2)^2 - 4 \times 2 \times (-3)}}{2 \times 2},$$
$$= \frac{2 \pm \sqrt{4 + 24}}{4},$$
$$= \frac{2 \pm \sqrt{28}}{4},$$
$$= \frac{2 \pm 2\sqrt{7}}{4},$$
$$= \frac{1 \pm \sqrt{7}}{2}.$$

From ① we can find y when $x = \frac{1+\sqrt{7}}{2}$.

$$y = x - 1,$$
$$\Rightarrow y = \frac{-1+\sqrt{7}}{2}.$$

Similarly, for $x = \frac{1-\sqrt{7}}{2}$ we obtain $y = \frac{-1-\sqrt{7}}{2}$.

Hence, the straight line intersects the circle at two points, namely $(x,y) = \left(\frac{1+\sqrt{7}}{2}, \frac{-1+\sqrt{7}}{2}\right)$ and $(x,y) = \left(\frac{1-\sqrt{7}}{2}, \frac{-1-\sqrt{7}}{2}\right)$.

Q8. From the information in the question we can form a pair of simultaneous equations which can be solved to find the cost of the two items. Let s denote a side plate and d denote a dinner plate; we have the following pair of simultaneous equations to solve.

$$12s + 6d = 170.40, \quad ①$$
$$d = 2s. \quad ②$$

Substituting ② into ① we see that,

$$12s + 12s = 170.40,$$
$$\Rightarrow 24s = 170.40,$$
$$\Rightarrow s = 7.10.$$

Using ② with $s = 7.10$ gives $d = 14.20$.

We conclude that a side plate costs £7.10 and a dinner plate £14.20.

Q9. From the question we can form the following two equations

$$3x + 2y = x + 4y, \quad ①$$
$$11 + 4x + 6y = 30. \quad ②$$

From ①, we have

$$3x + 2y = x + 4y,$$
$$\Rightarrow 2x = 2y,$$
$$\Rightarrow x = y.$$

Substituting this into ②,

$$11 + 4x + 6y = 30,$$
$$\Rightarrow 11 + 10x = 30,$$
$$\Rightarrow 10x = 19,$$
$$\Rightarrow x = 1.9.$$

Hence, the solution is $(x, y) = (1.9, 1.9)$.

Worked Solutions — Exercise 11.2

Q1. If we label the equations as follows,

$$y = x^2 + 1, \quad ①$$
$$y = -(x-2)^2 + 3, \quad ②$$

then setting ① equal to ② we have the following.

$$x^2 + 1 = -(x-2)^2 + 3$$
$$\Rightarrow \quad x^2 + 1 = -x^2 + 4x - 4 + 3$$
$$\Rightarrow \quad x^2 + 1 = -x^2 + 4x - 1$$
$$\Rightarrow \quad 2x^2 - 4x + 2 = 0$$
$$\Rightarrow \quad 2(x^2 - 2x + 1) = 0$$
$$\Rightarrow \quad 2(x-1)^2 = 0.$$

Thus, $x = 1$ is a repeated solution of the simultaneous equations. From Equation ① we have that $y = 2$ when $x = 1$.
This is shown graphically below.

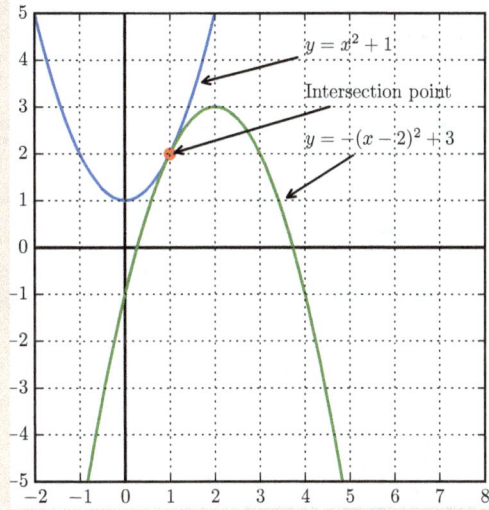

Q2. From the plot it appears that there is only one point of intersection.
This is incorrect and there are actually two points of intersection. Solving this pair of simultaneous equations algebraically lets us see this. To proceed, label the equations,

$$y = 12x^2 - 15x + 11, \quad ①$$
$$y = 10x - 2. \quad ②$$

Setting them equal, we obtain,

$$10x - 2 = 12x^2 - 15x + 11$$
$$\Rightarrow \quad 0 = 12x^2 - 25x + 13$$
$$\Rightarrow \quad = (12x - 13)(x - 1).$$

Thus, $x = \frac{13}{12}$ or $x = 1$. Using Equation ② we establish that the points of intersection are as follows:

$$(1, 8) \quad \text{and} \quad \left(\frac{13}{12}, \frac{53}{6}\right)$$

This question highlights the potential pitfalls of using a sketch to determine the solutions of a pair of simultaneous equations.

Q3. We proceed as usual and label the equations for ease of referencing.

$$\frac{1}{x} + \frac{1}{y} = 1, \quad ①$$
$$x^2 + y^2 = 8. \quad ②$$

From Equation ① we can obtain;

$$\frac{1}{x} + \frac{1}{y} = 1$$
$$\Rightarrow \quad \frac{1}{x} = 1 - \frac{1}{y}$$
$$\Rightarrow \quad x = \frac{1}{1 - \frac{1}{y}}$$
$$\Rightarrow \quad x = \frac{y}{y - 1}.$$

Substituting this into Equation ② we have,

$$\left(\frac{y}{y-1}\right)^2 + y^2 = 8,$$
$$\Rightarrow \quad \frac{y^2}{y^2 - 2y + 1} + y^2 = 8,$$
$$\Rightarrow \quad \frac{y^2 + y^4 - 2y^3 + y^2}{y^2 - 2y + 1} = 8,$$
$$\Rightarrow \quad 2y^2 + y^4 - 2y^3 = 8y^2 - 16y + 8,$$
$$\Rightarrow \quad y^4 - 2y^3 - 6y^2 + 16y - 8 = 0.$$

This quartic equation can then be factorised by inspection;

$$y^4 - 2y^3 - 6y^2 + 16y - 8 = 0,$$
$$\Rightarrow \quad (y^2 - 4y + 4)(y^2 + 2y - 2) = 0,$$
$$\Rightarrow \quad (y - 2)^2(y^2 + 2y - 2) = 0.$$

We see that there are three possible solutions for y: $y = 2$, $y = -1 - \sqrt{3}$ and $y = -1 - \sqrt{3}$. With these we can work out the corresponding values for the x

coordinate of the intersection points.

$$y = 2 \quad \Rightarrow \quad x = 2,$$
$$y = -1 - \sqrt{3} \quad \Rightarrow \quad x = \sqrt{3} - 1,$$
$$y = \sqrt{3} - 1 \quad \Rightarrow \quad x = -1 - \sqrt{3}.$$

Hence, the three points of intersection are,

$$(2,2), \quad \left(\sqrt{3} - 1, -1 - \sqrt{3}\right) \quad \text{and} \quad \left(-1 - \sqrt{3}, \sqrt{3} - 1\right)$$

Q4. Letting l denote the length, w denote the width we have the following pair of simultaneous equations to solve.

$$2l + 2w = 12, \quad ①$$
$$lw = 6 - \sqrt{8}. \quad ②$$

From ② we have $l = \frac{6-\sqrt{8}}{w}$; substituting this into ① gives

$$2\left(\frac{6-\sqrt{8}}{w}\right) + 2w = 12,$$
$$\Rightarrow \quad \frac{12 - 2\sqrt{8}}{w} + 2w = 12,$$
$$\Rightarrow \quad 2w^2 - 12w + 12 - 2\sqrt{8} = 0.$$

Solving this quadratic we obtain two possible values for w (both of which are positive, and so a physically reasonable): $w = 2 - \sqrt{2}$ and $w = 4 + \sqrt{2}$.
We use ① to find the corresponding values for the length. When $w = 2 - \sqrt{2}$, $l = 4 + \sqrt{2}$ and when $w = 4 + \sqrt{2}$, $l = 2 - \sqrt{2}$. Hence there are two physically reasonable solution pairs;

$$(l, w) = \left(4 + \sqrt{2}, 2 - \sqrt{2}\right),$$
$$(l, w) = \left(2 - \sqrt{2}, 4 + \sqrt{2}\right).$$

Q5. We have the following pair of simultaneous equations to solve,

$$10 = u + 2a, \quad ①$$
$$16 = u + 3.5a. \quad ②$$

Subtracting ① from ②,

$$6 = 1.5a,$$
$$\Rightarrow \quad \frac{6}{1.5} = a,$$
$$\Rightarrow \quad a = 4.$$

Substituting this value of a back into ① we find u,

$$10 = u + 2a$$
$$\Rightarrow \quad u = 2$$

Q6. We consider the following pair of simultaneous equations.

$$1.2 = \frac{150 - \mu}{\sigma}, \quad ①$$
$$-1.1 = \frac{120 - \mu}{\sigma}. \quad ②$$

Rearranging ①,

$$\sigma = \frac{150 - \mu}{1.2},$$

substituting this into ② gives,

$$-1.1 = \frac{120 - \mu}{\sigma}$$
$$\Rightarrow \quad -1.1 = \frac{120 - \mu}{\frac{150-\mu}{1.2}},$$
$$\Rightarrow \quad -1.1(150 - \mu) = 1.2(120 - \mu),$$
$$\Rightarrow \quad -165 + 1.1\mu = 144 - 1.2\mu,$$
$$\Rightarrow \quad \frac{23}{10}\mu = 309,$$
$$\Rightarrow \quad \mu = \frac{3090}{23}.$$

With this, we find the following value for σ,

$$\sigma = \frac{150 - \frac{3090}{23}}{1.2}$$
$$= \frac{300}{23}.$$

Hence, to three significant figures, $\mu = 134$ and $\sigma = 13.0$.

Q7. We consider the following three equations that have been obtained by resolving forces.

$$98 - T_1 = 10a \quad ①$$
$$T_1 - T_2 = 2a. \quad ②$$
$$T_2 - 49 = 5a \quad ③$$

From ① and ③ we obtain the following,

① $\Rightarrow$ $T_1 = 98 - 10a,$
③ $\Rightarrow$ $T_2 = 5a + 49.$

Substituting these into ② we have,

$$98 - 10a - (5a + 49) = 2a,$$
$$\Rightarrow \quad 98 - 15a - 49 = 2a,$$
$$\Rightarrow \quad 49 = 17a,$$
$$\Rightarrow \quad a = \frac{49}{17}.$$

Hence,

$$T_2 = 5 \times \frac{49}{17} + 49$$
$$= \frac{1078}{17},$$

and

$$T_1 = 98 - 10a$$
$$= \frac{1176}{17}.$$

Finally, rounding to one decimal place, as this is physically reasonable, our three solutions are $a \approx 2.9 \text{m s}^{-1}$, $T_1 \approx 69.2\text{N}$, $T_2 \approx 63.4\text{N}$.

Q8. For ease of reference we label the three equations as below

$$x + 3y + 1 = 0, \quad\quad\quad ①$$
$$(x-3)^2 + (y-2)^2 = 20, \quad\quad ②$$
$$y = \frac{1}{2}(x-3)^2 - 4. \quad\quad ③$$

To find the coordinates of all intersection points we work systematically and consider each possible pair of functions.

- **Parabola and Straight Line**

    From ① we can see that $x = -1 - 3y$. Substituting this into ③, we have,

    $$y = \frac{1}{2}(x-3)^2 - 4,$$
    $$\Rightarrow \quad y = \frac{1}{2}(-1 - 3y - 3)^2 - 4,$$
    $$\Rightarrow \quad 2y = (-3y - 4)^2 - 8,$$
    $$\Rightarrow \quad 2y = 9y^2 + 24y + 16 - 8,$$
    $$\Rightarrow \quad 0 = 9y^2 + 22y + 8,$$
    $$\Rightarrow \quad 0 = (9y + 4)(y + 2).$$

    Hence, $y = -\frac{4}{9}$ and $y = -2$.
    When $y = -\frac{4}{9}$, $x = \frac{1}{3}$ and when $y = -2$, $x = 5$. These values give us our first two points: $C = (5, -2)$ and $A = \left(\frac{1}{3}, -\frac{4}{9}\right)$.

- **Straight Line and Circle**

    Again, we have two points of intersection to find (we can use the coordinates for C found this time to check our previous answer). From ① we have that $x = -1 - 3y$, substituting this into the equation for the circle, ②;

$$(x-3)^2 + (y-2)^2 = 20,$$
$$\Rightarrow (-1-3y-3)^2 + (y-2)^2 = 20,$$
$$\Rightarrow (-3y-4)^2 + (y-2)^2 = 20,$$
$$\Rightarrow 9y^2 + 24y + 16 + y^2 - 4y + 4 = 20,$$
$$\Rightarrow 10y^2 + 20y = 0,$$
$$\Rightarrow 10y(y+2) = 0.$$

Hence, $y = 0$ and $y = -2$. Using these to find the corresponding x values we find the two points of intersection as $D = (-1, 0)$ and $C = 5, -2)$. Note that we have found C in multiple ways, giving us confidence in the answer.

- **Parabola and Circle**

We have four points to find in this case. Rearranging ②,

$$(x-3)^2 = 20 - (y-2)^2.$$

Substituting this into ③.

$$y = \frac{1}{2}(x-3)^2 - 4,$$
$$\Rightarrow y = \frac{1}{2}\left[20 - (y-2)^2\right] - 4,$$
$$\Rightarrow y = \frac{1}{2}\left[20 - y^2 + 4y - 4\right] - 4,$$
$$\Rightarrow 2y = 20 - y^2 + 4y - 4 - 8,$$
$$\Rightarrow y^2 - 2y - 8 = 0,$$
$$\Rightarrow (y-4)(y+2) = 0,$$

which leads to $y = 4$ or $y = -2$.
When $y = 4$,

$$8 = (x-3)^2 - 8$$
$$\Rightarrow 16 = (x-3)^2$$
$$\Rightarrow \pm 4 = (x-3)$$
$$\Rightarrow x = 3 \pm 4$$
$$\Rightarrow x = -1 \quad \text{or} \quad x = 7$$

This gives the points $B = (-1, 4)$ and $E = (7, 4)$.

When $y = -2$,
$$-4 = (x-3)^2 - 8$$
$$\Rightarrow \quad 4 = (x-3)^2$$
$$\Rightarrow \quad \pm 2 = (x-3)$$
$$\Rightarrow \quad x = 3 \pm 2$$
$$\Rightarrow \quad x = 5 \quad \text{or} \quad x = 1$$

This gives the points $F = (1, -2)$ and $E = (5, -2)$.
We have now found all the points, which are as follows,

$$A = \left(\frac{1}{3}, -\frac{4}{9}\right),$$
$$B = (-1, 4),$$
$$C = (5, -2),$$
$$D = (-1, 0),$$
$$E = (7, 4),$$
$$F = (1, -2).$$

Q9. Numbering our equations,

$$ax + by = e, \quad \text{①}$$
$$cx + dy = f. \quad \text{②}$$

Rearranging ① we see that $x = \frac{e-by}{a}$, substituting this into ②;

$$cx + dy = f,$$
$$\Rightarrow \quad c\left(\frac{e-by}{a}\right) + dy = f$$
$$\Rightarrow \quad \frac{ce - cby}{a} + dy = f$$
$$\Rightarrow \quad ce - cby + day = fa$$
$$\Rightarrow \quad y(da - cb) = fa - ce$$
$$\Rightarrow \quad y = \frac{fa - ce}{da - cb}.$$

We now use this expression for y to determine an expression for x, using our rearranged form of ①.

$$x = \frac{e - by}{a},$$
$$\Rightarrow x = \frac{e - b\left(\frac{fa-ce}{da-cb}\right)}{a},$$
$$\Rightarrow x = \frac{eda - ecb - bfa + bce}{a(da - cb)},$$
$$\Rightarrow x = \frac{(de - bf)a}{a(da - cb)},$$
$$\Rightarrow x = \frac{de - bf}{da - cb}.$$

Hence, our solution to the general pair of simultaneous equations is given by,

$$x = \frac{de - bf}{da - cb} \quad \text{and} \quad y = \frac{fa - ce}{da - cb}. \tag{2.1}$$

We shall use these expressions for x and y in the solutions of future questions.

Q10. Without loss of generality we let $n \in \mathbb{R}$ be the common difference in the arithmetic sequence, then using the notation of Question Q9. our terms are given by,

$$a = a,$$
$$b = a + n,$$
$$e = a + 2n,$$
$$c = a + 3n,$$
$$d = a + 4n,$$
$$f = a + 5n.$$

Using the expressions found in (2.1) we can find the solution in this case.

$$x = \frac{de - bf}{da - cb},$$
$$\Rightarrow x = \frac{(a + 4n)(a + 2n) - (a + n)(a + 5n)}{(a + 4n)a - (a + 3n)(a + n)},$$
$$\Rightarrow x = \frac{a^2 + bna + 8n^2 - (a^2 + 6na + 5n^2)}{a^2 + 4na - a^2 - 4na - 3n^2},$$
$$\Rightarrow x = \frac{3n^2}{-3n^2},$$
$$\Rightarrow x = -1.$$

$$y = \frac{fa-ce}{da-cb},$$
$$\Rightarrow y = \frac{(a+5n)a - (a+3n)(a+2n)}{(a+4n)a - (a+3n)(a+n)}$$
$$\Rightarrow y = \frac{a^2 + 5na - a^2 - 5na - 6n^2}{a^2 + 4na - a^2 - 4na - 3n^2}$$
$$\Rightarrow y = \frac{-6n^2}{-3n^2}$$
$$\Rightarrow y = 2$$

Hence, when a, b, e, c, d and f form an arithmetic sequence (in that order), the solution is always $(x,y) = (-1, 2)$.

Q11. For this question, we again use the expressions found in (2.1). We consider two cases; the first case being the "usual" Fibonacci sequence and the second being a general Fibonacci style sequence.

- **Case 1:** Let $a = 1$, $b = 1$, $e = 2$, $c = 3$, $d = 5$ and $f = 8$, then

$$x = \frac{de - bf}{da - cb},$$
$$\Rightarrow x = \frac{10 - 8}{5 - 3},$$
$$= \frac{2}{2},$$
$$= 1,$$

and

$$y = \frac{fa - ce}{da - cb},$$
$$\Rightarrow y = \frac{8 - 6}{5 - 3},$$
$$= \frac{2}{2},$$
$$= 1.$$

- **Case 2:** Here we make the following definitions based on two initial numbers $g, h \in \mathbb{R}$,

$$a = g,$$
$$b = h,$$
$$e = g + h,$$
$$c = g + 2h,$$
$$d = 2g + 3h,$$
$$f = 3g + 5h.$$

With this form of a Fibonacci sequence and using (2.1) we obtain, for x,

$$x = \frac{de - bf}{da - cb},$$

$$\Rightarrow \quad x = \frac{(2g + 3h)(g + h) - h(3g + 5h)}{g(2g + 3h) - h(g + 2h)},$$

$$\Rightarrow \quad x = \frac{2g^2 + 2gh + 3hg + 3h^2 - 3gh - 5h^2}{2g^2 + 3gh - hg - 2h^2},$$

$$\Rightarrow \quad x = \frac{2g^2 + 2gh - 2h^2}{2g^2 + 2gh - 2h^2},$$

$$\Rightarrow \quad x = 1.$$

Similarly, for y, we can obtain,

$$y = \frac{fa - ce}{da - cb},$$

$$\Rightarrow \quad y = \frac{(3g + 5h)g - (g + 2h)(g + h)}{(2g + 3h)g - h(g + 2h)},$$

$$\Rightarrow \quad y = \frac{3g^2 + 5hg - g^2 - gh - 2hg - 2h^2}{2g^2 + 3hg - hg - 2h^2},$$

$$\Rightarrow \quad y = \frac{2g^2 + 2gh - 2h^2}{2g^2 + 2gh - 2h^2},$$

$$\Rightarrow \quad y = 1.$$

Q12. We consider the following pair of simultaneous equations,

$$ax_1 + ax_2 = -b, \qquad \text{①}$$
$$ax_1 - ax_2 = -\sqrt{b^2 - 4ac}. \qquad \text{②}$$

Subtracting ② away from ①, we have,

$$2ax_2 = -b + \sqrt{b^2 - 4ac},$$

$$\Rightarrow \quad x_2 = \frac{-b + \sqrt{b^2 - 4ac}}{2a}.$$

Similarly, adding ① and ② gives,

$$2ax_1 = -b - \sqrt{b^2 - 4ac},$$

$$\Rightarrow \quad x_1 = \frac{-b - \sqrt{b^2 - 4ac}}{2a}.$$

It is apparent that these are the solutions obtained by the quadratic formula.

Q13. There are two approaches to this question, and we show both below.

- **Approach 1:**
  We can answer this question without solving any simultaneous equations. Notice that,
  $$\frac{1}{x} + \frac{1}{y} = \frac{y+x}{xy},$$
  hence,
  $$\frac{1}{x} + \frac{1}{y} = \frac{y+x}{xy}$$
  $$= \frac{x+y}{xy}$$
  $$= \frac{7}{2}.$$

- **Approach 2:**
  From ① we have $x = 7 - y$. Substituting this into ②,
  $$xy = 2,$$
  $$\Rightarrow (7-y)y = 2,$$
  $$\Rightarrow 7y - y^2 = 2,$$
  $$\Rightarrow 0 = y^2 - 7y + 2.$$

  Solving this equation results in $y = \frac{1}{2}\left(7 - \sqrt{41}\right)$ and $y = \frac{1}{2}\left(7 + \sqrt{41}\right)$. Then $x = \frac{1}{2}\left(7 + \sqrt{41}\right)$ and $x = \frac{1}{2}\left(7 - \sqrt{41}\right)$ respectively.
  Without loss of generality, let $x = \frac{1}{2}\left(7 + \sqrt{41}\right)$ and $y = \frac{1}{2}\left(7 - \sqrt{41}\right)$, then,
  $$\frac{1}{x} + \frac{1}{y} = \frac{2}{7 + \sqrt{41}} + \frac{2}{7 - \sqrt{41}}$$
  $$= \frac{14 - 2\sqrt{41} + 14 + 2\sqrt{41}}{49 - 41},$$
  $$= \frac{28}{8},$$
  $$= \frac{7}{2}.$$

This question shows that following an algebraic method is not always the most efficient method of solution.

Q14. First we use the information from the figure to determine an equation for each line or curve.

Green: $2x - 2y + 1 = 0,$

Aqua: $y = \frac{1}{2}x^2 + 1,$

Purple: $x = 3,$

Red: $y = -x + 6,$

Blue: $y = \frac{1}{2}x + 4.$

We can now find the coordinates of each point in turn.
- **Point A:**
  Point A is the intersection of the red and blue lines, and so we consider the following pair of simultaneous equations.
  $$y = -x + 6, \quad \text{①}$$
  $$y = \frac{1}{2}x + 4. \quad \text{②}$$
  We rearrange ② to be $x = 2y - 8$ and substitute into ①,
  $$y = -2y + 8 + 6,$$
  $$\Rightarrow \quad 3y = 14,$$
  $$\Rightarrow \quad y = \frac{14}{3}.$$
  When $y = \frac{14}{3}$, $x = \frac{4}{3}$ and so the coordinate of A is $\left(\frac{4}{3}, \frac{14}{3}\right)$.
- **Point B:**
  We can think of Point B in three different ways, each of varying difficulty. We present each method of solution here so that a comparison may be made.
  - Method 1:
    We consider the intersection of the aqua and blue lines, and so have the following pair of simultaneous equations.
    $$y = \frac{1}{2}x^2 + 1, \quad \text{①}$$
    $$y = \frac{1}{2}x + 4. \quad \text{②}$$
    Equating ① and ②,
    $$\frac{1}{2}x^2 + 1 = \frac{1}{2}x + 4,$$
    $$\Rightarrow \quad \frac{1}{2}x^2 - \frac{1}{2}x - 3 = 0,$$
    $$\Rightarrow \quad x^2 - x - 6 = 0,$$
    $$\Rightarrow \quad (x+2)(x-3) = 0.$$
    Hence, $x = 3$ or $x = -2$. From the figure it is clear that we are interested in $x = 3$. When $x = 3$, $y = \frac{11}{2}$, from ① and so the coordinates of point $B = \left(3, \frac{11}{2}\right)$.
  - Method 2:
    Point B is also the intersection of the aqua and purple lines. Since the purple line has equation $x = 3$, we can use the equation of the aqua line ($y = \frac{1}{2}x^2 + 1$) to find the y-coordinate of B. Thus, when $x = 3$, $y = \frac{11}{2}$, and so the coordinates of point $B = \left(3, \frac{11}{2}\right)$.
  - Method 3:
    Finally, we can consider B as the intersection of the purple and blue

lines and consider the pair of simultaneous equations,

$$x = 3, \qquad ①$$
$$y = \frac{1}{2}x + 4. \qquad ②$$

Substituting ① into ② we find that when $x = 3$, $y = \frac{11}{2}$. Hence the coordinated of point B are $\left(3, \frac{11}{2}\right)$.

Notice, that all three methods give the same answer as expected. The ability to choose the most efficient method is a skill that comes with practise.

- **Point C:**

We consider the intersection of the aqua and red lines, *i.e.*,

$$y = \frac{1}{2}x^2 + 1, \qquad ①$$
$$y = -x + 6. \qquad ②$$

From ② we see that $x = 6 - y$; upon substituting this into ①,

$$y = \frac{1}{2}(6 - y)^2 + 1,$$
$$\Rightarrow \quad 2y = 36 - 12y + y^2 + 2,$$
$$\Rightarrow \quad 0 = y^2 - 14y + 38,$$
$$\Rightarrow \quad 0 = (y - 7)^2 - 11.$$

Since this quadratic is in completed square form we can find that $y = 7 \pm \sqrt{11}$. From the figure it is clear that, in fact, $y = 7 - \sqrt{11}$. When $y = 7 - \sqrt{11}$,

$$x = 6 - (7 - \sqrt{11})$$
$$= \sqrt{11} - 1$$

The point C therefore has coordinates $(\sqrt{11} - 1, 7 - \sqrt{11}) \approx (2.32, 3.68)$.

- **Point D:**

Since D is the intersection of the red and green lines, we consider

$$y = -x + 6, \qquad ①$$
$$y = x + \frac{1}{2}. \qquad ②$$

Adding ① and ② we see that $2y = \frac{13}{2}$ which leads to $y = \frac{13}{4}$. When $y = \frac{13}{4}$, $x = \frac{11}{4}$ which means that the point D has coordinates $\left(\frac{11}{4}, \frac{13}{4}\right)$.

- **Point E:** This point is the intersection of the blue and green lines which have the following equations, respectively,

$$y = \frac{1}{2}x + 4, \qquad ①$$
$$2x - 2y + 1 = 0. \qquad ②$$

Substituting ① into ②, we have,

$$2x - 2\left(\frac{1}{2}x + 4\right) + 1 = 0,$$
$$\Rightarrow \quad 2x - x - 8 + 1 = 0,$$
$$\Rightarrow \quad x = 7.$$

When $x = 7$, using ① we obtain $y = \frac{7}{2} + 4 = \frac{15}{2}$. So, point E has coordinates $\left(7, \frac{15}{2}\right)$.

- **Point F:**
Point F is the intersection of the aqua and green lines; we consider,

$$y = \frac{1}{2}x^2 + 1, \quad ①$$
$$y = x + \frac{1}{2}. \quad ②$$

Equating these,

$$\frac{1}{2}x^2 + 1 = x + \frac{1}{2},$$
$$\Rightarrow \quad \frac{1}{2}x^2 - x + \frac{1}{2} = 0,$$
$$\Rightarrow \quad x^2 - 2x + 1 = 0.$$

This quadratic has a repeated root, $x = 1$ and when $x = 1$ we can, using ② calculate $y = \frac{3}{2}$.

Hence, point F has coordinates $\left(1, \frac{3}{2}\right)$.

Q15. (a) Assuming that the brakes work at a constant force, the distance will be proportional to the square of the speed, v, of the car, since in coming to a standstill the kinetic energy of a car of mass m, must be reduced to zero from $E = \frac{1}{2}mv^2$.

(b) Using the data for 20mph, 30mph and 70mph we obtain the following three simultaneous equations

$$400a + 20b + c = 12, \quad ①$$
$$900a + 30b + c = 23, \quad ②$$
$$4900a + 70b + c = 96. \quad ③$$

Here we have three equations with three unknowns. We first manipulate these three and eliminate one of the variables, leading to two equations with two unknowns. To this end, we subtract ① from ② to give,

$$500a + 10b = 11. \quad ④$$

We also subtract ② from ③,

$$4000a + 40b = 73. \quad ⑤$$

Rearranging ④,

$$500a + 10b = 11,$$
$$\Rightarrow \quad 500a = 11 - 10b,$$
$$\Rightarrow \quad 4000a = 88 - 80b.$$

This can now be substituted into ⑤ to obtain an equation where b is the only unknown variable.

$$88 - 80b + 40b = 73,$$
$$\Rightarrow \quad -40b = -15,$$
$$\Rightarrow \quad b = \frac{3}{8}.$$

We now have a value of b which can be used in ④ to find a value for the coefficient a.

$$500a + 10b = 11,$$
$$\Rightarrow \quad 500a = 11 - 10b,$$
$$\Rightarrow \quad 500a = 11 - \frac{30}{8},$$
$$\Rightarrow \quad 500a = \frac{29}{4},$$
$$\Rightarrow \quad a = \frac{29}{2000}.$$

Finally, we need to find the value of c; for simplicity we use ① for this.

$$400a + 20b + c = 12,$$
$$\Rightarrow \quad c = 12 - 400a - 20b,$$
$$\Rightarrow \quad c = 12 - \frac{29}{5} - \frac{15}{2},$$
$$\Rightarrow \quad c = -\frac{13}{10}.$$

Hence, for a speed v given in miles per hour, the stopping distance, d, in metres can be calculated using the the following formula,

$$d = \frac{29}{2000}v^2 + \frac{3}{8}v - \frac{13}{10} \tag{2.2}$$

(c) The value of c is unphysical since the distance required to stop a car that is not moving (*i.e.* when v in (2.2) is zero) cannot be negative.

3. Worked Solutions - Chapters 12 to 16

Worked Solutions — Exercise 12.1

Q1. (a) Rearranging the inequality gives,

$$4x - 5 \geq 15,$$
$$\Rightarrow \quad 4x \geq 20,$$
$$\Rightarrow \quad x \geq 5.$$

Therefore the set of values which satisfy this inequality is $\{x : x \geq 5\}$.

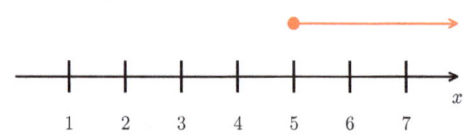

(b) Rearranging the inequality gives,

$$x + 5 < 3x + 2,$$
$$\Rightarrow \quad 3 < 2x,$$
$$\Rightarrow \quad x > \frac{2}{3}.$$

Therefore the set of values which satisfy the inequality is $\{x : x > \frac{2}{3}\}$.

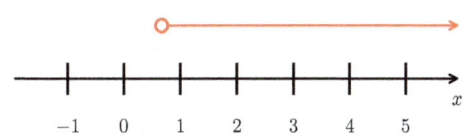

(c) Rearranging the inequality gives,

$$7 - x \leq 2x - 5,$$
$$\Rightarrow \quad 12 \leq 3x,$$
$$\Rightarrow \quad x \geq 4.$$

Therefore the set of values which satisfy the inequality is $\{x : x \geq 4\}$.

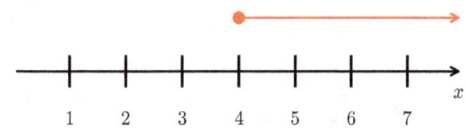

(d) Rearranging the inequality gives,

$$5 - 2x \geq 3 - x,$$
$$\Rightarrow \quad 2 \geq x.$$

Therefore the set of values which satisfy the inequality is $\{x : x \leq 2\}$.

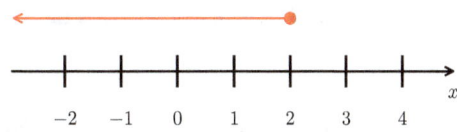

Q2. (a) Expanding brackets and rearranging the inequality gives,

$$3(x - 4) > 8,$$
$$\Rightarrow \quad 3x - 12 > 8,$$
$$\Rightarrow \quad 3x > 20,$$
$$\Rightarrow \quad x > \frac{20}{3}.$$

Therefore the set of values which satisfies this inequality is $\{x : x > \frac{20}{3}\}$.

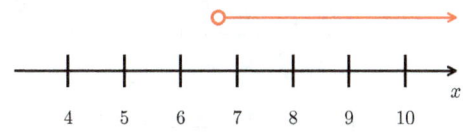

(b) Expanding brackets and rearranging the inequality gives,

$$5(2-x) + 2(3x+2) > 13,$$
$$\Rightarrow \quad 10 - 5x + 6x + 4 > 13,$$
$$\Rightarrow \quad 14 + x > 13,$$
$$\Rightarrow \quad x > -1.$$

Therefore the set of solutions which satisfy this inequality is $\{x : x > -1\}$.

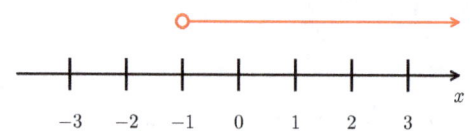

(c) Expanding brackets and rearranging the inequality gives,

$$3x - 6(2x-3) \leq 2(x-2),$$
$$\Rightarrow \quad 3x - 12x + 18 \leq 2x - 4,$$
$$\Rightarrow \quad -9x + 18 \leq 2x - 4,$$
$$\Rightarrow \quad 22 \leq 11x,$$
$$\Rightarrow \quad x \geq 2.$$

Therefore the set of solutions for this inequality is $\{x : x \geq 2\}$.

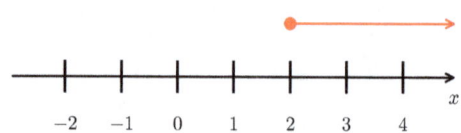

(d) Expanding brackets and rearranging the inequality gives,

$$2(x-3) + 4(1-x) < 3(2x+8) + 2(x-3),$$
$$\Rightarrow \quad 2x - 6 + 4x - 4 < 6x + 24 + 2x - 6,$$
$$\Rightarrow \quad 6x - 10 < 8x + 18,$$
$$\Rightarrow \quad -28 < 2x,$$
$$\Rightarrow \quad x > -14.$$

Therefore the set of solutions which satisfy this inequality is $\{x : x > -14\}$.

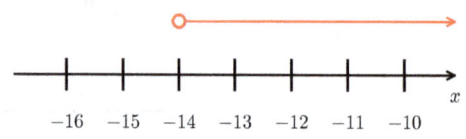

Q3. (a) Rearranging the inequality gives,

$$\frac{3}{4}x - 1 > 5,$$
$$\Rightarrow \quad \frac{3}{4}x > 6,$$
$$\Rightarrow \quad x > 8.$$

Therefore the set of solutions which satisfy the inequality is $\{x : x > 8\}$.

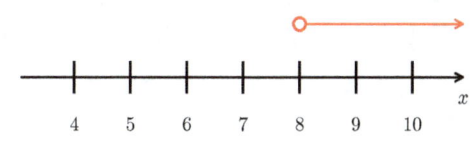

(b) Rearranging the inequality gives,

$$\frac{2x+1}{2} \geq \frac{3x-1}{2},$$
$$\Rightarrow \quad 2x + 1 \geq 3x - 1,$$
$$\Rightarrow \quad 2 \geq x.$$

Therefore the set of solutions which satisfy the inequality is $\{x : x \leq 2\}$.

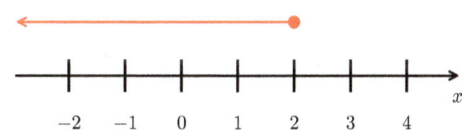

(c) Rearranging the inequality gives,

$$\frac{1}{3}(2x+1) > \frac{2}{5}(1-x),$$
$$\Rightarrow \quad 5(2x+1) > 6(1-x),$$
$$\Rightarrow \quad 10x + 5 > 6 - 6x,$$
$$\Rightarrow \quad 16x > 1,$$
$$\Rightarrow \quad x > \frac{1}{16}.$$

Therefore the set of solutions which satisfy this inequality is $\{x : x > \frac{1}{16}\}$.

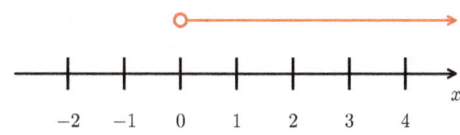

(d) Rearranging the inequality gives,

$$\frac{x+2}{4} < \frac{1}{3}(3x-2),$$
$$\Rightarrow \quad 3(x+2) < 4(3x-2),$$
$$\Rightarrow \quad 3x+6 < 12x-8,$$
$$\Rightarrow \quad 14 < 9x,$$
$$\Rightarrow \quad x > \frac{14}{9}.$$

Therefore the set of solutions which satisfies this inequality is $\{x : x > \frac{14}{9}\}$.

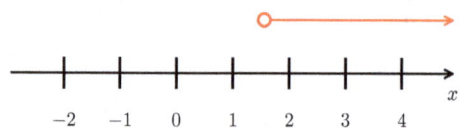

Q4. (a) Rearranging the inequality gives,

$$-2 < \frac{1}{3}x - 2 \leq 6,$$
$$\Rightarrow \quad 0 < \frac{1}{3}x \leq 8,$$
$$\Rightarrow \quad 0 < x \leq 24.$$

Therefore the set of values which satisfy the inequality is $\{x : 0 < x \leq 24\}$.

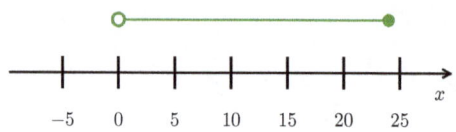

(b) Rearranging the inequality gives,

$$4 \leq \frac{1}{2}(3x+1) < 11,$$
$$\Rightarrow \quad 8 \leq 3x+1 < 22,$$
$$\Rightarrow \quad 7 \leq 3x < 21,$$
$$\Rightarrow \quad \frac{7}{3} \leq x < 7.$$

Therefore the set of solutions which satisfy this inequality is $\{x : \frac{7}{3} \leq x < 7\}$.

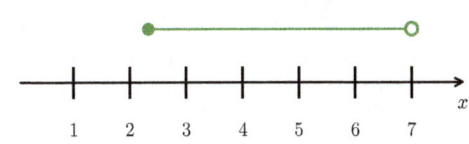

(c) Rearranging the inequality gives,

$$0 < \frac{x+9}{2} + 2(x+1) < 7,$$
$$\Rightarrow \quad 0 < x + 9 + 4(x+1) < 14,$$
$$\Rightarrow \quad 0 < x + 9 + 4x + 1 < 14,$$
$$\Rightarrow \quad 0 < 5x + 13 < 14,$$
$$\Rightarrow \quad -13 < 5x < 1,$$
$$\Rightarrow \quad -\frac{13}{5} < x < \frac{1}{5}.$$

Therefore the set of solutions which satisfy this inequality is $\{x : -\frac{13}{5} < x < \frac{1}{5}\}$.

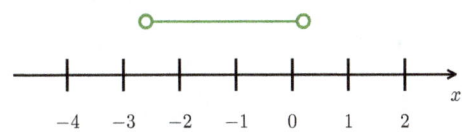

Worked Solutions — Exercise 12.2

Q1. (a) Rearranging the inequality gives $x^2 - 25 \leq 0$.

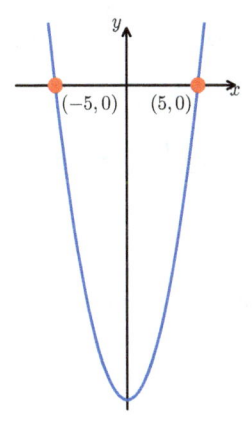

This factorises to give $(x+5)(x-5) \leq 0$. We can sketch this quadratic, as shown above. The set of solutions to the inequality are given when this quadratic is less than or equal to 0. Therefore the set of values for x which satisfies this inequality is $\{x : -5 \leq x \leq 5\}$.

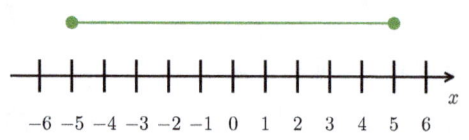

(b) Rearranging the inequality gives $x^2 - 9 > 0$. This factorises to give $(x-3)(x+3) > 0$. We can sketch this quadratic, as shown below.

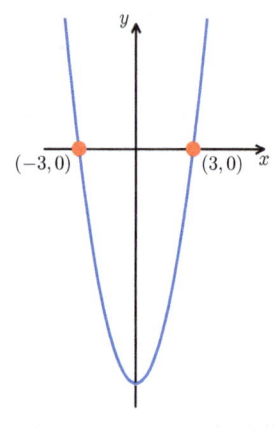

The set of solutions to the inequality are given when this quadratic is greater than 0. Therefore the set of values of x which satisfies this inequality is the disjoint union of two sets; $\{x : x < -3\}$ and $\{x : x > 3\}$.

(c) Rearranging the inequality gives $0 > x^2 - 16$. This factorises to give $(x-4)(x+4) < 0$. We can sketch this quadratic, as shown below.

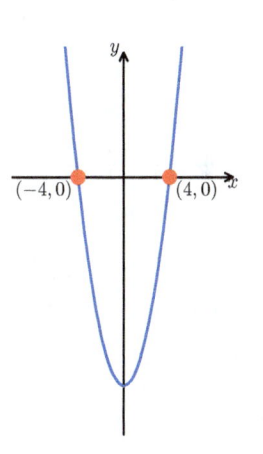

The set of solutions to the inequality are given when this quadratic is less than 0. Therefore the set of values of x which satisfies this inequality is $\{x : -4 \leq x \leq 4\}$.

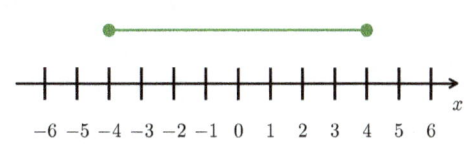

(d) Rearranging the inequality gives $2x^2 - 18 \leq 0$. This can be divided through by 2 to give $x^2 - 9 \leq 0$. This quadratic factorises to give $(x+3)(x-3) \leq 0$. We can sketch this quadratic, as shown below.

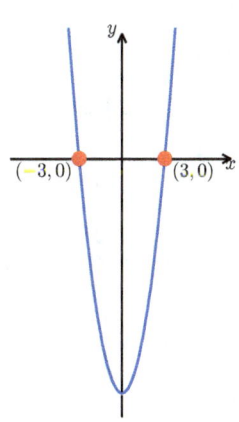

The set of solutions to the inequality are given when this quadratic is less than or equal to 0. Therefore the set of values for x which satisfies this inequality is $\{x : -3 \leq x \leq 3\}$.

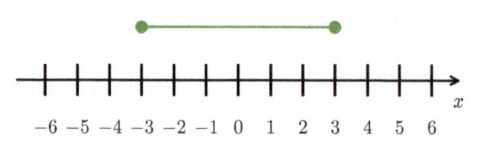

Q2. (a) The given inequality $x^2 - 7x - 18 < 0$ factorises to give $(x-9)(x+2) < 0$. We can sketch this quadratic, as shown below.

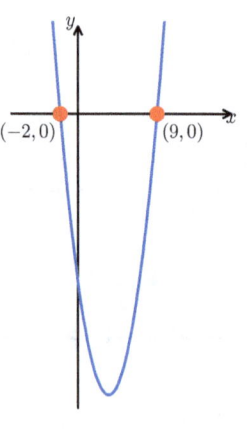

The set of solutions to the inequality are given when this quadratic is less than 0. Therefore the set of values for x which satisfies the inequality is $\{x : -2 < x < 9\}$.

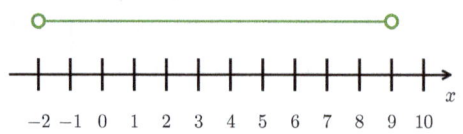

(b) Rearranging this inequality gives $x^2 + 3x - 10 \leq 0$, which factorises to give $(x+5)(x-2) \leq 0$. We can sketch this quadratic, as shown below.

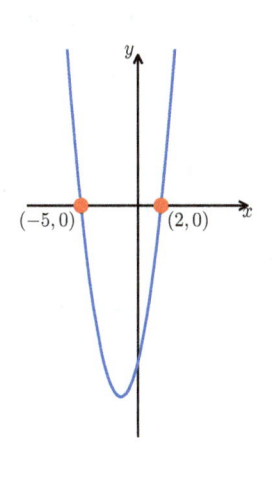

The set of solutions to the inequality are given when this quadratic is less than or equal to 0. Therefore the set of values for x which satisfies this inequality is $\{x : -5 \leq x \leq 2\}$.

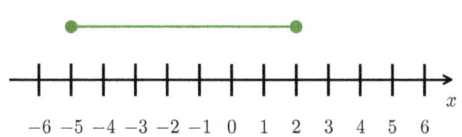

(c) Expanding and rearranging this inequality gives $x^2 + 9x - 10 \geq 0$, which factorises to give $(x+10)(x-1) \geq 0$. We can sketch this quadratic, as shown below.

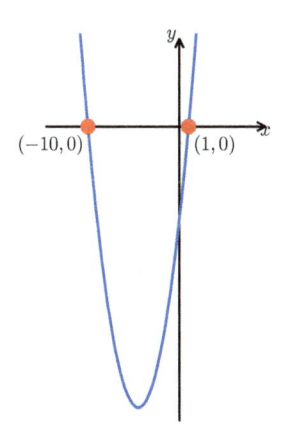

The set of solutions to the inequality are given when this quadratic is greater than or equal to 0. Therefore the set of values for x which satisfies this inequality is the disjoint union of two sets; $\{x : x \leq -10\}$ and $\{x : x \geq 1\}$.

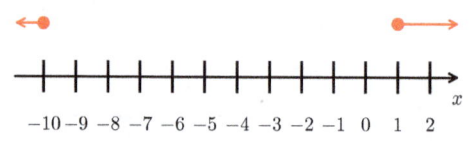

(d) Rearranging the inequality gives $4x^2 - 7x + 3 > 0$, which factorises to give $(4x - 3)(x - 1) > 0$. We can sketch this quadratic, as shown below.

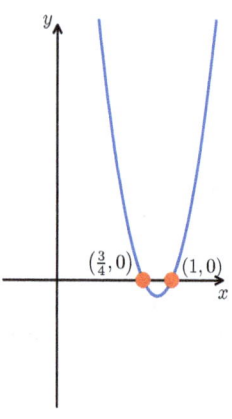

The set of solutions to the inequality are given when this quadratic is greater than 0. Therefore the set of values for x which satisfies this inequality is the disjoint union of two sets; $\{x : x < \frac{3}{4}\}$ and $\{x : x > 1\}$.

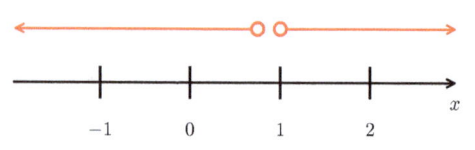

Worked Solutions — Exercise 12.3

Q1. (a) First, we find the set of solutions to the inequality $1 - x \leq 2x + 4$. By rearranging we have,

$$1 - x \leq 2x + 4,$$
$$\Rightarrow \quad -3 \leq 3x,$$
$$\Rightarrow \quad x \geq -1.$$

Therefore the set of solutions to this inequality is $\{x : x \geq -1\}$.
Next, we look for the set of solutions which satisfies $2(2x - 3) < 2$. By rearranging we have,

$$2(2x - 3) < 2,$$
$$\Rightarrow \quad 2x - 3 < 1,$$
$$\Rightarrow \quad 2x < 4,$$
$$\Rightarrow \quad x < 2.$$

Therefore the set of solutions to this inequality is $\{x : x < 2\}$.
Considering the solutions to each inequality (see the number line below), we can identify that the set of solutions which will satisfy both inequalities will be $\{x : -1 \leq x < 2\}$.

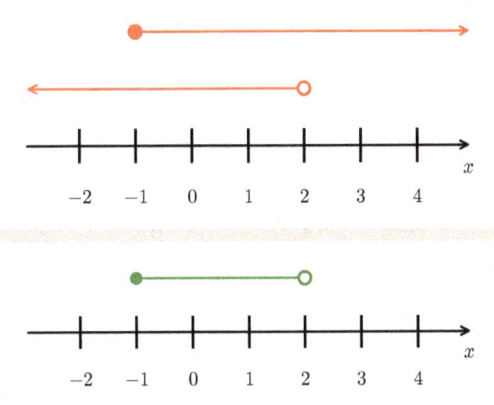

(b) To solve this pair of inequalities, first we look for the set of solutions which satisfies $4(x - 1) > \frac{1}{2}x$. Rearranging gives,

$$4(x - 1) > \frac{1}{2}x,$$
$$\Rightarrow \quad 8(x - 1) > x,$$
$$\Rightarrow \quad 8x - 8 > x,$$
$$\Rightarrow \quad 7x > 8,$$
$$\Rightarrow \quad x > \frac{8}{7}.$$

Therefore the set of solutions which satisfies this inequality is $\{x : x > \frac{8}{7}\}$.

Next, we consider the set of solutions to $x \geq \frac{2}{3}(5-x)$. By rearranging,

$$\begin{aligned} & x \geq \frac{2}{3}(5-x), \\ \Rightarrow\ & 3x \geq 2(5-x), \\ \Rightarrow\ & 3x \geq 10 - 2x, \\ \Rightarrow\ & 5x \geq 10, \\ \Rightarrow\ & x \geq 2. \end{aligned}$$

Therefore the set of solutions to this inequality is $\{x : x \geq 2\}$.
Considering the number line below, we can identify that the set of solutions which satisfies both inequalities is $\{x : x \geq 2\}$.

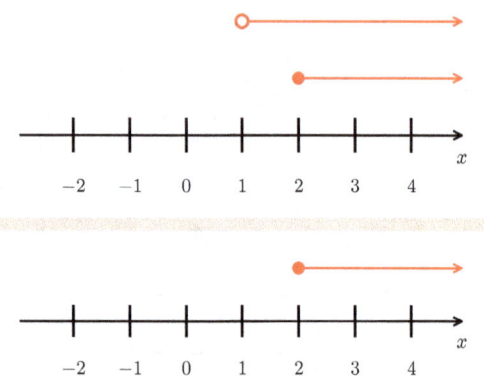

(c) First, we want to consider the set of values which satisfies $\frac{5}{3}x > 10$. By rearrangement, we can quickly deduce that the set of solutions to this inequality is $\{x : x > 6\}$.
Next, we consider the set of values which satisfy the inequality $3(1-x) \leq 2(3x+1)$. Expanding and rearranging gives,

$$\begin{aligned} & 3(1-x) \leq 2(3x+1), \\ \Rightarrow\ & 3 - 3x \leq 6x + 2, \\ \Rightarrow\ & 1 \leq 9x, \\ \Rightarrow\ & x \geq \frac{1}{9}. \end{aligned}$$

Therefore the set of solutions to this inequality will be $\{x : x \geq \frac{1}{9}\}$.
Considering the solutions to each inequality and using the number line below, we can see that the set of solutions satisfying both inequalities is $\{x : x > 6\}$.

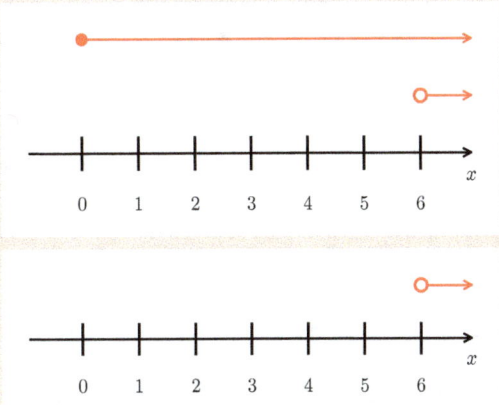

Q2. (a) To find the solutions which satisfy this pair of inequalities we consider each in turn. First, we consider the set of solutions to $x^2 - 3x > 4$. Rearranging gives $x^2 - 3x - 4 > 0$, which factorises to give $(x+1)(x-4) > 0$. We can sketch this quadratic, as shown below.

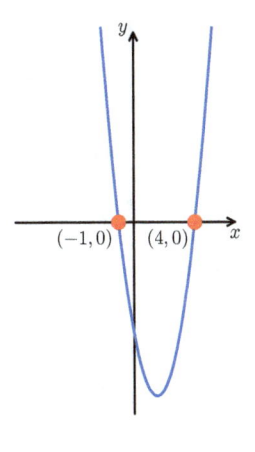

The set of solutions to the inequality are given when this quadratic is greater than 0. Therefore the set of solutions which satisfy this inequality is the disjoint union of two sets; $\{x : x < -1\}$ and $\{x : x > 4\}$.

Next we consider the second inequality, $\frac{2}{3}x < 2$. The solutions to this can be quickly deduced by manipulation to be $\{x : x < 3\}$.

Considering the solutions to both inequalities and using the number line below, we can see that the set of solutions which will satisfy both inequalities will be $\{x : x < -1\}$.

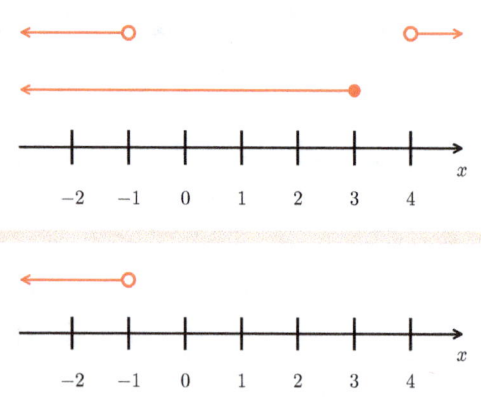

(b) Considering the first inequality, we look for the set of solutions which satisfies $x(x-5)+9 < 3$. Expanding brackets rearranging gives $x^2 - 5x + 6 < 0$. This factorises to give $(x-2)(x-3) < 0$. We can sketch this quadratic, as shown below.

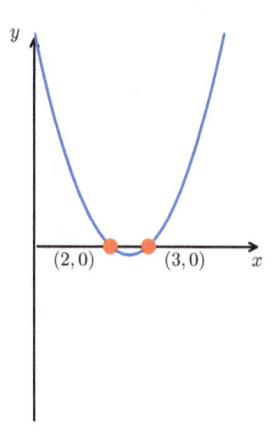

The set of solutions to the inequality are given when this quadratic is less than 0. Therefore the set of solutions which satisfy this inequality is $\{x : 2 < x < 3\}$.

By a similar process we want to find the set of solutions which satisfies $x^2 > 2(4-x)$. Expanding and rearranging gives $x^2 + 2x - 8 > 0$, which factorises to give $(x-2)(x+4) > 0$. This quadratic can be sketched, as shown below.

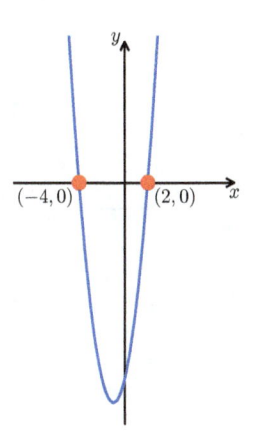

The set of solutions to the inequality are given when this quadratic is greater than 0. Therefore the set of solutions which satisfy this inequality is the disjoint union of two sets; $\{x : x > 2\}$ or $\{x : x < -4\}$.

Considering both set of solutions on the number line below, we can identify that the set of solutions which will satisfy both inequalities will be $\{x : 2 < x < 3\}$.

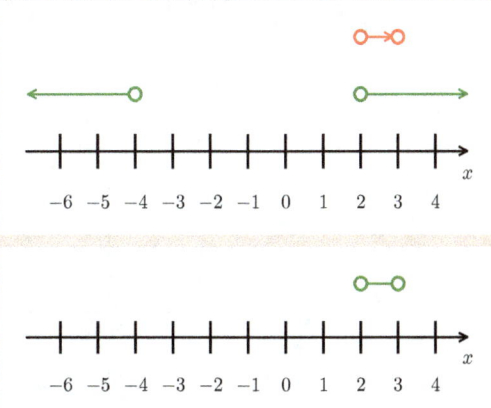

(c) First, let us consider the solutions to the inequality $\frac{1}{2}x(x+4) < \frac{2}{3}(4x+1)$. By expanding brackets and rearranging,

$$\frac{1}{2}x(x+4) < \frac{2}{3}(4x+1),$$
$$\Rightarrow \quad 3x(x+4) < 4(4x+1),$$
$$\Rightarrow \quad 3x^2 + 12x < 16x + 4,$$
$$\Rightarrow \quad 3x^2 - 4x - 4 < 0.$$

This factorises to give $(3x+2)(x-2) < 0$. We can sketch this quadratic, as shown below.

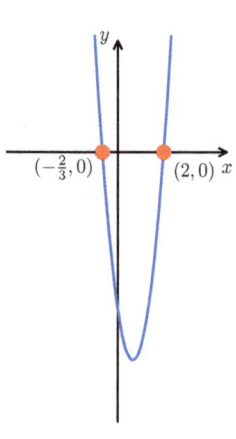

The set of solutions to the inequality are given when this quadratic is less than 0. Therefore the set of solutions which satisfy this inequality is $\{x : -\frac{2}{3} < x < 2\}$.

Next, we consider the set of solutions which satisfy the inequality $x^2 + 4x > x$. Rearranging gives $x^2 + 3x > 0$, which can be factorised to give $x(x+3) > 0$. We can sketch this quadratic, as shown below.

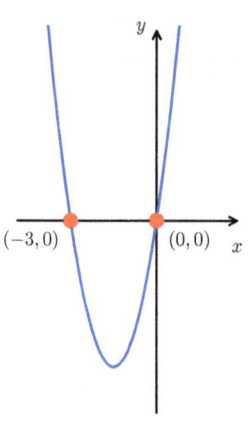

The set of solutions to the inequality are given when this quadratic is greater than 0. Therefore the set of solutions which satisfy this inequality is the disjoint union of two sets; $\{x : x < -3\}$ and $\{x : x > 0\}$.

Finally, considering the number line below which represents the solutions to both of the given inequalities, we can identify that the set of solutions which satisfy both inequalities will be $\{x : 0 < x < 2\}$.

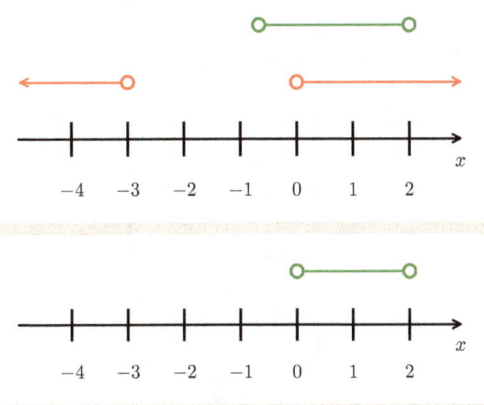

Worked Solutions — Exercise 12.4

For the solutions given below the method suggested in Example 12.10 is used.

Q1. (a) The region which requires shading is where the values of y are greater than the boundary line $y = 3x - 6$, and therefore the boundary is plotted as a dotted line and the region *above* the line is shaded (as below).

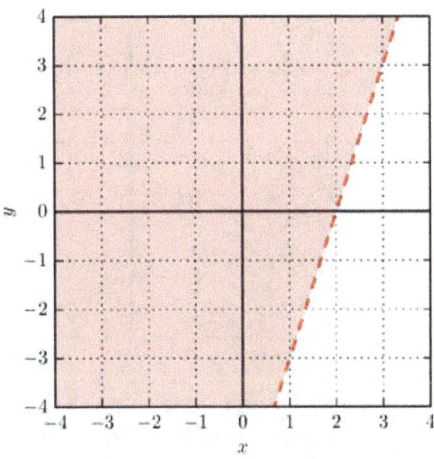

(b) The region we are considering here is where all values of y are less than or equal to the boundary line $y = 3 - x$. Therefore the boundary line is plotted as a solid line to indicate that the boundary is include, and the region *below* the line is shaded (as below).

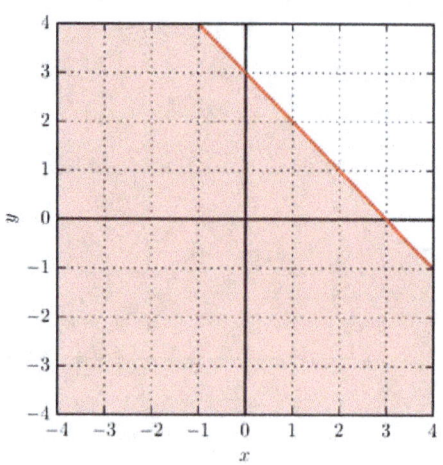

(c) The region which requires shading is where all values of y are greater than or equal to the boundary line $y = 1 - 2x$. Therefore the boundary line is plotted as a solid line and the region *above* the line is shaded (as below).

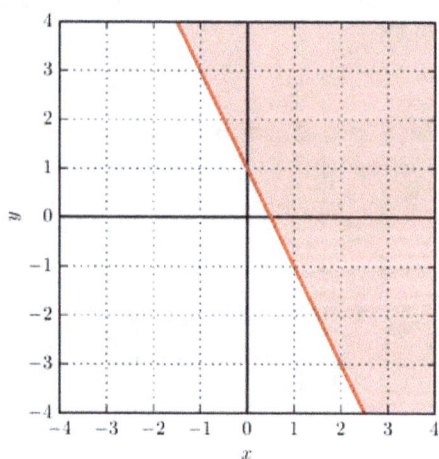

Q2. (a) The region which requires shading is where the values of y are greater than or equal to the boundary $y = x^2 - 10x + 24$, and therefore the boundary is plotted as a solid line. The region which will be shaded will be *above* the boundary.

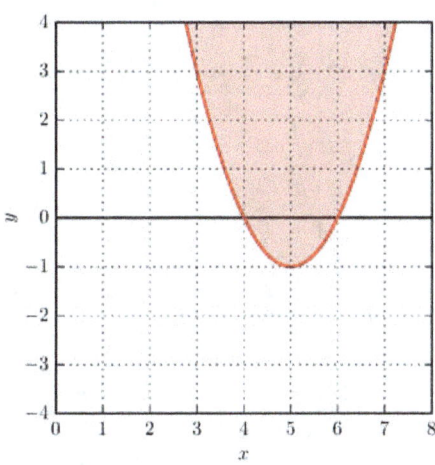

(b) The region which needs to be shaded is where the values of y are less than the boundary $y = x(3-x)$. The boundary line is plotted as a dotted line to indicate that they are not included in the solution, and the region *below* the boundary is shaded.

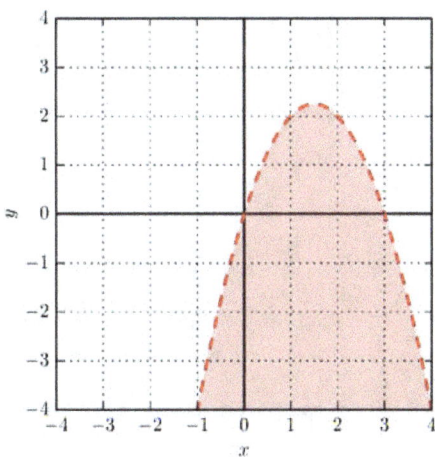

(c) The region to be shaded is the values of y which are less than or equal to the boundary $y = x^2 - 3x + 7$, therefore the boundary is a solid line. The region to be shaded will be *below* the boundary line.

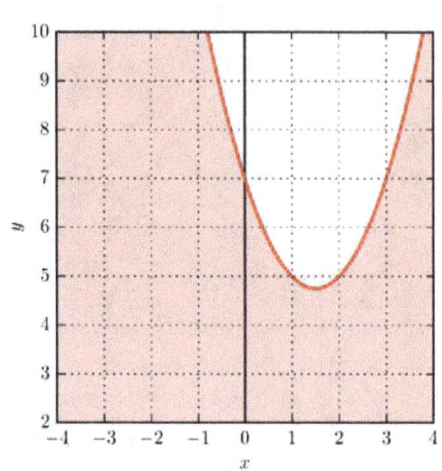

Q3. (a) The region to be shaded here is all values of y which are less than or equal to the boundary $y = 3x$ and greater than the boundary $y = -x - 2$. Therefore, the region below the solid boundary line $y = 3x$ and above the dotted boundary line $y = -x - 2$ is shaded.

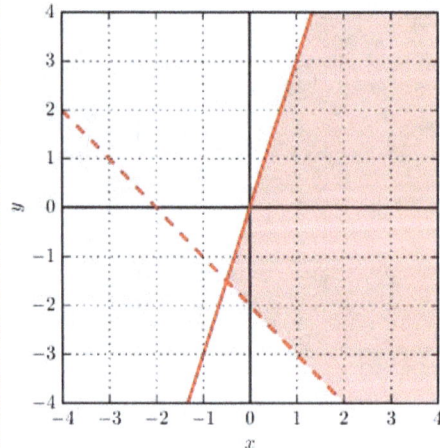

(b) The region which requires shading is the values of y such that they are greater than the boundary $y = x^2 - 3x - 5$ and less than the boundary $y = 1 - x$. Therefore, the region is shaded above the dotted boundary $y = x^2 - 3x - 5$ and below the dotted boundary line $y = 1 - x$.

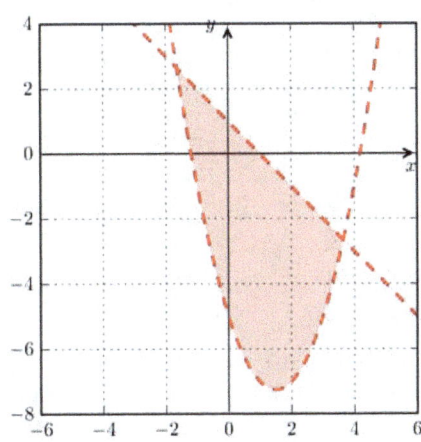

(c) The region to shade is where the values of y are greater than or equal to the boundary $y = x^2 + 3$ *and* less than the boundary $y = 5 + 2x - x^2$. So the region below the solid boundary $y = x^2 + 3$ *and* below the dotted boundary $y = 5 + 2x - x^2$ is shaded.

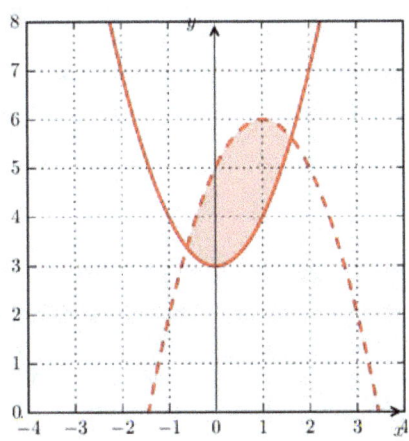

Worked Solutions — Exercise 12.5

Q1. This question has been designed to open some discussion and debate. Obviously, any reasonable suggestion would be accepted as a solution. In other words, a combination of inequalities of the form:
- $y \leq a$ (where a is a positive constant value);
- $y \geq -x - b$ (where b is a positive constant value);

- $y \leq -(x-c)^2 + d$ (where c and d are positive constant values).

The image in the question was generated using the inequalities $y \leq 3$, $y \geq -x - 2$ and $y \leq 5 - (x-3)^2$.

Q2. The quickest way to find the correct choice will be to solve each inequality in turn and compare solutions on a number line.

First we consider $3(1-x) < 2$. Expanding and rearranging gives,

$$\begin{aligned} & 3(1-x) < 2, \\ \Rightarrow \quad & 3 - 3x < 2, \\ \Rightarrow \quad & 1 < 3x, \\ \Rightarrow \quad & x > \frac{1}{3}. \end{aligned}$$

Therefore the set of solutions which satisfies this inequality is $\{x : x > \frac{1}{3}\}$.

Next we consider the inequality $x^2 - 4x - 5 \geq 0$. This quadratic factorises to give $(x-5)(x+1) \geq 0$. We can sketch this quadratic, as shown below.

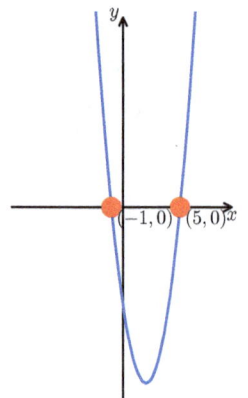

The set of solutions to the inequality are given when this quadratic is greater than or equal to 0. Therefore the set of solutions which satisfies this inequality is the disjoint union of two sets; $\{x : x \leq -1\}$, $\{x : x \geq 5\}$.

Comparing the solutions to both inequalities on the number line below, we can see that the set of solutions which satisfy both inequalities will be $\{x : x \geq 5\}$.

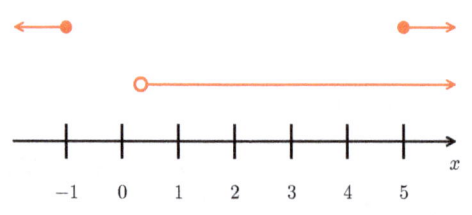

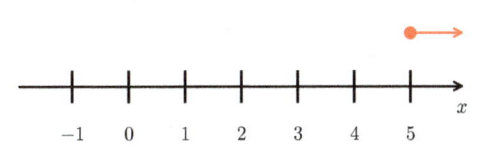

Therefore, from the given choices, we must select option (d) since the solutions $\{x : x > 8\}$ lie in this region.

Q3. (a) Let the height of the book be x. Then the width of the book will be $x - 6$, and therefore the perimeter can be expressed as $x + x + (x - 6) + (x - 6) \leq 60$. Thus,

$$x + x + (x - 6) + (x - 6) \leq 60,$$
$$\Rightarrow 4x - 12 \leq 60,$$
$$\Rightarrow 4x \leq 72,$$
$$\Rightarrow x \leq 18.$$

Since x is a length, this means that x must be positive. Therefore the set of solutions is $\{x : 0 < x \leq 18\}$.

(b) The thickness of the book is a misleading piece of information that does not add anything to our mathematical problem. Instead we focus on the fact that the surface area of the front is at least 160cm. Therefore we can write the inequality $x(x-6) \geq 160$, which is the second inequality involving x. Expanding the brackets and rearranging gives the inequality $x^2 - 6x - 160 \geq 0$. The quadratic factorises to give $(x - 16)(x + 1) \geq 0$. We can sketch this quadratic, as shown below.

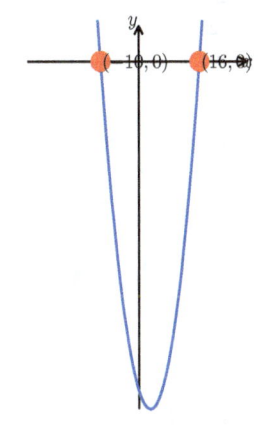

The set of solutions to the inequality are given when this quadratic is greater than or equal to 0. Therefore the set of solutions to this inequality is the disjoint union of two sets; $\{x : x \geq 16\}$ and $\{x : x \leq -10\}$. However, as in part (a), we must ensure that x is positive, since it is a length. Thus, the only acceptable solutions for this inequality are $\{x : x \geq 16\}$.

(c) Comparing the solutions to both inequalities on the number line below, it is clear to see that $\{x : 16 \leq x \leq 18\}$.

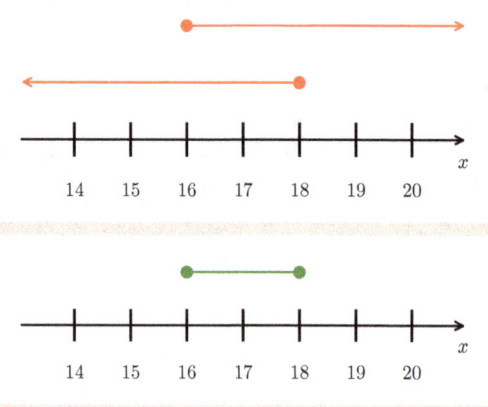

Worked Solutions — Exercise 13.1

Q1. (a) $x^2 + y^2 = 4$;
(b) $x^2 + y^2 = 16$;
(c) $(x-3)^2 + (y-3)^2 = 1$;
(d) $(x+1)^2 + (y-2)^2 = 36$;
(e) $(x+4)^2 + (y+5)^2 = 9$;
(f) $(x-6)^2 + (y+4)^2 = 25$.

Q2. (a) Centre $(0,0)$, radius $2\sqrt{2}$;
(b) Centre $(0,0)$, radius 2. Rearrange so that $x^2 + y^2 = 4$.
(c) Centre $(0,0)$, radius $2\sqrt{3}$. Rearrange so that $x^2 + y^2 = 12$;
(d) This is not an equation of a circle. Rearranging gives $x^2 + y^2 = -3$;
(e) Centre $(4,2)$, radius 2;
(f) Centre $(3,3)$, radius 3. We have used the fact that $(3-x)^2 = (x-3)^2$;
(g) Centre $(-1,0)$, radius $\sqrt{5}$. We have that $x^2 + 2x + 1 = (x+1)^2$. Hence, the equation rearranges to $(x+1)^2 + y^2 = 5$;
(h) Centre $(0,2)$, radius 6. We have $y^2 - 4y + 4 = (y-2)^2$, so the equation rearranges to $x^2 + (y-2)^2 = 36$.

Worked Solutions — Exercise 13.2

Q1. (a) By completing the square, the equation can be rearranged so that

$$x^2 + 8x + y^2 = 20$$
$$\Rightarrow (x+4)^2 - 16 + y^2 = 20,$$
$$\Rightarrow (x+4)^2 + y^2 = 36.$$

The centre is $(-4, 0)$ and the radius is 6.

(b) $y^2 - 4y = (y-2)^2 - 4$. Hence, the equation can be rearranged so that

$$x^2 + y^2 - 4y = 12,$$
$$\Rightarrow x^2 + (y-2)^2 - 4 = 12,$$
$$\Rightarrow x^2 + (y-2)^2 = 16.$$

The centre is $(0, 2)$ and the radius is 4.

(c) By completing the square, the equation can be rearranged so that

$$x^2 + 10x + y^2 - 12y = 20,$$
$$\Rightarrow (x+5)^2 - 25 + (y-6)^2 - 36 = 20,$$
$$\Rightarrow (x+5)^2 + (y-6)^2 = 81.$$

The centre is $(-5, 6)$ and the radius is 9.

(d) By completing the square, the equation can be rearranged so that

$$x^2 - 2x + y^2 - 2y + 4 = 0,$$
$$\Rightarrow (x-1)^2 - 1 + (y-1)^2 - 1 + 4 = 0$$
$$\Rightarrow (x-1)^2 - 1 + (y-1)^2 = -2.$$

This is not the equation of a circle.

(e)
$$2x^2 - 4x + 2y^2 + 4x = -2,$$
$$\Rightarrow x^2 - 2x + y^2 + 2x = -1,$$
$$\Rightarrow (x-1)^2 - 1 + (y+1)^2 - 1 = -1,$$
$$\Rightarrow (x-1)^2 + (y+1)^2 = 1.$$

The centre is $(1, -1)$, the radius is 1.

(f) The coefficients of x^2 and y^2 are different, so this cannot be the equation of a circle.

By completing the square we obtain

$$x^2 - 16x + 4y^2 - 16y = 4,$$
$$\Rightarrow (x-4)^2 - 16 + 4(y-2)^2 + 16 = 4,$$
$$\Rightarrow (x-4)^2 + 4(y-2)^2 = 4,$$
$$\Rightarrow (x-4)^2 + 4(y-2)^2 = 4.$$

This is actually the equation of an ellipse, which we plot below

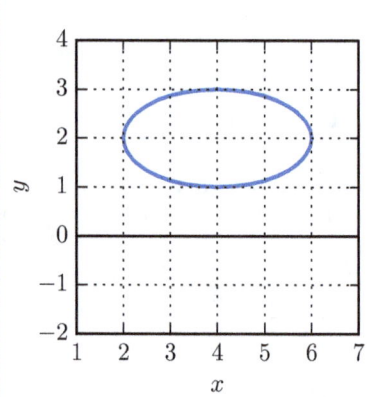

Q2. (a) The centre of the circle can be found using

$$C = \frac{A+B}{2} = \frac{((5,2)+(10,-4))}{2} = \left((\frac{15}{2},-1\right).$$

We can then find the length of the diameter as follows

$$|\overrightarrow{AB}| = \sqrt{(10-5)^2 + (-4-2)^2}$$
$$= \sqrt{5^2 + 6^2}$$
$$\sqrt{61}.$$

Hence, the radius of the circle is $r = \frac{\sqrt{61}}{2}$. The equation of the circle is

$$\left(x - \frac{15}{2}\right)^2 + (y+1)^2 = r^2 = \frac{61}{4} = 15\frac{1}{4}.$$

(b) The centre of the circle can be found using

$$C = \frac{A+B}{2} = \frac{((11,2)+(16,4))}{2} = \left(\frac{27}{2}, 3\right).$$

We can then find the length of the diameter as follows

$$|\overrightarrow{AB}| = \sqrt{(16-11)^2 + (4-2)^2}$$
$$= \sqrt{5^2 + 2^2}$$
$$\sqrt{29}.$$

Hence, the radius of the circle is $r = \frac{\sqrt{29}}{2}$. The equation of the circle is

$$\left(x - \frac{27}{2}\right)^2 + (y-3)^2 = r^2 = \frac{29}{4}.$$

(c) The centre of the circle can be found using
$$C = \frac{A+B}{2} = \frac{((-5,4)+(-1,-6))}{2} = (-3,-1).$$

We can then find the length of the diameter as follows
$$|\overrightarrow{AB}| = \sqrt{(-1-(-5))^2 + (-6-4)^2}$$
$$= \sqrt{(-3)^2 + (-10)^2}$$
$$\sqrt{116}.$$

Hence, the radius of the circle is $r = \frac{\sqrt{116}}{2}$. The equation of the circle is
$$\left(x - \frac{27}{2}\right)^2 + (y-3)^2 = r^2 = \frac{116}{4} = 29.$$

(d) The centre of the circle can be found using
$$C = \frac{A+B}{2} = \frac{((1,6)+(10,3))}{2} = \left(\frac{11}{2}, \frac{9}{2}\right).$$

We can then find the length of the diameter as follows
$$|\overrightarrow{AB}| = \sqrt{(10-1)^2 + (3-6)^2}$$
$$= \sqrt{(9)^2 + (-3)^2}$$
$$\sqrt{90}.$$

Hence, the radius of the circle is $r = \frac{\sqrt{90}}{2}$. The equation of the circle is
$$\left(x - \frac{11}{2}\right)^2 + \left(y - \frac{9}{2}\right)^2 = r^2 = \frac{90}{4} = \frac{45}{2}.$$

Q3. (a)
$$x^2 - 14x + y^2 - 6y + 58 = 16,$$
$$\Rightarrow \quad (x-7)^2 - 49 + (y-3)^2 - 9 + 58 = 16,$$
$$\Rightarrow \quad (x-7)^2 + (y-3)^2 = 16 + 9 + 49 - 58 = 16.$$

The circle is centred at $(7,3)$ and has radius 4.

(b) In order to determine whether the point $(4,3)$ lies inside or outside of the circle, we check how far from the circle's centre it is. This distance is given by
$$\sqrt{(7-4)^2 + (3-3)^2} = 3 < 4.$$

The point therefore lies inside the circle.

(c) In order to determine whether or not the circle crosses the y-axis, we set $x = 0$ in the circle's equations and attempt to find any values of y that satisfy the resultant equation:

$$(-7)^2 + (y-3)^2 = 16,$$
$$\Rightarrow \quad 49 + (y-3)^2 = 16,$$
$$\Rightarrow \quad (y-3)^2 = 16 - 49 < 0.$$

There are no real y-values that satisfy the above, hence, the circle does not intersect the y-axis.

(d) To find where the circle intersects the x-axis, we set $y = 0$ in the circle's equation and find the corresponding x-values:

$$(x-7)^2 + (0-3)^2 = 16,$$
$$\Rightarrow \quad (x-7)^2 + 9 = 16,$$
$$\Rightarrow \quad (x-7)^2 = 7,$$
$$\Rightarrow \quad x - 7 = \pm\sqrt{7},$$
$$\Rightarrow \quad x = 7 \pm \sqrt{7}.$$

The points of intersection are then $P(7-\sqrt{7}, 0)$ and $Q(7+\sqrt{7}, 0)$. As they are on the x-axis, the length $|PQ|$ is just $|7+\sqrt{7} - (7-\sqrt{7})| = 2\sqrt{7}$.

Q4. We complete the square for the equation of the second circle to obtain

$$x^2 - 10x + y^2 - 8y + 41 = 16,$$
$$\Rightarrow \quad (x-5)^2 - 25 + (y-4)^2 - 16 + 41 = 16,$$
$$\Rightarrow \quad (x-5)^2 + (y-4)^2 = 16 + 16 + 25 - 41,$$
$$\Rightarrow \quad (x-5)^2 + (y-4)^2 = 16.$$

Hence, both circles have radius 4. The first circle has centre $C_1 = (-2, -1)$ and the second has centre $C_2 = (5, 4)$. The distance between C_1 and C_2 is

$$|C_1 C_2| = \sqrt{(5-(-2))^2 + (4-(-1))^2}$$
$$= \sqrt{7^2 + 5^2}$$
$$= \sqrt{49 + 25} = \sqrt{74}.$$

Now, $\sqrt{74} > 8$ and hence the distance between the centres is greater than the sum of the radii. In this case, the circles do not intersect. The two circles are shown below.

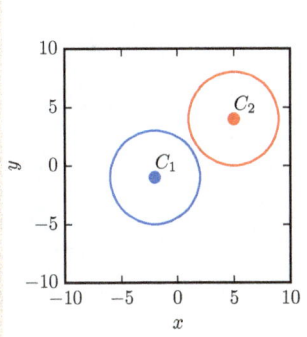

Q5. (a) We complete the square to obtain

$$x^2 - 10x + y^2 - 8y + 16 = 0,$$
$$\Rightarrow (x-5)^2 - 25 + (y-4)^2 - 16 + 16 = 0,$$
$$\Rightarrow (x-5)^2 + (y-4)^2 = 25.$$

Hence, we have an equation of the circle and the centre is $C = (5, 4)$.

(b) From the equation above, we see that the radius $r = 5$. As the centre is at $(5, 4)$ the circle must touch the y-axis only at the point $(0, 4)$.

(c) The distance from the centre of the circle to the origin $|OC|$ is

$$|OC| = \sqrt{5^2 + 4^2}$$
$$= \sqrt{41}.$$

Now, the distance $|CP| = r = 5$. Hence, as O, P and C are collinear, we have

$$|OP| = |OC| - |CP| = \sqrt{41} - 5.$$

(d) We find the points of intersection with the x-axis by noticing that $(x, 0)$, $(5, 0)$ and $(5, 4)$ is a right angled triangle with hypotenuse of length $r = 5$. We then have

$$(5-x)^2 + 4^2 = 5^2.$$

This is a Pythagorean triple, with $5 - x = 3$, $x = 2$ and $A = (2, 0)$ The area of the triangle OAC is then $\frac{1}{2} \times 2 \times 4 = 4$.

A plot showing the circle and the triangle OAC is shown below.

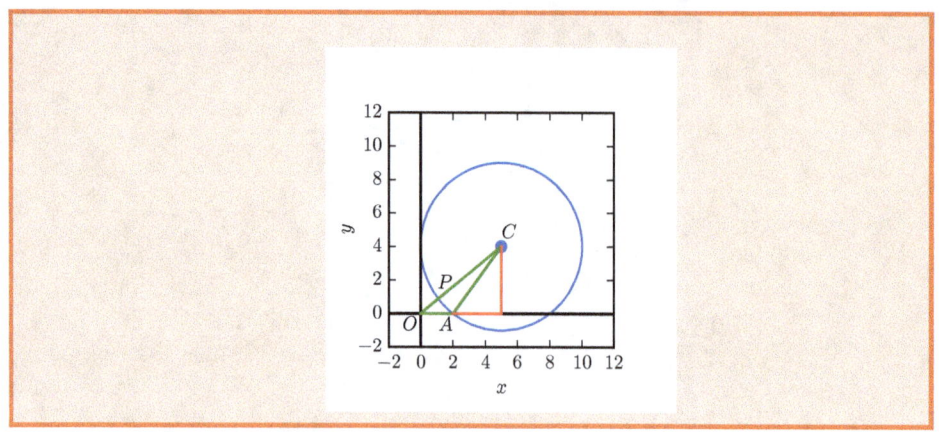

Worked Solutions — Exercise 13.3

Q1. The shortest distance from the centre to the chord is the length of the line which is perpendicular to the chord and passes through the centre. We know that this line bisects the chord and we have a right angled triangle, with hypotenuse of length r, and one side of length $c/2$. The length a we seek thus satisfies Pythagoras' theorem

$$r^2 = a^2 + \left(\frac{c}{2}\right)^2$$
$$\Rightarrow a = \sqrt{r^2 - \frac{c^2}{4}}.$$

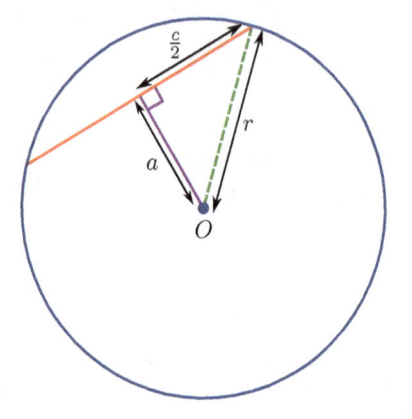

Q2. The solution to this problem is just a rearrangement of the solution to previous problem. Hence

$$r^2 = a^2 + \left(\frac{c}{2}\right)^2$$
$$\Rightarrow \quad c = 2\sqrt{r^2 - a^2}.$$

Q3. (a) Triangle ABC is right-angled due to results in Section 13.2. $|AB| = 2r$ and $|BC| = \frac{3r}{2}$. Hence, by Pythagoras' theorem, $|CA| = \sqrt{4r^2 - 9r^2/4} = \frac{\sqrt{7}r}{2}$. Now, $\overrightarrow{FG}$ is a tangent to the circle and, hence, must be perpendicular to the vector OE. As $\overrightarrow{AC}$ is parallel to $\overrightarrow{FG}$, then $\overrightarrow{OD}$ must be perpendicular to $\overrightarrow{AC}$. Thus, from Section 13.3, D is the midpoint of $\overrightarrow{AC}$ and $b = \frac{|CA|}{2} = \frac{\sqrt{7}r}{4}$.

(b) As $\angle CDO$ is a right-angle, the triangle AOD is a similar triangle to ABC with all lengths half that of ABC. Therefore, $c = \frac{|BC|}{2} = \frac{3r}{4}$.

Q4. Consider the equilateral triangle ABC shown below and circle centred at O. Using properties of the equilateral triangles, we know the perpendicular bisector of AB will pass through point C. As AB is also a chord of the circle, we know that the perpendicular bisector will pass through the centre of the circle.

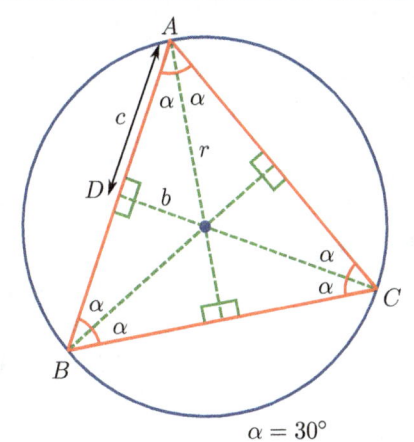

$\alpha = 30°$

(a) We know that $|AB| = 2c$. c can be calculated by using trigonometry and noticing that the hypotenuse of the triangle ADO is of length r. $c = r\cos(30) = \frac{\sqrt{3}r}{2}$. Hence, the sides are of length $\sqrt{3}r$.

(b) From above, the base of the equilateral triangle has length $\sqrt{3}r$ and the perpendicular height is given by $|DC| = b + r$. Now, $b = r\sin(30) = \frac{r}{2}$ and $|DC| = \frac{3r}{2}$. The area of the triangle is then $\frac{1}{2} \cdot \sqrt{3}r \cdot \frac{3r}{2} = \frac{3\sqrt{3}r^2}{4}$.

Q5. (a) Let O be the centre of the ring. The line AB is a tangent to the hole, and so the line OP meets it at a right angle.

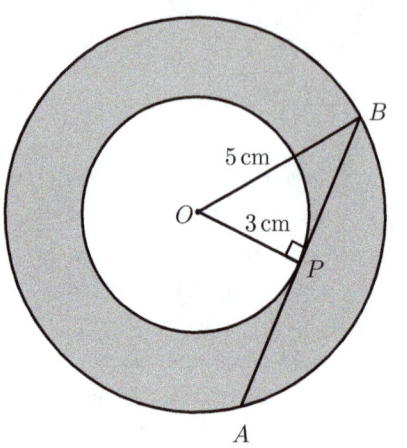

Therefore, BPO is a right angle triangle and the length of BP is given by

$$|BP| = \sqrt{5^2 - 3^2} = 4 \text{ cm}.$$

The length of AP is also equal to 4 cm. We can see this either by symmetry, or by noting that OP is the perpendicular from the centre of the circle to the chord AB, and therefore bisects it.

Therefore the length of AB is 8 cm.

(b) From our previous answer, we know that OPA is a right angle triangle, with $|OA| = 5$cm and $|AP| = 4$cm. Therefore, if θ is the angle at OAP, then $\cos(\theta) = \frac{4}{5}$.

The surface is a tangent to the ring, touching it at the point A. The radius OA is perpendicular to the tangent, and so OA is a vertical line.

Let C be the point where the perpendicular from B meets the surface. Let h be the length of BC. This is the height of the point B.

Since OA and BC are both perpendicular to the surface, they are parallel with each other.

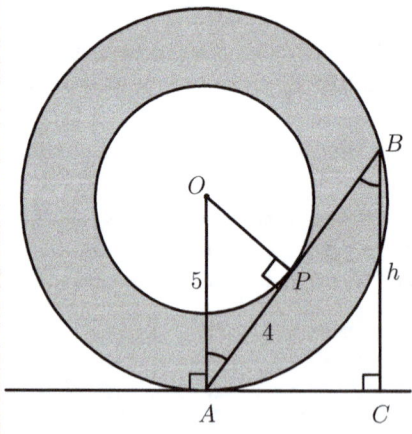

Therefore, the angles OAP and ABC are alternate angles, both equal to θ. The length of AB is 8 cm and so

$$\cos(\theta) = \frac{4}{5} = \frac{h}{8} \implies h = \frac{32}{5} = 6.4 \text{ cm}.$$

Q6. (a) We complete the square for x and y.

$$(x-2)^2 - 4 + (y+1)^2 - 1 = k,$$
$$(x-2)^2 + (y+1)^2 = k + 5.$$

This describes a circle if $(k+5) > 0$, that is, if $k > -5$.

(b) When $k = 11$, the equation becomes $(x-2)^2 + (y+1)^2 = 16$, which describes a circle of radius 4, centred at $(2, -1)$.

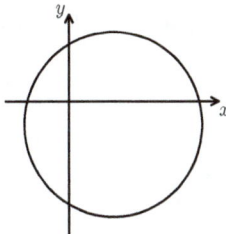

(c) When $k = -5$, the equation becomes $(x-2)^2 + (y+1)^2 = 0$. This equation represents a single point at $(2, -1)$.

Geometrically, this can be thought of as a circle of radius zero. Algebraically, we can solve the equation directly. Since we have two non-negative quantities which have a sum of zero, they must both be equal to zero. That is, we have $(x-2)^2 = 0$ and $(y+1)^2 = 0$. The only solution to these equations are $x = 2$ and $y = -1$, corresponding to the point $(2, -1)$.

Q7. (a) Each of the four sides of the rectangle are chords of the circle. Therefore, the perpendicular bisectors of each side passes through the centre of the circle. That is, the line from the midpoint of AB to the midpoint of CD passes through the centre. The line joining the midpoints of BC and DA also passes through the centre.

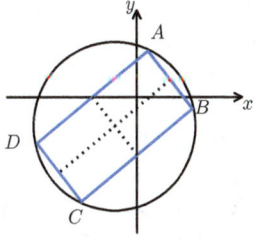

These lines meet at the centre of the rectangle, and so the centre of the rectangle is also the centre of the circle. We can easily calculate the centre of the rectangle by calculating the midpoint of either diagonal.

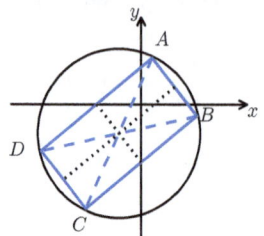

For example, the midpoint of the line AC is given by

$$\frac{A+C}{2} = \left(\frac{1-5}{2}, \frac{4-9}{2}\right) = \left(-2, -\frac{5}{2}\right).$$

The line AC is a diameter of the circle. Its length is given by

$$\sqrt{(-5-1)^2 + (-9-4)^2} = \sqrt{36+169} = \sqrt{205}.$$

The radius is therefore equal to $\frac{1}{2}\sqrt{205}$ and the equation of the circle S is

$$(x+2)^2 + \left(y+\frac{5}{2}\right)^2 = \frac{205}{4}.$$

(b) The length of the line AB is equal to $\sqrt{4^2 + 5^2} = \sqrt{41}$, therefore the equation of the circle S_2 is

$$(x-1)^2 + (y-4)^2 = 41.$$

To show that the point E lies on the intersection of the two circles, we must show that it satisfies both equations.

$$(-5.4+2)^2 + (3.8+2.5)^2 =$$
$$(-3.4)^2 + (6.3)^2 = 11.56 + 39.69 = 51.25 = \frac{205}{4}.$$

Therefore E lies on S_1.

$$(-5.4-1)^2 + (3.8-4)^2 =$$
$$(-6.4)^2 + (-0.2)^2 = 40.96 + 0.04 = 41.$$

Therefore E also lies on S_2.

Q8. (a) The lines forming the cross-section of the cone are tangents to the ball. Therefore, the radius from the centre of the circle to the point of contact is at right angles to the cone. By symmetry, the line from the apex to the centre of the circle must bisect the angle at the apex.

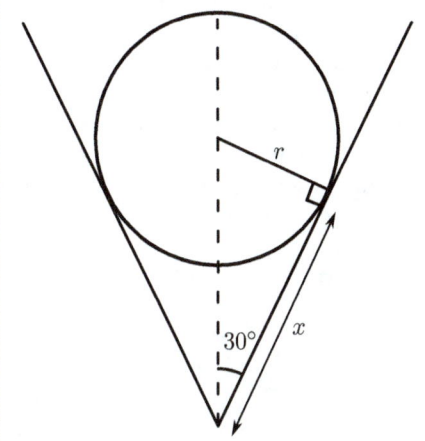

Therefore,
$$\tan(30°) = \frac{1}{\sqrt{3}} = \frac{r}{x},$$
$$\implies x = r\sqrt{3}.$$

(b) If the distance from the apex to the centre of the ball is h, then
$$h^2 = r^2 + x^2,$$
$$\implies h = \sqrt{r^2 + \left(r\sqrt{3}\right)^2} = \sqrt{r^2 + 3r^2} = 2r.$$

(c) The largest ball which hits the first ball will also touch the surface of the cone. The balls will stack on top of each other as shown below.

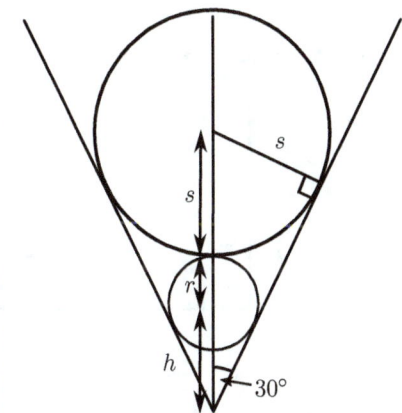

Again by symmetry, the line from the apex through the centre of the second ball bisects the angle at the apex, and therefore also passes through the centre of the first ball.

The distance from the apex to the centre of the second ball can be split into three lengths. Let s be the radius of the second ball.
- The distance from the apex to the centre of the first ball, $h = 2r$.
- The distance from the centre of the first ball to its top, r.
- The distance from the point where the balls touch to the centre of the first ball, s.

We therefore have

$$\sin(30°) = \frac{1}{2} = \frac{s}{2r + r + s},$$
$$3r + s = 2s,$$
$$s = 3r.$$

Therefore, a ball with radius three times greater will just touch the first ball when it comes to rest in the cone.

There is another way to calculate this radius, without performing any further calculations. We found that $h = 2r$. This means that the distance underneath the smaller ball is equal to its radius, r. In other words, the distance underneath a ball is equal to its radius. We now note that the larger ball has a distance of $3r$ underneath it: the diameter of the smaller ball, $2r$, and the space below it, r.

If the larger ball has a distance of $3r$ underneath it, its radius must be equal to $3r$.

Worked Solutions — Exercise 14.1

Q1. We use Pythagoras' theorem and the definitions of the trigonometric ratios to answer these questions.

(a) Using the given information we can construct the diagram below.

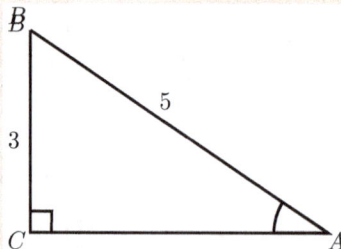

By Pythagoras,

$$AC = \sqrt{5^2 - 3^2}$$
$$= \sqrt{16}$$
$$= 4$$

Using the definitions of the trigonometric ratios, we can now say that,

$$\sin(A) = \frac{3}{5}$$
$$\cos(A) = \frac{4}{5}$$
$$\tan(A) = \frac{3}{4}$$
$$\sin(B) = \frac{4}{5}$$
$$\cos(B) = \frac{3}{5}$$
$$\tan(B) = \frac{4}{3}$$
$$|AB| = 5$$
$$|AC| = 4$$
$$|BC| = 3$$

(b) Using the given information we can construct the diagram below. Note that the lengths in blue are not physical lengths, they represent the trigonometric ratios.

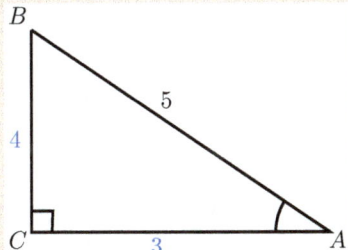

Using the definitions of the trigonometric ratios, we can now say that,

$$BC = 0.1 \times \sin(A)$$
$$= 0.1 \times \frac{4}{5}$$
$$= \frac{2}{25}$$
$$= 0.08,$$
$$AC = 0.1 \times \cos(A)$$
$$= 0.1 \times \frac{3}{5}$$
$$= \frac{3}{50}$$
$$= 0.06.$$

To summarise,

$$\sin(A) = \frac{4}{5}$$
$$\cos(A) = \frac{3}{5}$$
$$\tan(A) = \frac{4}{3}$$
$$\sin(B) = \frac{3}{5}$$
$$\cos(B) = \frac{4}{5}$$
$$\tan(B) = \frac{3}{4}$$
$$|AB| = 0.1\,\text{m}$$
$$|AC| = 0.06\,\text{m}$$
$$|BC| = 0.08\,\text{m}$$

(c) Using the given information we can construct the diagram below. Note that the lengths in blue are not physical lengths, they represent the trigonometric ratios.

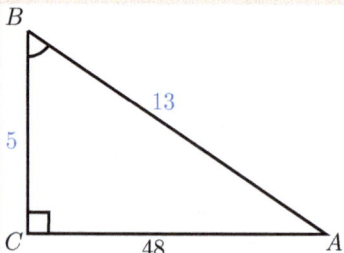

Using the definitions of the trigonometric ratios, we can now say that,

$$\sin(B) = \frac{12}{13}$$
$$\cos(B) = \frac{5}{13}$$
$$\tan(B) = \frac{12}{5}.$$

$$BC = \frac{48}{\sin(B)}$$
$$= \frac{48}{\frac{12}{13}}$$
$$= 52,$$
$$AC = \frac{48}{\tan(B)}$$
$$= \frac{48}{\frac{12}{5}}$$
$$= 20.$$

To summarise,

$$\sin(A) = \frac{5}{13}$$
$$\cos(A) = \frac{12}{13}$$
$$\tan(A) = \frac{5}{12}$$
$$\sin(B) = \frac{12}{13}$$
$$\cos(B) = \frac{5}{13}$$
$$\tan(B) = \frac{12}{5}$$
$$|AB| = 52\,\text{mm}$$
$$|AC| = 48\,\text{mm}$$
$$|BC| = 20\,\text{mm}$$

Q2. From the given information we draw the following diagram.

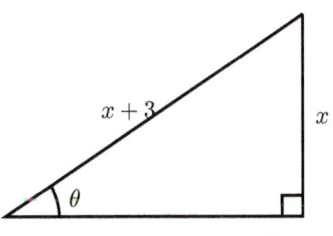

As $\theta = 30°$, $\sin(\theta) = \frac{1}{2}$. Hence,

$$\sin(\theta) = \frac{\text{opposite}}{\text{hypotenuse}}$$
$$\Rightarrow \quad \frac{1}{2} = \frac{x}{x+3}$$
$$\Rightarrow \quad x + 3 = 2x$$
$$\Rightarrow \quad x = 3.$$

Q3. From the given information we draw the following triangle.

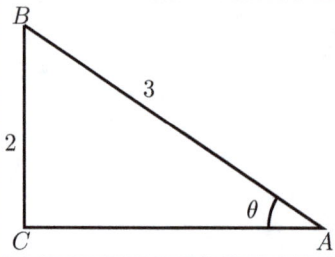

Using Pythagoras' Theorem,

$$|AC| = \sqrt{3^2 - 2^2}$$
$$= \sqrt{5}.$$

Hence,

$$\cos(\theta) = \frac{\sqrt{5}}{3}$$
$$\tan(\theta) = \frac{2}{\sqrt{5}}$$

Q4. From the given information we draw the following triangle.

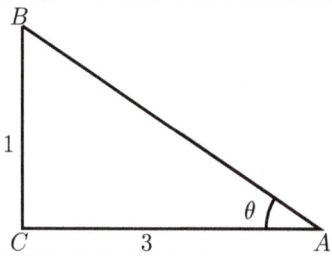

Using Pythagoras' Theorem,

$$|AB| = \sqrt{3^2 + 1^2}$$
$$= \sqrt{10}.$$

Hence,

$$\sin(\theta) = \frac{1}{\sqrt{10}}$$
$$\cos(\theta) = \frac{3}{\sqrt{10}}$$

Q5.

(a)

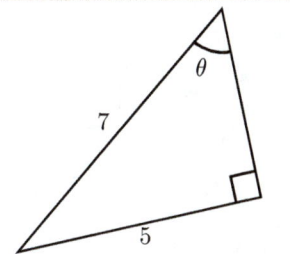

From the diagram,

$$\sin(\theta) = \frac{5}{7}$$
$$\Rightarrow \quad \theta = \arcsin\left(\frac{5}{7}\right)$$
$$= 45.58°$$

(b)

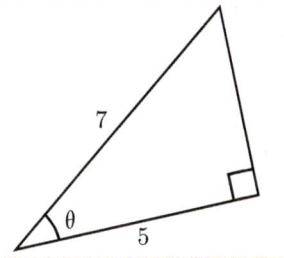

From the diagram,

$$\cos(\theta) = \frac{5}{7}$$
$$\Rightarrow \quad \theta = \arccos\left(\frac{5}{7}\right)$$
$$= 44.41°$$

(c)

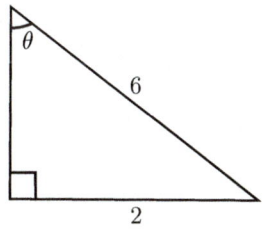

From the diagram,
$$\sin(\theta) = \frac{2}{6}$$
$$\Rightarrow \quad \theta = \arcsin\left(\frac{2}{6}\right)$$
$$= 19.47°$$

(d)

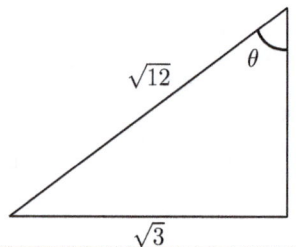

From the diagram,
$$\sin(\theta) = \frac{\sqrt{3}}{\sqrt{12}}$$
$$= \frac{\sqrt{3}}{2\sqrt{3}}$$
$$= \frac{1}{2}$$

Hence,
$$\theta = \arcsin\left(\frac{1}{2}\right)$$
$$= 30°$$

Q6. (a) For the left hand situation.

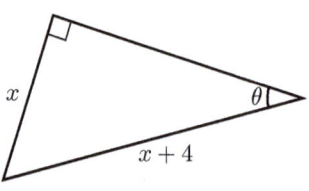

Similarly to Question 2, we note that if $\theta = 30°$, then $\sin(\theta) = \frac{1}{2}$. And so,

$$\frac{x}{x+4} = \frac{1}{2}$$
$$\Rightarrow \quad 2x = x + 4$$
$$\Rightarrow \quad x = 4.$$

Hence the length of the hypotenuse is 4.

(b) For the right hand situation.

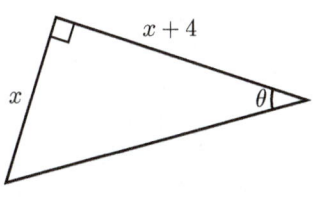

Noting that $\theta = 30°$ implies that $\tan(\theta) = \frac{1}{\sqrt{3}}$.

$$\frac{1}{\sqrt{3}} = \frac{x}{x+4}$$
$$\Rightarrow \quad x + 4 = \sqrt{3}x$$
$$\Rightarrow \quad 4 = \left(\sqrt{3} - 1\right)x$$
$$\Rightarrow \quad x = \frac{4}{\sqrt{3} - 1}$$

Q7. (a)

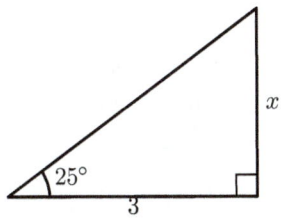

$$\tan(25) = \frac{x}{3}$$
$$\Rightarrow \quad x = 3 \times \tan(25)$$
$$= 1.398922974$$
$$\approx 1.40$$

(b)

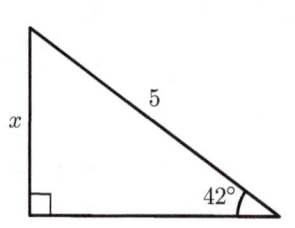

$$\sin(42) = \frac{x}{5}$$
$$\Rightarrow \quad x = 5 \times \sin(42)$$
$$= 3.345653932$$
$$\approx 1.36$$

(c)

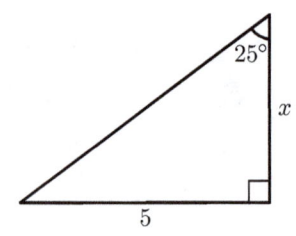

$$\tan(25) = \frac{5}{x}$$
$$\Rightarrow \quad x = \frac{5}{\tan(25)}$$
$$= 10.7225346$$
$$\approx 10.72$$

(d)

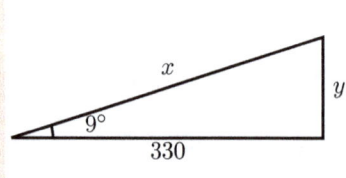

$$\cos(9) = \frac{330}{x}$$
$$\Rightarrow x = \frac{330}{\cos(9)}$$
$$= 334.1134815$$
$$\approx 334.11$$

And,
$$\tan(9) = \frac{y}{330}$$
$$\Rightarrow y = 330 \times \tan(9)$$
$$= 52.26686531$$
$$\approx 52.27$$

Q8. From the information we construct the mathematical diagram below.

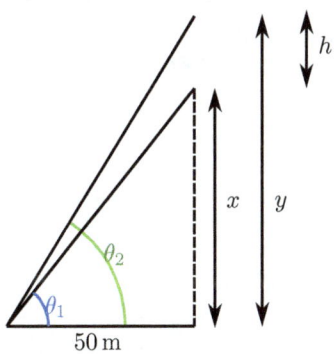

To find x,
$$\tan(\theta_1) = \frac{\text{opposite}}{\text{adjacent}}$$
$$= \frac{x}{50}$$
$$\Rightarrow x = 50 \times \tan(\theta_1)$$
$$\Rightarrow x = 50 \times \tan(72.6)$$
$$= 159.550194$$
$$\approx 159.55 \text{ m}.$$

To find y,

$$\tan(\theta_1) = \frac{\text{opposite}}{\text{adjacent}}$$
$$= \frac{y}{50}$$
$$\Rightarrow \quad y = 50 \times \tan(\theta_2)$$
$$\Rightarrow \quad y = 50 \times \tan(74.8)$$
$$= 184.0305728$$
$$\approx 184.03 \text{ m}.$$

Hence the distance between the top of the tower and the restaurant is

$$h \approx 184.03 - 159.55 = 24.4 \text{ m}.$$

Worked Solutions — Exercise 14.2

Q1. The sketches are shown on the graph below. (a) blue curve, (b) red curve, (c) green curve and (d) purple curve.

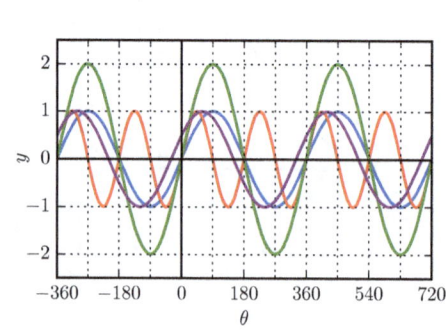

Q2. The sketches are shown on the graph below. (a) blue curve, (b) red curve, (c) green curve and (d) purple curve.

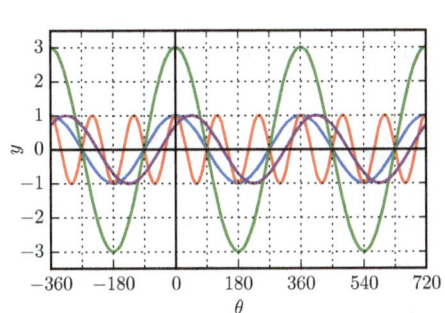

Q3. The sketches are shown on the graph below. (a) blue curve, (b) red curve, (c) green curve and (d) purple curve.

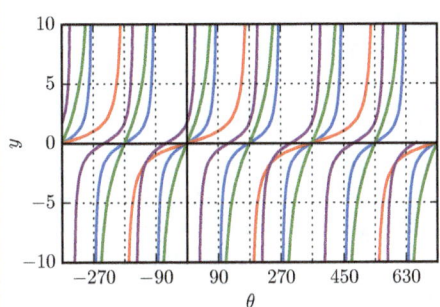

Q4. $\sin(x)$ is a periodic function with period $360°$, hence $\sin(60) = \sin(60 + 360) = \sin(60 - 360)$. Adding any other multiple of 360 to 60 leads to a value outside of the interval $[-540, 540]$.

In addition, $\sin(x) = \sin(180 - x)$, hence, $\sin(60) = \sin(180 - 60) = \sin(120)$. We then again use the periodicity of $\sin(x)$ to see that $\sin(120) = \sin(120 + 360) = \sin(120 - 360)$, adding other multiples of 360 lead to values outside of the interval $[-540, 540]$. The values of x are therefore

$$x = -300°, \quad -240°, \quad 60°, \quad 120°, \quad 420°, \quad 480°.$$

Q5. $\cos(x)$ is a periodic function with period $360°$, hence $\cos(120) = \sin(120 + 360) = \sin(120 - 360)$. Adding any other multiple of 360 to 120 leads to a value outside of the interval $[-540, 540]$.

In addition, $\cos(x) = \cos(-x)$, hence, $\cos(120) = \cos(-120)$. We then again use the periodicity of $\cos(x)$ to see that $\sin(-120) = \sin(-120 + 360) = \sin(-120 - 360)$, adding other multiples of 360 lead to values outside of the interval $[-540, 540]$. The values of x are therefore

$$x = -480°, \quad -240°, \quad 120°, \quad 120°, \quad 240°, \quad 480°.$$

Q6. $\tan(x)$ is a periodic function with period $180°$, hence $\tan(60) = \tan(60 + 180) = \tan(60 - 180) = \tan(60 - 360)$. Adding any other multiple of 180 to 60 leads to a value outside of the interval $[-360, 360]$. Over an interval of width $180°$, $\tan(x)$ has no repeated values. Hence, the only possible values of x are

$$x = -300°, \quad -120°, \quad 60°, \quad 240°.$$

Q7. We first find those values θ such that $\tan(\theta) = \tan(45°)$ and then find x such that $3x = \theta$. As we seek $-360 \leq x \leq 360$, we need to find $1080 = -3 \times 360 \leq \theta \leq 3 \times 360 = 1080$. Using the periodicity of $\tan(\theta)$ we have

$$\tan(45) = \tan(45 + 180) = \tan(45 + 360) = \tan(45 + 540) = \tan(45 + 720)$$
$$= \tan(45 + 900) = \tan(45 - 180) = \tan(45 - 360) = \tan(45 - 540)$$
$$= \tan(45 - 720) = \tan(45 - 900) = \tan(45 - 1080).$$

Hence,

$$\theta = 45, \quad 225°, \quad 405°, \quad 585°,$$
$$765°, \quad 945°, \quad -135°, \quad -315°,$$
$$-495°, \quad -675°, \quad -855°, \quad -1035°.$$

Using $x = \theta/3$ we have

$$x = 15°, \quad 75°, \quad 135°, \quad 195°,$$
$$255°, \quad 155°, \quad -45°, \quad -105°,$$
$$-165°, \quad -225°, \quad -285°, \quad -345°.$$

Q8. (a) The gradient of the line is $\frac{1}{\sqrt{3}}$, which means that $\tan(\theta) = \frac{1}{\sqrt{3}}$. This is a standard triangle and $\theta = 30°$. However, the point P has x-coordinate -3 and, therefore, the angle between the positive x-axis and OP must be $30 + 180 = 210°$. Now, as $\tan(\theta) = \frac{\text{opposite}}{\text{adjacent}}$ and we know that the adjacent side of the triangle is length 3, we have

$$\text{opposite} = \text{adjacent} \times \frac{1}{\sqrt{3}} = \frac{3}{\sqrt{3}} = \sqrt{3}.$$

Hence, as the angle $210°$ lies in the third quadrant, the y-coordinate of P is $\sqrt{3}$.

(b) In this case, as the x-coordinate of Q is 2, then the angle between the positive x-axis and OQ must be $30°$. We again use $\tan(\theta) = \frac{\text{opposite}}{\text{adjacent}}$ and the length of the adjacent side is 2, hence,

$$\text{opposite} = \text{adjacent} \times \frac{1}{\sqrt{3}} = \frac{2}{\sqrt{3}}.$$

The y-coordinate of Q is therefore $\frac{2}{\sqrt{3}}$.
A sketch of the situation is shown below.

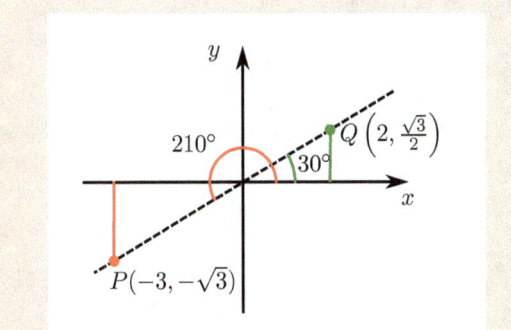

Worked Solutions — Exercise 14.3

Q1. (a)

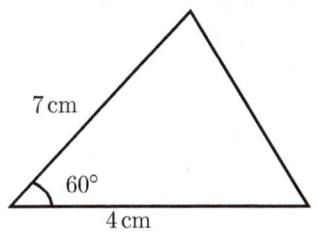

$$\text{Area} = \frac{1}{2} ab \sin(C)$$
$$\Rightarrow \text{Area} = \frac{1}{2} \times 7 \times 4 \times \sin(60)$$
$$= \frac{1}{2} \times 7 \times 4 \times \frac{\sqrt{3}}{2}$$
$$= 7\sqrt{3}$$
$$\approx 12.12 \, \text{cm}^2.$$

(b)

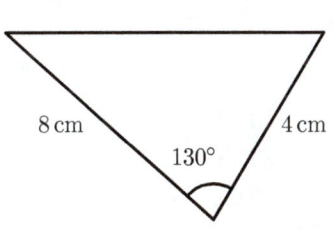

$$\text{Area} = \frac{1}{2}ab\sin(C)$$
$$\Rightarrow \text{Area} = \frac{1}{2} \times 8 \times 4 \times \sin(130)$$
$$= 12.25671109$$
$$\approx 12.26\,\text{cm}^2.$$

(c)

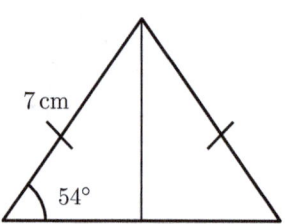

We first find the angle at the apex of the triangle, $18 - -54 - 54 = 72°$

$$\text{Area} = \frac{1}{2}ab\sin(C)$$
$$\Rightarrow \text{Area} = \frac{1}{2} \times 7 \times 7 \times \sin(72)$$
$$= 23.30088465$$
$$\approx 23.30\,\text{cm}^2.$$

(d)

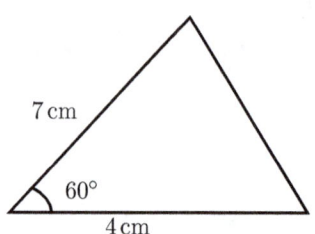

$$\text{Area} = \frac{1}{2}ab\sin(C)$$
$$\Rightarrow \text{Area} = \frac{1}{2} \times 3 \times 8 \times \sin(85)$$
$$= 11.95433638$$
$$= 7\sqrt{3}$$
$$\approx 11.95\,\text{cm}^2.$$

Q2. (a) i. We first use Pythagoras' theorem to find the perpendicular height, h, of the triangle.

$$h = \sqrt{6^2 - 5^2}$$
$$\sqrt{36 - 25}$$
$$= \sqrt{11}$$

Hence, the area of the triangle is given by,

$$\text{Area} = \frac{1}{2} \times 5 \times \sqrt{11}$$
$$= \frac{5\sqrt{11}}{2}$$
$$\approx 8.29 \text{ square units}$$

ii.
$$\text{Area} = \frac{1}{2} \times 5 \times 6 \times \sin 33.56$$
$$= 8.292148886$$
$$\approx 8.29 \text{ square units}$$

(b) There are less calculations involved in this instance when using the general formula for the area of a triangle.

Q3. An equilateral triangle has all angles the same length, x say, and all interior angles are $60°$. Since the area is $16\sqrt{3}$, we have that

$$16\sqrt{3} = \frac{1}{2} \times x \times x \times \sin(60)$$
$$= \frac{1}{2}x^2 \frac{\sqrt{3}}{2}$$
$$\Rightarrow \quad 64\sqrt{3} = x^2\sqrt{3}$$
$$\Rightarrow \quad x^2 = 64$$
$$\Rightarrow \quad x = 8.$$

Q4. We first calculate the missing angle in the traingle, $180 - 55 - 55 = 70°$. Then, applying the formula for the area of a triangle,

$$A = \frac{1}{2}ab\sin(C)$$
$$\Rightarrow \quad 21 = \frac{1}{2}x \times x \times \sin(70)$$
$$\Rightarrow \quad \frac{x^2}{2} = \frac{21}{\sin(70)}$$
$$\Rightarrow \quad x^2 = \frac{42}{\sin(70)}$$
$$\Rightarrow \quad \quad = 44.69546644.$$

Hence,

$$x = 6.685466808$$
$$\approx 6.7\,\text{cm}$$

Q5.

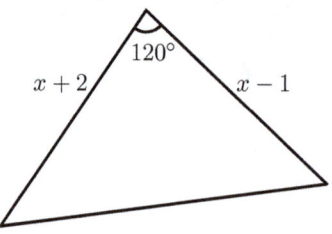

With reference to the picture above, and using the formula for the area of a general triangle.

$$A = \frac{1}{2}ab\sin(C)$$
$$\Rightarrow \quad 10\sqrt{3} = \frac{1}{2}(x+2)(x-1)\sin(120)$$
$$\Rightarrow \quad 10\sqrt{3} = \frac{1}{2}(x+2)(x-1)\frac{\sqrt{3}}{2}$$
$$\Rightarrow \quad 40 = x^2 + x - 2$$
$$\Rightarrow \quad 0 = x^2 + x - 42$$
$$\Rightarrow \quad 0 = (x-6)(x+7).$$

Since the length must be positive $x = 6\,\text{cm}$.

Q6.

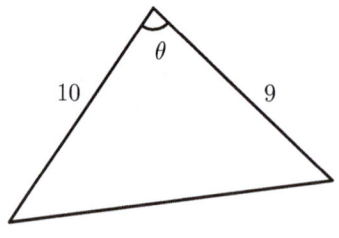

From the above, we can form an equation to find θ.

$$A = \frac{1}{2}ab\sin(C)$$
$$\Rightarrow \quad 35 = \frac{1}{2}10 \times 9 \times \sin(\theta)$$
$$\Rightarrow \quad 70 = 90\sin(\theta)$$
$$\Rightarrow \quad \sin(\theta) = \frac{70}{90}$$
$$= \frac{7}{9}$$

So $\theta \approx 51.06°$ or $\theta \approx 128.94°$.

Worked Solutions — Exercise 14.4

Q1. (a) If the angles are exact, then no, this cannot be a feasible triangle, as the sum of angles is 181.

(b) If the angles are all correct to the nearest degree, then we can use the sine rule to check whether we have a feasible triangle. Let $A = 53°$, $B = 64°$, $C = 64°$ and $a = 6.00$, $b = 7.21$ and $c = 7.32$. We have

$$\frac{\sin(A)}{a} = 0.1331\ldots,$$
$$\frac{\sin(B)}{b} = 0.1246\ldots,$$
$$\frac{\sin(C)}{c} = 0.1227\ldots.$$

As the above values are all different (and not close), then the sine rule is not satisfied and we do not have a feasible triangle.

In fact, we could have seen this without having to use the sine rule at all. We have a triangle which is *nearly* isosceles, assuming that the two angles of 64° are not exact. However, we do not have a triangle where two of the sides are of the same length, to the same degree of accuracy.

When testing with the sine rule, technically we should have checked that it was not possible to achieve equality of ratios with the angles B and C in the interval $[63.5, 64.5)$ and A in the interval $[52.5, 53.5]$ and the lengths a, b and c in the intervals $[5.995, 6.005)$, $[7.205, 7.215)$ and $[7.315, 7.325)$, respectively.

Q2. We use the sine rule in all parts of this question.

(a)
$$|AC| = b = 8, \quad \text{opposite } \angle ABC = 60°,$$
$$|AB| = c = x, \quad \text{opposite } \angle BCA = 45°.$$

Hence,
$$\frac{x}{\sin(45)} = \frac{8}{\sin(60)},$$
$$\Rightarrow \quad x = \frac{8\sin(45)}{\sin(60)}$$
$$= \frac{8 \cdot \frac{1}{\sqrt{2}}}{\frac{\sqrt{3}}{2}}$$
$$= \frac{8 \cdot 2\frac{1}{\sqrt{2}}}{\sqrt{3}}$$
$$= \frac{8\sqrt{2}}{\sqrt{3}}$$
$$= 6.53 \quad \text{to 2 d.p.}$$

(b)
$$|AB| = c = 73, \quad \text{opposite } \angle BCA = 70°,$$
$$|BC| = a = x, \quad \text{opposite } \angle CAB = 30°.$$

Hence,
$$\frac{x}{\sin(30)} = \frac{7.3}{\sin(70)},$$
$$\Rightarrow \quad x = \frac{7.3 \cdot \frac{1}{2}}{\sin(70)}$$
$$= 3.88 \quad \text{to 2 d.p.}$$

(c)
$$|AB| = c = 22.4, \quad \text{opposite } \angle BCA = 40°,$$
$$|CA| = b = x, \quad \text{opposite } \angle ABC = 130°.$$

Hence,
$$\frac{x}{\sin(130)} = \frac{22.4}{\sin(40)},$$
$$\Rightarrow \quad x = \frac{22.4 \cdot \sin(130)}{\sin(40)}$$
$$= 26.70 \quad \text{to 2 d.p.}$$

(d)
$$|AC| = b = 9, \quad \text{opposite } \angle ABC = 50°,$$
$$|AB| = c = x, \quad \text{opposite } \angle BCA = 70°.$$

Hence,
$$\frac{x}{\sin(70)} = \frac{9}{\sin(50)},$$
$$\Rightarrow \quad x = \frac{9 \cdot \sin(70)}{\sin(50)}$$
$$= 11.04 \quad \text{to 2 d.p.}$$

(e)
$$|BC| = a = 12, \quad \text{opposite } \angle CAB = 100°,$$
$$|AB| = c = x, \quad \text{opposite } \angle BCA = 30°.$$

Hence,
$$\frac{x}{\sin(30)} = \frac{12}{\sin(100)},$$
$$\Rightarrow \quad x = \frac{12 \cdot \sin(30)}{\sin(100)}$$
$$= 6.09 \quad \text{to 2 d.p.}$$

Q3. We use the sine rule for the majority of the parts to this question.

(a)
$$|AB| = c = 6, \quad \text{opposite } \angle BCA = \theta,$$
$$|BC| = a = 7, \quad \text{opposite } \angle CAB = 30°.$$

Hence,
$$\frac{\sin(\theta)}{6} = \frac{\sin(30)}{7},$$
$$\Rightarrow \quad \sin(\theta) = \frac{6\sin(30)}{7}$$
$$\Rightarrow \quad \theta = \sin^{-1}\left(\frac{6\sin(30)}{7}\right)$$
$$= \sin^{-1}\left(\frac{3}{7}\right)$$
$$= 25.4° \quad \text{to 1 d.p.}$$

(b)
$$|AB| = c = \sqrt{79}, \quad \text{opposite } \angle BCA = \theta,$$
$$|BC| = a = 7, \quad \text{opposite } \angle CAB = 45°.$$

Hence,
$$\frac{\sin(\theta)}{\sqrt{79}} = \frac{\sin(45)}{7},$$
$$\Rightarrow \quad \sin(\theta) = \frac{\sqrt{79}}{7\sqrt{2}}$$
$$\Rightarrow \quad \theta = \sin^{-1}\left(\frac{\sqrt{79}}{7\sqrt{2}}\right)$$
$$= 63.9° \quad \text{to 1 d.p.}$$

(c)
$$|AC| = b = 8, \quad \text{opposite } \angle ABC = \theta,$$
$$|BC| = a = 7, \quad \text{opposite } \angle CAB = 50°.$$

Hence,
$$\frac{\sin(\theta)}{8} = \frac{\sin(50)}{7},$$
$$\Rightarrow \quad \sin(\theta) = \frac{8\sin(50)}{7}$$
$$\Rightarrow \quad \theta = \sin^{-1}\left(\frac{8\sin(50)}{7}\right)$$
$$= 61.1° \quad \text{to 1 d.p.}$$

(d) For this question we are given two angles $\angle BCA = 73°$ and $\angle CAB = 30°$. Hence,
$$\angle ABC = 180 - 73 - 30$$
$$= 77°.$$

(e)
$$|CA| = b = 9, \quad \text{opposite } \angle ABC = \theta,$$
$$|BC| = a = 11, \quad \text{opposite } \angle CAB = 72°.$$

Hence,
$$\frac{\sin(\theta)}{9} = \frac{\sin(72)}{11},$$
$$\Rightarrow \quad \sin(\theta) = \frac{9\sin(72)}{11}$$
$$\Rightarrow \quad \theta = \sin^{-1}\left(\frac{9\sin(72)}{11}\right)$$
$$= 51.1° \quad \text{to 1 d.p.}$$

Q4. (a) Referring to the figure below, we see that the angle $CBA = 45 + 20 = 65°$.

(b) We similarly find that $\angle ACB = 180 - 65 - 50 = 65°$. Immediately, noticing that we have an isosceles triangle, we have

$$|AC| = |AB| = 8 \text{ miles}.$$

(c) To find the remaining length $|BC|$, we use the chain rule

$$\frac{|BC|}{\sin(50)} = \frac{8}{\sin(65)}$$
$$\Rightarrow \quad |BC| = \frac{8\sin(50)}{\sin(65)}$$
$$= 6.8 \text{ miles to 1 d.p.}$$

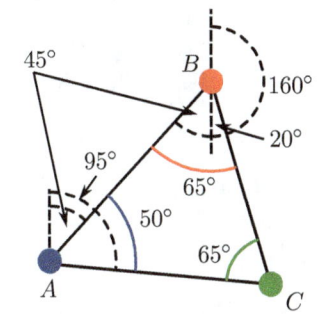

Q5. We first label the diagram of the situation below.

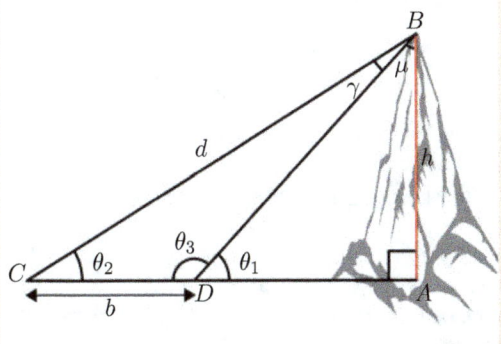

From the information given we know $\theta_1 = 5.75°$, $\theta_2 = 3.37°$ and $b = 50\,\text{km} = 50\,000\,\text{km}$.

We then calculate some of the missing angles.

- Since θ_1 and θ_3 lie on a straight line,

$$\theta_3 = 180 - \theta_1,$$
$$= 174.25°.$$

- Considering the triangle DBC, we can calculate γ as follows.

$$\gamma = 180 - 174.25 - 3.37,$$
$$= 2.89°.$$

Since we know all angles in triangle DBC and one of the sides we can use the sine rule to find the length d.

$$\frac{d}{\sin(174.25)} = \frac{50000}{\sin(2.38)},$$
$$\Rightarrow \quad d = \frac{50\sin(174.25)}{\sin(2.38)}$$
$$= 120\,630.340\ldots$$

Finally, d is the hypotenuse of the right angled triangle ABC, and so we can use right angled trigonometry to determine the height of Mount Everest.

$$\sin(3.37) = \frac{h}{d},$$
$$\Rightarrow \quad h = 120630.340\sin(3.37)$$
$$= 7091.096\ldots$$
$$\approx 7091\,\text{m}.$$

This answer is not very close to the accepted height of Mount Everest. As we now see, the answer is very sensitive to small changes in the sizes of the measured angles.

If $\theta_1 = 5.05°$, then we can perform the same calculations as above. We find:

$$\theta_3 = 180 - 5.05 = 174.95°,$$
$$\gamma = 180 - 174.95° - 3.37 = 1.68°,$$
$$d = \frac{50\sin(174.95)}{\sin(1.68)} = 150\,124.607\ldots,$$
$$h = 150124.607\ldots\sin(3.37) = 8824.8\ldots.$$

With these measurements, the height of Everest is $8825\,\text{m}$ to the nearest metre, which is much closer to the accepted $8848\,\text{m}$.

Q6. Side AB is opposite angle $\angle ACB$ and BC is opposite $\angle CAB$. Using the sine rule,

we therefore have
$$\frac{x}{\frac{1}{\sqrt{6}}} = \frac{x+2}{\sin(60)},$$
$$\Rightarrow \quad x\sqrt{6} = \frac{2(x+2)}{\sqrt{3}},$$
$$\Rightarrow \quad \frac{x\sqrt{3}\sqrt{6}}{\sqrt{3}} = \frac{2(x+2)}{\sqrt{3}},$$
$$\Rightarrow \quad 3\sqrt{2}x = 2x + 4,$$
$$\Rightarrow \quad (3\sqrt{2} - 2)x = 4,$$
$$\Rightarrow \quad x = \frac{4}{3\sqrt{2} - 2}.$$

Worked Solutions — Exercise 14.5

Q1. (a) Consider the figure below

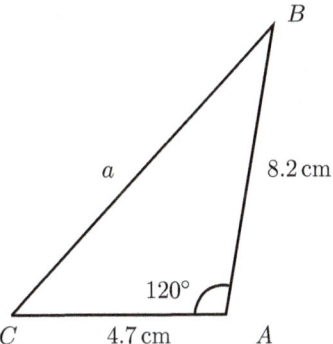

Applying the cosine rule,
$$a^2 = b^2 + c^2 - 2bc\cos(A)$$
$$\Rightarrow \quad a^2 = 4.7^2 + 8.2^2 - 2 \times 4.7 \times 8.2 \times \cos(120)$$
$$= \frac{12787}{100}$$

Hence,
$$a = 11.3079618$$
$$\approx 11.31 \text{ cm}$$

(b) Consider the figure below

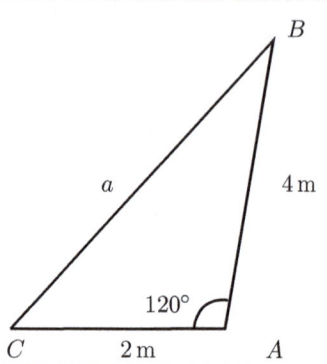

Applying the cosine rule,

$$a^2 = b^2 + c^2 - 2bc\cos(A)$$
$$\Rightarrow a^2 = 4^2 + 2^2 - 2 \times 4 \times 2 \times \cos(60)$$
$$= 12$$

Hence,

$$a = \sqrt{12}$$
$$= 2\sqrt{3}$$
$$\approx 3.46 \, \text{m}$$

(c) Consider the figure below

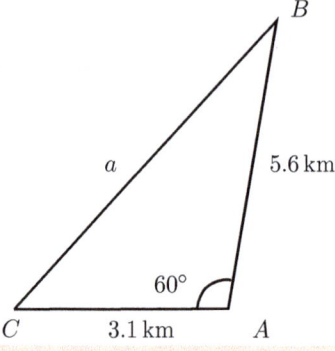

Applying the cosine rule,

$$a^2 = b^2 + c^2 - 2bc\cos(A)$$
$$\Rightarrow a^2 = 3.1^2 + 5.6^2 - 2 \times 3.1 \times 5.6 \times \cos(50)$$
$$= 18.65241419$$

Hence,
$$a = 14.318844081$$
$$\approx 4.31 \text{ft}$$

Q2. With reference to the figure below.

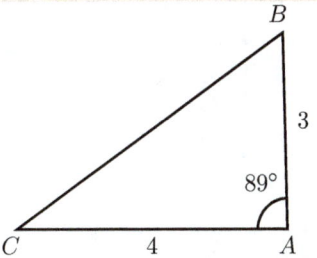

(a) Applying the cosine rue.
$$a^2 = b^2 + c^2 - 2bc\cos(A)$$
$$\Rightarrow \quad a^2 = 3^2 + 4^2 - 2 \times 3 \times 4 \times \cos(89)$$
$$= 24.58114225$$

Hence,
$$a = 4.957937297$$
$$\approx 4.96 \text{ cm}$$

(b) If this tringle was approximated by a right-angled triangle, the longest side would have length 5 cm. Hence, the percentage error is given by,
$$\text{Percentage Error} \approx \left(\frac{5 - 4.96}{5}\right) \times 100$$
$$= 0.84\%$$

Q3. Using the information given we can construct the following diagram of the described situation. The lighthouse is located at A and there are two ships located at B and C.

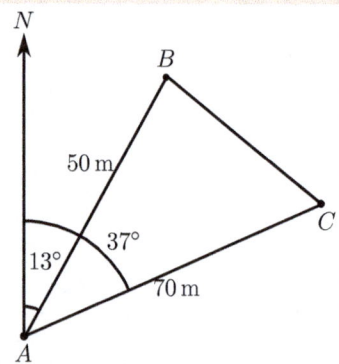

From this physical diagram we can construct a "paired down" mathematical diagram containing only the information we need to know.

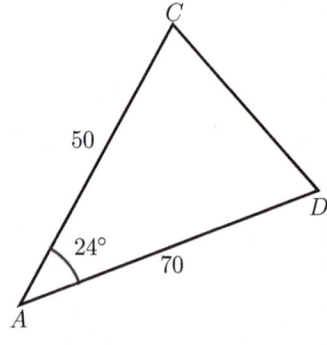

Using the cosine rule,

$$a^2 = b^2 + c^2 - 2bc\cos(A)$$
$$\Rightarrow a^2 = 50^2 + 70^2 - 2 \times 50 \times 70 \times \cos(24)$$
$$= 1005.181797.$$

Hence,

$$a = 3170460213$$
$$\approx 31.7\,\text{m}.$$

Q4. We construct the diagram below.

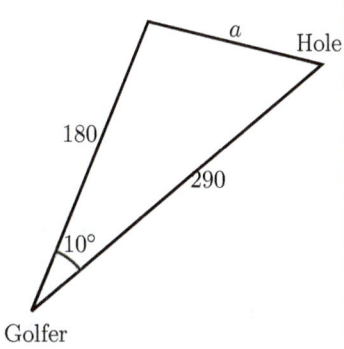

Applying the cosine rule.

$$a^2 = b^2 + c^2 - 2bc\cos(A)$$
$$\Rightarrow a^2 = 290^2 + 180^2 - 2 \times 180 \times 290 \times \cos(10)$$
$$= 13686.07059.$$

Hence,

$$a = 116.9874805$$
$$\approx 117.$$

So, the ball is 117 m away from the hole.

Q5. (a) With reference to the picture below

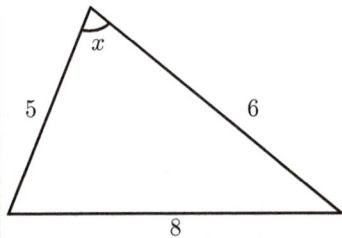

$$\cos(x) = \frac{5^2 + 6^2 - 8^2}{2 \times 5 \times 6}$$
$$= -\frac{1}{20}$$

Hence,

$$x = \arccos\left(-\frac{1}{20}\right)$$
$$= 92.86598398$$
$$\approx 92.87°$$

(b) With reference to the picture below

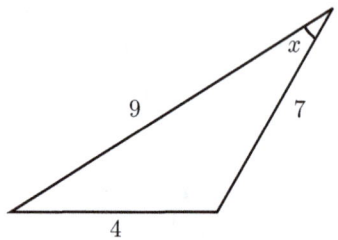

$$\cos(x) = \frac{9^2 + 7^2 - 4^2}{2 \times 9 \times 7}$$
$$= \frac{19}{21}$$

Hence,

$$x = \arccos\left(\frac{19}{21}\right)$$
$$= 25.2087653$$
$$\approx 25.21°$$

(c) With reference to the picture below

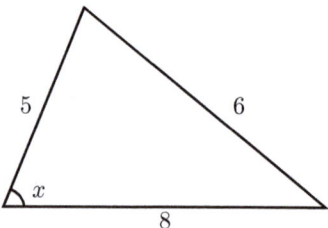

$$\cos(x) = \frac{5^2 + 8^2 - 6^2}{2 \times 5 \times 8}$$
$$= \frac{53}{80}$$

Hence,

$$x = \arccos\left(\frac{53}{80}\right)$$
$$= 48.50918314$$
$$\approx 48.51°$$

(d) With reference to the picture below

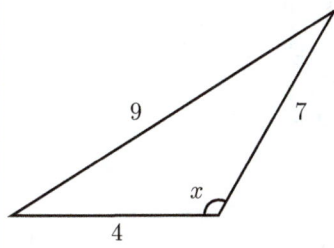

$$\cos(x) = \frac{4^2 + 7^2 - 9^2}{2 \times 4 \times 7}$$
$$= -\frac{2}{7}$$

Hence,

$$x = \arccos\left(-\frac{2}{7}\right)$$
$$= 106.6015496$$
$$\approx 106.60°$$

Q6. (a) With reference to the picture below.

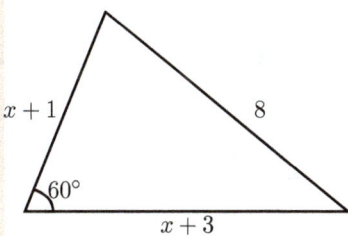

Applying the cosine rule we find that,

$$c^2 = b^2 + a^2 - 2ba\cos(C)$$
$\Rightarrow \qquad 8^2 = (x+3)^2 + (x+1)^2 - 2(x+3)(x+1)\cos(60°)$
$\Rightarrow \qquad 64 = x^2 + 6x + 9 + x^2 + 2x + 1 - 2(x^2 + 4x + 3) \times \frac{1}{2}$
$\Rightarrow \qquad 64 = x^2 + 6x + 9 + x^2 + 2x + 1 - x^2 - 4x - 3$
$\Rightarrow \qquad 64 = x^2 + 4x + 7$
$\Rightarrow \quad x^2 + 4x - 57 = 0.$

(b) Using the quadratic formula,

$$x = \frac{-4 \pm \sqrt{16 - 4 \times 1 \times (-57)}}{2}$$
$$= \frac{-4 \pm \sqrt{244}}{2}$$
$$= \frac{-4 \pm \sqrt{4}\sqrt{61}}{2}$$
$$= -2 \pm \sqrt{61}.$$

Since lengths cannot be negative, $x = -2 + \sqrt{61}$. Hence, the unknown sides have the following lengths.

$$x + 1 = -1 + \sqrt{61}$$
$$x + 3 = 1 + \sqrt{61}.$$

Q7. Applying the cosine rule in the situation shown below,

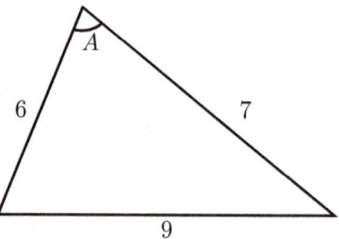

$$\cos(A) = \frac{6^2 + 7^2 - 9^2}{2 \times 6 \times 7}$$
$$= \frac{4}{84}$$
$$= \frac{1}{21}$$

Q8. The information given in the question leads to the diagram below

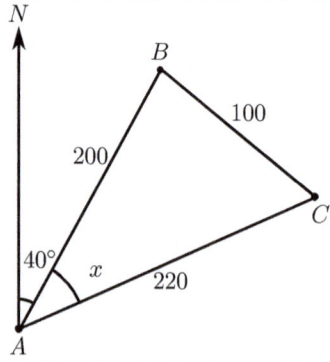

Applying the cosine rule,

$$\cos(x) = \frac{200^2 + 220^2 - 100^2}{2 \times 200 \times 220}$$
$$= \frac{49}{55}$$

Hence,

$$x = \arccos\left(\frac{49}{55}\right)$$
$$= 27.01229396$$
$$\approx 27°.$$

Therefore, the bearing of C from A is $40 + 27 = 67°$.

Worked Solutions — Exercise 15.1

Q1. (a)

$$\text{Gradient of Chord } AB = \frac{y_B - y_A}{x_B - x_A}$$
$$= \frac{\frac{27}{2} - \frac{1}{2}}{3 - 1}$$
$$= \frac{13}{2}$$
$$= 6.5.$$

(b)

$$\text{Gradient of Chord } AB = \frac{y_B - y_A}{x_B - x_A}$$
$$= \frac{\frac{125}{16} - \frac{1}{2}}{\frac{5}{2} - 1}$$
$$= \frac{39}{8}$$
$$= 4.875.$$

(c)

$$\text{Gradient of Chord } AB = \frac{y_B - y_A}{x_B - x_A}$$
$$= \frac{4 - \frac{1}{2}}{2 - 1}$$
$$= \frac{7}{2}$$
$$= 3.5.$$

(d)

$$\text{Gradient of Chord } AB = \frac{y_B - y_A}{x_B - x_A}$$
$$= \frac{\frac{343}{128} - \frac{1}{2}}{\frac{7}{4} - 1}$$
$$= \frac{93}{32}$$
$$= 2.90625.$$

(e)

$$\text{Gradient of Chord } AB = \frac{y_B - y_A}{x_B - x_A}$$
$$= \frac{\frac{27}{16} - \frac{1}{2}}{\frac{3}{2} - 1}$$
$$= \frac{19}{8}$$
$$= 2.375.$$

(f)

$$\text{Gradient of Chord } AB = \frac{y_B - y_A}{x_B - x_A}$$
$$= \frac{\frac{125}{128} - \frac{1}{2}}{\frac{5}{4} - 1}$$
$$= \frac{61}{32}$$
$$= 1.90625.$$

(g)

$$\text{Gradient of Chord } AB = \frac{y_B - y_A}{x_B - x_A}$$
$$= \frac{\frac{1331}{2000} - \frac{1}{2}}{\frac{11}{10} - 1}$$
$$= \frac{331}{200}$$
$$= 1.655.$$

From the values the gradient of the chord is decreasing, likely to 1.5, but further work would be required to confirm this.

Q2.
$$\begin{aligned}\frac{dx^5}{dx} &= \lim_{h\to 0}\frac{(x+h)^5-x^5}{h}\\ &= \lim_{h\to 0}\frac{(x^5+5x^4h+10x^3h^2+10x^2h^3+5xh^4+5h^5)-x^5}{h}\\ &= \lim_{h\to 0}\frac{5x^4h+10x^3h^2+10x^2h^3+5xh^4+5h^5}{h}\\ &= \lim_{h\to 0}5x^4+10x^3h+10x^2h^2+5xh^3+5h^4\\ &= 5x^4.\end{aligned}$$

Q3. Let $f(x)=\frac{1}{x}$, then

$$\begin{aligned}f'(x) &= \lim_{h\to 0}\frac{f(x+h)-f(x)}{h}\\ &= \lim_{h\to 0}\frac{\left(\frac{1}{x+h}\right)-\frac{1}{x}}{h}\\ &= \lim_{h\to 0}\frac{x-(x+h)}{hx(x+h)}\\ &= \lim_{h\to 0}\frac{-h}{hx(x+h)}\\ &= \lim_{h\to 0}-\frac{1}{x(x+h)}\\ &= -\frac{1}{x^2}.\end{aligned}$$

Q4. (a) When $x=5$,
$$\begin{aligned}y &= 3x^2\\ \Rightarrow\quad y &= 3\times 5^2\\ &= 75.\end{aligned}$$

Hence the point $(5,75)$ lies on the curve $y=3x^2$.

(b)
$$\begin{aligned}m &= \frac{d(3x^2)}{dx}\\ &= \lim_{h\to 0}\frac{3(x+h)^2-3x^2}{h}\\ &= \lim_{h\to 0}\frac{3(x^2+2xh+h^2)-3x^2}{h}\\ &= \lim_{h\to 0}\frac{6xh+h^2}{h}\\ &= \lim_{h\to 0}6x+3h.\end{aligned}$$

At the point A, $x = 5$, and hence,
$$m = \lim_{h \to 0} 30 + 3h.$$

(c) As $h \to 0$, $m \to 30$.

Q5. Let $f(x) = c$, for some constant value $c \in \mathbb{R}$.
$$\frac{df}{dx} = \lim_{h \to 0} \frac{f(x+h) - f(x)}{h}$$
$$= \lim_{h \to 0} \frac{c - c}{h}$$
$$= \lim_{h \to 0} 0$$
$$= 0.$$

Q6. Let $f(x) = 3x^2 + 5x$, then
$$f'(x) = \lim_{h \to 0} \frac{f(x+h) - f(x)}{h}$$
$$= \lim_{h \to 0} \frac{3(x+h)^2 + 5(x+h) - (3x^2 + 5x)}{h}$$
$$= \lim_{h \to 0} \frac{3x^2 + 6xh + 3h^2 + 5x + 5h - 3x^2 - 5x}{h}$$
$$= \lim_{h \to 0} \frac{6xh + 3h^2 + 5h}{h}$$
$$= \lim_{h \to 0} 6x + 3h + 5$$
$$= 6x + 5.$$

The functions (blue) are shown with their derivatives (red) in the graphs below.

(a)

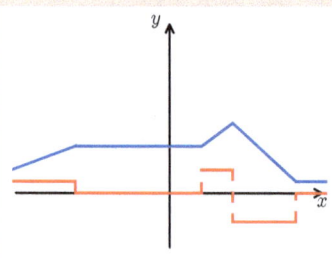

(b)

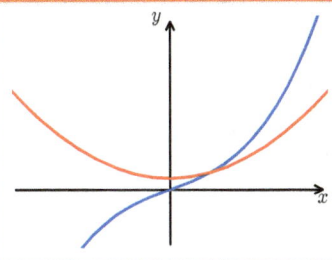

Q7. The function $f(x) = x^2 + x - 12$ is a quadratic.
(a) Note that,

$$x^2 + x - 12 = \left(x + \frac{1}{2}\right)^2 - \frac{1}{4} - 12$$
$$= \left(x + \frac{1}{2}\right)^2 - \frac{49}{4}.$$

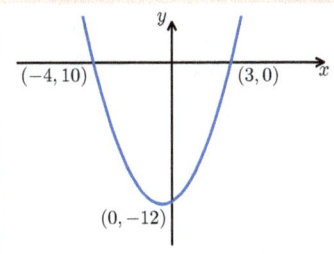

(b) The derivative is shown in red on the sketch below.

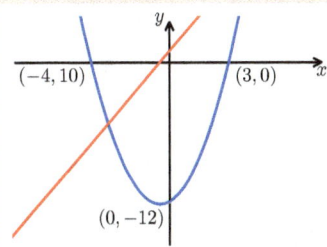

(c) At the vertex of the quadratic the gradient is zero.

Worked Solutions — Exercise 15.2

Q1. In this question we apply the fact that $y = x^n$ has derivative $\frac{dy}{dx} = nx^{n-1}$.
(a)
$$f(x) = x^6$$
$$\Rightarrow f'(x) = 6x^5$$

(b)
$$y = x^8$$
$$\Rightarrow \frac{dy}{dx} = 8x^7$$

(c)
$$f(x) = x^9$$
$$\Rightarrow f'(x) = 9x^8$$

(d)
$$y = x^{-4}$$
$$\Rightarrow \frac{dy}{dx} = -4x^{-5}$$

(e)
$$f(x) = x^{-7}$$
$$\Rightarrow f'(x) = -7x^{-8}$$

(f)
$$y = x^{-4}$$
$$\Rightarrow \frac{dy}{dx} = -4x^{-5}$$

(g)
$$f(x) = x^{\frac{1}{2}}$$
$$\Rightarrow f'(x) = \frac{1}{2}x^{-\frac{1}{2}}$$

(h)
$$y = x^{\frac{1}{5}}$$
$$\Rightarrow \frac{dy}{dx} = \frac{1}{5}x^{-\frac{4}{5}}$$

(i)
$$f(x) = x^{\frac{3}{4}}$$
$$\Rightarrow f'(x) = \frac{3}{4}x^{-\frac{1}{4}}$$

(j)
$$y = x^3 \times x^4$$
$$= x^7$$
$$\Rightarrow \frac{dy}{dx} = 7x^6$$

(k)
$$f(x) = x^6 \times x^{-2}$$
$$= x^4$$
$$\Rightarrow f'(x) = 4x^3$$

(l)
$$y = x^4 \times x^{\frac{1}{2}}$$
$$= x^{\frac{9}{2}}$$
$$\Rightarrow \frac{dy}{dx} = \frac{9}{2} x^{\frac{7}{2}}$$

(m)
$$f(x) = \frac{x^7}{x^4}$$
$$= x^3$$
$$\Rightarrow f'(x) = 3x^2$$

(n)
$$y = \frac{x^8}{x^2}$$
$$= x^6$$
$$\Rightarrow \frac{dy}{dx} = 6x^5$$

(o)
$$f(x) = \frac{x^7}{x^4}$$
$$= x^3$$
$$\Rightarrow f'(x) = 3x^2$$

(p)
$$y = \frac{x^8}{x^2}$$
$$= x^6$$
$$\Rightarrow \frac{dy}{dx} = 6x^5$$

(q)
$$f(x) = \frac{x^9}{x^{10}}$$
$$= x^{-1}$$
$$\Rightarrow f'(x) = -x^{-2}$$

(r)
$$y = \frac{x^4 \times x^5}{x^3}$$
$$= \frac{x^9}{x^3}$$
$$= x^6$$
$$\Rightarrow \frac{dy}{dx} = 6x^5$$

(s)
$$f(x) = \frac{x^7 \times x^3}{x}$$
$$= \frac{x^10}{x}$$
$$= x^9$$
$$\Rightarrow f'(x) = 9x^8$$

(t)
$$y = \frac{x^4}{x^3 \times x^7}$$
$$= \frac{x^4}{x^10}$$
$$= x^{-6}$$
$$\Rightarrow \frac{dy}{dx} = -6x^{-7}$$

(u)
$$f(x) = \frac{x^{\frac{1}{2}} \times x^{\frac{1}{4}}}{x}$$
$$= \frac{x^{\frac{3}{4}}}{x}$$
$$= x^{-\frac{1}{4}}$$
$$\Rightarrow f'(x) = -\frac{1}{4}x^{-\frac{5}{4}}$$
$$= -\frac{1}{4x^{\frac{5}{4}}}$$

(v)
$$y = \frac{x^{\frac{4}{3}} \times x^{\frac{7}{2}}}{x^4}$$
$$= \frac{x^{\frac{29}{6}}}{x^4}$$
$$= x^{\frac{5}{6}}$$
$$\Rightarrow \frac{dy}{dx} = \frac{5}{6}x^{-\frac{1}{6}}$$

Q2. Using the rule $y = ax^n \Rightarrow \frac{dy}{dx} = anx^{n-1}$.

(a)
$$y = 6x$$
$$\Rightarrow \frac{dy}{dx} = 6$$

(b)
$$f(x) = 7x^3$$
$$\Rightarrow f'(x) = 21x^2$$

(c)
$$y = 4x^7$$
$$\Rightarrow \frac{dy}{dx} = 28x^6$$

(d)
$$f(x) = 4x^{-3}$$
$$\Rightarrow f'(x) = -12x^{-4}$$

(e)
$$y = 12x^{-4}$$
$$\Rightarrow \frac{dy}{dx} = -48x^{-5}$$

(f)
$$f(x) = 7x^{-5}$$
$$\Rightarrow f'(x) = -35x^{-6}$$

(g)
$$y = -6x^{-3}$$
$$\Rightarrow \frac{dy}{dx} = 18x^{-4}$$

(h)
$$f(x) = -2x$$
$$\Rightarrow f'(x) = -2$$

(i)
$$y = -5x^{-1}$$
$$\Rightarrow \frac{dy}{dx} = 5x^{-6}$$

(j)
$$f(x) = \frac{1}{2}x^{\frac{1}{4}}$$
$$\Rightarrow f'(x) = \frac{1}{8}x^{-\frac{3}{4}}$$

(k)
$$y = -\frac{1}{4}x^{-2}$$
$$\Rightarrow \frac{dy}{dx} = \frac{1}{2}x^{-3}$$

(l)
$$f(x) = -\frac{1}{8}x^{-\frac{4}{5}}$$
$$\Rightarrow f'(x) = \frac{4}{40}x^{-\frac{9}{5}}$$
$$= \frac{1}{10}x^{-\frac{9}{5}}$$

Q3. We differentiate and then evaluate at the required point.

(a)
$$y = 4x^5$$
$$\Rightarrow \frac{dy}{dx} = 20x^4.$$

Hence, evaluating at $x = 4$,
$$\frac{dy}{dx}(4) = 20 \times 4^4$$
$$= 5120$$

(b)
$$y = 3x^2 + 3x - 5$$
$$\Rightarrow \frac{dy}{dx} = 6x + 3.$$

Hence, evaluating at $x = -2$,
$$\frac{dy}{dx}(-2) = 6 \times (-2) + 3$$
$$= -9$$

(c)
$$y = \frac{5x^4 + 2x}{x^3}$$
$$= 5x + 2x^{-2}$$
$$\Rightarrow \frac{dy}{dx} = 5 - 4x^{-3}.$$

Hence, evaluating at $x = 1$,
$$\frac{dy}{dx}(1) = 5 - \frac{4}{1^3}$$
$$= 1$$

(d)
$$y = 2x^3 + 4x - 5$$
$$\Rightarrow \frac{dy}{dx} = 6x^2 + 4$$

Hence, evaluating at $x = \frac{13}{27}$,
$$\frac{dy}{dx}\left(\frac{13}{27}\right) = 6 \times \left(\frac{13}{27}\right)^2 + 4$$
$$= \frac{1310}{243}$$

Q4. In this question, we differentiate the function and find the values of x for which $f'(x) < 0$ and $f'(x) > 0$. If $f'(x) < 0$ the function is decreasing, if $f'(x) > 0$ the function is increasing and if $f'(x) = 0$, the function is stationary.
(a)
$$f(x) = 2x + 5;$$
$$\Rightarrow f'(x) = 2,$$

hence, $f(x)$ is increasing for all $x \in \mathbb{R}$.
(b)
$$f(x) = x^2 + 2x + 1;$$
$$\Rightarrow f'(x) = 2x + 2$$
$$= 2(x+1).$$

$f'(x) < 0$ and hence $f(x)$ is decreasing for $x < -1$, $f'(x) > 0$ and hence $f(x)$ is increasing for $x > -1$. $f(x)$ is stationary for $x = -1$.
(c)
$$f(x) = x^3 + 2x + 6;$$
$$\Rightarrow f'(x) = 3x^2 + 5.$$

$f'(x) > 0$ and hence $f(x)$ is decreasing for all $x \in \mathbb{R}$.
(d)
$$f(x) = x^4 + 6x^2 + 3;$$
$$\Rightarrow f'(x) = 4x^3 + 12x$$
$$= 4x \underbrace{(x^2 + 4)}_{>0}.$$

$f'(x) < 0$ and hence $f(x)$ is decreasing for $x < 0$, $f'(x) > 0$ and hence $f(x)$ is increasing for $x > 0$. $f(x)$ is stationary at $x = 0$.

Q5. For this question, we use $\sqrt{x} = x^{1/2}$, $\sqrt[3]{x} = x^{1/3}$ and $1/x^a = x^{-a}$. Then we use the fact that the derivative of a sum of terms is equal to the derivative of each term summed.
 (a) $\frac{dy}{dx} = 12x^3 + 6x^2 + 4$;
 (b) $f'(x) = 12x^2 + 2x$;
 (c) $\frac{dy}{dx} = 36x^5 - 20x^4 + 9x^2 + 8x + 1$;
 (d) $f'(x) = \frac{3}{2}x^2 + \frac{4}{3}x - \frac{3}{4}$;
 (e) $\frac{dy}{dx} = 3x^3 + \frac{4}{3}x - \frac{1}{5}$;
 (f) $f'(x) = \frac{35}{3}x^4 + \frac{8}{3}x^3 + \frac{9}{4}x^2 - x + 2$;
 (g) $\frac{dy}{dx} = \frac{3}{4}x^{-\frac{1}{2}} + 2x^{\frac{3}{2}}$;
 (h) $f'(x) = \frac{28}{15}x^{\frac{4}{3}} + \frac{12}{25}x^{-\frac{1}{5}} - \frac{2}{9}x^{-\frac{1}{3}}$;
 (i) $\frac{dy}{dx} = \frac{18}{25}x^{\frac{1}{6}} - \frac{1}{2}x^{-\frac{1}{4}} + \frac{1}{6}x^{-\frac{1}{2}}$;
 (j) $f'(x) = -16x^{-5} + 6x^{-3} + 2x^{-4}$;

(k) $\frac{dy}{dx} = 3 + 2x^{-2} + 12x^{-3}$;

(l) $f'(x) = 8x + 3 + \frac{7}{3}x^{-2} - \frac{20}{7}x^{-3}$;

(m) $\frac{dy}{dx} = \frac{10}{12}x^{\frac{1}{4}} + \frac{4}{10}x^{-\frac{1}{2}} + \frac{1}{5x^{\frac{3}{2}}} + \frac{9}{16x^{\frac{7}{4}}}$;

(n) $f'(x) = \frac{8}{3}x - x^{-\frac{1}{2}} - \frac{3}{2}x^{-\frac{3}{2}} - \frac{3}{4\sqrt{x}} + \frac{4}{9x^{\frac{4}{3}}}$;

(o) $\frac{dy}{dx} = 7x^6 - \frac{10}{12}x^{\frac{1}{4}} + \frac{1}{3\sqrt{x}} + \frac{1}{x^{\frac{6}{5}}}$

Q6. In parts (a)-(l), we multiply out the brackets and then differentiate. In parts (m)-(x), we simplify the expression and then differentiate.

(a)
$$y = x(x^2 - 3x + 2)$$
$$= x^3 - 3x^2 + 2x,$$
$$\Rightarrow \quad \frac{dy}{dx} = 3x^2 - 6x + 2$$
$$= 3x(x-2) + 2.$$

(b)
$$f(x) = 4x(2x^2 + 3x - 4)$$
$$= 8x^3 + 12x^2 - 16x,$$
$$\Rightarrow \quad f'(x) = 24x^2 + 24x - 16$$
$$= 8(3x^2 + 3x - 2).$$

(c)
$$y = 3x^2(4x^3 + 2x)$$
$$= 12x^5 + 6x^3,$$
$$\Rightarrow \quad \frac{dy}{dx} = 60x^4 + 18x^2$$
$$= 6x^2(10x^2 + 3).$$

(d)
$$f(x) = (3x-4)(2x+1)$$
$$= 6x^2 - 5x - 4,$$
$$\Rightarrow \quad f'(x) = 12x - 5.$$

(e)
$$y = (2x-6)(2x+4)$$
$$= 4x^2 - 4x - 24,$$
$$\Rightarrow \quad \frac{dy}{dx} = 8x - 4$$
$$= 4(2x-1).$$

(f)
$$f(x) = (3x+4)(4x+1)$$
$$= 12x^2 + 19x + 4,$$
$$\Rightarrow f'(x) = 24x + 19.$$

(g)
$$y = (2x^2+5)(3x+1)$$
$$= 6x^3 + 2x^2 + 15x + 5,$$
$$\Rightarrow \frac{dy}{dx} = 18x^2 + 4x + 15$$
$$= 2x(9x+2) + 15.$$

(h)
$$f(x) = (3x^2+5)(2x-5)$$
$$= 6x^3 - 15x^2 + 10x - 25,$$
$$\Rightarrow f'(x) = 18x^2 - 30x + 10$$
$$= 2(9x^2 - 15x + 5).$$

(i)
$$y = (3x^2+4)(3x^2-5)$$
$$= 9x^4 - 3x^2 - 20,$$
$$\Rightarrow \frac{dy}{dx} = 36x^3 - 6x$$
$$= 6x(6x^2 - 1).$$

(j)
$$f(x) = \left(\frac{1}{x}+5\right)(2x-3)$$
$$= 10x - 13 - \frac{3}{x},$$
$$\Rightarrow f'(x) = 10 + \frac{3}{x^2}.$$

(k)
$$y = \left(\frac{2}{x}-5\right)\left(\frac{3}{x}+1\right)$$
$$= -5 - \frac{13}{x} + \frac{6}{x^2},$$
$$\Rightarrow \frac{dy}{dx} = \frac{13}{x^2} - \frac{12}{x^3}$$
$$= \frac{13x - 12}{x^3}.$$

(l)
$$f(x) = \left(2x + \frac{1}{x}\right)\left(\frac{1}{x^2} + 4x\right)$$
$$= 8x^2 + \frac{2}{x} + \frac{1}{x^3} + 4,$$
$$\Rightarrow \quad f'(x) = 16x - \frac{2}{x^2} - \frac{3}{x^4}.$$

(m)
$$y = \frac{3x+4}{x} = 3 + 4x^{-1},$$
$$\Rightarrow \quad \frac{\mathrm{d}y}{\mathrm{d}x} = -4x^{-2}$$
$$= -\frac{4}{x^2}.$$

(n)
$$f(x) = \frac{6x+7}{2x}$$
$$= 3 + \frac{7x^{-1}}{2},$$
$$\Rightarrow \quad f'(x) = -\frac{7x^{-2}}{2}$$
$$= -\frac{7}{2x^2}.$$

(o)
$$y = \frac{8x + 9x^2}{2x} = 4 + \frac{9x}{2},$$
$$\Rightarrow \quad \frac{\mathrm{d}y}{\mathrm{d}x} = \frac{9}{2}.$$

(p)
$$f(x) = \frac{8x + 7x^2}{2x^2}$$
$$= 4x^{-1} + \frac{7}{2},$$
$$\Rightarrow \quad f'(x) = -4x^{-2}$$
$$= -\frac{4}{x^2}.$$

(q)
$$y = \frac{6x^3 + 3x}{3x^3} = 2 + x^{-2},$$
$$\Rightarrow \quad \frac{\mathrm{d}y}{\mathrm{d}x} = -2x^{-3} = -\frac{2}{x^3}.$$

(r)
$$f(x) = \frac{7x^4 + 3x^2 + 6x}{2x^2}$$
$$= \frac{7}{2}x^2 + \frac{3}{2} + 3x^{-1},$$
$$\Rightarrow f'(x) = 7x - 3x^{-2}$$
$$= 7x - \frac{3}{x^2}.$$

(s)
$$y = \frac{2x^3 + 4x}{\sqrt{x}}$$
$$= 2x^{5/2} + 4x^{1/2},$$
$$\Rightarrow \frac{dy}{dx} = 5x^{3/2} + 2x^{-1/2}$$
$$= 5x^{3/2} + \frac{2}{x^{1/2}}$$
$$= \frac{5x^2 + 2}{\sqrt{x}}.$$

(t)
$$f(x) = \frac{4x^2 - 3x + 2}{\sqrt[3]{x}}$$
$$= 4x^{5/3} - 3x^{2/3} + 2x^{-1/3},$$
$$\Rightarrow f'(x) = \frac{20}{3}x^{2/3} - 2x^{-1/3} - \frac{2}{3}x^{-4/3}$$
$$= \frac{20}{3}x^{2/3} - \frac{2}{\sqrt[3]{x}} + \frac{3}{3x^{4/3}}$$
$$= \frac{2(10x^2 - 3x - 1)}{3x^{4/3}}.$$

(u)
$$y = \frac{3x^4 + 2x^2 + 4x}{3\sqrt{x}}$$
$$= x^{7/2} + \frac{2}{3}x^{3/2} + \frac{4}{3}x^{1/2},$$
$$\Rightarrow \frac{dy}{dx} = \frac{7}{2}x^{5/2} + x^{1/2} + \frac{2}{3}x^{-1/2}$$
$$= \frac{7}{2}x^{5/2} + x^{1/2} + \frac{2}{3\sqrt{x}}$$
$$= \frac{21x^3 + 6x + 4}{6\sqrt{x}}.$$

(v)
$$f(x) = \frac{4x^3 + 3x + 2}{2x^{2/3}}$$
$$= 2x^{7/3} + \frac{3}{2}x^{1/3} + x^{-2/3},$$
$$\Rightarrow f'(x) = \frac{14}{3}x^{4/3} + \frac{x^{-2/3}}{2} - \frac{2x^{-5/3}}{3}$$
$$= \frac{28x^3 + 3x - 4}{6x^{5/3}}.$$

(w)
$$y = \frac{x^7 + 6x^2 + 5x + 3}{3x^{2/5}}$$
$$= \frac{1}{3}x^{33/5} + 2x^{8/5} + \frac{5x^{3/5}}{3} + x^{-2/5},$$
$$\Rightarrow \frac{\mathrm{d}y}{\mathrm{d}x} = \frac{11}{5}x^{28/5} + \frac{16}{5}x^{3/5} + x^{-2/5} - \frac{2}{5}x^{-7/5}$$
$$= \frac{11x^7 + 16x^2 + 5x - 2}{5x^{7/5}}.$$

(x)
$$f(x) = \frac{2x^3 + 3x + 4}{3x^{5/3}}$$
$$= \frac{2}{3}x^{4/3} + x^{-2/3} + \frac{4}{3}x^{-5/3},$$
$$\Rightarrow f'(x) = \frac{8}{9}x^{1/3} - \frac{2}{3}x^{-5/3} - \frac{20}{9}x^{-8/3}$$
$$= \frac{2(4x^3 - 3x - 10)}{9x^{\frac{8}{3}}}.$$

Q7. (a)
$$y = x^{1/2}$$
$$\Rightarrow \frac{\mathrm{d}y}{\mathrm{d}x} = \frac{1}{2}x^{-1/2}$$
$$\Rightarrow \frac{\mathrm{d}^2y}{\mathrm{d}x^2} = -\frac{1}{4}x^{-3/2} = -\frac{1}{4x^{3/2}}.$$

At $x = 2$, $\frac{\mathrm{d}^2y}{\mathrm{d}x^2} = -\frac{1}{4\sqrt{8}} = -\frac{1}{8\sqrt{2}}.$

(b)
$$y = x^2 + 2\sqrt{x} = x^2 + 2x^{1/2},$$
$$\Rightarrow \frac{\mathrm{d}y}{\mathrm{d}x} = 2x + x^{-1/2}$$
$$\Rightarrow \frac{\mathrm{d}^2y}{\mathrm{d}x^2} = 2 - \frac{x^{-3/2}}{2} = 2 - \frac{1}{2x^{3/2}}.$$

At $x=2$, $\frac{d^2y}{dx^2} = 2 - \frac{1}{2\sqrt{8}} = \frac{8\sqrt{2}-1}{4\sqrt{2}}$.

(c)
$$y = x^3 + 5x + 6,$$
$$\Rightarrow \frac{dy}{dx} = 3x^2 + 5$$
$$\Rightarrow \frac{d^2y}{dx^2} = 6x.$$

At $x=2$, $\frac{d^2y}{dx^2} = 12$.

Worked Solutions — Exercise 16.1

Q1. (a) We know that
$$\frac{d}{dx}(x^4) = 4x^3$$

Therefore, we can use the Fundamental Theorem of Calculus to deduce that one antiderivative of $y = x^3$ is $\frac{1}{4}x^4$.

In order to capture all possible solutions we need to add a constant, so the antiderivative of $y = x^3$ is
$$\frac{1}{4}x^4 + c$$

(b) The area under the curve up to x is
$$A(x) = \frac{1}{4}x^4 + c.$$

We need to find the unknown constant, c. We can see that when $x = 0$, $A = 0$. Substituting back into the equation above we obtain $c = 0$. Therefore, the area is
$$A(2) = \frac{1}{4}(2)^4 = \frac{1}{4}(16) = 4.$$

(c) First, sketch the curve and the rectangles we are using for the approximation.

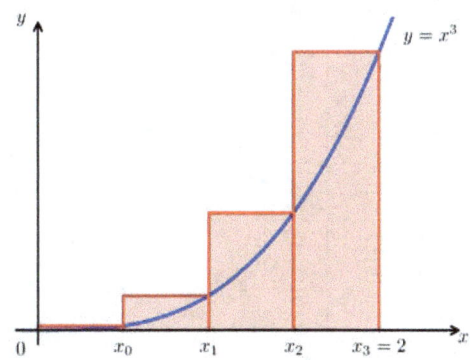

The end-points are given by

$x_1 = 0.5$,
$x_2 = 1$,
$x_3 = 1.5$, and
$x_4 = 2$.

The heights of the rectangles are calculated using $y = x_i^3$:

$y_1 = 0.125$,
$y_2 = 1$,
$y_3 = 3.375$, and
$y_4 = 8$.

The width of each rectangle is $\delta x = 0.5$, therefore, the area of each rectangle is given by $\delta x \cdot y_i$:

$$A \approx 0.5(0.125 + 1 + 3.375 + 8) = 6.25.$$

(d) The accuracy is given by the difference between the precise area, calculated using the antiderivative, and the area approximated using the rectangle method, divided by the precise area.

$$\frac{|4 - 6.25|}{4} = 0.5625.$$

Q2. (a) First, calculate the approximation to the area using the rectangle method evaluated at the midpoint of each rectangle.

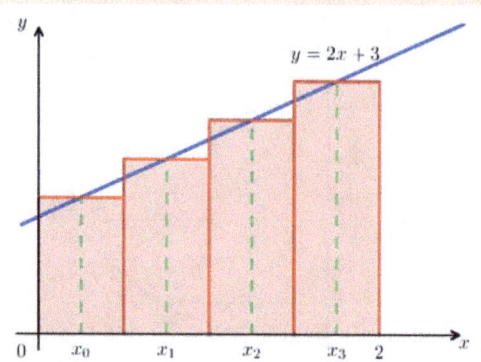

The midpoints are at

$x_1 = 0.25,$
$x_2 = 0.75,$
$x_3 = 1.25,$ and
$x_4 = 1.75.$

The heights of the rectangles are equal to $y_i = 2x_i + 3$:

$y_1 = 3.5,$
$y_2 = 4.5,$
$y_3 = 5.5,$ and
$y_4 = 6.5.$

The width of each rectangle is $\delta x = 0.5$, therefore, the area of each rectangle is $\delta x \cdot y_i$:

$$A \approx 0.5(3.5 + 4.5 + 5.5 + 6.5) = 10.$$

(b) Now we use the antiderivative method to calculate the area. We know that

$$\frac{\mathrm{d}}{\mathrm{d}x}(x^2 + x) = 2x + 1.$$

Therefore, we can use the Fundamental Theorem of Calculus to deduce that one antiderivative of $y = 2x + 3$ is $x^2 + 3x$. In order to capture all possible solutions we need to add a constant, so the antiderivative is

$$x(x + 3) + c.$$

This gives us the area under the curve up to x as

$$A(x) = x(x + 3) + c.$$

When $x = 0$, $A = 0$, therefore, $c = 0$.
Evaluating for the area up to $x = 2$ gives
$$A(2) = 2(2+3) = 10.$$

(c) Since $y = 2x+3$ is a straight line, we can also use geometric area formulae to compute the area. The shape bounded by $y = 2x+3$, the x-axis, the y-axis, and $x = 2$ is a trapezium.

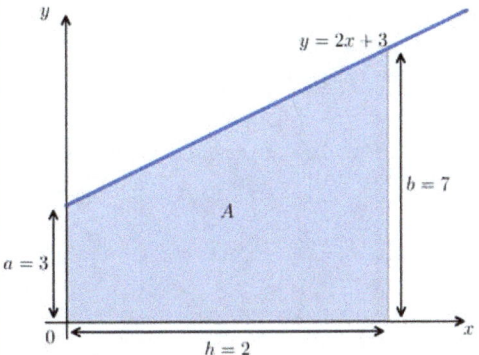

The area of a trapezium is given by
$$A = \frac{a+b}{2} \cdot h = \frac{3+7}{2} \cdot 2 = 10.$$

The area calculated with each of the three methods is $A = 10$. Therefore, the error of the rectangle method in this case is 0. This is because $y = f(x)$ is a straight line so each rectangle has the same amount of area above $f(x)$ as below it.

Worked Solutions — Exercise 16.2
Q1. (a) The indefinite integral is $x^4 + c$.
   (b) The integrand is $4x^3$.
   (c) The constant of integration is c.
   (d) The integration variable is x.
Q2. The following solutions show every step in the process, however, some students may be able to skip some of the steps. Students may use any letter to represent the constant of integration provided it is not x (or t where relevant), or e to avoid confusion with the exponential.
   (a) First use (16.7):
$$\int 3x^2 \, dx = 3 \int x^2 \, dx.$$

From Formula 16.1:
$$\int x^2 \, dx = \frac{1}{3}x^3 + c.$$

Therefore,
$$\int 3x^2 \, dx = 3 \cdot \frac{1}{3}x^3 + 3c = x^3 + k.$$

(b) Using (16.7)
$$\int 6x^{3/2} \, dx = 6 \int x^{3/2} \, dx$$

Fractional powers of x are treated the same as integer powers, therefore we can use Formula 16.1 as usual:
$$\int x^{3/2} \, dx = \frac{2}{5}x^{5/2} + c.$$

Therefore,
$$\int 6x^{3/2} \, dx = 6 \cdot \frac{2}{5}x^{5/2} + 6c = \frac{12}{5}x^{5/2} + k.$$

(c) First we expand the integrand
$$(5x+2)(x^2-3) = 5x^3 + 2x^2 - 15x - 6.$$

Therefore, using Formulae 16.2, we have
$$\int (5x+2)(x^2-3) \, dx = \int 5x^3 + 2x^2 - 15x - 6 \, dx$$
$$= 5 \int x^3 \, dx + 2 \int x^2 \, dx - 15 \int x \, dx - 6 \int 1 \, dx.$$

From Formula 16.1
$$\int x^3 \, dx = \frac{1}{4}x^4 + c_1,$$
$$\int x^2 \, dx = \frac{1}{3}x^3 + c_2,$$
$$\int x \, dx = \frac{1}{2}x^2 + c_3,$$
$$\int 1 \, dx = x + c_4.$$

Therefore,
$$\int (5x+2)(x^2-3) \, dx = \frac{5}{4}x^4 + 5c_1 + \frac{2}{3}x^3 + 2c_2 - \frac{15}{2}x^2 - 15c_3 - 6x - 6c_4$$
$$= \frac{5}{4}x^4 + \frac{2}{3}x^3 - \frac{15}{2}x^2 - 6x + k.$$

(d) First expand the brackets of the integrand:
$$x(x^2 + 2) = x^3 + 2x.$$

Next use (16.8) and (16.7):
$$F(x) = \int x^3 + 2x \, dx = \int x^3 \, dx + 2 \int x \, dx.$$

From Formula 16.1
$$\int x^3 \, dx = \frac{1}{4}x^4 + c_1$$
$$\int x \, dx = \frac{1}{2}x^2 + c_2.$$

Therefore,
$$F(x) = \frac{1}{4}x^4 + c_1 + \frac{2}{2}x^2 + 2c_2 = \frac{1}{4}x^4 + x^2 + k.$$

We are told that $F(x) = 1$ when $x = 1$. We can use this information to find the actual value of k for this problem by substituting back into the solution above.
$$1 = \frac{1}{4}(1)^4 + 1^2 + k = \frac{5}{4} + k.$$

Rearranging we obtain
$$k = 1 - \frac{5}{4} = -\frac{1}{4}$$

Substituting back into the general solution we obtain the solution particular to this problem:
$$F(x) = \frac{1}{4}(x^4 + 4x^2 - 1).$$

(e) The dt shows that the variable of integration in this problem is t. Therefore, we can use Formula 16.1 with t in place of x as follows:
$$\int t^3 \, dt = \frac{1}{4}t^4 + c.$$

(f) We know that
$$\frac{1}{x^3} = x^{-3}.$$

Therefore, we can use Formula 16.1 immediately:
$$\int \frac{1}{x^3} \, dx = \int x^{-3} \, dx = -\frac{1}{2}x^{-2} + c.$$

(g) The dt shows that we must integrate with respect to the variable t. Therefore, we treat any other values in the problem (in this case, x^4) as constants. We first use (16.7):

$$\int x^4 \, dt = x^4 \int 1 \, dt.$$

Then, using Formula 16.1 we have

$$\int 1 \, dt = t + c.$$

Therefore,

$$\int x^4 \, dt = x^4(t + c).$$

(h) First expand the brackets in the integrand:

$$\left(\frac{1}{x^2} + 3\right)(x^2 - 1) = 1 + 3x^2 - \frac{1}{x^2} - 3 = 3x^2 - x^{-2} - 2.$$

Therefore, using Formulae 16.2

$$\int \left(\frac{1}{x^2} + 3\right)(x^2 - 1) \, dx = 3 \int x^2 \, dx - \int x^{-2} \, dx - 2 \int 1 \, dx.$$

Applying Formula 16.1 to each term on the right hand side we get

$$\int x^2 \, dx = \frac{1}{3}x^3 + c_1,$$

$$\int x^{-2} \, dx = -x^{-1} + c_2,$$

$$\int 1 \, dx = x + c_3.$$

Therefore,

$$\int \left(\frac{1}{x^2} + 3\right)(x^2 - 1) \, dx = 3 \cdot \frac{1}{3}x^3 + 3c_1 - (-x^{-1} + c_2) - 2x - 2c_3$$

$$= x^3 + \frac{1}{x} - 2x + k.$$

We are told that $F(3) = 21$. Substituting into our solution above we obtain

$$21 = 27 + \frac{1}{3} - 6 + k.$$

Rearranging we see that $k = -\frac{1}{3}$. Therefore, our full solution is

$$\int \left(\frac{1}{x^2} + 3\right)(x^2 - 1) \, dx = x^3 + \frac{1}{x} - 2x - \frac{1}{3}.$$

4. Worked Solutions - Chapters 17 to 21

Worked Solutions — Exercise 17.1

Q1. The similarities of the graphs are:
- Both graphs have values for all $x \in \mathbb{R}$
- Both graphs have a y-intercept at $(0, 1)$.
- Both graphs grow very large, very quickly.
- There are no negative values for $f(x)$ or $g(x)$, and both graphs tend to zero as x approaches $-\infty$

The difference in the graphs is that for $g(x)$, the graph increases at a faster rate than $f(x)$.

Q2. The graphs should look like this:

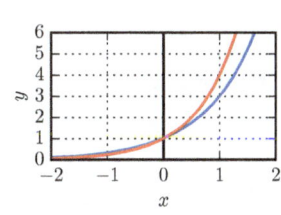

(a) The red curve
(b) The blue curve

Q3. Both the graphs for (a) and (c) will look like this:

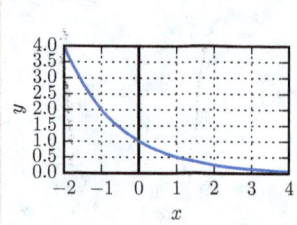

(b) This graph is a 'downhill' shape. It approaches zero as x approaches $+\infty$.
(d) Both graph are the same. This is because:

$$y = \frac{1}{2}^x = (2^{-1})^x = 2^{-x}.$$

Q4. (a) The distinguishing features of an exponential graph are:
- The graphs have a y-intercept at $(0,1)$
- The domain is $x \in \mathbb{R}$
- The range is $f(x) > 0$
- The graph is increasing when $a > 1$ and decreasing when $0 < a < 1$
- The graphs are asymptotic to the x-axis as x approaches $-\infty$ when $a > 1$ and as x approaches ∞ when $0 < a < 1$
- The graphs are smooth and continuous.

(b) $a > 0$ otherwise it could lead to calculations such as $-2^{\frac{1}{2}}$, which has no real answer. $a \neq 1$ because when $a = 1$, the answer will always be 1, and therefore the function will not be exponential.

Worked Solutions — Exercise 17.2

Q1. (b)
Q2. (d)
Q3. (d)
Q4. For $V = 10\,000 \times 1.024^t$:
(a) £10,000
(b) The multiplier is 1.024, therefore the *interest rate* is $1.024 - 1 = 0.24 = 2.4\%$
(c)

$$V = 10000 \times 1.024^4$$
$$= 10995.12$$

(d) Using the TABLE function on a calculator for $V = 10\,000 \times 1.024^t$, it can be seen that for:

$$t = 29, V = 19892,$$
$$= 30, V = 20370$$

Therefore, the initial investments doubles after 30 years.
(e) After 8 years there is $V = 10000 \times 1.024^8 = 12089$ left in the account.
If half of this is removed, then there is now £6044.50 left in the account.
The investor now leaves this in for a further 5 years, at the same interest rate:
So $V = 6044.5 \times 1.024^5 = 6805.50$.

Q5. Find the growth factor between each piece of data.

Year	Value	Growth Factor
2000	£2700	
2001	£3240	1.20
2002	£3890	1.20
2003	£4670	1.20
2004	£5600	1.20
2005	£6720	1.20

All growth factors are 1.20 to 3 s.f. and therefore the growth is approximately exponential.

(a) The approximate percentage increase of the value each year is 20%.
(b) $V = 2700 \times 1.2^t$.
(c) The value in 2008:

$$V = 2700 \times 1.2^8,$$
$$= 8629.73.$$

Q6. Any scenario where the initial value is 5.4 and the growth factor is 1.06. This could be also be any situation with a percentage increase of 6%.

Q7. Comparing consecutive years' populations gives a common growth factor of 1.013 or 1.014.
Using this can give a model of $P = 138.8 \times 1.013^t$ where P is the population over t years.
Using the TABLE function on the calculator with this model shows that the population may exceed 200 million 29 years after 2006, that is 2035.
The answer is after 27 years (2033) if the growth factor of 1.014 is used.

Q8. There are several ways to answer this.
One possible model is to say that the 7 cells double every 40 minutes and therefore a possible equation could be,

$$B = 7 \times 2^t,$$

where B is the number of bacteria after t lots of 40 minute intervals.
Using this model, we need to see how many 40 minute intervals there are in 10 hours:

$10 \times 60 \div 40 = 15$

So we can use the formula with $t = 15$:

$$B = 7 \times 2^{15} = 229376.$$

This shows that the estimate of 2 million cells is not sensible.

Worked Solutions — Exercise 17.3

Q1. Answers below
- (a) 32
- (b) 0.32
- (c) The percentage decrease is $1 - 0.32 = 0.68 = 68\%$

Q2. Answers below
- (a) $I = 200 \times 0.7^t$
- (b) After 4 hours they have $I = 200 \times 0.7^4 = 48.02$mg left in their system. Once they take another tablet, they will then have 248.02mg.
- (c) After a further 4 hours they have $I = 248.02 \times 0.7^4 = 59.55$mg left in their system. Once they take another tablet, they will then have 259.55mg.

Q3. Answers below
- (a) $V = 64000 \times 0.86^t$
- (b) $V = 64000 \times 0.86^2 = 47334.40$
- (c) See graph below

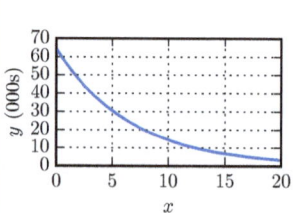

- (d) From the graph, drawing a horizontal line across at 32000, an estimate can be made between 4 and 5 years.

Worked Solutions — Exercise 17.4

Q1. Graphs shown below.
- (a) $y = e^{2x}$

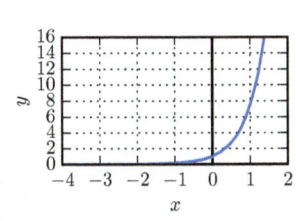

(b) $y = e^{-3x}$

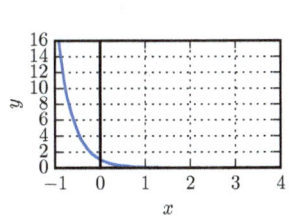

(c) $y = \frac{3}{2}e^{-2x}$

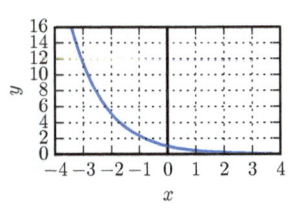

(d) $y = e^{\frac{x}{2}}$

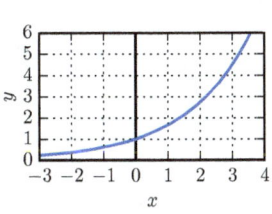

Q2. $V = 24\,000 e^{-0.2t}$
  (a) The original value is £24 000.
  (b) $V = 24\,000 e^{-0.2 \times 3} = 13171$ (nearest £)
  (c) Using the TABLE function on the calculator and the function $V = 24\,000 e^{-0.2t}$, we can see that after 3 years it will be worth £13 171, and after 4 years it will be worth £10 783, therefore, it will first be less than half its value after 4 years.

(d) The graph is shown below.

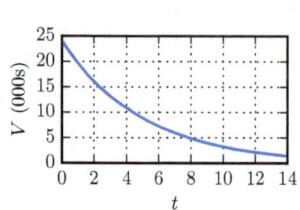

Q3. Using the TABLE function on the calculator and the function $P = 12\,000e^{-0.4t}$, we can see that it will take 6 years for there to be 1089 owls and 7 years for there to be 730 owls. Therefore, it takes 7 years to fall below 1000 owls for the first time.

Q4. (a) At time $t = 0$,

$$I = 150 - 120e^{-0.16 \times 0},$$
$$= 150 - 120,$$
$$= 30.$$

(b) When $t = 10$,

$$I = 150 - 120e^{-0.16 \times 10},$$
$$= 125.77.$$

We would expect around 125/126 sheep to be infected after 10 days.

(c) As $t \to \infty$, $e^{-0.16t} \to 0$, hence $I \to 150 - 120 \times 0 = 150$. The model predicts that eventually the whole population of sheep will become infected.

(d) A sketch showing the salient features is shown below.

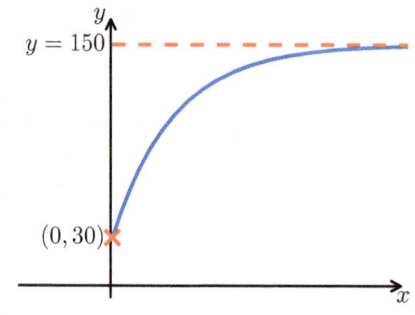

Worked Solutions — Exercise 19.1

Q1. (a) Taking the inverse sine gives us a solution in the first quadrant,

$$\theta = \sin^{-1}(0.338) = 19.8°.$$

There is another solution in the second quadrant, which we can find either by sketching out a graph of the sine function, or drawing the angles on the unit circle. In either case, we find that

$$\theta = 180 - 19.8 = 160.2°.$$

The sine function is negative in the third and fourth quadrants, and so the only solutions in the given range are $\theta = 19.8°, 160.2°$.

(b) Taking the inverse cosine of both sides of this equation gives us the solution

$$2\theta = \cos^{-1}(0.848) = 32.01°.$$

This is the solution in the first quadrant. The cosine function is positive in the fourth quadrant as well, and so there is another solution,

$$2\theta = (360 - 32.01)° = 327.99°.$$

Therefore, the full set of solutions is given by $2\theta = (32.01 + 360n)°$ and $2\theta = (327.99 + 360n)°$ for any integer n.

Putting these two solutions together, we have

$$\theta = \begin{cases} (16.0 + 180n)°, \\ (164.0 + 180n)°, \end{cases}$$

for any $n \in \mathbb{Z}$. We must select all of the values for which $-180° < \theta < 180°$. From the first set of solutions, θ lies in the given range when $n = -1$ and $n = 0$, giving $\theta = -164.0°$ and $\theta = 16.0°$. From the second set of solutions, we obtain the values $\theta = -16.0°$ and $\theta = 164.0°$. Therefore we have

$$\theta = \pm 164.0°, \quad \pm 16.0°.$$

(c) Taking the inverse cosine, we have the solution $\theta - 20° = 60°$. There is also a solution in the fourth quadrant, given by $\theta - 20° = -60°$. We can find other solutions by adding multiples of $360°$ to these, but none of these solutions will give values of θ lying in the specified range.

Therefore the solutions in the range are $\theta = 80°$ and $\theta = -40°$.

(d) Taking the inverse tangent will give some solution in the second or fourth quadrants. Calculators may give the result $-79.7°$ or $100.3°$. If, for example, we start with the result $-79.7°$, then the full set of solutions is given by

$$(-79.7 + 180n)° \quad \text{for } n \in \mathbb{Z}.$$

This will give the same set of results, whichever value is taken as the initial solution.

The solutions in the given range are $\theta = 280.3°$ and $\theta = 460.3°$.

(e) Taking the inverse sine of the equation gives us the solution

$$4\theta + 25° = -7.47°.$$

Calculators may give this angle as $352.53°$ instead. Both of these solutions refer to the same point in the fourth quadrant. There is another solution in the third quadrant which we can express as $187.47°$.

There is therefore one set of solutions of the form $4\theta + 25° = (-7.47 + 360n)°$ and another set of the form $4\theta + 25° = (187.47 + 360n)°$ for $n \in \mathbb{Z}$. We can therefore give the full set of solutions as

$$\theta = \begin{cases} \frac{1}{4}(-7.47 - 25 + 360n) = (-8.12 + 90n)°, \\ \frac{1}{4}(187.47 - 2540.62 + 360n) = (40.62 + 90n)°, \end{cases}$$

for any $n \in \mathbb{Z}$. The first form of solution does not give any values in the required range. The second form of solution gives the result $\theta = 40.6°$.

(f) We can transform the cosine into a sine using the identity $\cos(x) = \sin(x + 90°)$. This gives us

$$2\sin(2\theta) + 3\sin(2\theta) = 5\sin(2\theta) = 2.4.$$

Therefore, $\sin(2\theta) = 0.48$. This has solutions in the first quadrants with $2\theta = (28.69 + 360n)°$, and in the second quadrant with $2\theta = (151.31 + 360n)°$. We can therefore write the solutions as

$$\theta = \begin{cases} \frac{1}{2}(28.69 + 360n) = (14.34 + 180n)°, \\ \frac{1}{2}(151.31 + 360n) = (75.66 + 180n)°, \end{cases}$$

for any $n \in \mathbb{Z}$. The only values with $|\theta| < 90°$ are with $n = 0$, giving solutions $\theta = 14.3°$ and $\theta = 75.7°$.

Q2. The equation $\cos(x) = 0.6$ has solutions $53.13°$ in the first quadrant and $306.87°$ in the fourth quadrant. Therefore, the set of possible solutions can be written as

$$a\theta = \begin{cases} 53.13 - 25 + 360n = (28.13 + 360n)°, \\ 306.87 - 25 + 360n = (281.87 + 360n)°, \end{cases}$$

for any $n \in \mathbb{Z}$.

The smallest positive solution is $\theta = 28.13/a$. There must be at least one solution in the range $[0°, 10°]$, and so we want to find a value of a for which $28.13/a$ is smaller than $10°$. This gives us the inequality $28.13 < 10a$, and so $a \geq 3$.

The solutions when $a = 3$ and $n = 0$ are $\theta = 9.38°$ and $\theta = 93.96°$. For $n = 1$, the solutions are $\theta = 129.38°$ and $\theta = 213.96°$ and the remaining positive solutions will be larger still. Therefore, for $a = 3$ we have one solution in the range $[0°, 10°]$ and exactly two solutions with $\theta \in [0°, 100°]$, as required.

When $a = 4$ and $n = 0$, we have the solutions $\theta = 7.03°$ and $\theta = 70.47°$. For $n = 1$, we have the solutions $\theta = 97.03°$ and $\theta = 160.47°$. Therefore, there are now more than two solutions in the range $\theta \in [0°, 100°]$. As a increases, we will have more solutions in this range, and so $a = 3$ is the only possible value with the required number of values in each range.

The corresponding solutions in the given range are $\theta = 9.38°$ and $\theta = 93.96°$.

Q3. (a) Taking square roots gives us $3\cos(\theta) = \pm 2$. The equation $\cos(\theta) = \frac{2}{3}$ gives us solutions $\theta = 41.8°$ and $\theta = 138.2°$. The solutions to $\cos(\theta) = -\frac{2}{3}$ are $\theta = -41.8°$ and $\theta = -138.2°$. Therefore, the full set of solutions is $\theta \in \{-138.2°, -41.8°, 41.8°, 138.2°\}$.

(b) We can factorise this equation to give

$$(3\sin(\theta) - 1)(\sin(\theta) + 2) = 0.$$

This gives us the solutions $\sin(\theta) = \frac{1}{3}$ and $\sin(\theta) = -2$. Since sine takes values in the range $[-1, +1]$, we only need to consider the equation $\sin(\theta) = \frac{1}{3}$. In the given range, this has the solutions $\theta = 19.5°$ and $\theta = 160.5°$.

(c) This factorises in the same way as the previous question to give

$$(3\tan(\theta) - 1)(\tan(\theta) + 2) = 0.$$

Since the tangent function can take any real value, we will obtain solutions from both of the two expressions in the factorised equation.

The first expression is equal to zero when $\tan(\theta) = \frac{1}{3}$. This gives us the solutions $\theta = 18.4°$ and $\theta = -161.6°$.

The second expression is zero when $\tan(\theta) = -2$. From this, we obtain the solutions $\theta = -63.44°$ and $\theta = 116.57°$.

Therefore the complete set of solutions in the given range is given by

$$\theta \in \{-161.6°, -63.44°, 18.4°, 116.57°\}.$$

(d) We can write this equation as $\cos^2(\theta) = 1$ and take the square root of both sides. This gives is $\cos(\theta) = \pm 1$. We can find the solutions to this equation by sketching a graph of the cosine function. We see that the solutions are given by $\theta \in \{-180°, 0°, 180°\}$.

(e) We can transform the $\cos^2$ term into a $\sin^2$ using the identity $\sin^2(\theta) + \cos^2(\theta) = 1$.

$$\begin{aligned} 6\cos^2(\theta) - \sin(\theta) - 4 &= 6\left(1 - \sin^2(\theta)\right) - \sin(\theta) - 4 \\ &= -6\sin^2(\theta) - \sin(\theta) + 2 \\ &= -(2\sin(\theta) - 1)(3\sin(\theta) + 2) = 0. \end{aligned}$$

Therefore θ is a solution to the equation if $\sin(\theta) = \frac{1}{2}$ or $\sin(\theta) = -\frac{2}{3}$. From $\sin(\theta) = \frac{1}{2}$, we find the solutions $30°$ and $150°$. Finally, $\sin(\theta) = -\frac{2}{3}$ when $\theta = -41.8°$ or $\theta = -138.2°$. The complete set of solutions in the given range is given by

$$\theta \in \{-138.2°, -41.8°, 30°, 150°\}.$$

(f) We can transform the $\sin^2$ term into a $\cos^2$ using the identity $\sin^2(\theta) + \cos^2(\theta) = 1$.

$$\begin{aligned} 6\sin^2(\theta) - 5\cos(\theta) - 7 &= 6\left(1 - \cos^2(\theta)\right) - 5\cos(\theta) - 7 \\ &= -6\cos^2(\theta) - 5\cos(\theta) - 1 \\ &= -(2\cos(\theta) + 1)(3\cos(\theta) + 1) = 0. \end{aligned}$$

Therefore θ is a solution to the equation if $\cos(\theta) = -\frac{1}{2}$ or $\cos(\theta) = -\frac{1}{3}$. Solving $\cos(\theta) = -\frac{1}{2}$, we find the solutions $120°$ and $-120°$. Finally, $\cos(\theta) = -\frac{1}{3}$ when $\theta = 109.47°$ or $\theta = -109.47°$. The complete set of solutions in the given range is given by

$$\theta \in \{-120°, -109.47°, 109.47°, 120°\}.$$

(g) The equation can be factorised to obtain

$$(\tan(2\theta) - 2)(\tan(2\theta) + 3) = 0.$$

Therefore any solution to $\tan(2\theta) = 2$ or $\tan(2\theta) = -3$ will be a solution to the original equation.
One solution to $\tan(2\theta) = 2$ is $2\theta = 63.43°$. The period of the tangent function is $180°$ and so we can also identify the solutions $2\theta = -296.57°$, $2\theta = -115.57°$ and $2\theta = 243.43°$.
Similarly, we can solve $\tan(2\theta) = -3$ to find a solution $2\theta = -71.57°$. Using the periodicity of the tangent function, this also allows us to calculate the solutions $\tan(2\theta) = -251.57°$, $\tan(2\theta) = 108.43°$ and $\tan(2\theta) = 288.43°$. Combining these two sets of results, and dividing by two to obtain values of θ, we have the full set of solutions,

$$\theta \in \{-148.3°, -125.8°, -58.3°, -35.8°, 31.7°, 54.2°, 121.7°, 144.2°\}.$$

Q4. We note that the value of the left hand side of the equation is undefined if $\cos(\theta) = 0$. If we multiply both sides by $\cos(\theta)$ we have

$$3\sin(\theta) + 2 = 4\cos(\theta) + 6\cos(\theta)\sin(\theta),$$

which we can rewrite as

$$6\cos(\theta)\sin(\theta) + 4\cos(\theta) - 3\sin(\theta) - 2 = 0.$$

This can then be factorised as

$$(2\cos(\theta) - 1)(3\sin(\theta) + 2) = 0.$$

Therefore, θ is a solution to the equation if $\cos(\theta) = \frac{1}{2}$ or $\sin(\theta) = -\frac{2}{3}$.
The solution to $\cos(\theta) = \frac{1}{2}$ with the smallest absolute value is $\theta = 60°$. The solution to $\sin(\theta) = -\frac{2}{3}$ with the smallest absolute value is $\theta = -41.8°$. Therefore the solution with the smallest absolute value is $\theta = -41.8°$.

Q5. Dividing through by $\cos(2\theta)$ gives us the equation $1 = 3\tan(2\theta)$, or $\tan(2\theta) = \frac{1}{3}$. This gives us a solution $2\theta = 18.43°$. Since the tangent function is periodic and repeats every $180°$, we have a set of solutions $2\theta = (18.43 + 180n)°$ for any $n \in \mathbb{Z}$. Dividing by two gives us the solutions $\theta = (9.2 + 90n)°$ which gives us four solutions in the given range, $\theta \in \{9.2°, 99.2°, 189.2°, 279.2°\}$.

Q6. (a) Using the identity $\cos(\theta) = \sin(\theta + 90°)$,

$$\sin(45°) = \sin(-45° + 90°) = \cos(-45°) = \cos(45°).$$

Alternatively, since $\tan(45°) = 1$, we know that $\sin(45°) = \cos(45°)$. Therefore,

$$\sin^2(45°) + \cos^2(45°) = \sin^2(45°) + \sin^2(45°) = 2\sin^2(45°) = 1.$$

And therefore, $\sin(45°) = \frac{1}{\sqrt{2}}$.

(b) The solutions to $2\sin^2(\theta) = 1$ are given by $\sin(\theta) = \frac{1}{\sqrt{2}}$ and $\sin(\theta) = -\frac{1}{\sqrt{2}}$. We already have the solution in the first quadrant, $45°$. Since we want to find solutions giving positive and negative values, the remaining solutions are the corresponding angles in the other three quadrants.

The full set of solutions is given by $\theta \in \{45°, 135°, 225°, 315°\}$.

Worked Solutions — Exercise 19.2

Q1.
$$\frac{\sin^2(\theta)}{\tan^2(\theta)} = \frac{\sin^2(\theta)}{\frac{\sin^2(\theta)}{\cos^2(\theta)}},$$
$$= \frac{\sin^2(\theta)\cos^2(\theta)}{\sin^2(\theta)},$$
$$= \cos^2(\theta),$$
$$= 1 - \sin^2(\theta).$$

Q2.
$$f(x) = \tan^2(x)\cos^4(x),$$
$$= \frac{\sin^2(x)}{\cos^2(x)}\cos^4(x),$$
$$= \sin^2(x)\cos^2(x),$$
$$= \sin^2(x)(1 - \sin^2(x)),$$
$$= \sin^2(x) - \sin^4(x).$$

Q3. First we note the following,

$$\cos(\theta)\tan(\theta) = \cos(\theta)\frac{\sin(\theta)}{\cos(\theta)},$$
$$= \sin(\theta).$$

Hence,

$$\cos(\theta)\tan(\theta) = \frac{\sqrt{3}}{2},$$
$$\Rightarrow \sin(\theta) = \frac{\sqrt{3}}{2}.$$

Thus, $\theta = 60°, 120°$.

Q4. We first seek to simplify the left hand side of the equation we need to solve. To this end, we apply the trigonometric identity (19.3),

$$\frac{1 - 2\cos^2(\theta) + \cos^4(\theta)}{\sin^2(\theta)} = \frac{(1 - \cos^2(\theta))^2}{\sin^2(\theta)},$$
$$= \frac{(1 - \cos^2(\theta))^2}{1 - \cos^2(\theta)},$$
$$= 1 - \cos^2(\theta).$$

Using the above,

$$\frac{1 - 2\cos^2(\theta) + \cos^4(\theta)}{\sin^2(\theta)} = \frac{1}{2},$$
$$\Rightarrow 1 - \cos^2(\theta) = \frac{1}{2},$$
$$\Rightarrow \cos^2(\theta) = \frac{1}{2},$$
$$\Rightarrow \cos(\theta) = \frac{1}{\sqrt{2}}.$$

Using the periodicity of $\cos(\theta)$ we see that $\theta \in \{45°, 315°\}$.

Q5. (a) Starting from the left hand side,

$$\frac{\cos^4(\theta) - \sin^4(\theta)}{\cos^2(\theta)} = \frac{\left(\cos^2(\theta) + \sin^2(\theta)\right)\left(\cos^2(\theta) - \sin^2(\theta)\right)}{\cos^2(\theta)},$$
$$= \frac{\cos^2(\theta) - \sin^2(\theta)}{\cos^2(\theta)},$$
$$= \frac{\cos^2(\theta)}{\cos^2(\theta)} - \frac{\sin^2(\theta)}{\cos^2(\theta)},$$
$$= 1 - \tan^2(\theta).$$

(b) Using the result shown above,

$$\frac{\cos^4(\theta) - \sin^4(\theta)}{\cos^2(\theta)} = \frac{1}{2},$$
$$\Rightarrow \quad 1 - \tan^2(\theta) = \frac{1}{2},$$
$$\Rightarrow \quad \tan^2(\theta) = \frac{1}{2},$$
$$\Rightarrow \quad \tan(\theta) = \frac{1}{\sqrt{2}}.$$

As $\tan(\theta)$ has period $180°$, there are three solutions in the range $0° \leq \theta \leq 540°$, namely $\theta = 35.26°, 215.26°, 395.26°$.

Q6. We first consider,

$$(\cos(x) + \sin(x))^3 = \cos^3(x) + 3\sin(x)\cos^2(x) + 3\sin^2(x)\cos(x) + \sin^3(x),$$
$$= \cos^3(x) + 3\sin(x)\cos^2(x) + 3(1 - \cos^2(x))\cos(x)$$
$$+ \sin(x)(1 - \cos(x)),$$
$$= \cos^3(x) + 3\sin(x)\cos^2(x) + 3\cos(x) - 3\cos^3(x)$$
$$+ \sin(x) - \sin(x)\cos^2(x),$$
$$= 3\cos(x) - 2\cos^3(x) + 2\sin(x)\cos^2(x) + \sin(x).$$

Hence,

$$f(x) = (\cos(x) + \sin(x))^3 - \sin(x)\left(2\cos^2(x) + 1\right),$$
$$= 3\cos(x) - 2\cos^3(x) + 2\sin(x)\cos^2(x) + \sin(x)$$
$$- \sin(x)\left(2\cos^2(x) + 1\right),$$
$$= 3\cos(x) - 2\cos^3(x) + 2\sin(x)\cos^2(x) + \sin(x)$$
$$- 2\sin(x)\cos^2(x) - \sin(x),$$
$$= 3\cos(x) - 2\cos^3(x).$$

Worked Solutions — Exercise 20.1

Q1. (a) Differentiating we obtain $\frac{dy}{dx} = 2x$. When $x = 2$ we get $y = 9$ and $\frac{dy}{dx} = 4$. The equation of the tangent is,

$$y - 9 = 4(x - 2)$$
$$y - 9 = 4x - 8$$
$$-4x + y = 1.$$

(b) Differentiating we obtain $\frac{dy}{dx} = 3 + 2x - 3x^2$. When $x = -1$ we get $y = -1$

and $\frac{dy}{dx} = -2$. The equation of the tangent is,
$$y - (-1) = -2(x - (-1))$$
$$y + 1 = -2x - 2$$
$$2x + y = -3.$$

(c) Differentiating we obtain $\frac{dy}{dx} = 2x + 4x^{-3}$. When $x = -2$ we get $y = \frac{7}{2}$ and $\frac{dy}{dx} = -\frac{9}{2}$. The equation of the tangent is,
$$y - \frac{7}{2} = -\frac{9}{2}(x - (-2))$$
$$2y - 7 = -9x - 18$$
$$9x + 2y = -11.$$

(d) Differentiating we obtain $\frac{dy}{dx} = \cos(x)$. When $x = \frac{\pi}{3}$ we get $y = \frac{\sqrt{3}}{2}$ and $\frac{dy}{dx} = \frac{1}{2}$. The equation of the tangent is,
$$y - \frac{\sqrt{3}}{2} = \frac{1}{2}(x - \frac{\pi}{3})$$
$$2y - \sqrt{3} = x - \frac{\pi}{3}$$
$$-x + 2y = \sqrt{3} - \frac{\pi}{3}.$$

(e) Differentiating we obtain $\frac{dy}{dx} = \frac{4}{x} - 1$. When $x = 1$ we get $y = -1$ and $\frac{dy}{dx} = 3$. The equation of the tangent is,
$$y - (-1) = 3(x - 1)$$
$$y + 1 = 3x - 3$$
$$-3x + y = -4.$$

Q2. (a) Expanding first we get $y = x^2 - x - 6$ then differentiate to obtain $\frac{dy}{dx} = 2x - 1$. When $x = -1$ we get $y = -4$ and $\frac{dy}{dx} = -3$, hence the gradient of the normal is $\frac{1}{3}$. The equation of the normal is,
$$y - (-4) = \frac{1}{3}(x - (-1))$$
$$3y + 12 = x + 1$$
$$-x + 3y = -11.$$

(b) Differentiating we obtain $\frac{dy}{dx} = 2x + 2$. When $x = \frac{1}{2}$ we get $y = -\frac{7}{4}$ and $\frac{dy}{dx} = 3$, hence the gradient of the normal is $-\frac{1}{3}$. The equation of the normal is,

$$y - \left(-\frac{7}{4}\right) = -\frac{1}{3}\left(x - \frac{1}{2}\right)$$
$$3y + \frac{21}{4} = -x + \frac{1}{2},$$
$$-x + 3y = -\frac{23}{4},$$
$$-4x + 12y = -19$$

(c) Simplifying first we get $y = x^{\frac{3}{2}} - 3x^{\frac{1}{2}}$ then differentiate to obtain $\frac{dy}{dx} = \frac{3}{2}x^{\frac{1}{2}} - \frac{3}{2}x^{-\frac{1}{2}}$.

When $x = 4$ we get $y = 2$ and $\frac{dy}{dx} = \frac{9}{4}$, hence the gradient of the normal is $-\frac{4}{9}$. The equation of the normal is,

$$y - 2 = -\frac{4}{9}(x - 4)$$
$$9y - 18 = -4x + 16$$
$$4x + 9y = 34.$$

(d) Differentiating we obtain $\frac{dy}{dx} = 2e^{2x}$. When $x = 0$ we get $y = 1$ and $\frac{dy}{dx} = 2$, hence the gradient of the normal is $-\frac{1}{2}$. The equation of the normal is,

$$y - 1 = -\frac{1}{2}x$$
$$2y - 2 = -x$$
$$x + 2y = 2.$$

(e) Differentiating we obtain $\frac{dy}{dx} = 2\cos(2x) + \sin(x)$. When $x = \frac{\pi}{6}$ we get $y = 0$ and $\frac{dy}{dx} = \frac{3}{2}$, hence the gradient of the normal is $-\frac{2}{3}$. The equation of the normal is,

$$y = -\frac{2}{3}\left(x - \frac{\pi}{6}\right)$$
$$3y = -2x + \frac{\pi}{3}$$
$$2x + 3y = \frac{\pi}{3}.$$

Q3. First find where the curve intersects the coordinate axes. When $x = 0$, $y = 6$ and when $y = 0$, $x = -3$. There are no other intersections with the axes. Expanding we get $y = x^3 + 4x^2 + 5x + 6$ then differentiate to obtain $\frac{dy}{dx} = 3x^2 + 8x + 5$. When $x = -3$, $\frac{dy}{dx} = 8$ and when $x = 0$, $\frac{dy}{dx} = 5$. The equation of the first tangent is,

$$y = 8(x - (-3))$$
$$y = 8x + 24.$$

The equation of the second tangent is,

$$y - 6 = 5x$$
$$y = 5x + 6.$$

To find the intersection of these two tangents, solve as simultaneous equations.

$$8x + 24 = 5x + 6$$
$$3x = -18$$
$$x = -6$$

Substituting $x = -6$ into either tangent equation gives $y = -24$.

Q4. Differentiating we obtain $\frac{dy}{dx} = \frac{1}{3}x^2 - 1$. When $x = 3$ we get $y = 1$ and $\frac{dy}{dx} = 2$. The equation of the tangent is,

$$y - 1 = 2(x - 3)$$
$$y - 1 = 2x - 6$$
$$y = 2x - 5.$$

The tangent line crosses the axes at $(0, -5)$ and $\left(\frac{5}{2}, 0\right)$, hence the area bounded by the tangent and coordinate axes is $\frac{1}{2} \times 5 \times \frac{5}{2} = \frac{25}{4}$.

Q5. If $y = 15x + k$ is a tangent then we need the value of x on the curve such that the gradient is 15. Differentiating we obtain $\frac{dy}{dx} = -\frac{2}{x^3} - 1$.

$$15 = -\frac{2}{x^3} - 1$$
$$16 = -\frac{2}{x^3}$$
$$x^3 = -\frac{1}{8}$$
$$x = -\frac{1}{2}.$$

When $x = -\frac{1}{2}$ we get $y = \frac{9}{2}$. Substituting these into $y = 15x + k$ we obtain $k = 12$.

Q6. Differentiating we obtain $\frac{dy}{dx} = 3x^2 + 4x$. When $x = -1$ we get $y = 0$ and $\frac{dy}{dx} = -1$, hence the gradient of the normal is 1. The equation of the normal is $y = x + 1$. Equate the original curve and the normal line to find the other intersections.

$$x + 1 = x^3 + 2x^2 - 1$$
$$0 = x^3 + 2x^2 - x - 2.$$

We know that $x = -1$ is a root, hence by the factor theorem, $(x+1)$ is a factor and the equation can be written as $0 = (x+1)(Ax^2 + Bx + C)$. By equating coefficients, $A = 1$, $C = -2$ and $A + B = 2$ so $B = 1$. Finally we have $0 = (x+1)(x^2 + x - 2)$ which can be further factorised to $0 = (x+1)(x-1)(x+2)$, therefore the x-coordinates of the other intersections are $x = -2$ and $x = 1$.

Q7. Differentiating we obtain $\frac{dy}{dx} = 3x^2 - 18x + 25$. When $x = p$, $y = p^3 - 9p^2 + 25p - 17$ and $\frac{dy}{dx} = 3p^2 - 18p + 25$. The equation of a tangent at any point $x = p$ is,

$$y - (p^3 - 9p^2 + 25p - 17) = (3p^2 - 18p + 25)(x - p).$$

We know this tangent passes through the point $(1, 0)$ so we can substitute $x = 1$ and $y = 0$ then solve for p.

$$-(p^3 - 9p^2 + 25p - 17) = (3p^2 - 18p + 25)(1 - p)$$
$$-p^3 + 9p^2 - 25p + 17 = 3p^2 - 18p + 25 - 3p^3 + 18p^2 - 25p$$
$$2(p^3 - 6p^2 + 9p - 4) = 0$$

We know $p = 1$ is a solution so we can use the factor theorem to factorise further giving,

$$2(p - 1)(p - 1)(p - 4) = 0.$$

Hence $p = 4$.

Worked Solutions — Exercise 20.2

Q1. (a)
$$\frac{dy}{dx} = 4x - 7$$
$$0 = 4x - 7$$
$$x = frac74.$$

(b)
$$y = x^3 + 5x^2 + 3x + 15$$
$$\frac{dy}{dx} = 3x^2 + 10x + 3$$
$$0 = 3x^2 + 10x + 3$$
$$0 = (3x + 1)(x + 3) \quad \Rightarrow \quad x = -\frac{1}{3}, \ x = -3.$$

(c)
$$\frac{dy}{dx} = 3x^2 - 12x + 3$$
$$0 = 3x^2 - 12x + 3$$
$$x = \frac{12 \pm \sqrt{12^2 - 4 \times 3 \times 3}}{2 \times 3}$$
$$x = \frac{12 \pm 6\sqrt{3}}{6}$$
$$x = 2 \pm \sqrt{3}.$$

(d)
$$\frac{dy}{dx} = 12x^2 - 22x - 20$$
$$0 = 12x^2 - 22x - 20$$
$$0 = 2(3x + 2)(2x - 5) \quad \Rightarrow \quad x = -\frac{2}{3}, \ x = \frac{5}{2}.$$

(e) $$\frac{dy}{dx} = 12x^3 + 12x^2 - 24x$$
$$0 = 12x^3 + 12x^2 - 24x$$
$$0 = 12x(x+2)(x-1) \quad \Rightarrow \quad x = -2, \; x = 0, \; x = 1.$$

(f) $$\frac{dy}{dx} = 5x^4 - 5$$
$$0 = 5x^4 - 5$$
$$0 = 5(x+1)(x-1)(x^2+1) \quad \Rightarrow \quad x = -1, \; x = 1.$$

(g) $$y = 4x - 3 + \frac{2}{x}$$
$$\frac{dy}{dx} = 4 - \frac{2}{x^2}$$
$$0 = 4 - \frac{2}{x^2}$$
$$x^2 = \frac{1}{2}$$
$$x = \pm \frac{\sqrt{2}}{2}.$$

(h) $$\frac{dy}{dx} = 7\left(\frac{1}{7x}\right) - 2x + 1$$
$$0 = \frac{1}{x} - 2x + 1$$
$$0 = 1 - 2x^2 + x$$
$$2x^2 - x - 1 = 0$$
$$(2x+1)(x-1) = 0 \quad \Rightarrow \quad x = -\frac{1}{2}, \; x = 1.$$

Notice here that $\ln(7x)$ is not defined for negative values of x so we reject $x = -\frac{1}{2}$. There is only one turning point at $x = 1$.

Q2. (a) Differentiating each term of the polynomial gives
$$g'(x) = 2x - 6.$$

The turning point of g occurs when the derivative is zero.
$$2x - 6 = 0 \Rightarrow x = 3.$$

(b) The value of g at its turning point is $g(3) = 3^2 - 12 + 11 = 8$.

(c) For large values of $|x|$, the polynomial is dominated by the x^2 term, and so $g(x) \to \infty$ is positive. Therefore, the turning point is the minimum value of the polynomial.
Alternatively, the gradient is negative for $x < 3$ and is positive for $x > 3$. Therefore, the minimum value of the polynomial g is $g(3) = 8$ and so $g(x) > 0$ for all x.

Worked Solutions — Exercise 20.3

Q1. (a) $\frac{d^2y}{dx^2} = 4$. This is always positive hence the stationary point is a minimum.

(b) $\frac{d^2y}{dx^2} = 6x + 10$. When $x = -\frac{1}{3}$, $\frac{d^2y}{dx^2} = -8$ so this is a maximum. When $x = 3$, $\frac{d^2y}{dx^2} = 8$ so this is a minimum.

(c) $\frac{d^2y}{dx^2} = 6x - 12$. When $x = 2 - \sqrt{3}$, $\frac{d^2y}{dx^2} = -6\sqrt{3}$ so this is a maximum. When $x = 2 + \sqrt{3}$, $\frac{d^2y}{dx^2} = 6\sqrt{3}$ so this is a minimum.

(d) $\frac{d^2y}{dx^2} = 24x - 22$. When $x = -\frac{2}{3}$, $\frac{d^2y}{dx^2} = -38$ so this is a maximum. When $x = \frac{5}{2}$, $\frac{d^2y}{dx^2} = 38$ so this is a minimum.

(e) $\frac{d^2y}{dx^2} = 36x^2 + 24x - 24$. When $x = -2$, $\frac{d^2y}{dx^2} = -72$ so this is a minimum. When $x = 0$, $\frac{d^2y}{dx^2} = -24$ so this is a maximum. When $x = 1$, $\frac{d^2y}{dx^2} = 36$ so this is a minimum.

(f) $\frac{d^2y}{dx^2} = 20x^3$. When $x = -1$, $\frac{d^2y}{dx^2} = -20$ so this is a maximum. When $x = 1$, $\frac{d^2y}{dx^2} = 20$ so this is a minimum.

(g) $\frac{d^2y}{dx^2} = \frac{4}{x^3}$. When $x = -\frac{\sqrt{2}}{2}$, $\frac{d^2y}{dx^2} = -8\sqrt{2}$ so this is a maximum. When $x = \frac{\sqrt{2}}{2}$, $\frac{d^2y}{dx^2} = 8\sqrt{2}$ so this is a minimum.

(h) $\frac{d^2y}{dx^2} = -\frac{1}{x^2} - 2$. When $x = 1$, $\frac{d^2y}{dx^2} = -3$ so this is a maximum.

Q2. (a) $\frac{dy}{dx} = 5x^4 - 4x^3 - 12x^2$

$0 = 5x^4 - 4x^3 - 12x^2$

$0 = x^2(5x^2 - 4x - 12)$

$0 = x^2(5x + 6)(x - 2) \Rightarrow x = -\frac{6}{5},\ x = 0,\ x = 2.$

$\frac{d^2y}{dx^2} = 20x^3 - 12x^2 - 24x$. When $x = -\frac{6}{5}$, $\frac{d^2y}{dx^2} = -\frac{576}{25}$ so this is a maximum. When $x = 2$, $\frac{d^2y}{dx^2} = 64$ so this is a minimum. When $x = 0$, $\frac{d^2y}{dx^2} = 0$ which is inconclusive so we should check the value of $\frac{dy}{dx}$ near $x = 0$.

x	-1	0	1
$\frac{dy}{dx}$	-3	0	-11

We see the gradient is negative, then zero, then negative so the stationary point at $x = 0$ is an inflection.

(b) $\frac{dy}{dx} = 32x - x^{-\frac{2}{3}}$

$0 = 32x - x^{-\frac{2}{3}}$

$x^{-\frac{2}{3}} = 32x$

$1 = 32x^{\frac{5}{3}}$

$x = \frac{1}{8}$

$\frac{d^2y}{dx^2} = 32 + \frac{2}{3}x^{-\frac{5}{3}}$. When $x = \frac{1}{8}$, $\frac{d^2y}{dx^2} = \frac{160}{3}$ so this is a minimum.

(c) $$\frac{dy}{dx} = -x^{-2} + 3x^{-4}$$
$$0 = -\frac{1}{x^2} + \frac{3}{x^4}$$
$$\frac{1}{x^2} = \frac{3}{x^4}$$
$$x^2 = 3$$
$$x = \pm\sqrt{3}$$

$\frac{d^2y}{dx^2} = x^{-3} - 12x^{-5}$. When $x = -\sqrt{3}$, $\frac{d^2y}{dx^2} = 0.577$ so this is a minimum. When $x = \sqrt{3}$, $\frac{d^2y}{dx^2} = -0.577$ so this is a maximum.

(d) $$\frac{dy}{dx} = -e^{-x} + 2$$
$$0 = -e^{-x} + 2$$
$$e^{-x} = 2$$
$$x = -\ln(2)$$

$\frac{d^2y}{dx^2} = e^{-x}$. When $x = -\ln(2)$, $\frac{d^2y}{dx^2} = 2$ so this is a minimum.

Q3.
$$\frac{dy}{dx} = 3 - 3x^2$$
$$3 - 3x^2 > 0$$
$$3(x+1)(x-1) > 0 \quad \Rightarrow \quad -1 < x < 1.$$

Q4.
$$\frac{dy}{dx} = 4x^3 - 4x$$
$$4x^3 - 4x < 0$$
$$4x(x+1)(x-1) < 0 \quad \Rightarrow \quad x < -1, \ 0 < x < 1.$$

Q5. The volume of a cylinder is $V = \pi r^2 h$ and since we already know that $V = 3000$ we can express h in terms of r as follows, $h = \frac{3000}{\pi r^2}$. The area which needs to be covered is a circle on top and the curved surface around the height of the cake so we have $A = \pi r^2 + 2\pi rh = \pi r^2 + \frac{6000}{r}$.

$$\frac{dA}{dr} = 2\pi r - 6000r^{-2}$$
$$0 = 2\pi r - 6000r^{-2}$$
$$\frac{6000}{r^2} = 2\pi r$$
$$r = \sqrt[3]{\frac{3000}{\pi}}.$$

$\frac{d^2A}{dr^2} = 2\pi + 12000r^{-3}$. When $r = \sqrt[3]{\frac{3000}{\pi}}$, $\frac{d^2A}{dr^2}$ is positive so this is a minimum and we find that $A = 914\,\text{cm}^2$.

Q6. Expanding first we get $y = x^2 - 4x + 4$ then differentiate to obtain $\frac{dy}{dx} = 2x - 4$. When $x = p$ we get $y = (p-2)^2$ and $\frac{dy}{dx} = 2(p-2)$. The equation of the tangent is,

$$y - (p-2)^2 = 2(p-2)(x-p)$$

When $x = 0$ we have,
$$y = 2(p-2)(-p) + (p-2)^2$$
$$y = 4p - 2p^2 + p^2 - 4p + 4$$
$$y = 4 - p^2 = (2+p)(2-p).$$

When $y = 0$ we have,
$$x = -\frac{(p-2)^2}{2(p-2)} + p$$
$$x = \frac{-(p-2)}{2} + p$$
$$x = \frac{p+2}{2}.$$

The area bounded by the tangent and the coordinate axes will be a triangle.
$$A = \frac{1}{2}\left(\frac{p+2}{2}\right)(2+p)(2-p)$$
$$A = \frac{8 + 4p - 2p^2 - p^3}{4}$$
$$A = 2 + p - \frac{1}{2}p^2 - \frac{1}{4}p^3.$$

We can now differentiate A to find the maximum area.
$$\frac{dA}{dp} = 1 - p - \frac{3}{4}p^2$$
$$0 = 1 - p - \frac{3}{4}p^2$$
$$3p^2 + 4p - 4 = 0$$
$$(3p-2)(p+2) = 0 \quad \Rightarrow \quad p = -2, \ p = \frac{3}{2}.$$

$\frac{d^2A}{dp^2} = -1 - \frac{3}{2}p$. When $p = -2$, $\frac{d^2A}{dp^2} = 2$ so this is a minimum. When $p = \frac{3}{2}$, $\frac{d^2A}{dp^2} = -\frac{13}{4}$ so this is a maximum. The area when $p = \frac{3}{2}$ is $\frac{49}{32}$.

Q7. $V = x(30 - 2x)(30 - 2x) = 4x^3 - 120x^2 + 900x$
$$\frac{dV}{dx} = 12x^2 - 240x + 900$$
$$0 = 12x^2 - 240x + 900$$
$$0 = x^2 - 20x + 75$$
$$0 = (x-5)(x-15) \quad \Rightarrow \quad x = 5, \ x = 15.$$

Clearly if $x = 15$ then all the card has been cut away so we are only interested in $x = 5$. $\frac{d^2V}{dx^2} = 24x - 240$. When $x = 5$, $\frac{d^2V}{dx^2} = -120$ so this is a maximum, hence the maximum volume is $2000 \, \text{cm}^3$.

Worked Solutions — Exercise 21.1

Q1.
$$\int_0^4 x^2\,dx = \left[\frac{1}{3}x^3 + c\right]_0^4 = \left(\frac{1}{3}4^3 + c\right) - \left(\frac{1}{3}0^3 + c\right) = \frac{64}{3}.$$

Q2.
$$\int_1^2 x+1\,dx = \int_1^2 x\,dx + \int_1^2 1\,dx$$
$$= \left[\frac{1}{2}x^2 + c_1\right]_1^2 + \left[x + c_2\right]_1^2$$
$$= \left(\frac{1}{2}2^2 + c_1\right) - \left(\frac{1}{2}1^2 + c_1\right) + (2 + c_2) - (1 + c_2)$$
$$= 2 - \frac{1}{2} + 2 - 1$$
$$= \frac{5}{2}.$$

Q3. (a)
$$\int_1^4 x\,dx = \left[\frac{1}{2}x^2 + c\right]_1^4 = \left(\frac{1}{2}4^2 + c\right) - \left(\frac{1}{2}1^2 + c\right) = \frac{15}{2}.$$

(b)
$$\int_0^3 -x^2\,dx = \int_3^0 x^2\,dx$$
$$= \left[\frac{1}{3}x^3 + c\right]_3^0$$
$$= \left(\frac{1}{3}0^3 + c\right) - \left(\frac{1}{3}3^3 + c\right)$$
$$= -9.$$

(c)
$$\int_2^1 x^3\,dx = \left[\frac{1}{4}x^4 + c\right]_2^1 = \left(\frac{1}{4}1^4 + c\right) - \left(\frac{1}{4}2^4 + c\right) = -\frac{15}{4}.$$

(d)
$$\int_2^3 x^3 - x^2 \, dx = \int_2^3 x^3 \, dx + \int_3^2 x^2 \, dx$$
$$= \left[\frac{1}{4}x^4 + c_1\right]_2^3 + \left[\frac{1}{3}x^3 + c_2\right]_3^2$$
$$= \left(\frac{1}{4}3^4 + c_1\right) - \left(\frac{1}{4}2^4 + c_1\right) + \left(\frac{1}{3}2^3 + c_2\right)$$
$$- \left(\frac{1}{3}3^3 + c_2\right)$$
$$= \frac{81}{4} - \frac{16}{4} + \frac{8}{3} - \frac{27}{3}$$
$$= \frac{119}{12}.$$

(e)
$$\int_1^2 x + x^4 \, dx = \int_1^2 x \, dx + \int_1^2 x^4 \, dx$$
$$= \left[\frac{1}{2}x^2 + c_1\right]_1^2 + \left[\frac{1}{5}x^5 + c_2\right]_1^2$$
$$= \left(\frac{1}{2}2^2 + c_1\right) - \left(\frac{1}{2}1^2 + c_1\right) + \left(\frac{1}{5}2^5 + c_2\right)$$
$$- \left(\frac{1}{5}1^5 + c_2\right)$$
$$= \frac{4}{2} - \frac{1}{2} + \frac{32}{5} - \frac{1}{5}$$
$$= \frac{77}{10}.$$

Q4. We know that $y = x$ is above the x-axis for all x between $x = 2$ and $x = 50$, therefore, the area is given by

$$A = \int_2^{50} x \, dx$$
$$= \left[\frac{1}{2}x^2 + c\right]_2^{50}$$
$$= \frac{2500}{2} - \frac{4}{2}$$
$$= 1248.$$

In order to calculate the area using geometric formulae, we first plot the graph of $y = x$:

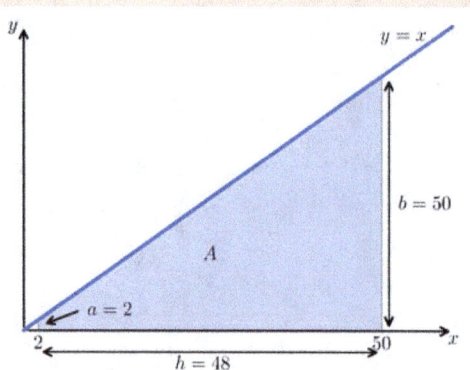

The area required is that of a trapezium:

$$A = \frac{(a+b)}{2} \cdot h = \frac{2+50}{2} \times 48 = 1248.$$

Q5. First we sketch the curve $y = \sqrt{x+1}$.

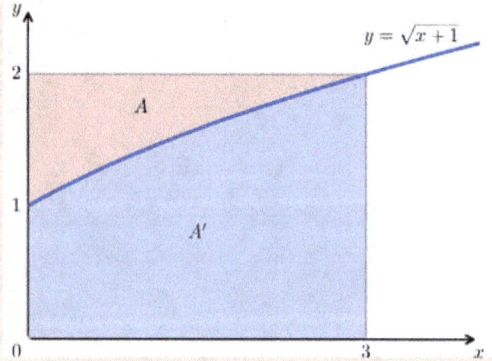

The area between the curve and the y-axis is the same as the usual area problem if we treat the y-axis in this problem as the x-axis in the formulae we defined above. Therefore, if $x = f(y)$, we can say that

$$A = \int_1^2 f(y)\,\mathrm{d}y.$$

Now we rearrange $y = \sqrt{x+1}$ to find x in terms of y, or $x = f(y)$. Squaring both sides:

$$x + 1 = y^2.$$

Subtracting 1 from both sides:

$$x = y^2 - 1.$$

We use this to find A:

$$\begin{aligned}
A &= \int_1^2 f(y)\,dy \\
&= \int_1^2 y^2 - 1\,dy \\
&= \int_1^2 y^2\,dy + \int_2^1 1\,dy \\
&= \left[\frac{1}{3}y^3 + c_1\right]_1^2 + \left[y + c_2\right]_2^1 \\
&= \left(\frac{1}{3}2^3 + c_1\right) - \left(\frac{1}{3}1^3 + c_1\right) + (1 + c_2) - (2 + c_2) \\
&= \frac{8}{3} - \frac{1}{3} + 1 - 2 \\
&= \frac{4}{3}.
\end{aligned}$$

Looking back at our plot we can see that $A + A'$ is equal to the area of a rectangle of width 3 and height 2:

$$A + A' = 3 \times 2 = 6.$$

Therefore, the area between $y = \sqrt{x+1}$ and the x-axis between the limits $x = 1$ and $x = 3$ is

$$A' = 6 - A = 6 - \frac{4}{3} = \frac{14}{3}.$$

Q6. First we plot the function, $f(x) = -3x^{1/3}$.

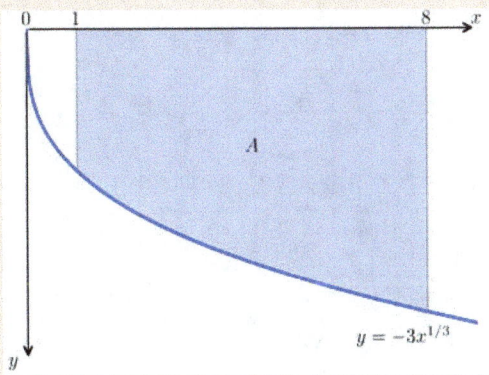

The curve is below the x-axis, therefore

$$A = -\int_1^8 f(x)\,dx$$
$$= -\int_1^8 -3x^{1/3}\,dx$$
$$= \int_1^8 3x^{1/3}\,dx$$
$$= \left[\frac{3}{4}3x^{4/3} + c\right]_1^8$$
$$= \left(\frac{9}{4}8^{4/3} + c\right) - \left(\frac{9}{4}1^{4/3} + c\right)$$
$$= \frac{135}{4}.$$

Q7. The price is quoted per cubic metre, therefore we need to find the volume of the box. The volume of the box is given by the depth of the box multiplied by the area of the cross-section. We can find the area of the cross-section by finding the area under $f(x)$ and adding to the area of the rectangular section below the nominal x-axis.

First we find the area of the rectangular section which has width 1m and height 0.3m:

$$A_{\text{rect}} = 1 \times 0.3 = 0.3\text{m}^2.$$

Now we find the area of the irregularly shaped part of the cross-section. This is given by the area between $f(x)$, the top of A_{rect} (the x-axis) and the limits $x = 0$ and $x = 1\text{m}$.

$$A_{\text{irr}} = \int_0^1 2x^3 - 3x^2 + 1\,dx$$
$$= \int_0^1 2x^3\,dx + \int_1^0 3x^2\,dx + \int_0^1 1\,dx$$
$$= \left[\frac{1}{4}2x^4 + c_1\right]_0^1 + \left[\frac{1}{3}3x^2 + c_2\right]_1^0 + \left[x + c_3\right]_0^1$$
$$= \left[\frac{1}{2}x^4 + c_1\right]_0^1 + \left[x^2 + c_2\right]_1^0 + \left[x + c_3\right]_0^1$$
$$= \left(\frac{1}{2}1^4 + c_1\right) - \left(\frac{1}{2}0^4 + c_1\right) + (0^2 + c_2) - (1^2 + c_2)$$
$$\quad + (1 + c_3) - (0 + c_3)$$
$$= 0.5\text{m}^2.$$

Therefore, the cross-sectional area of the box is

$$A = A_{\text{rect}} + A_{\text{irr}} = 0.3 + 0.5 = 0.8\text{m}^2.$$

The volume of the box is

$$A \times \text{depth} = 0.8 \times 0.75 = 0.6 \text{m}^3.$$

The cost of transporting the box is

$$\text{Cost} = 0.6 \text{m}^3 \times £4.30 = £2.58.$$

Q8. First we plot the curve.

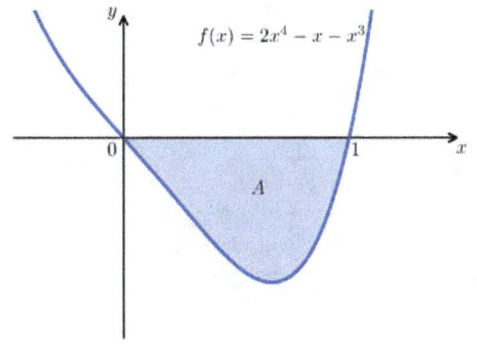

Therefore, the area A is completely below the x-axis and

$$\begin{aligned}
A &= -\int_0^1 f(x)\,dx \\
&= -\int_0^1 2x^4 - x - x^3\,dx \\
&= -\left(\int_0^1 2x^4\,dx + \int_1^0 x\,dx + \int_1^0 x^3\,dx\right) \\
&= -\left(\left[\frac{2}{5}x^5 + c_1\right]_0^1 + \left[\frac{1}{2}x^2 + c_2\right]_1^0 + \left[\frac{1}{4}x^4 + c_3\right]_1^0\right) \\
&= -\left(\left(\frac{2}{5}1^5 + c_1\right) - \left(\frac{2}{5}0^5 + c_1\right) + \left(\frac{1}{2}0^2 + c_2\right) - \left(\frac{1}{2}1^2 + c_2\right)\right. \\
&\qquad\left. + \left(\frac{1}{4}0^4 + c_3\right) - \left(\frac{1}{4}1^4 + c_3\right)\right) \\
&= -\left(\frac{2}{5} - \frac{1}{2} - \frac{1}{4}\right) \\
&= \frac{7}{20}.
\end{aligned}$$

Q9. First plot the curve. We know from examining the function that $f(x)$ crosses the x-axis at $x = -1/2$, 0, 1, 2, and 0.

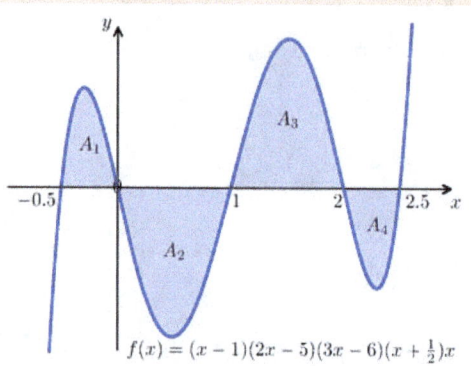

From the plot we see that there are four different area sections in the region of interest, alternating above and below the x-axis. Therefore, we need to calculate each area separately and sum to obtain the total area.

For each area calculation we will need the integral of $f(x)$, therefore we first find the indefinite integral that we will use each time. To make the integration easier we use the expanded version of $f(x)$.

$$\int 6x^5 - 30x^4 + 40.5x^3 - 1.5x^2 - 15x \, dx = \frac{6}{6}x^6 - \frac{30}{5}x^5 + \frac{40.5}{4}x^4$$
$$- \frac{1.5}{3}x^3 - \frac{15}{2}x^2 + c$$
$$= x^6 - 6x^5 + 10.125x^4 - 0.5x^3$$
$$- 7.5x^2 + c$$
$$= x^2(x^4 - 6x^3 + 10.125x^2$$
$$- 0.5x - 7.5) + c.$$

Next we turn our attention to each area calculation. Firstly, we look at A_1, which is above the x-axis.

$$A_1 = \int_{-0.5}^{0} f(x) \, dx$$
$$= \left[x^2(x^4 - 6x^3 + 10.125x^2 - 0.5x - 7.5) + c\right]_{-0.5}^{0}$$
$$= (0 + c) - ((-0.5)^2((-0.5)^4 - 6(-0.5)^3 + 10.125(-0.5^2)$$
$$- 0.5(-0.5) - 7.5) + c)$$
$$= 0.9765625.$$

A_2 is below the x-axis, therefore

$$\begin{aligned}A_2 &= -\int_0^1 f(x)\,\mathrm{d}x \\ &= -\left[x^2(x^4 - 6x^3 + 10.125x^2 - 0.5x - 7.5) + c\right]_0^1 \\ &= -\left((1^2(1^4 - 6(1)^3 + 10.125(1^2) - 0.5 - 7.5) + c) - (0 + c)\right) \\ &= -(-2.875) \\ &= 2.875.\end{aligned}$$

A_3 is above the x-axis, therefore

$$\begin{aligned}A_3 &= \int_1^2 f(x)\,\mathrm{d}x \\ &= \left[x^2(x^4 - 6x^3 + 10.125x^2 - 0.5x - 7.5) + c\right]_1^2 \\ &= (2^2(2^4 - 6(2)^3 + 10.125(2)^2 - 0.5(2) - 7.5) + c) \\ &\qquad - (1^2(1^4 - 6(1)^3 + 10.125(1^2) - 0.5 - 7.5) + c) \\ &= (0 + c) - (-2.875 + c) \\ &= 2.875.\end{aligned}$$

A_4 is below the x-axis, therefore

$$\begin{aligned}A_4 &= -\int_2^{2.5} f(x)\,\mathrm{d}x \\ &= -\left[x^2(x^4 - 6x^3 + 10.125x^2 - 0.5x - 7.5) + c\right]_2^{2.5} \\ &= -\left((2.5^2(2.5^4 - 6(2.5)^3 + 10.125(2.5)^2 - 0.5(2.5) - 7.5) + c)\right. \\ &\qquad \left. - (2^2(2^4 - 6(2)^3 + 10.125(2)^2 - 0.5(2) - 7.5) + c)\right) \\ &= -((-0.9765625 + c) - (0 + c)) \\ &= 0.9765625.\end{aligned}$$

We can now sum to find the total area:

$$\begin{aligned}A &= A_1 + A_2 + A_3 + A_4 \\ &= 0.9765625 + 2.875 + 2.875 + 0.9765625 \\ &= 7.703125 \\ &= 7.70 \text{ to 2 decimal places.}\end{aligned}$$

Q10. First we plot the graph of $f(x) = x\lfloor x \rfloor$.

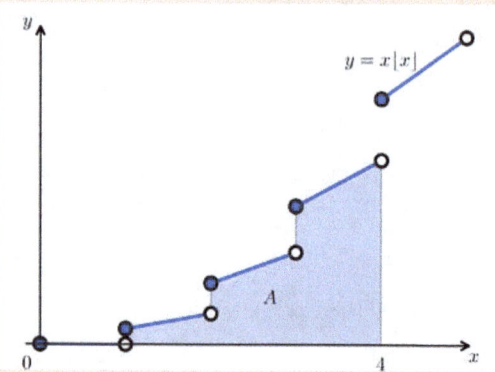

From the figure we can see that the function is not continuous. Therefore, we need to divide the region into four sections in order to calculate the area. The sections can be defined by the following intervals for x: $[0, 1)$, $[1, 2)$, $[2, 3)$, and $[3, 4)$.

For x in $[0, 1)$, $f(x) = x\lfloor x \rfloor = 0$ and

$$A_0 = \int_0^1 f(x)\,dx = \int_0^1 0\,dx = 0.$$

For x in $[1, 2)$, $f(x) = x\lfloor x \rfloor = 1x = x$ so

$$\begin{aligned} A_1 &= \int_1^2 x\,dx \\ &= \left[\frac{1}{2}x^2 + c\right]_1^2 \\ &= \left(\frac{1}{2}2^2 + c\right) - \left(\frac{1}{2}1^2 + c\right) \\ &= \frac{3}{2}. \end{aligned}$$

For x in $[2, 3)$, $f(x) = x\lfloor x \rfloor = 2x$. Therefore,

$$\begin{aligned} A_2 &= \int_2^3 2x\,dx \\ &= \left[\frac{1}{2}2x^2 + c\right]_2^3 \\ &= \left[x^2 + c\right]_2^3 \\ &= (9 + c) - (4 + c) \\ &= 5. \end{aligned}$$

For x in $[3, 4)$, $f(x) = x\lfloor x \rfloor = 3x$. Therefore,

$$\begin{aligned}
A_3 &= \int_3^4 3x \, \mathrm{d}x \\
&= \left[\frac{1}{2}3x^2 + c\right]_3^4 \\
&= \left[\frac{3}{2}x^2 + c\right]_3^4 \\
&= \left(\frac{3}{2}4^2 + c\right) - \left(\frac{3}{2}3^2 + c\right) \\
&= \frac{21}{2}.
\end{aligned}$$

Now we are ready to calculate the total area:

$$A = A_0 + A_1 + A_2 + A_3 = 0 + \frac{3}{2} + 5 + \frac{21}{2} = 17.$$

To generalise for x in $[0, a)$ we observe that the total area is the sum of the areas of a series of trapezia. We recall that the area of a trapezium is given by $h \cdot (a+b)/2$. In each trapezium $h = 1$. For trapezium i (where the first trapezium is $i = 0$):

$$\begin{aligned}
a &= f(i) = i\lfloor i \rfloor = i^2 \\
b &= f(i) = (i+1)\lfloor i \rfloor = i(i+1)
\end{aligned}$$

For the calculation of b we have used $\lfloor i \rfloor$ because the point $x = b$ is not strictly in the trapezium that we are looking at (refer back to the filled and empty circles in the figure above).

We know that the integral of $f(x)$ between $x = 0$ and $x = a$ is equal to the area under $f(x)$, therefore,

$$\begin{aligned}
\int_0^a x\lfloor x \rfloor \, \mathrm{d}x &= \sum_{i=0}^{a-1} \frac{i^2 + i(i+1)}{2} \cdot 1 \\
&= \sum_{i=0}^{a-1} i^2 + \frac{1}{2}i.
\end{aligned}$$

5. Worked Solutions - Chapters 22 to 27

Worked Solutions — Exercise 22.1

Q1. (a) The population is the set of all the cheeses which have reached the correct age. A sample is a randomly chosen, smaller subset of the cheeses.

(b) He says that he starts with the first cheese. This means that the sample is not being randomly chosen: he always chooses the cheeses in positions 1, 21, 41, ... He should select his first cheese randomly from the first twenty cheeses.

Also, the shelves hold sixty cheeses each, so wherever he starts his sample, cheeses from the ends of the shelf will always be under- or over-represented in the sample. This may affect his overall results.

A better method would be to use stratified sampling, and choose three random cheeses from each shelf. This would not take significantly more time than his current method.

Q2. (a) The sample could be constructed using opportunity sampling. Since we cannot force healthy people to try the drug, the sample group can only be composed of those people willing to take part. The disadvantage is that the group is self-selecting, and so is unlikely to be particularly representative of the general population.

(b) The first trials of a new drug are conducted on small sample groups because there is a small chance of very serious side effects being seen. Since the group is small and self-selected, we will have low confidence in the results being seen. If there is a 0.1% chance of a serious reaction, we are unlikely to see it during the trial. If the small trial does not show any significant problems with the drug, larger trials can be performed.

Q3. (a) The school could gather the names of all pupils taking the exam and list them in a random order. They could then take the sample to be the first

twenty names on the list.
- (b) In simple random sampling, each choice should be independent. For the method described, after four pupils have been chosen from one class, no-one else in the class will be selected. Therefore, the choices are not independent.

Q4. (a) We estimate the population mean with the sample mean.
$$\frac{16.3 + 16.6 + 17.0 + 17.3 + 17.1 + 17.4}{6} = \frac{101.7}{6} = 16.95 \text{ pounds.}$$

- (b) The values in the sample are fairly close together. This may be because the fish in the lake are similar sizes. In this case, our estimated mean could be reasonably accurate.
- (c) The sample is very small. A larger sample would increase the accuracy of the estimate.
  The sample has been constructed using opportunity sampling, with no attempt to measure a representative sample of the fish in the lake. This could be improved by capturing fish at different locations within the lake.

Q5. The researcher constructed two samples and obtained two different sample means. The different values may have come about by chance. Different samples will give different results. If the population variance is very high, then two sample means can have very different values.

Alternatively, the different values may have come about because he constructed the samples using opportunity sampling at two different times. It could be that one, or both, of the samples were not representative of the overall population.

He could improve his survey by improving his sampling technique. For example, he could find the proportion of people in different age categories in the overall population, and use quota sampling to ensure that his sample matches these proportions.

Worked Solutions — Exercise 23.1

Q1. The mode can be read directly from the chart.

There are 32 data points, so the median is given by the value mid-way between the sixteenth and seventeenth values. Both of these values lie within the households with two children, and so the median is equal to 2.

If we write X_i for the number of households with i children, then the mean is given by

$$\mu = \frac{\sum i X_i}{\sum X_i} = \frac{(1 \times 12) + (2 \times 14) + (3 \times 5) + (4 \times 1)}{12 + 14 + 5 + 1}$$
$$= \frac{12 + 28 + 15 + 4}{32} = \frac{59}{32} = 1.84$$

to two decimal places.

Q2. The bar chart should show the following data.

Fuel	Gas	Electricity	Oil	LPG
Frequency	57	32	8	3

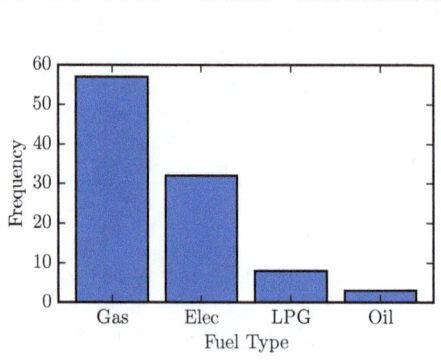

Q3. The bar chart is shown below.

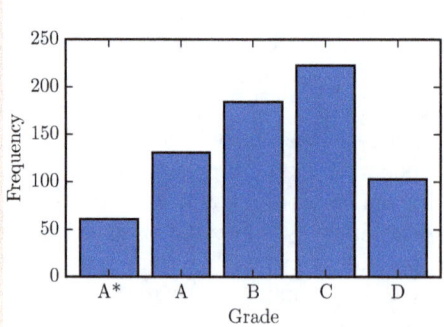

We can write out a cumulative frequency table.

Grade	A*	A	B	C	D
Cumulative frequency	61	192	376	599	702

There are 702 exam results and so the central two data points are at positions 351 and 352. The cumulative frequency table shows us that these two points both lie in the B grade category, and so this is the median.

Q4. Assuming there are no driverless cars in our sample, the range of data is $\{1, 2, 3\}$. Let X_i be the number of cars with i occupants. Let m be the median value and M be the mode.

The mode is less than the median, $M < m$. Since they must both be values from the set $\{1, 2, 3\}$, we can say that $m \neq 1$ and $M \neq 3$.

If $m = 3$ then at least half of the data points must be equal to three, since this is the highest value in the range. That is, $X_3 \geq 9$ and so $X_1 + X_2 \leq 8$. But this implies that 3 is also the mode, which we have already ruled out. Therefore the median must be equal to 2 and the mode equal to 1.

Since there are twice as many data points equal to the mode as there are data points equal to the median, we have $X_1 = 2X_2$. In particular, X_1 is even. Also, it must be the case that $X_1 < 9$, else X_1 would also be the median.

Suppose $X_1 \leq 6$. This means that $X_2 = \frac{1}{2}X_1 \leq 3$ and so $X_1 + X_2 \leq 9$. This implies $X_3 \geq 7$, and the mode is equal to 3. This contradicts our result that $M = 1$ and so $X_1 > 6$. Therefore, the only possible value is $X_1 = 8$, from which we calculate that $X_2 = 4$ and $X_3 = 5$.

The bar chart should show the following data.

Occupants	1	2	3
Frequency	8	4	5

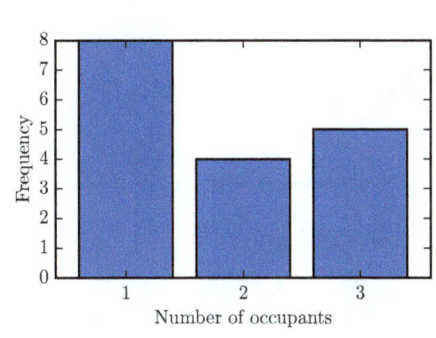

Q5. A This data is unimodal, with a clear peak at 3. Almost all of the data is within a distance of 2 of the mode, so the data at value 9 can be considered to be an outlier.

B This chart also shows a clear peak. The data spreads out more gradually from the mode than in Chart A, so we say that it has higher variation.

C The values 2, 7 and 8 are the most common in the data set, but there is no clear peak. The differences in the frequencies are most likely to be due to chance.

D There are two clear local maxima here, so both values can be considered to be modes. The distribution is bimodal.

Worked Solutions — Exercise 23.2

Q1. The bar chart data is shown in the following dot plot.

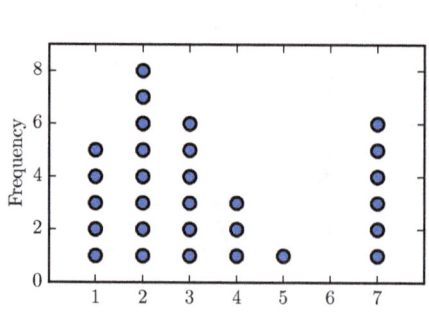

Q2. (a) Here are the results shown in a dot plot

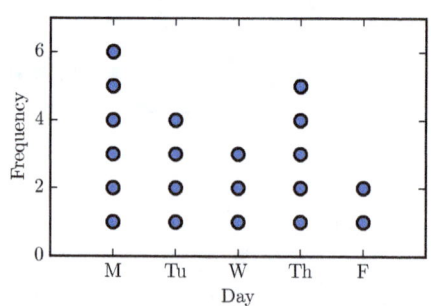

(b) The mean number of people cycling to work is given by:
$$\frac{6+4+3+5+2}{5} = \frac{20}{5} = 4 \text{ people.}$$

(c) The days of the week, arranged in order of increasing numbers of people cycling, are {Friday, Wednesday, Tuesday, Thursday, Monday}. Therefore the median value occurs on the Tuesday.

Q3. (a) In the following dot plot, the boys' results are shown as blue dots, and the girls' results in red.

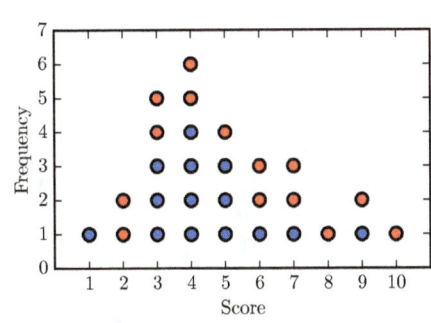

(b) The modal score, which we can read directly from the plot, is equal to 4.

(c) We can use the plot to calculate the girls' median score. There are fourteen red dots and so, taking the scores in ascending order, the median score is the midpoint of the seventh and eighth values. These are equal to 5 and 6 and so the median is equal to 5.5.

Q4. (a) The company's performance is shown in the following dot plot.

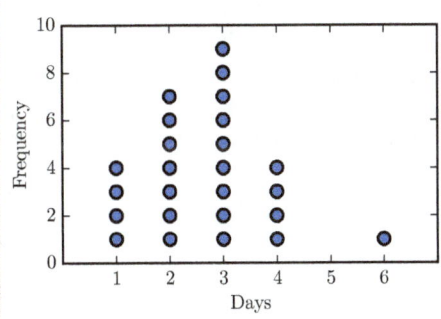

(b) The mean delivery time is calculated as follows:

$$\frac{(1 \times 4) + (2 \times 7) + (3 \times 9) + (4 \times 4) + (6 \times 1)}{25} =$$
$$\frac{4 + 14 + 27 + 16 + 6}{25} = \frac{67}{25} = 2.68 \text{ days.}$$

(c) Of the 25 parcels in the sample, 20 were delivered within the target time. That is, 80% were delivered on time.

(d) A measurement of the company's performance is an attempt to measure customer satisfaction. The mean delivery time is not a good way to do this. If the sample is representative of the overall service, then one parcel out of every five is not delivered in the agreed time. This means that 20% of customers are likely to be unhappy with the service.

Parcels which are delivered early, lower the value of the mean. But those customers whose parcels were delivered late will not be reassured by being

> told that many other parcels were delivered early.
>
> A better measurement would be to track the percentage of parcels delivered within the target time.

Worked Solutions — Exercise 23.3

Q1. (a) The range of values, after rounding, is £14 000 to £95 000 and so the stems must range from 1 to 9 with no gaps. The lines for values starting with 6 and 7 must be present and left blank. We obtain the following plot, where $1|4 = £14\,000$.

```
1 | 4 5
2 | 0 3 5 7 7 7 8
3 | 0 0 0 1 2 3 5 5 6 7 7 8
4 | 1 1 4 4 6 8 8
5 | 2 8
6 |
7 |
8 | 5
9 | 5
```

(b) There are 32 data points, so the median is the mean of the data points at positions 15 and 16. These are both equal to £35 000, and so this is the median. We could have gone back to the original data and produced a median of £35 125, but this implies a level of accuracy which is not supported by the data in general.

Q2. The data is given to two decimal places, so the stem of the data will be the integer part and the first decimal place. There are no data points for 3.5 kg, so we must leave a blank row in the plot. We obatin the following plot, where $3.0|6$ represents 3.06 kg

```
3.0 | 6 8
3.1 | 4 6 7 9
3.2 | 0 0 1 3 6 8
3.3 | 2 8 8
3.4 | 4 9
3.5 |
3.6 | 0
```

Q3. In this stem-and-leaf plot, $6|3$ represents $63\,\mu\text{g m}^{-3}$.

```
 6 | 3
 7 |
 8 | 2 4
 9 | 1 1 8
10 | 0 3 4 8 9
11 | 2 3
12 | 4
```

There are 14 data points, and the sum of the data is 1382. The mean is given by

$$\frac{1382}{14} = 98.7 \,\mu g\, m^{-3}$$

to one decimal place.

The median, m, is the mean of the data values in locations 7 and 8.

$$m = \frac{100 + 103}{2} = 101.5 \,\mu g\, m^{-3}.$$

Q4. Results of men's 100 m semi-finals, where 9.8|6 represents 9.86 s.

```
 9.8 | 6
 9.9 | 2 4 5 7 8
10.0 | 1 1 1 3 5 5 7 8 8
10.1 | 1 2 3 3 6 7
10.2 | 3
```

There are two heats of 7 and one of 8, making a total of 22 data points. The mean is

$$\frac{221.06}{22} = 10.05 \,s$$

to two decimal places.

The median is the mean of the data values in locations 11 and 12. These are both equal to 10.05 s, and so this is the value of the median.

Q5. Results of mental agility test, , where 2|9|1 represents a score of 92 in the placebo group and 91 in the tonic group.

```
         Placebo group   |    | Tonic group
                   6  4  |  8 |
                6  1  0  |  9 | 1 4
                8  4  3  | 10 | 2 2 8
          8  8  4  3  2  | 11 | 0 4 5 9
                   7  4  2| 12 | 2 2 3 4 7 8
                      2  0| 13 | 0 3 8 9
                         7  3| 14 | 0 1
                            4| 15 |
```

There are 21 people in each group, so the median value is the eleventh value. For the group taking the tonic, the median is 122. For the group taking the placebo, the median is 114.

Worked Solutions — Exercise 23.4

Q1. We can calculate the heights of the bars by extending the table to show the width and the frequency density.

Range	Frequency	Width	Frequency Density
$0 \leq x < 10$	3	10	0.3
$10 \leq x < 20$	7	10	0.7
$20 \leq x < 25$	11	5	2.2
$25 \leq x < 35$	15	10	1.5
$35 \leq x < 40$	6	5	1.2
$40 \leq x < 50$	6	10	0.6
$50 \leq x < 70$	6	20	0.3
$70 \leq x < 100$	3	30	0.1

The histogram is shown below.

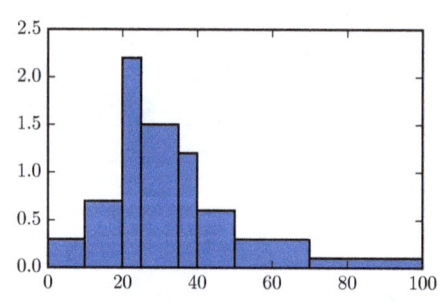

Q2. (a) The frequency density of the first class is 1.2 and this has a height of 6 cm. Therefore, the height of each bar in centimetres is 5 times the frequency density. The density of the 10 to 20 class is 2.8 so it must have a height of 14 cm.

(b) The bar for the range 30 to 40 is 12 cm high, so the frequency density is 2.4. The width of the class is 10 and so the total frequency is 24.

(c) The width of the final class is 30 and this is represented by a bar of width 1.5 cm. Therefore the bar for the range 50 to 70, with width 20, will be 1 cm wide.

(d) There are 120 data points in total, and so $y = 12$. Therefore the frequency density of the final class is 0.4 and so the height is 2 cm.

The histogram is shown below.

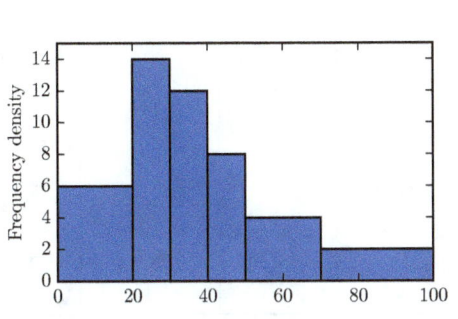

Q3. We can extend the table as follows and use it to plot the histogram.

Range (s)			Width	Frequency Density
$0 \leq$	x	< 5	5	3735
$5 \leq$	x	< 10	5	3226
$10 \leq$	x	< 15	5	3419
$15 \leq$	x	< 30	15	1390
$30 \leq$	x	< 60	30	573
$60 \leq$	x	< 120	60	167

The histogram is shown below.

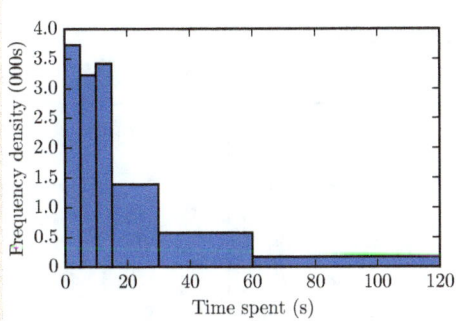

Q4. The minimum legal weight of a coin is 122.5 grains. Mr Miller said that the lightest coin was 0.207 or 0.208 grains heavier than this. We will assume that the lightest coin was 122.707 grains, which is 0.567 grains below the standard weight. Since we do not have any information about the heaviest coin, we will also assume that the heaviest coin was 0.567 grains above the standard weight.

This gives us the following table, from which we can plot the histogram.

Deviation (grains)	Frequency	Width	Frequency Density
$-0.567 \le d < -0.26525$	209	0.30175	692
$-0.26525 \le d < -0.2$	362	0.06525	5548
$-0.2 \le d < -0.1$	1261	0.1	12610
$-0.1 \le d < 0$	3023	0.1	30230
$0 \le d < 0.1$	2631	0.1	26310
$0.1 \le d < 0.2$	1733	0.1	17330
$0.2 \le d < 0.26525$	536	0.06525	8215
$0.26525 \le d < 0.567$	245	0.30175	812

The histogram is shown below.

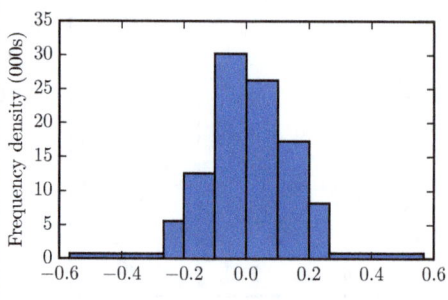

Worked Solutions — Exercise 23.5

Q1. For data set A, we can extend the table to give the cumulative frequencies.

Range			Frequency	Cumulative Frequency
$0 \le$	x	< 25	80	80
$25 \le$	x	< 50	134	214
$50 \le$	x	< 75	186	400
$75 \le$	x	< 100	497	897
$100 \le$	x	< 125	1534	2431
$125 \le$	x	< 150	3975	6406
$150 \le$	x	< 175	2865	9271
$175 \le$	x	< 200	729	10000

Then we plot the known values and sketch a smooth line between the points. The estimated median is given by the value when the cumulative frequency is equal to

5000. From the graph below, this gives us an estimated median of $x = 142$.

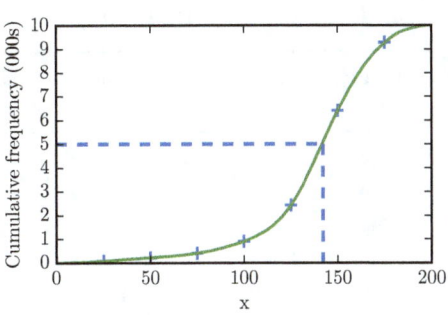

Repeating this for data set B, we have the following table.

Range			Frequency	Cumulative Frequency
$0 \leq$	x	< 25	2435	2435
$25 \leq$	x	< 50	1354	3789
$50 \leq$	x	< 75	843	4632
$75 \leq$	x	< 100	244	4876
$100 \leq$	x	< 125	358	5234
$125 \leq$	x	< 150	1358	6592
$150 \leq$	x	< 175	2079	8671
$175 \leq$	x	< 200	1329	10000

From which we can draw the following graph, and read off an estimated mean of $x = 112$.

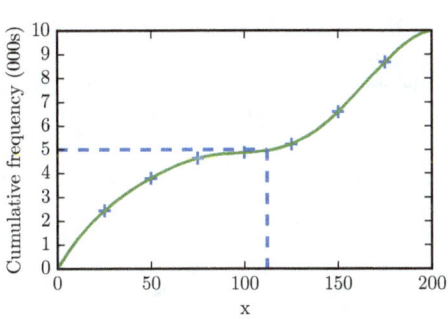

Data set B is bimodal and its cumulative frequency graph does not have the usual shape. The data points near the median are further apart than they are in data set A. This means that the gradient of the cumulative frequency near the median is much smaller in data set B. Small changes in the way that we draw the curve lead to bigger changes in the estimate of the median. Therefore, we would expect the estimate for data set A to be more accurate than the estimate for data set B.

Q2. First, we will extend the table with a column for the cumulative frequency.

Range	Frequency	Cumulative frequency
$0 \le x < 100$	23	23
$100 \le x < 200$	107	130
$200 \le x < 250$	284	414
$250 \le x < 300$	435	849
$300 \le x < 400$	348	1197
$400 \le x < 500$	231	1428
$500 \le x < 600$	95	1523

There are 1523 data points and so our estimate for the median will be data value X_{762}. This is in the class range 250 to 300. Our estimate of the cumulative frequency for this class is given by a straight line connecting $(x_1, y_1) = (250, 414)$ and $(x_2, y_2) = (300, 849)$.

We want to find the x co-ordinate of the point (x_3, y_3) with $y_3 = 762$.

$$\frac{y_2 - y_1}{x_2 - x_1} = \frac{y_3 - y_1}{x_3 - x_1} \implies \frac{849 - 414}{300 - 250} = \frac{762 - 414}{x_3 - 250}$$
$$\implies \frac{435}{50} = \frac{348}{x_3 - 250}$$
$$\implies x_3 - 250 = \frac{50 \times 348}{435} = 40$$
$$\implies x_3 = 290$$

Q3. We already have a column for the cumulative frequency values for the data. There are 836 values, so our estimate for the median will be the mean of our estimates for values X_{418} and X_{419}. We can read the estimate $X_{418} = 6$ directly from the table. Note that the table does not give the exact value: it tells us that $X_{418} \le 6 < X_{419}$. The value 6 is our estimate.

We will calculate the estimate of X_{419} using linear interpolation on the line segment joining $(12, 418)$ and $(16, 598)$. Let x be our estimate of X_{419}, and then

$$\frac{598 - 418}{16 - 12} = \frac{419 - 418}{x - 12} \implies \frac{180}{4} = \frac{1}{x - 12}$$
$$\implies x - 6 = \frac{4}{180}$$
$$\implies x = 6.02$$

to two decimal places.

Our estimate for the median is the mean of our two estimates, and so is equal to 6.01.

Q4. We will calculate an estimate for X_{5000} using linear interpolation between $(4855, 0)$

and $(7486, 0.1)$. Our estimate x is then

$$\frac{7486 - 4855}{0.1 - 0} = \frac{5000 - 4855}{x - 0} \implies \frac{2631}{0.1} = \frac{145}{x}$$
$$\implies x = \frac{145}{26310}$$
$$\implies x = 0.0055$$

to four decimal places. The data points are very dense in this part of the range so, to this level of accuracy, we would take X_{5001} to be equal to 0.0055 to four decimal places. Our estimate for the median weight is found by adding this to the standard weight, $123.274 + 0.0055 = 123.2795$ grains.

Worked Solutions — Exercise 23.6

Q1. (a) If we write the ordered results of the students in Class A as $\{A_1, A_2, \ldots, A_{30}\}$, then the quartiles are given by

$$Q_1 = A_8 = 51, \qquad Q_2 = \frac{1}{2}(A_{15} + A_{16}) = 64.5, \qquad Q_3 = A_{23} = 75.$$

The interquartile range is $75 - 51 = 24$, so any data points below $51 - 36 = 15$ or above $75 + 36 = 111$ are classed as outliers. There are no such data points, so the whiskers of the box will cover the full range of data from 18 to 87.
Class B has 19 pupils and so the quartiles are given by:

$$Q_1 = B_5 = 46, \qquad Q_2 = B_{10} = 55, \qquad Q_3 = B_{15} = 82.$$

The interquartile range is $82 - 46 = 36$. A data point is an outlier if its distance from the interval (Q_1, Q_3) is greater than $1.5 \times 36 = 54$. Since all of the data points lie inside $(-8, 118)$, the whiskers of the box will cover the full range of data from 27 to 92.
Class C has 32 pupils, so the quartiles are given by

$$Q_1 = C_8 = 60, \qquad Q_2 = \frac{1}{2}(C_{15} + C_{16}) = 76, \qquad Q_3 = C_{23} = 85.$$

The interquartile range is $85 - 60 = 25$ and so an outlier is any point below $60 - 37.5 = 22.5$ or above $85 + 37.5 = 122.5$. Therefore, the lowest two data points, 18 and 20, are outliers. The whiskers will cover the rest of the data, from 37 to 95.

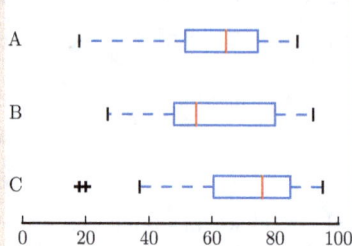

(b) Class C has the highest values for all three of its quartiles, so we would say that overall it was the highest performing class.

Q2. We have results from 29 plants without fertiliser, ranging from 0.2 kg to 2.0 kg. The median is at position 15 and the quartiles are at positions 8 and 23:

$$Q_1 = 1.2\,\text{kg}, \qquad Q_2 = 1.4\,\text{kg}, \qquad Q_3 = 1.7\,\text{kg}.$$

The interquartile range is $1.7 - 1.2 = 0.5$kg. Therefore, data points which lie below 0.45 kg or above 2.45 kg are outliers. In this data set, the lowest data point is an outlier.

We have 26 results from the plants which were given the fertiliser, ranging from 0.5 kg to 2.6 kg. The median lies between the data points at positions 13 and 14 and the quartiles are at positions 7 and 20:

$$Q_1 = 1.0\,\text{kg}, \qquad Q_2 = 1.2\,\text{kg}, \qquad Q_3 = 1.6\,\text{kg}.$$

The interquartile range is $1.6 - 1.0 = 0.6$kg. Therefore, data points which lie below 0.1 kg or above 2.5 kg are outliers. In this data set, the highest data point is an outlier.

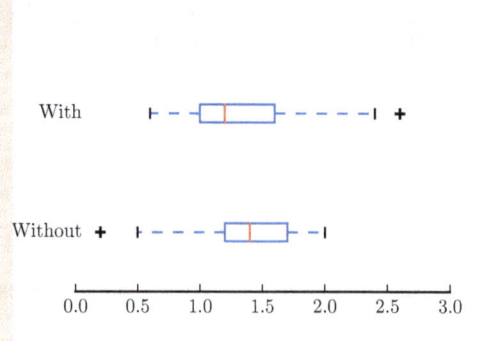

The gardener saw mixed results from his tests with the fertiliser.

All three quartiles are lower for the fertilised plants, indicating that most plants had lower yields.

The results suggest that the fertiliser had a positive effect at the extremes: the entire range is higher when fertiliser is added. The highest yielding plants yield more, and the lowest yielding plants also do better, when the fertiliser is used.

Q3. There are 35 washers in each batch, and so the quartiles are given by the size of the washers at positions 9, 18 and 27. For the old machine, this is

$$Q_1 = 14.84\,\text{mm}, \qquad Q_2 = 14.92\,\text{mm}, \qquad Q_3 = 15.11\,\text{mm}.$$

For the new machine, the figures are

$$Q_1 = 14.73\,\text{mm}, \qquad Q_2 = 15.03\,\text{mm}, \qquad Q_3 = 15.15\,\text{mm}.$$

This gives us the following box plots.

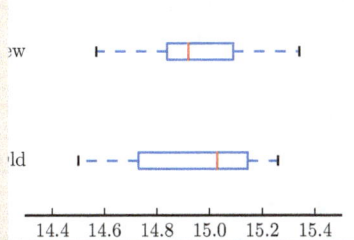

The median size of the washers from the new machine is closer to the target size of 15 mm, being 0.03 mm too large, compared to 0.08 mm too small. The total range of the sizes from the two machines are very close (0.76 mm from the old machine and 0.77 mm from the new machine).

However, the box plot clearly shows us that the interquartile range is larger for the new machine, suggesting that the new machine is less consistent. The interquartile range of the old machine is 0.27 mm and for the new machine it is 0.42 mm. Based on this data set, we would not recommend buying the new machine.

Q4. (a) We first extend the table to show the cumulative frequency.

Journey time (minutes)	Frequency	Cumulative Frequency
$40 \leq x < 50$	6	6
$50 \leq x < 60$	5	11
$60 \leq x < 70$	15	26
$70 \leq x < 80$	9	35
$80 \leq x < 90$	7	42
$90 \leq x < 105$	5	47
$100 \leq x < 110$	3	50

Now we can estimate the quartiles by estimating the journey time when the cumulative frequency is equal to 12.5, 25 and 37.5 using linear interpolation. The lower quartile, Q_1, lies on the line segment between 60 min and 70 min. This line passes through the points $(60, 11)$ and $(70, 26)$. We can use the equation $(y_1 - y_0) = m(x_1 - x_0)$ to find the gradient, m.

$$m = \frac{26 - 11}{70 - 60} = 1.5.$$

The line also passes through $(Q_1, 12.5)$ so we can use the equation of the line again, this time with the points $(60, 11)$ and $(Q_1, 12.5)$, to find our estimate of the lower quartile.

$$(12.5 - 11) = 1.5(Q_1 - 60)$$
$$1.5 = 1.5(Q_1 - 60)$$
$$Q_1 = 61$$

The same calculation with the points $(60, 11)$ and $(Q_2, 25)$ gives us the estimate $Q_2 = 69.3$ to one decimal place.

To find our estimate of the upper quartile, we calculate the gradient of the line segment between 80 min and 90 min.

$$m = \frac{42 - 35}{90 - 80} = 0.7$$

Then we can substitute the co-ordinates of $(80, 35)$ and $(Q_3, 37.5)$ into the equation of the line.

$$(37.5 - 35) = 0.7(Q_3 - 80)$$
$$2.5 = 0.7(Q_1 - 80)$$
$$Q_3 = 83.6$$

Our estimates of the quartiles, to one decimal place, are

$$Q_1 = 61.0, \quad Q_2 = 69.3, \quad Q_3 = 83.6.$$

(b) The estimate of the skew coefficient is given by

$$\frac{Q_3 - 2Q_2 + Q_1}{Q_3 - Q_1} = \frac{83.6 - (2 \times 69.3) + 61.0}{83.6 - 61.0} = \frac{6.0}{22.6} = 0.27$$

to two decimal places.
The skew is positive.

Worked Solutions — Exercise 23.7

Q1. We calculate $y = (x - 972)/133$.

x	440	706	972	1371	1770	2036	2302
y	-4	-2	0	3	6	8	10
y^2	16	4	0	9	36	64	100

Therefore, $\sum y = 21$ and $\sum y^2 = 229$, which gives us

$$\mu_Y = \frac{21}{7} = 3.$$

The variance is given by

$$\sigma_Y^2 = \frac{229}{7} - 3^2 = 23.714,$$

and so the standard deviation is equal to 4.87 to two decimal places. Reversing the coding gives us $\mu_X = 133\mu_Y + 972 = 1371$ and $\sigma_X = 133\mu_Y = 647.7$ to one decimal place.

Q2. (a) We will use the midpoint (m_i) of each range to estimate the sum of the rates, and the sum of the squares of the rates.

Hourly rate (£)	m_i	Freq. (f_i)	$f_i m_i$	$f_i m_i^2$
$8 \leq x < 10$	9	30	270	2430
$10 \leq x < 30$	20	26	520	10400
$30 \leq x < 40$	35	16	560	19600
$40 \leq x < 50$	45	12	540	24300
$50 \leq x < 70$	60	8	480	28800
$70 \leq x < 100$	85	6	510	43350
$100 \leq x < 200$	150	0	0	0
$200 \leq x < 300$	250	2	500	125000

This gives us $\sum f_i = 100$, $\sum f_i m_i = 3380$ and $\sum f_i m_i^2 = 253880$. Therefore we can estimate the mean to be

$$\mu = \frac{\sum f_i m_i}{\sum f_i} = \frac{3380}{100} = £33.80 \text{ an hour.}$$

The estimated variance is given by

$$\sigma^2 = \frac{\sum f_i m_i^2}{\sum f_i} - \mu^2 = \frac{253880}{100} - 1142.44 = 1396.36.$$

Taking the square root, we estimate the standard deviation to be £37.36 an hour.

(b) The mean is not a good measure to use in this case. The right hand tail of the data is very long and for highly asymmetric data sets, the mean is not a good description of the hourly rate. In this case, we can see that almost one third of the employees earn less than a third of the mean rate. The salaries of the senior managers has increased the mean hourly rate so that it doesn't represent the salary of the vast majority of the workers well.76

Q3. (a) To calculate the mean and standard deviation of Nixon's speech, we can extend the table to find the sum of the lengths and the sum of the squares of the lengths.

Length (x)	Freq (f)	fx	fx^2	Length (x)	Freq (f)	fx	fx^2
1	54	54	54	8	91	728	5824
2	482	964	1928	9	58	522	4698
3	444	1332	3996	10	32	320	3200
4	352	1408	5632	11	25	275	3025
5	244	1220	6100	12	4	48	576
6	171	1026	6156	13	4	52	676
7	142	994	6958	14	1	14	196

The speech is 2104 words long, and we have $\sum fx = 8957$ and $\sum fx^2 = 49019$. Therefore the mean for Nixon's speech is given by

$$\mu_N = \frac{\sum fx}{2104} = \frac{8957}{2104} = 4.26 \text{ letters}$$

to two decimal places. The variance is given by

$$\sigma_N^2 = \frac{\sum fx^2}{2104} - \mu_N^2 = \frac{49019}{2104} - 18.12 = 5.175,$$

and so the standard deviation is $\sigma_N = \sqrt{5.175} = 2.27$ letters, to two decimal places.

Repeating the calculations for Trump's speech, we have $\sum fx = 6682$ and $\sum fx^2 = 38500$. His speech was 1457 words long. The mean for Trump's speech is given by

$$\mu_T = \frac{\sum fx}{1457} = \frac{6682}{1457} = 4.59 \text{ letters to two decimal places.}$$

The variance is given by

$$\sigma_T^2 = \frac{\sum fx^2}{1457} - \mu_T^2 = \frac{38500}{1457} - 21.03 = 5.392,$$

and so the standard deviation is $\sigma_T = \sqrt{5.392} = 2.32$ letters, to two decimal places.

(b) We have been given the summary statistics for Lincoln's speech, so we can put these straight into the formulae. The mean, to two decimal places, is given by

$$\mu_L = \frac{\sum fx}{3623} = \frac{16932}{3623} = 4.67 \text{ letters.}$$

The variance is given by

$$\sigma_L^2 = \frac{\sum fx^2}{3623} - \mu_L^2 = \frac{106966}{3623} - 21.84 = 7.683,$$

and so the standard deviation is $\sigma_L = \sqrt{7.683} = 2.77$ letters, to two decimal places.

(c) These results do not suggest that there is an overall trend to longer or shorter words in the speeches. The difference between the oldest and most recent speeches is less than 0.9 of a letter.

There is some evidence to suggest that the more recent speeches do not contain as many very long words. The standard deviation is highest for Lincoln's speech, indicating he tended to use words whose length was further from the mean. Since all words contain at least one letter, this implies that his speech included more long words than the other two speeches.

Q4. To calculate our estimates, we must find the mid-point m of each class. For each class we can estimate the sum of the data points, and the sum of the square of the data points.

Speed (mph)	Frequency (f)	mid-point (m)	fm	fm^2
$10 \leq x < 20$	23	15	315	4725
$20 \leq x < 30$	242	25	6050	151250
$30 \leq x < 35$	156	32.5	4940	160550
$35 \leq x < 40$	184	37.5	6900	258750
$40 \leq x < 45$	160	42.5	6800	289000
$45 \leq x < 50$	76	47.5	3420	162450
$50 \leq x < 60$	62	55	3355	184525
$60 \leq x < 65$	8	62.5	500	31250

From this, we can calculate the estimates $\sum X_i = 32280$ and $\sum X_i^2 = 1242500$. A total of $N = 900$ speeds were recorded.

We estimate the values for the mean and variance as

$$\mu = \frac{1}{N}\sum X_i = \frac{32280}{900} = 35.87 \text{mph},$$

$$\sigma^2 = \frac{1}{N}\sum X_i^2 - \mu^2 = \frac{1242500}{900} - 1286.42 = 94.14,$$

both to two decimal places.

Our estimate for the standard deviation is $\sigma = \sqrt{94.19} = 9.70$mph, to two decimal places.

Q5. The mid-points for the first two classes are 27.5 and 32.5. Therefore,

$$a(27.5 - b) = -15 \quad \text{and} \quad a(32.5 - b) = -5.$$

Subtracting these equations gives the result $5a = 10$ and hence $a = 2$.

We can now substitute this value back into $a(27.5 - b) = -15$. Solving the equation $2(27.5 - b) = -15$ gives us the result $b = 35$.

To estimate the mean and standard deviation of the electricity demand, we first estimate the mean and variance of the coded data. There are 8194 data points.

We estimate the mean as

$$\mu_Y = \frac{\sum Y_i}{8194} = \frac{82387}{8194} = 10.05$$

to two decimal places. Our estimate of the variance is given by

$$\sigma_Y^2 = \frac{\sum Y_i^2}{f_i} - \mu_Y^2 = \frac{2525560}{8194} - 101 = 207.22,$$

also to two decimal places, and so we estimate $\sigma_Y = 14.40\,\text{GW}$.
We can then undo the coding to estimate the values for the original data.

$$\mu_X = \frac{\mu_Y}{a} + b = \frac{10.05}{2} + 35 = 40.03\,\text{GW},$$
$$\sigma_X = \frac{\sigma_Y}{a} = \frac{14.40}{2} = 7.20\,\text{GW},$$

both to two decimal places.

Worked Solutions — Exercise 23.8

Q1. (a) The results have been given in order, so we can see that the median is equal to 86.
Summing the results gives a total of 1447, so the mean value is 72.35.
(b) Data has a negative skew if its left hand tail is either longer or fatter than its right hand tail. We can classify a data set as having negative skew if its mean is less than its median. Alternatively, we can see the skew by plotting a histogram or box plot.
(c) Many pupils did very well in this test, with a majority scoring over 85%. This means that there was no possibility of having a long right hand tail, since the maximum possible score is 100%. The test is failing to differentiate between the most able students.

Q2. (a) First, we calculate the summary statistics $\sum X_i$ and $\sum X_i^2$.

x_i	1	2	3	4	5	6	7
f_i	2	18	123	372	349	50	1
$f_i x_i$	2	36	369	1488	1745	300	7
$f_i x_i^2$	2	72	1107	5952	8725	1800	49

In this table, f_i represents the number of data points equal to x_i. We find $\sum X_i = 3947$ and $\sum X_i^2 = 17707$, which gives us:

$$\mu = \frac{\sum X_i}{\sum f_i} = \frac{3947}{915} = 4.314$$

$$\sigma^2 = \frac{\sum X_i^2}{\sum f_i} - \mu^2 = \frac{17707}{915} - 18.608 = 0.744$$

$$\sigma = \sqrt{0.744} = 0.863$$

to three decimal places.

(b) The mode of the data is equal to 4 and so the skew coefficient is given by

$$\text{skew} = \frac{(\text{mean} - \text{mode})}{\sigma} = \frac{4.314 - 4}{0.863} = 0.234$$

to three decimal places.

Q3. (a) To estimate the median, we first calculate the cumulative frequencies.

Age (years)			Frequency (f)	Cumulative frequency
	x	< 1	18	18
$1 \leq$	x	< 2	23	41
$2 \leq$	x	< 3	28	69
$3 \leq$	x	< 4	85	154
$4 \leq$	x	< 5	121	275
$5 \leq$	x	< 6	276	551
$6 \leq$	x	< 7	321	672
$7 \leq$	x	< 8	355	1227
$8 \leq$	x	< 9	340	1567
$9 \leq$	x	< 10	133	1700

We see that the middle point lies somewhere between 7 and 8 years. The line on the cumulative frequency graph in this section joins $(x_1, y_1) = (7, 672)$ and $(x_2, y_2) = (8, 1227)$. Therefore its gradient is equal to

$$\text{gradient} = \frac{y_2 - y_1}{x_2 - x_1} = \frac{1227 - 672}{8 - 7} = 555.$$

This line passes through the point $(x_3, y_3) = (m, 850)$ and we must find the value of m. Since the gradient of the line is constant, we have

$$\frac{y_3 - y_1}{x_3 - x_1} = \frac{850 - 672}{m - 7} = 555.$$

Therefore $555m = 178 + 3885 = 4063$ and so the median equals 7.32 years to two decimal places.

(b) From the summary statistics we can calculate the mean μ and the standard deviation. We obtain

$$\mu = \frac{\sum X_i}{1700} = \frac{11376}{1700} = 6.69 \text{ years}$$

$$\sigma = \sqrt{\frac{\sum X_i^2}{1700} - \mu^2} = \sqrt{\frac{82171}{1700} - 44.78} = \sqrt{3.56} = 1.89 \text{ years}$$

both to two decimal places. Now we can calculate that the skew coefficient is equal to

$$\frac{\mu - m}{\sigma} = \frac{6.69 - 7.32}{1.89} = -0.33.$$

Worked Solutions — Exercise 24.1

Q1. (a) We would expect a positive correlation here, with the test scores as the response variable.

(b) It would be reasonable to expect no correlation here, since there is no obvious causal connection between a film's title and its popular appeal. However, it could be argued that films which are part of a franchise tend to have longer titles *and* bigger audiences, so we could make a case for some weak positive correlation.

(c) There have been studies showing that people who exercise frequently generally take less sick leave, so we are justified in saying that we expect a negative correlation. Even so, the relationship is likely to be much more complex than the connection between, for example, sunshine and ice cream sales. Depending on their chosen activity, staff could suffer from exercise related injuries. Low levels of exercise will have no measurable effect. Some staff will have underlying health problems which are unconnected to general fitness.

Q2. The scatter graph shows a weak positive correlation.

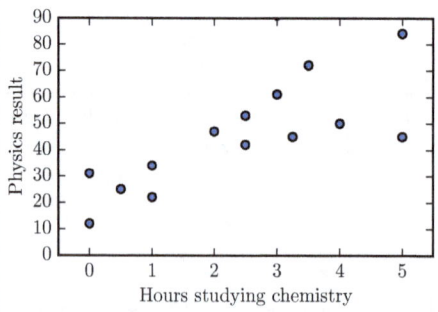

It is unlikely that studying for the chemistry test has a direct effect on a student's physics result. The correlation between studying for the chemistry test and the score on the physics test is probably explained by a third variable: the conscientiousness of the student. That is, those students who studied most for one test probably also studied for the other.

Q3. (a) A strong negative correlation between HDL levels and incidence of heart disease means that people with high HDL levels are less likely to suffer from heart disease than people with lower levels.

(b) The correlation does not prove that higher HDL levels are preventing heart disease. It could be that other factors are causing higher HDL levels *and* reducing heart disease. Since higher HDL levels are associated with other healthy activities, such as exercising and having a good diet, it is likely that the healthy lifestyle is causing the high HDL level and protecting against heart disease.

Q4. (a) There is a clear positive correlation in the data, but it is fairly weak.

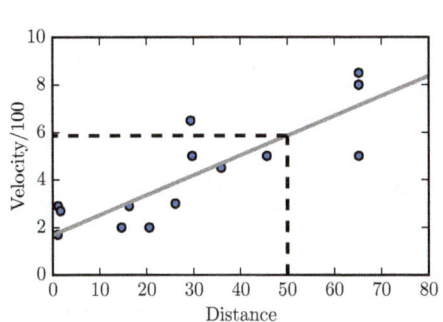

(b) Since the velocity of a galaxy is proportional to its distance, we would expect the data to be strongly positively correlated. This suggests that the figures that Hubble used were not very accurate. (Hubble expressed surprise that he was able to find any relationship at all, given the quality of the data. He said that for "such scanty material, so poorly distributed, the results are fairly definite.")

(c) Given the weakness of the correlation, it is not clear exactly where we should draw the line to show the relationship. One example is shown above.

We could argue that there is one data point which we know exactly: the earth is not moving relative to itself. This would suggest that any linear relationship must pass through the origin. However, that is not something we can deduce from the data we have.

From the line we have drawn, we would predict that a galaxy at a distance of 50 million light years would be travelling away from the earth at around $600 \,\text{km}\,\text{s}^{-1}$. We should not try to give a more accurate figure, given the low correlation of the data.

Worked Solutions — Exercise 24.2

Q1. (a) The scatter graph indicates a strong positive correlation between the length and the weight of the frogs.

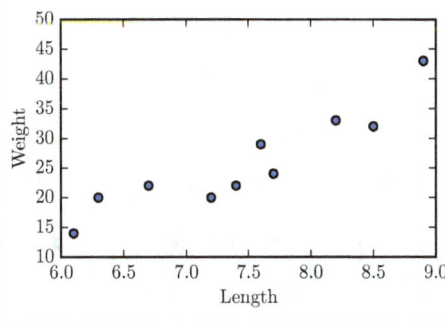

(b) For a frog which weighs 30 g, we estimate that the length l will satisfy $30 = 8.39l - 36.7$. Therefore, $8.39l = 66.7$ and so we estimate $l = 7.9$ cm to one decimal place.

(c) The values suggested by the scientist fit the suggested regression equation. However, the estimate is beyond the range of the observed values. The relationship may not hold so far from the observed values, and so should be treated with caution.

Q2. (a) We would assume that the age of the car affects its price, so the age is the explanatory variable, and the price is the response variable.

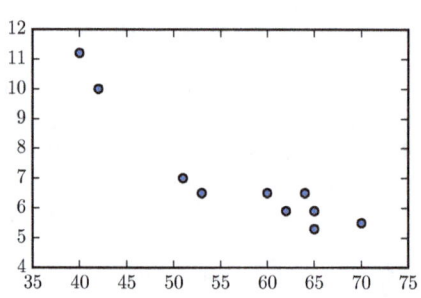

The graph shows a strong negative correlation.

(b) First, we calculate the product of the data values.

A_i	40	42	51	53	60	62	64	65	65	70
P_i	11.2	10	7	6.5	6.5	5.9	6.5	5.9	5.3	5.5
$A_i P_i$	448	420	357	344.5	390	365.8	416	383.5	344.5	385

We can then calculate the summary statistics, $\sum A_i = 572$, $\sum P_i = 70.3$ and $\sum A_i P_i = 3854.3$. From these, we can calculate the covariance.

$$\sigma_{AP} = \frac{1}{10}\sum A_i P_i - \left(\frac{10}{N}\sum A_i\right)\left(\frac{1}{10}\sum P_i\right)$$

$$= \frac{3854.3}{10} - \frac{572}{10} \cdot \frac{70.3}{10} = 385.43 - 402.12 = -16.69.$$

The covariance is negative, as we would expect for negatively correlated data.

(c) The gradient of the line is given by

$$m = \frac{\sigma_{AP}}{\sigma_A^2} = \frac{-16.69}{9.72^2} = -0.1767.$$

This value is measured in thousands of pounds per month, and it represents the price drop of a typical car in one month. This value indicates that the cars were losing around £177 in value each month.

Q3. (a) The scatter graph suggests that there is no significant correlation between a film's title length and its box office takings.

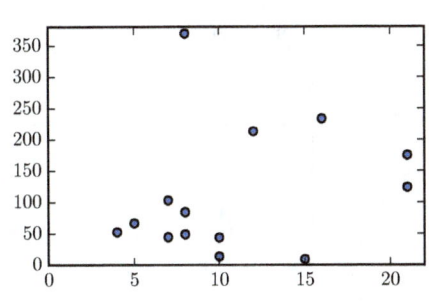

(b) First we must calculate the mean of each variable separately.

$$\mu_l = \frac{1}{15}\sum l_i = \frac{166}{15} = 11.07 \text{ letters,}$$
$$\mu_b = \frac{1}{15}\sum b_i = \frac{2128.8}{15} = \$141.92\text{m.}$$

The covariance of the data is given by

$$\sigma_{lb} = \frac{1}{15}\sum l_i b_i - \mu_l\mu_b = \frac{26536.4}{15} - 1571.1 = 198.0.$$

(c) To find the correlation coefficient, we need to calculate the variance of each variable.

$$\sigma_l^2 = \frac{1}{15}\sum l_i^2 - \left(\frac{1}{15}\sum l_i\right)^2 = \frac{2234}{15} - \left(\frac{166}{15}\right)^2 = 26.46,$$
$$\sigma_b^2 = \frac{1}{15}\sum b_i^2 - \left(\frac{1}{15}\sum b_i\right)^2 = \frac{613430}{15} - \left(\frac{2128.8}{15}\right)^2 = 20754.$$

Therefore the correlation coefficient is given by

$$\rho = \frac{\sigma_{lb}}{\sigma_l \sigma_b} = \frac{\sigma_{lb}}{\sqrt{\sigma_l^2 \sigma_b^2}} = \frac{198.0}{\sqrt{26.46 \times 20754}} = 0.27,$$

to two decimal places. This is a low value for positively correlated data, much closer to zero than one, and so this confirms our observation that there is no significant correlation.

Worked Solutions — Exercise 25.1

Q1. (a) The following graph shows the relationship between oil reserves (on the x-axis) and oil production (on the y-axis) for selected countries.

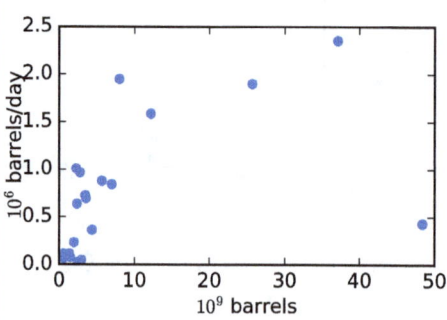

(b) There is a reasonably strong positive correlation between a country's oil reserves and oil production.

(c) The oil production from Libya in 2015 is significantly lower than would be expected. Possible reasons include:
- War, terrorism or other political instability.
- Sanctions imposed by other countries.
- Misreporting of reserves.

(d) The scatter diagram would suggest that the production in Oman was around 800 thousand barrels per day.

(e) Venezuela's production rate was only slightly higher than Nigeria's. However, its reserves are almost ten times the size of Nigeria's. If the correlation shown in the scatter graph were to continue, we would expect Venezuela's production rate to be much higher.

Q2. (a) The sum of the figures given for oil production is equal to 8.446×10^7 barrels per day. We divide this by the number of data points to obtain the mean production rate of 8.446×10^6 barrels per day.

(b) The reported oil reserve figures, in order, are

$$\{28.6, 29.6, 29.7, 29.8, 29.8, 30.2, 30.5, 31.2, 32.1, 33.9\}.$$

The middle two values are 29.8 and 30.2. Therefore, the median value of reported oil reserves is 30.0 thousand million barrels.

(c) The median would be a better choice than the mean.
There is a sudden drop in Mexico's stated reserves, giving two outlier values in the data set. For asymmetric distributions like this, the outlying values tend to have an unreasonably large effect on the mean value. The median will be a more representative value.

(d) Possible reasons for such a sudden drop in the reported reserves include:
- A sharp drop in the price of oil. This could reduce the amount of oil which could be extracted profitably.
- A revision to incorrect or over-optimistic estimates.

Although, theoretically, the difference could be due to a large amount of the oil having been produced during 1997, this is not likely. The average production rate would be around 70 million barrels per day, which would double the total world production.

Q3. (a) The blue line represents the production from the United Kingdom, and the red line represents Kuwait.
- Kuwait dropped its oil production significantly, by around 60%, during the 1980s. Reducing the supply would tend to push up the price.
- Following the Piper Alpha disaster in 1988, the UK's oil production fell by around half a million barrels of oil a day. It took about four years for the output to recover.
- The Iraqi invasion of Kuwait in 1990 stopped almost all oil production in the country. However, production recovered within a year or two.

(b) The oil production from the United Kingdom fell sharply after the peak around the year 2000. This could be due to falling oil prices, but we know that there have been periods of high oil prices since then. The more likely explanation is that production costs have risen. The most likely reason for rising costs, is that the remaining oil is much harder to extract.

(c) The graph shows that Kuwait's mean rate of production between 2004 and 2015 was over 2.5 million barrels per day. This means that the country produced over ten thousand million barrels in this time, or 10% of the stated reserves. It is not likely that additional reserves which were exactly equal to the oil produced were identified each year. Therefore, the stated values of the oil reserves are unlikely to be reliable.

Q4. (a) We must choose five points at random, and this is best done by using a computer, or some physical method such as drawing a piece of paper from a bag. Attempting to name numbers at random is not a reliable method. Numbers should be selected *with* replacement. For example, we might select $\{1991, 1999, 2002, 2003, 2003\}$. This would give us a sample mean of 1.9775×10^6 barrels per day.

(b) When we calculate the mean of five points selected at random, this sample mean will not be the same as the mean of the entire population. It could lie anywhere between the two extreme points, 1.8642×10^6 and 2.0302×10^6 barrels per day. If we take a large number of samples, the mean of these sample means will be close to the population mean.

If we use a sampling method without replacement, the sample mean will lie between 1.8960×10^6 and 2.0079×10^6 barrels per day. A large number of sample means using such a method will *not* have a mean which tends to the population mean.

(c) To obtain a systematic sample, we can select a random starting point and then select every third point along. For example, if we start from the year 1994, we would have the data points $\{1864.2, 1936.3, 1994.1, 1951.5, 1894.6\}$. This gives a sample mean of 1.9281×10^6 barrels per day.

(d) Calculating the percentage increase for the years 1990 to 2005 gives us fifteen data points.

Year	Consumption	Percentage increase
1990	1211.1	
1991	1232.7	1.78
1992	1296.1	5.14
1993	1312.5	1.26
1994	1411.7	7.55
1995	1579.5	11.88
1996	1699.0	7.56
1997	1829.5	7.68
1998	1965.8	7.45
1999	2138.3	8.77
2000	2258.8	5.63
2001	2285.5	1.18
2002	2413.4	5.59
2003	2485.3	2.97
2004	2555.5	2.82
2005	2605.6	1.96

The median value is 5.59%.

(e) We could make an estimate for the consumption in 2015 by assuming that the consumption will increase at 5.59% per year. Over ten years, this gives us a rate of

$$\text{Rate} = (1.0559)^{10} \times 2605.6 = 4488.9 \text{ thousand barrels per day.}$$

Therefore we estimate that the consumption in 2015 will be 4.4489×10^6 barrels per day.

(f) If the rate of consumption increases at 5.59% per year, and it doubles in N years, then N must satisfy the equation $(1.0559)^N = 2$. Therefore, $N \log_2 1.0559 = 1$ and so

$$N = \frac{1}{\log_2 1.0559} = 12.7 \text{ years.}$$

Therefore, at this rate of increase, India's oil consumption will double every twelve to thirteen years.

Suppose that after growing for k years at this same rate, India's consumption is equal to 84 726 thousand barrels per day. This means that

$$(1.0559)^k \times 2605.6 = 84726$$
$$(1.0559)^k = \frac{84726}{2605.6} = 32.5169.$$

Hence, $k \log_e 1.0559 = \log_e 32.5169$

and so $k = \dfrac{\log_e 32.5169}{\log_e 1.0559} = 64$ years.

Therefore, if India were to continue growing at this rate, by 2069 it would require the equivalent of the entire global output of 2005.

Q5. (a) The data must be arranged into classes. The range of the data is 37.6 to 79.1 million tonnes of carbon dioxide. One way of dividing this is as follows.

Range	Frequency	Width
$35 \leq x < 40$	1	5
$40 \leq x < 45$	3	5
$45 \leq x < 55$	5	10
$55 \leq x < 60$	5	5
$60 \leq x < 65$	6	5
$65 \leq x < 70$	4	5
$70 \leq x < 80$	1	10

These classes gives us the following histogram.

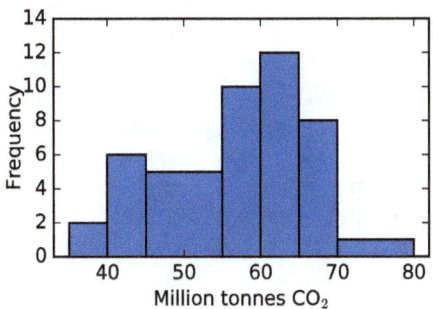

(b) We can copy the data for the two ranges into a spreadsheet and list the data in increasing order. This allows us to identify the three quartiles and the interquartile range.

	1965 to 1989	1991 to 2015
Q_1	26.5	35.7
Q_2	27.9	37.2
Q_3	30.0	37.7
IQR	3.5	2.0

We will identify outliers using the rule that the whiskers must not be more than 1.5 times the length of box. This gives us the following minimum and maximum values points, which are not considered to be outliers.

	1965 to 1989	1991 to 2015
min	21.3	71.9
max	32.7	93.0

Therefore, both sets of data have three outliers at the lower end of the data. The left hand whiskers will extend to the lowest point within the range. This gives us the following box plots.

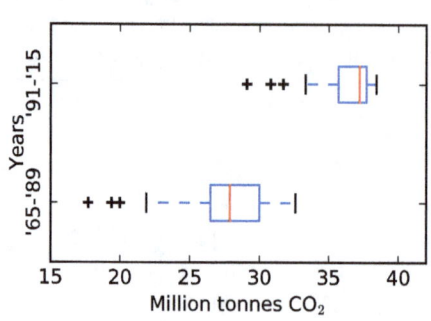

(c) Although both countries are oil producers, Norway produces around ten times as much as Denmark. Oil production was significantly higher oil in the years 1991 to 2015 compared with the years 1965 to 1989.

(d) The box plots show that Denmark's CO_2 emissions have dropped slightly, while Norway's have clearly increased. Therefore, the graphs tend to support the statement that oil production is positively correlated with carbon dioxide emissions. If we assume that carbon dioxide emissions are positively correlated with oil use, then the graph supports the statement.

(e) These graphs only look at two countries, and this sample size is not enough to draw a general conclusion. The difference we see could be due to other reasons, such as different government policies on emission reductions. Even if there is a link in this case, it does not necessarily hold in general.

Q6. (a) The data gives us the following graph.

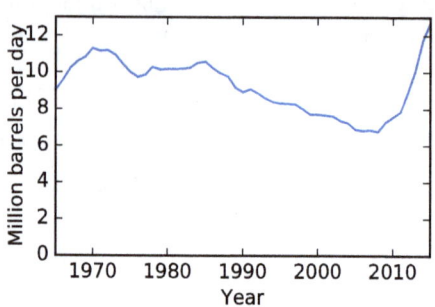

The graph is bimodal. Production reaches a (local) maximum output in 1970, which is followed by a gentle drop in production. In 2009, the output began to increase dramatically until production exceeded the previous maximum value.

(b) The most likely reason for the sudden increase in production is that the price of oil has increased. This can encourage investment to extract oil in areas which would not give a profit at lower prices.

Sudden increases in production can happen at the end of a period of war or political instability. Neither of these reasons are likely to apply to the United States.

Q7. (a) The United States was the largest emitter from 1965 to 2005. After 2006, China was the largest emitter. We can check the data directly to find this, or we can use a spreadsheet to find the answer automatically.

> **Use of Technology 5.1 — Using a spreadsheet to find the maximum**
> To do this automatically, we can add a spreadsheet row which gives us the maximum value in each column. We can then add another row which reports the row which contains this value. Finally, we can use this row number to look up the country name. The exact details for doing this will vary between spreadsheets.

(b) We can plot the emission data for China against the size of its economy to obtain the following graph.

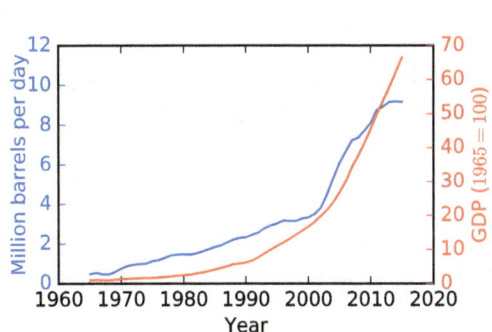

This graph suggests that the Chinese government has succeeded in curbing carbon emissions while the economy continued to grow.

Worked Solutions — Exercise 26.1

Q1. (a) Travelling at $0.9\,\text{m s}^{-1}$, it will take $10\,\text{s}$ to cover $9\,\text{m}$.

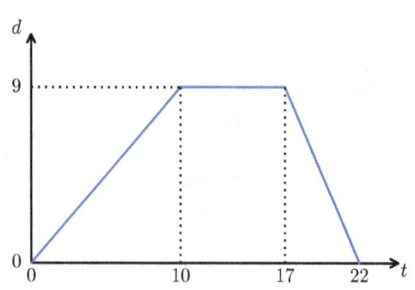

(b) The speed on the return journey is given by the gradient of the line segment between $17\,\text{s}$ and $22\,\text{s}$.
$$v = \frac{9-0}{22-17} = 1.8\text{ms}^{-1}.$$

Q2. (a) The velocity is given by the gradient of the graph. For this straight line segment, this is calculated as follows.
$$\text{speed} = \frac{15-0}{10-0} = 1.5\text{ms}^{-1}.$$

(b) The object is $5\,\text{m}$ from point B at time $t = 37.5\text{s}$. We calculate the gradient along this line segment as follows.
$$\text{speed} = \frac{30-10}{40-30} = 2\text{ms}^{-1}.$$

(c) The displacement is constant in the time interval $10 \leq t \leq 20$, and so the object is not moving.

(d) At time $t = 25\text{s}$, the line is sloping downwards, so we expect the velocity to be negative.
$$\text{velocity} = \frac{10-15}{30-20} = -0.5\text{ms}^{-1}.$$

A velocity of $-1.5\,\text{m s}^{-1}$ indicates that the object is moving back towards point A with a speed of $1.5\,\text{m s}^{-1}$.

Q3. (a) The acceleration is shown by the gradient of the curve. Therefore, the greatest forward acceleration is at the point where the curve has the greatest positive gradient. This is at time 0, when the car is first released.

(b) The greatest speed is when the absolute value of v is greatest. This is at time $t = t_0$.

(c) The car hits the obstacle at time $t = t_1$. It decelerates quickly and bounces off the obstacle. It travels a short way backwards and comes to rest.

Worked Solutions — Exercise 26.2

Q1. From the question, we have

$$u = 50\,\text{ms}^{-1},$$
$$t = 30\,\text{s},$$
$$s = 800\,\text{m}.$$

In this case, we can rearrange $s = ut + \frac{a}{2}t^2$ to find an expression for a:

$$a = 2\left(\frac{s - ut}{t^2}\right). \tag{5.1}$$

Substituting our values for u, s and t into the above gives

$$\begin{aligned}a &= 2\left(\frac{800 - 50 \cdot 30}{30^2}\right) \\ &= 2\left(\frac{800 - 1500}{900}\right) \\ &= 2\left(\frac{-700}{900}\right) \\ &= -1\frac{5}{9}\,\text{ms}^{-2}.\end{aligned}$$

In other words, the car decelerates at $1\frac{5}{9}\,\text{ms}^{-2}$.

Now that we have the acceleration, we can use the formula $v = u + at$ to find the car's speed at $t = 30\,\text{s}$. We have

$$\begin{aligned}v &= 50 - 1\frac{5}{9} \cdot 30 \\ &= 3\frac{1}{3}\,\text{ms}^{-1}.\end{aligned}$$

That is, the car is travelling in a forward direction with speed $3\frac{1}{3}\,\text{ms}^{-1}$.

Q2. Let $r_A(t)$ be the position of particle A at time t and assume that it starts from the origin so that $r_A(0) = 0$. Then, we have that

$$r_A(t) = 20t + t^2.$$

Similarly, let $r_B(t)$ be the position of particle B at time t. We know that B start 60 m ahead of A and is moving with constant velocity, hence

$$r_B(t) = 60 + 30t.$$

We need to find the time at which $r_A = r_B$. Hence, equating the above, we have

$$20t + t^2 = 60 + 30t$$
$$\Rightarrow t^2 - 10t - 60 = 0.$$

By completing the square, we find

$$(t-5)^2 - 85 = 0$$
$$\Rightarrow \qquad t = \pm\sqrt{85} + 5 \text{ s}.$$

We have two solutions, but one is negative. We therefore conclude that the particles will collide after $\sqrt{85}+5$ s. Note, if prior to time $t=0$ the particles had been moving with the same velocities/acceleration, they would have been in contact at time $t = -\sqrt{85}+5$ s.

An illustration of the situation is shown below together with a plot of the positions of the two particles against time.

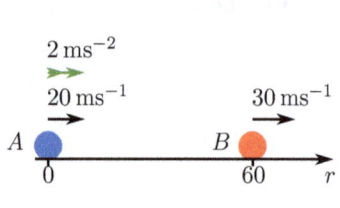
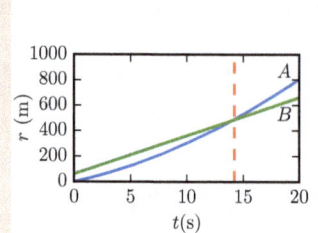

Q3. Let particle A have position r_A and particle B have position r_B. For simplicity, let A be at the origin at time $t = 0$ s. r_A therefore has equation

$$r_A = 10t + \frac{1}{2}t^2.$$

We do not yet know the starting location of particle B, but let us say $r_B = x$ m at time $t = 0$ s. This scenario is shown below.

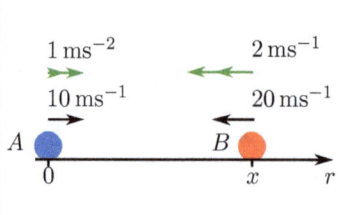

The equations of motion thus give

$$r_B = x - 20t - t^2.$$

Now, at time $t = 20$ s, we have that $r_A = r_B$. Hence, we can equate our expressions for r_A and r_B at time $t = 20\,\mathrm{s}$ and rearrange to find x:

$$10 \cdot 20 + \frac{1}{2}20^2 = x - 20 \cdot 20 - 20^2,$$
$$\Rightarrow \quad 200 + 200 = x - 400 - 400,$$
$$\Rightarrow \quad 400 = x - 800,$$
$$\Rightarrow \quad x = 1200.$$

Therefore, $r_B = 1200\,\mathrm{m}$ at time $t = 0\,\mathrm{m}$. In other words, the particles were initially 1200 m apart.

Q4. Let S be the displacement of the bullet and upwards represent a positive displacement. From the equations of motion, we have

$$S = 300t - \frac{1}{2}9.8t^2,$$

because gravity acts in the negative direction. The bullet is in contact with the ground when $S = 0$, so we find t such that

$$0 = 300t - \frac{1}{2}9.8t^2$$
$$= t(300 - 4.9t).$$

This yields two solutions $t = 0\,\mathrm{s}$ and $t = \frac{300}{4.9} = 61.22\,\mathrm{s}$ to 2 d.p. The first shows that the bullet started with a displacement of zero, while the second shows the bullet was in flight for 61.22 s. Now, as the height of the bullet is a parabola, we know that the maximum height will occur halfway through the flight time, *i.e.* when $t = \frac{300}{2 \cdot 4.9}\,\mathrm{s}$. The displacement at this time is

$$S = 300 \cdot \frac{300}{9.8} - \frac{1}{2}9.8\left(\frac{300}{9.8}\right)^2$$
$$= 4592.\ldots.$$

The maximum height of the bullet is therefore 4592 m to 4 s.f. Note, the exact time $t = \frac{300}{9.8}\,\mathrm{s}$ was used in the above calculation, rather than $t = \frac{61.22}{2}\,\mathrm{s}$.
A plot of the height of the bullet against time is shown below.

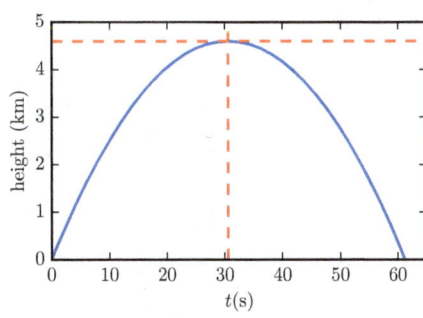

Q5. Let us assume that at time t the car has displacement S. The equations of motions state that
$$S = ut + \frac{1}{2}at^2.$$
At time $t = 4\,\text{s}$ we have $S = 200\,\text{m}$ and at time $t = 7\,\text{s}$ we have $S = 400\,\text{m}$. Inserting these values into the above equation, we have the following set of simultaneous equations:
$$200 = 4u + \frac{1}{2}a4^2 = 4u + 8a, \quad \text{①}$$
$$400 = 7u + \frac{1}{2}a7^2 = 7u + \frac{49}{2}a, \quad \text{②}$$
for the acceleration a and initial velocity u. By multiplying ① by 7 and ② by 4 we can eliminate u:
$$1400 = 28u + 56a,$$
$$1600 = 28u + \frac{196}{2}a,$$
$$\Rightarrow \quad 200 = (98 - 56)\,a,$$
$$\Rightarrow \quad a = \frac{200}{42} = \frac{100}{21}.$$

The acceleration of the car is therefore $a = \frac{100}{21} = 4.762\,\text{ms}^{-2}$ to 3 d.p. Inserting the above value for a into ①, we find
$$200 = 4u + 8 \cdot \frac{100}{21},$$
$$\Rightarrow \quad u = 50 - 2 \cdot \frac{100}{21}.$$

The car therefore has initial velocity $u = 40.476\,\text{ms}^{-1}$ to 3 d.p. We can then use the equation for S to find the time at which the displacement is 600 m:
$$ut + \frac{1}{2}at^2 = 600,$$
$$\Rightarrow \quad -\frac{1}{2}at^2 - ut + 600 = 0,$$
$$\Rightarrow \quad t^2 + \frac{2u}{a}t - \frac{1200}{a} = 0,$$
$$\Rightarrow \quad \left(t + \frac{u}{a}\right)^2 - \frac{u^2}{a^2} - \frac{1200}{a} = 0,$$
$$\Rightarrow \quad \left(t + \frac{u}{a}\right)^2 = \frac{u^2}{a^2} + \frac{1200}{a},$$
$$\Rightarrow \quad t + \frac{u}{a} = \pm\sqrt{\frac{u^2}{a^2} + \frac{1200}{a}},$$
$$\Rightarrow \quad t = \pm\sqrt{\frac{1200}{a} + \frac{u^2}{a^2}} - \frac{u}{a}$$

We are only interested in the positive solution above. Inserting the values of a and u into the above gives $t = 9.505\ldots$ s. In other words, the car takes $2.505\,\text{s}$ to complete the next $200\,\text{m}$ to 3 d.p.

A plot showing the displacement of the car against time is shown below.

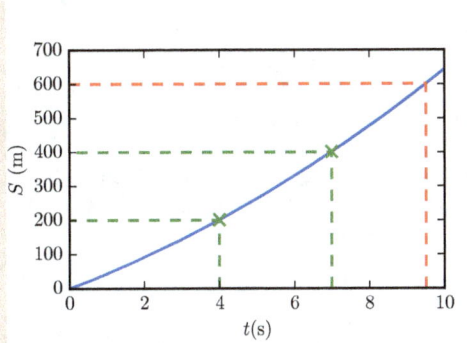

Q6. Let the position of particle A be r_A and the position of particle B be r_B. Also, let us assume that the ground is centred at the origin and a position above the ground is positive. The scenario is shown in the figure below.

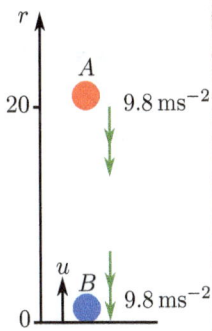

The equations of motion reveal that

$$r_A = 20 - \frac{1}{2}9.8t^2,$$
$$r_B = ut - \frac{1}{2}9.8t^2,$$

where u is the initial velocity of particle B. By equating these positions and setting $t = 1$, we can find the velocity at which B has to be fired.

$$20 - \frac{1}{2}9.8 = u - \frac{1}{2}9.8,$$
$$\Rightarrow \quad u = 20.$$

Particle B must be fired at $20\,\text{ms}^{-1}$.

Q7. We first convert the accelerations to ms^{-2}. There are $1000\,\text{m}$ in a km and $3600\,\text{s}$ in one hour. Hence, dragster A accelerates at $a_A = 205\,\text{kmh}^{-1}\text{s}^{-1} = 205 \times 1000/3600 = \frac{1025}{18} = 56.94\ldots\text{ms}^{-2}$. Similarly, dragster B accelerates at $a_B = 198\,\text{kmh}^{-1}\text{s}^{-1} = 198 \times 1000/3600 = 55\,\text{ms}^{-2}$. Using the equations of motion, we find that, after the periods of acceleration, the dragsters A and B have respective speeds

$$v_A = 2.79 \times \frac{1025}{18} = 158.875\,\text{ms}^{-1},$$
$$v_B = 2.89 \times 55 = 158.95\,\text{ms}^{-1}.$$

We can then use $v^2 = u^2 + 2as$ rearranged, with $u = 0$ in both cases, to find the distances travelled by the two dragsters over their period of acceleration:

$$s_A = \frac{v_A^2}{2a_A} = 221.630\,625\,\text{m},$$
$$s_B = \frac{v_B^2}{2a_B} = 229.682\,75\,\text{m}.$$

The dragsters complete the remaining distances at their maximum speeds, we have

$$t_A = \frac{305 - 221.630625}{158.875} + 2.79 = 3.3147\ldots\text{s},$$
$$t_B = \frac{305 - 229.68275}{158.95} + 2.89 = 3.3608\ldots\text{s}.$$

Hence, dragster A wins the race and the time gap is $0.0461\,\text{s}$ to 4 d.p.

Q8. To solve this question, we calculate the time at which the ball first impacts the ground and at what speed it is travelling, then find its speed upon rebound and then calculate the time until the next impact. As the ball is dropped, it has initial speed $0\,\text{ms}^{-1}$ and initial height $10\,\text{m}$. Hence, we can find the speed v_1 upon first impact as follows

$$v_1^2 = 2as$$
$$= 2 \times 9.8 \times 10,$$
$$\Rightarrow v_1 = \sqrt{196} = 14\,\text{ms}^{-1}.$$

The time taken for the ball to hit the ground for the first time t_1 is given by

$$s = \frac{1}{2}at_1^2,$$
$$\Rightarrow 10 = \frac{1}{2}9.8 \times t_1^2,$$
$$\Rightarrow t_1 = \sqrt{\frac{20}{9.8}} = \frac{10}{7}\text{s}.$$

The ball rebounds with speed $v_2 = 0.8v_1$ and we are looking to find the the time

$t_2 \neq 0$ such that the displacement of the ball is $s = 0$. In this case, we use

$$s = ut_2 + \frac{1}{2}at_2^2,$$
$$\Rightarrow \quad 0 = 0.8v_1t_2 - \frac{1}{2}9.8t_2^2,$$
$$\Rightarrow \quad 0 = 0.8 \cdot 14 - 4.9t_2,$$
$$\Rightarrow \quad t_2 = \frac{56}{4.9 \cdot 5} = \frac{16}{7}\text{s}.$$

The time taken for the ball to hit the floor for the second time is $t = t_1 + t_2 = \frac{10}{7} + \frac{16}{7} = \frac{26}{7}$s.

The plots below show the velocity of the ball and its height against time, respectively.

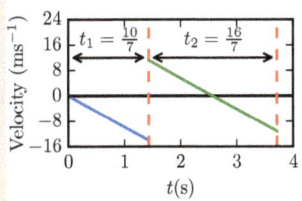 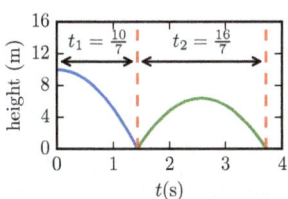

Q9. (a) The object travels 16.25 m during the first 10 s. This distance is given by the area under the graph between $t = 0$ and $t = 10$.

$$\text{distance} = 16.25 = \frac{1}{2} \times 10 \times u = 5u.$$

Therefore, the speed at time $t = 6$ is given by $u = 3.25 \text{ms}^{-1}$.

The speed in the interval $13 < t < 17$ is 2ms^{-1}, and so the maximum speed in the interval $0 \leq t \leq 24$ is 3.25ms^{-1}.

(b) During the interval $0 \leq t \leq 10$, the object is moving away from its starting point. It reaches its furthest distance from the start at $t = 10$s, when it has travelled 16.25 m.

After time $t = 10$s, the object starts to move towards its starting point. The total distance travelled is calculated as follows.

$$\text{distance} = \left(\frac{1}{2} \times (13 - 10) \times 2\right) + ((17 - 13) \times 2)$$
$$+ \left(\frac{1}{2} \times (24 - 17) \cdot 2\right)$$
$$= 3 + 8 + 7 = 18\text{m}.$$

This means that during this time, the object first travels the 16.25 m back to its starting point and then travels a further $(18 - 16.25) = 1.75$m in the other direction. Therefore the time at which the object is the furthest distance from its starting point is at $t = 10$s.

(c) The acceleration in the interval $17 \leq t \leq 24$ is given by the gradient of the line.
$$\text{acceleration} = \frac{0 - (-2)}{24 - 17} = \frac{2}{7}\text{ms}^{-2}.$$

(d) We need to show that the object has travelled the 16.25 m back to the starting point in the time interval $10 \leq t \leq 20.5$.
First we calculate the velocity, w, at time $t_0 = 20.5\,\text{s}$.

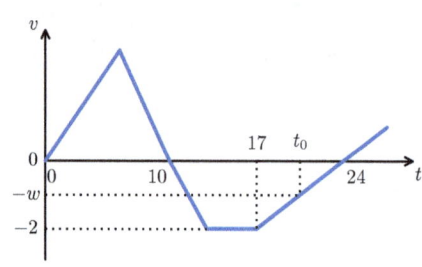

The acceleration in the interval $17 \leq t \leq 24$ is $\frac{2}{7}\text{ms}^{-2}$.
$$\frac{2}{7} = \frac{0 - w}{24 - 20.5} = \frac{-w}{3.5} \implies w = -1\text{ms}^{-1}.$$

From this, we can calculate the distance travelled in the interval $20.5 \leq t \leq 24$ by finding the area under the curve.
$$\text{distance} = \frac{1}{2} \times (24 - 20.5) \times 1 = 1.75\text{m}.$$

We know that the object travels 18 m in the interval $10 \leq t \leq 24$ and so the distance travelled in $10 \leq t \leq 20.5$ is $(18 - 1.75) = 16.25$m.
Therefore at time $t = 20.5$s, the object has travelled 16.25 m and has returned to the starting point.

(e) We know that the object is a distance of 1.75 m behind the starting point at time $t = 24$s. We want to find the time t_1 such that the object travels 1.75 m in the interval $[24, t_1]$.
At time t_1, the velocity is equal to $\frac{2}{7}(t_1 - 24)\text{ms}^{-1}$ and the distance travelled since $t - 24$s is calculated as follows.
$$\text{distance} = \frac{1}{2} \times (t_1 - 24) \times \frac{2(t_1 - 24)}{7} = 1.75,$$
$$\implies \frac{(t_1 - 24)^2}{7} = 1.75,$$
$$\implies (t_1 - 24)^2 = 12.25,$$
$$\implies t_1 - 24 = 3.5 \implies t_1 = 27.5\text{s}.$$

Q10. (a) Constant acceleration and deceleration is shown as a straight line on a velocity-time graph. Constant velocity is shown as a horizontal line. Therefore, we can sketch the following graph.

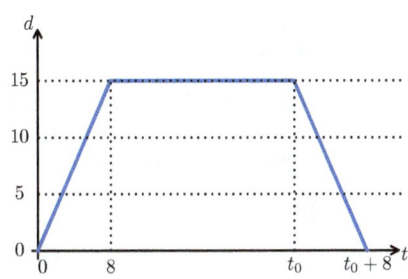

From this graph, we can calculate t_0. The distance covered is equal to the area under the graph, and this is given as 420 m.

$$\frac{1}{2} \times 8 \times 15 + 15(t_0 - 8) + \frac{1}{2} \times 8 \times 15 = 420,$$
$$\Rightarrow \quad 120 + 15(t_0 - 8) = 420,$$
$$\Rightarrow \quad 15(t_0 - 8) = 300,$$
$$\Rightarrow \quad t_0 - 8 = 20 \Rightarrow t_0 = 28\,\text{s}.$$

(b) The motorbike sets off at time $t = 8$s. It accelerates up to a maximum velocity of $x\,\text{ms}^{-1}$ until time $t = 20$s. At this time, it has travelled $\frac{12x}{2} = 6x$. Over the same time, the distance covered by the car is given by:

$$\text{displacement} = \frac{1}{2} \times 8 \times 15 + 15(20 - 8) = 60 + 180 = 240.$$

Therefore, $6x = 240 \implies x = 40$ and so the motorbike accelerates to $40\,\text{ms}^{-1}$ over 12 s. We therefore calculate the acceleration as $\frac{40}{12} = \frac{10}{3}\,\text{ms}^{-2}$.

(c) The car travels a total of 420 m and so travels $420 - 240 = 180$m after time $t = 20$s.

The motorbike therefore travels 180 m as it decelerates from a velocity of $40\,\text{ms}^{-1}$ in some time t_1. The distance travelled is given by:

$$\frac{1}{2} \times 40 t_1 = 180 \implies t_1 = 9\,\text{s}.$$

Therefore, the motorbike comes to rest at time $t_1 + 20 = 29$s.

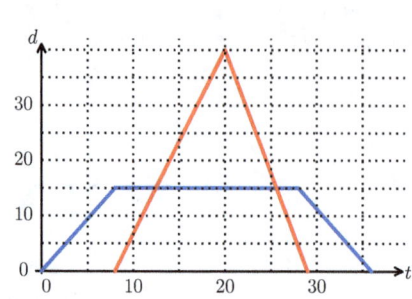

Worked Solutions — Exercise 26.3

Q1. For an object with initial velocity $v(0) = u$ and constant acceleration a, we have

$$v(t_1) = v(0) + \int_0^{t_1} a\,dt$$
$$= u + [at]_0^{t_1}$$
$$= u + at_1.$$

Now, t_1 is a *dummy* variable here, so can be replaced with t to give the constant acceleration formula:

$$v(t) = u + at.$$

We integrate this again to find the displacement:

$$s(t_1) = \int_0^{t_1} v(t)\,dt$$
$$= \int_0^{t_1} (u + at)\,dt$$
$$= \left[ut + \frac{1}{2}at^2\right]_0^{t_1}$$
$$= ut_1 + \frac{1}{2}at_1^2.$$

Again, t_1 is a dummy variable and can be replaced with t to give the constant acceleration formula:

$$s(t) = ut + \frac{1}{2}at^2.$$

Q2. We use integration to find

$$s(t_1) = \int_0^{t_1} v(t)\,dt$$
$$= \int_0^{t_1} (-t^3 + 2t - 10)\,dt$$
$$= \left[-\frac{t^4}{4} + t^2 - 10t\right]_0^{t_1}$$
$$= -\frac{t_1^4}{4} + t_1^2 - 10t_1.$$

Here, t_1 is a dummy variable. We can replace it with any variable we like, so $s(t) = -\frac{t^4}{4} + t^2 - 10t$. At time $t_2 = 2$, the particle's displacement is

$$s(2) = -\frac{2^4}{4} + 2^2 - 2 \cdot 10 = -4 + 4 - 20 = -20.$$

Q3. The particle starts from rest, so we have

$$v(t_1) = \int_0^{t_1} a(t)\,dt$$
$$= \int_0^{t_1} (4t + 2)\,dt$$
$$= \left[2t^2 + 2t\right]_0^{t_1}$$
$$= 2t_1^2 + 2t_1.$$

t_1 is a dummy variable, so $v(t) = 2t^2 + 2t$.

To find the displacement, we integrate the velocity to find

$$s(t_1) = \int_0^{t_1} v(t)\,dt$$
$$= \int_0^{t_1} (2t^2 + 2t)\,dt$$
$$= \left[\frac{2t^3}{3} + t^2\right]_0^{t_1}$$
$$= \frac{2t_1^3}{3} + t_1^2.$$

Again, t_1 is a dummy variable, so $s(t) = \frac{2t^3}{3} + t^2$.

Q4. Let the origin be at the initial location of particle A. The velocity of particle A

satisfies

$$v_A(t_1) = \int_0^{t_1} a_A(t)\,dt$$

$$= \int_0^{t_1} -t^{1/2}\,dt$$

$$= \left[-\frac{2}{3}t^{3/2}\right]_0^{t_1}$$

$$= -\frac{2}{3}t_1^{3/2},$$

$$\Rightarrow \quad v_A(t) = -\frac{2}{3}t^{3/2}.$$

We integrate again to find the position of particle A:

$$r_A(t_1) = \int_0^{t_1} v_A(t)\,dt$$

$$= \int_0^{t_1} -\frac{2}{3}t^{3/2}\,dt$$

$$= \left[-\frac{4}{15}t^{5/2}\right]_0^{t_1}$$

$$= -\frac{4}{15}t_1^{5/2},$$

$$\Rightarrow \quad r_A(t) = -\frac{4}{15}t^{5/2}.$$

We work similarly to find the velocity of particle B:

$$v_B(t_1) = \int_0^{t_1} a_B(t)\,dt$$

$$= \int_0^{t_1} (t^{3/2} + 3)\,dt$$

$$= \left[\frac{2}{5}t^{5/2} + 3t\right]_0^{t_1}$$

$$= -\frac{2}{5}t_1^{5/2} + 3t_1,$$

$$\Rightarrow \quad v_B(t) = -\frac{2}{5}t^{5/2} + 3t.$$

To find the position of particle B we make use of the fact that it starts 20 m away from particle A and this will be in the positive direction. We therefore have

$$r_B(t_1) = 20 + \int_0^{t_1} v_B(t)\,dt$$

$$= 20 + \int_0^{t_1} \left(\frac{2}{5}t^{5/2} + 3t\right) dt$$

$$= 20 + \left[\frac{4}{35}t^{7/2} + \frac{3}{2}t^2\right]_0^{t_1}$$

$$= 20 + \frac{4}{35}t_1^{7/2} + \frac{3}{2}t_1^2,$$

$$\Rightarrow \quad r_B(t) = 20 + \frac{4}{35}t_1^{7/2} + \frac{3}{2}t_1^2.$$

At time $t = 5\,\text{s}$, we have $r_A = -\frac{4}{15} \cdot 5^{5/2}$ and $r_B = 20 + \frac{4}{35} \cdot 5^{7/2} + \frac{3}{2} \cdot 5^2$. The distance between them is given by

$$r_B - r_A = 20 + \frac{4}{35} \cdot 5^{7/2} + \frac{3}{2} \cdot 5^2 - \left(-\frac{4}{15} \cdot 5^{5/2}\right) = 104.35\ldots.$$

The particles are $104.35\,\text{m}$ apart to 2 d.p.

A plot of the positions of particles A and B and their separation $|r_B - r_A|$ is below.

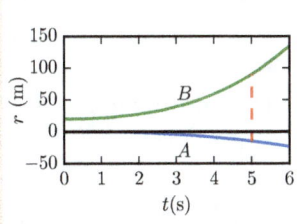
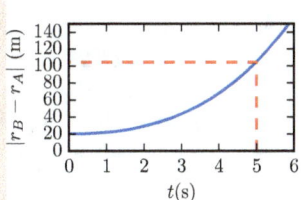

Q5. We first find expressions for the sprinter's velocity, $v(t)$, and displacement, $s(t)$, over the first $2.5\,\text{s}$ of the race. We use integration and the fact that the sprinter will start from rest to find

$$v(t_1) = \int_0^{t_1} a(t)\,dt$$

$$= \int_0^{t_1} 2.1t^2\,dt$$

$$= \left[\frac{2.1}{3}t^3\right]_0^{t_1}$$

$$= \frac{2.1}{3}t_1^3,$$

$$\Rightarrow \quad v(t) = \frac{2.1}{3}t^3.$$

Similarly, we find

$$s(t_1) = \int_0^{t_1} v(t)\,dt$$
$$= \int_0^{t_1} \frac{2.1}{3} t^3 \,dt$$
$$= \left[\frac{2.1}{12} t^4\right]_0^{t_1}$$
$$= \frac{2.1}{12} t_1^4,$$
$$\Rightarrow \quad s(t) = \frac{2.1}{12} t^4.$$

After $2.5\,\text{s}$, the sprinter will have travelled $s(2.5) = 6.8359375\,\text{m}$ and will have reached a speed of $v(2.5) = 10.9375\,\text{ms}^{-1}$. The total time taken for the whole $100\,\text{m}$ is therefore $2.5 + t_2$, where t_2 is the time taken to complete the remaining $100 - 6.8359375\,\text{m}$ at $10.9375\,\text{ms}^{-1}$. We therefore have

$$t_2 = \frac{100 - 6.8359375}{10.9375} = 8.51785\ldots.$$

Hence the total time taken to complete $100\,\text{m}$ is $2.5 + 8.51785\ldots = 11.02\,\text{s}$ to 2 d.p.

Worked Solutions — Exercise 27.1

Q1. (a) The ball falls to the ground due to a weight force exerted on the ball.
  (b) The hammer pushes the nail and therefore exerts a pushing force on it.
  (c) As the brake pads squeeze the disc they exert a compression force on the disc.
  (d) The two teams are pulling on the rope, resulting in a tension force in the rope.
  (e) The engine exerts a driving force on the bicycle.
  (f) The cyclist pushes the pedal down, thereby exerting a pushing force on the pedal.

Q2. The joists are subject to compression forces between the roof and the ground.

Q3. (a) We know that

$$W = mg.$$

Therefore, the weight of the man when standing on Earth is

$$W = 75 \times 9.8 = 735\,\text{N}.$$

(b) When the man is standing on Mars the same equation, $W = mg$ applies, however, we now use $g = 3.73\,\text{ms}^{-2}$:

$$W = 75 \times 3.73 = 279.75\,\text{N}.$$

Notice that, although the man's weight has changed by standing on Mars, his mass has remained constant.

Q4. (a) We use Newton's Second Law to find the pushing force:

$$F = ma$$
$$= 3 \times 2$$
$$= 6 \text{ N}.$$

(b) We know that the weight is given by $W = mg$. Taking $g = 9.8 \text{ ms}^{-2}$ and converting the mass of the ball to kg:

$$W = mg$$
$$= 0.02 \times 9.8$$
$$= 0.196 \text{ N}.$$

(c) Firstly, we need to find the acceleration. To do this we use the equations of constant acceleration. Specifically, $v = u + at$. Rearranging for a we have

$$a = \frac{v - u}{t} = \frac{60 - 0}{10} = 6 \text{ ms}^{-2}.$$

Next, we use $F = ma$ to find the driving force:

$$F = ma$$
$$= 1300 \times 6$$
$$= 7800 \text{ N}.$$

Q5. Firstly, we rearrange $F = ma$ to find the acceleration:

$$a = \frac{F}{m} = \frac{12}{3} = 4 \text{ ms}^{-2}.$$

Now we use one of the equations of constant acceleration to find the distance the box travels. We know the initial velocity, $u = 2 \text{ ms}^{-1}$, the acceleration, $a = 4 \text{ ms}^{-2}$, and the time $t = 10 \text{ s}$. Therefore, we use

$$s = ut + \frac{1}{2}at^2$$
$$= 2 \times 10 + \frac{1}{2} \times 4 \times 10^2$$
$$= 20 + 200$$
$$= 220 \text{ m}.$$

Q6. (a) The box is subject to a weight force and a tension force in the rope. The forces diagram is

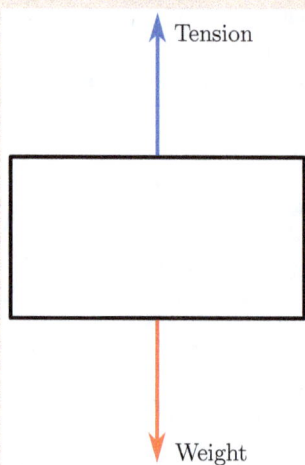

(b) There are two objects here that we must draw the forces for: the car and the trailer. Each is subject to a separate weight force, and to a tension force in the rope. The car is also subject to a driving force.

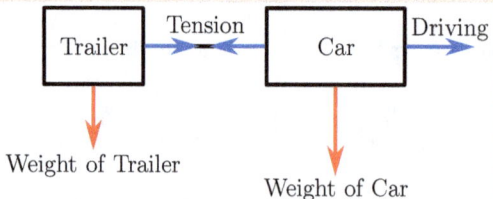

Some students may say that the car and trailer move together and, therefore, may be modelled as one particle with the following forces diagram. This is correct, as we will see in the section on Connected Particles.

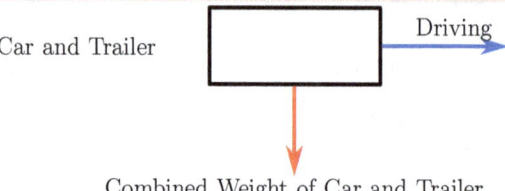

(c) The elevator car is subject to two forces: weight and tension in the cable. The forces diagram is

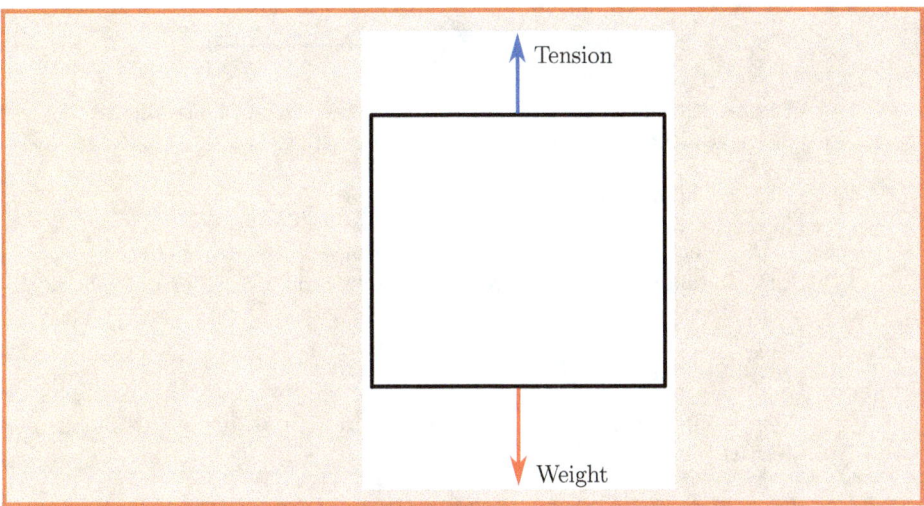

Worked Solutions — Exercise 27.2

Q1. Object (a), a ball that is dropped from a height of 0.5 m above the ground is subject to a weight force vertically downwards. This force is not balanced by any other force therefore the resultant force is equal to the weight force and is non-zero. The ball is accelerating and is not in equilibrium.

Object (b), the car travelling up a hill at a constant speed of $50\,\mathrm{km\,s^{-1}}$ is not accelerating. Therefore, by $F = ma$ the resultant force on it must be zero and the car is in equilibrium.

Object (c), the box that is lifted from the ground with an acceleration of $0.2\,\mathrm{m\,s^{-1}}$ is accelerating and therefore has a non-zero resultant force. The box is not in equilibrium.

Object (d), the box that is sliding down a slope at an increasing speed is accelerating and therefore has a non-zero resultant force. The box is not in equilibrium.

The answer is (b).

Q2. The resultant force is given by $F = ma$, where $m = 500\,\mathrm{g} = 0.5\,\mathrm{kg}$ and $a = 4\,\mathrm{m\,s^{-2}}$. Therefore, the resultant force is

$$F = 0.5 \times 4 = 2\,\mathrm{N}.$$

The answer is (d).

Q3. The acceleration is given by rearranging $F = ma$ to obtain $a = F/m$ where $m = 0.4\,\mathrm{kg}$ and $F = 25\,\mathrm{N}$. Therefore, the acceleration of the box is

$$a = \frac{F}{m} = \frac{25}{0.4} = 62.5\,\mathrm{m\,s^{-2}}$$

The answer is (a).

Q4. (a) Modelling the centre of the rope as a particle we can draw the following diagram of the forces:

The resultant force is given by the sum of the forces, taking forces going to the right as positive. Therefore, the resultant force is

$$F = 785 - 632 = 153 \text{ N}$$

to the right, or, in the direction of the team pulling with 785 N.

(b) First we find the resultant force in the x-direction, taking forces to the right as positive:

$$F_x = F_2 + F_3 - F_5 = 4 + 3 - 8 = -1 \text{ N}.$$

Next we find the resultant force in the y-direction, taking upwards forces as positive:

$$F_y = F_4 - F1 = 6 - 4 = 2 \text{ N}.$$

Now we draw the right angled triangle that shows the resultant force.

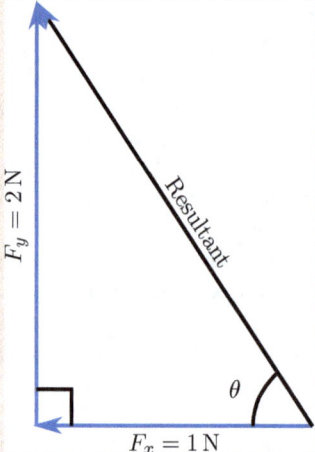

Now we use Pythagoras' Theorem in order to calculate the magnitude of the resultant:

$$F = \sqrt{F_x^2 + F_y^2} = \sqrt{(-1)^2 + 2^2} = \sqrt{3} = 1.73 \text{ N}$$

to 2 decimal places. Finally we calculate the direction of the resultant as the angle θ shown in the diagram above:

$$\theta = \tan^{-1} \frac{|F_y|}{|F_x|} = \tan^{-1} \left(\frac{2}{1}\right) = 63.43°$$

to 2 decimal places.

(c) The resultant force is given by the sum of the $\mathbf{F_i}$. Therefore,

$$\begin{aligned}\mathbf{R} &= \mathbf{F_1} + \mathbf{F_2} + \mathbf{F_3} + \mathbf{F_4} \\ &= (-5\mathbf{j}) + (-1\mathbf{i} + 3\mathbf{j}) + (10\mathbf{i}) + (-6\mathbf{i} - 1\mathbf{j}) \\ &= (-1 + 10 - 6)\mathbf{i} + (-5 + 3 - 1)\mathbf{j} \\ &= 3\mathbf{i} - 3\mathbf{j} \,\mathrm{N}.\end{aligned}$$

(d) The resultant force is given by the sum of the $\mathbf{F_i}$. Therefore,

$$\begin{aligned}\mathbf{R} &= \mathbf{F_1} + \mathbf{F_2} + \mathbf{F_3} + \mathbf{F_4} + \mathbf{F_5} + \mathbf{F_6} \\ &= \begin{pmatrix}0\\5\end{pmatrix} + \begin{pmatrix}0\\-5\end{pmatrix} + \begin{pmatrix}5\\0\end{pmatrix} + \begin{pmatrix}1\\7\end{pmatrix} + \begin{pmatrix}-6\\-5\end{pmatrix} + \begin{pmatrix}-3\\-1\end{pmatrix} \\ &= \begin{pmatrix}0+0+5+1-6-3\\5-5+0+7-5-1\end{pmatrix} \\ &= \begin{pmatrix}-3\\1\end{pmatrix}\,\mathrm{N}.\end{aligned}$$

Q5. The component form of the resultant is given by the sum of the $\mathbf{F_i}$. Therefore,

$$\begin{aligned}\mathbf{R} &= \mathbf{F_1} + \mathbf{F_2} + \mathbf{F_3} + \mathbf{F_4} + \mathbf{F_5} \\ &= \begin{pmatrix}0\\-4\end{pmatrix} + \begin{pmatrix}3\\-2\end{pmatrix} + \begin{pmatrix}2\\0\end{pmatrix} + \begin{pmatrix}1\\4\end{pmatrix} + \begin{pmatrix}-6\\3\end{pmatrix} \\ &= \begin{pmatrix}0+3+2+1-6\\-4-2+0+4+3\end{pmatrix} \\ &= \begin{pmatrix}0\\1\end{pmatrix}\,\mathrm{N}.\end{aligned}$$

We need to find the magnitude and direction of the resultant. The magnitude is given by

$$|\mathbf{R}| = \sqrt{\mathbf{R}_i^2 + \mathbf{R}_j^2} = \sqrt{0^2 + 1^2} = \sqrt{1} = 1\,\mathrm{N}.$$

We can see by inspection that the direction of the resultant is vertically upwards, because the horizontal component of $\mathbf{R}$ is zero and the vertical component is positive. However, we show how to calculate it here for completeness. We would normally calculate the direction from

$$\tan\theta = \frac{\mathbf{R}_j}{\mathbf{R}_i},$$

however, here this would require us to divide by zero which is not possible. Therefore, we use one of the other trigonometric identities and the magnitude of our resultant. Then

$$\sin\theta = \frac{\mathbf{R}_j}{|\mathbf{R}|} = \frac{1}{1}$$

and

$$\theta = \sin^{-1} 1 = 90°$$

which is vertically upwards.

Q6. Firstly, we use $F = ma$ to find the magnitude of the resultant force. In order to do this we need to know m. Since $W = mg$ we can say that

$$m = \frac{W}{g} = \frac{13,000}{10} = 1300\,\text{kg}.$$

Now, using $\mathbf{F} = m\mathbf{a}$, the resultant is:

$$\mathbf{F} = 1,300 \times (-3\mathbf{i} + 0.7\mathbf{j})\text{N} = -3,900\mathbf{i} + 910\mathbf{j}\text{N}.$$

We know that the resultant is equal to the sum of the individual forces. Therefore, we can find $\mathbf{D}$ as follows:

$$\begin{aligned}
\mathbf{D} &= \mathbf{R} - \mathbf{W} - \mathbf{F} - \mathbf{N} \\
&= (-3,900\mathbf{i} + 910\mathbf{j}) - (-13,000\mathbf{j}) - (3,000\mathbf{i} - 700\mathbf{j}) - (2,000\mathbf{i} + 11,000\mathbf{j}) \\
&= (-3,900 - 3,000 - 2,000)\mathbf{i} + (910 + 13,000 + 700 - 11,000)\mathbf{j} \\
&= (-8,900\mathbf{i} + 3,610\mathbf{j})\text{N}.
\end{aligned}$$

Q7. When the rope is cut the only force acting on the box will be its weight. Since $W = mg$, we know that the acceleration of the box will be equal to acceleration due to gravity which is $g = 9.8\,\text{ms}^{-2}$.

6. Worked Solutions - Chapters 28 to 31

Worked Solutions — Exercise 28.1

Q1. The normal reaction force of a box on a horizontal surface is equal and opposite to the weight. The mass of the box is $m = 50\,\text{g} = 0.05\,\text{kg}$ so the weight force acting on the box is

$$W = mg = 0.05 \times 9.8 = 0.49\,\text{N}.$$

The weight force is vertically downwards. Therefore, the answer is (b), 0.49 N vertically upwards.

Q2. The box is subject to four forces: weight, normal reaction, pushing and friction. As the box is on a horizontal surface, the weight and the normal reaction force balance each other. Therefore, the resultant force will be horizontal, in the direction of the pushing force. Friction acts to oppose motion, therefore:

$$F = P - F_r = 10 - 2.5 = 7.5\,\text{N}.$$

The answer is (c), 7.5 N in the direction of the pushing force.

Q3. When the rocket forces air out of its base it creates an equal and opposite thrust force that acts to push the rocket vertically upwards with a force of $F_{\text{rocket}} = 1000\,\text{N}$.
The rocket is also subject to a weight force vertically downwards of

$$W = mg = 15 \times 9.8 = 147\,\text{N}.$$

When the rocket loses contact with the ground the normal reaction force vanishes, therefore, the resultant force is given by:

$$F = F_{\text{rocket}} - W = 1,000 - 147 = 853\,\text{N}.$$

Therefore, the answer is (a), $F = 853\,\text{N}$ vertically upwards.

Q4. When the rocket forces air out of the back of the it generates an equal and opposite thrust force pushing the box forwards with force of $F_{\text{box}} = 35\,\text{N}$. As the surface is horizontal, the thrust force and the friction force act horizontally and the weight and normal reaction forces act vertically. The weight and normal reaction forces will balance each other out and, therefore, the resultant force is given by

$$F = F_{\text{box}} - F_r = 35 - 10 = 25\,\text{N}.$$

Q5. As the box is on a horizontal surface the normal reaction force will be equal and opposite to the weight force. We know that

$$W = mg = 3 \times 9.8 = 29.4\,\text{N},$$

therefore, the normal reaction force is $R = 29.4\,\text{N}$ vertically upwards.

Q6. The normal reaction force acts perpendicular to the plane and its magnitude is equal to the force that the box exerts on the plane in a direction perpendicular to the plane. Therefore, the magnitude of the normal reaction force is $R = 5\sqrt{2}\,\text{N}$.

Q7. As the box is in equilibrium we know that the resultant force must be zero. The resultant force is given by the sum of the vector forces acting on the box, therefore,

$$\mathbf{F} = \mathbf{W} + \mathbf{R} + \mathbf{P} + \mathbf{F_r} = 0.$$

We rearrange to find the friction force, F_r:

$$\mathbf{F_r} = (0\mathbf{i} + 0\mathbf{j}) - \mathbf{W} - \mathbf{R} - \mathbf{P}$$
$$= -(-50\mathbf{j}) - (-21.7\mathbf{i} + 12.5\mathbf{j}) - (29.295\mathbf{i} + 33.125\mathbf{j})$$
$$= (-7.595\mathbf{i} - 4.375\mathbf{j})\,\text{N}.$$

Q8. In order to find the final velocity of the box we need to find the acceleration of the box, using $F = ma$. We therefore begin by finding the resultant force on the box.

The box is subject to four forces: weight and normal reaction forces are vertical, whilst the pushing and friction forces are horizontal. The weight and normal reation forces balance each other out. The direction of motion must be the positive direction for forces and acceleration. Therefore, the resultant force is

$$F = P - F_r = 3 - 9 = -6\,\text{N}.$$

Rearranging $F = ma$ to find the acceleration we obtain

$$a = \frac{F}{m} = \frac{-6}{3} = -2\,\text{ms}^{-2}.$$

As the acceleration is negative, this means that the box is decelerating.

The deceleration is constant, therefore, we can use the equations of constant acceleration to find the final velocity. We know $u = 3\,\text{ms}^{-2}$, $a - 2\,\text{ms}^{-2}$, and $s = 1.25\,\text{m}$, so we will use the equation $v^2 = u^2 + 2as$ to find the final velocity v.

$$v^2 = 3^2 + 2 \times (-2) \times 1.25$$
$$= 9 - 5$$
$$= 4$$

Therefore, the final velocity is $v = 2\,\text{ms}^{-1}$.

Q9. In order to maintain equilibrium the resultant force must be $F = 0\,\text{N}$. The box is subject to four forces: the vertical weight and normal reaction force, which balance each other, and the horizontal pushing force and friction force. Therefore, the resultant force is given by

$$F = P - F_r = 0.$$

Therefore, in order to maintain equilibrium, $F_r = P = 6\,\text{N}$.

Q10. (a) As the plane is smooth we assume that the friction force is $F_r = 0\,\text{N}$.
(b) As the ball is in a vacuum we assume that there is no air resistance and $F_\text{air} = 0\,\text{N}$.
(c) As the tow rope is light we assume that its weight is $W = 0\,\text{N}$.

Q11. Our modelling assumptions mean that we can ignore the weight of the rope and the pulley, that the tension in the rope is constant along its length and that there is no friction between the pulley and the rope. We would expect the mass of $8\,\text{kg}$ to move downwards and the mass of $5\,\text{kg}$ to move upwards. Therefore, we have the following forces diagrams:

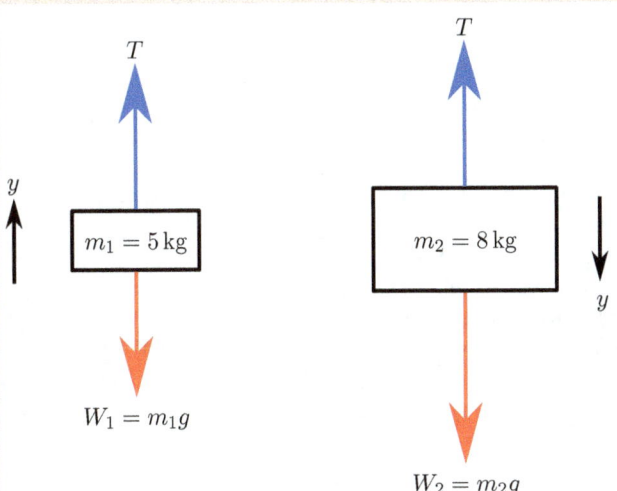

We now write down the equations of the resultant forces for each mass:

$$F_1 = T - W_1 \tag{6.1}$$
$$F_2 = W_2 - T. \tag{6.2}$$

We can calculate W_1 and W_2:

$$W_1 = m_1 g = 5 \times 9.8 = 49\,\text{N}$$
$$W_2 = m_2 g = 8 \times 9.8 = 78.4\,\text{N}.$$

As the two masses are connected we know that they will have the same acceleration, so substituting for $F = ma$, and our calculated values of W_1 and W_2 into equations (6.1) and (6.2), we obtain

$$5a = T - 49 \tag{6.3}$$
$$8a = 78.4 - T. \tag{6.4}$$

We now have two equations with two unknowns that we can solve simultaneously to find a and T. First, we add the equations together:

$$5a + 8a = T - 49 + 78.4 - T$$

which simplifies to

$$13a = 29.4.$$

Therefore, $a = 2.26\,\text{ms}^{-2}$ to 2 decimal places. Substituting back into equation (6.3) we can find T:

$$5 \times \frac{29.4}{13} = T - 49.$$

Rearranging:

$$T = 5 \times \frac{29.4}{13} + 49 = 60.31\,\text{N to 2 d.p.}.$$

We find the resultant force on each mass by substituting our full value for T and W_i into equations (6.1) and (6.2):

$$F_1 = T - W_1 = 60.30\ldots - 49 = 11.31\,\text{N to 2 d.p.}$$
$$F_2 = W_2 - T = 78.4 - 60.30\ldots = 18.09\,\text{N to 2 d.p.}.$$

Q12. Our modelling assumptions mean that we can ignore the weight of the rope and the pulley, that the tension in the rope is constant along its length and that there is no friction between the pulley and the rope. We would expect the mass of 25 kg to move towards the edge of the desk and the mass of 2 kg to move upwards. Therefore, we have the following forces diagrams:

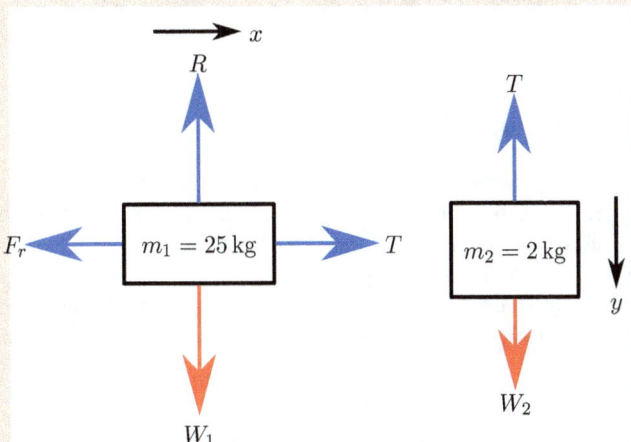

Now we set up the equations for the resultant forces on each mass:

$$F_1 = T - F_r$$
$$F_2 = W_2 - T.$$

We can calculate W_2

$$W_2 = m_2 g = 2 \times 9.8 = 19.6 \, \text{N}.$$

Substituting W_2, our given value for F_r, and for $F = ma$ into the equations for the resultant forces we obtain:

$$250a = T - 10 \qquad (6.5)$$
$$2a = 19.6 - T. \qquad (6.6)$$

Adding the equations together we obtain

$$250a + 2a = T - 10 + 19.6 - T = 9.6.$$

Rearranging we find the acceleration:

$$a = \frac{9.6}{252} = 0.038 \, \text{N to 2 d.p..}$$

We substitute this back into equation (6.5) to find T:

$$250 \times \frac{9.6}{252} = T - 10.$$

Therefore,

$$T = 250 \times \frac{9.6}{252} + 10 = 19.52 \, \text{N to 2 d.p..}$$

We use $F = ma$ to find the resultant force on each mass:

$$F_1 = 250 \times \frac{9.6}{252} = 9.52\,\text{N to 2 d.p.}$$
$$F_2 = 2 \times \frac{9.6}{252} = 0.076\,\text{N to 2 d.p..}$$

Q13. Our modelling assumptions mean that we can ignore the weight of the rope and pulley, that the tension in the rope is constant along its length and that there is no friction between the pulley and the rope. We would expect mass m_1 to move upwards and masses m_2 and m_3 to move down. As m_2 and m_3 do not move relative to one another, they may be modelled as a single particle of mass $m_s = m_2 + m_3 = 0.7\,\text{kg}$. Therefore, we have the following force diagrams:

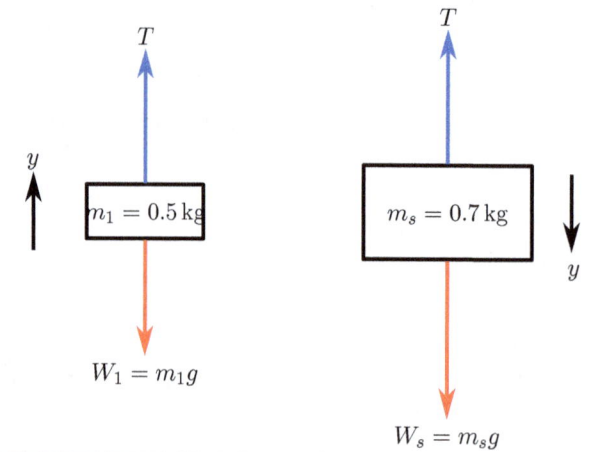

We write down the equations for the resultant forces

$$F_1 = T - W_1$$
$$F_s = W_s - T.$$

We calculate W_1 and W_s:

$$W_1 = m_1 g = 0.5 \times 9.8 = 4.9\,\text{N}$$
$$W_s = m_s g = 0.7 \times 9.8 = 6.86\,\text{N}.$$

As the masses are all connected they will all have the same acceleration. Therefore, we substitute for $F = ma$, and our calculated values of W_1 and W_s into our equations for the resultant forces:

$$0.5a = T - 4.9 \qquad (6.7)$$
$$0.7a = 6.86 - T. \qquad (6.8)$$

Next we add equations (6.7) and (6.8) together:

$$0.5a + 0.7a = T - 4.9 + 6.86 - T.$$

Simplifying we obtain

$$1.2a = 1.96.$$

Therefore,

$$a = \frac{1.96}{1.2} = 1.63 \,\text{N to 2 d.p.}.$$

We substitute the full value for a back into equation (6.7) to find T:

$$0.5 \times \frac{1.96}{1.2} = T - 4.9.$$

Rearranging we find T:

$$T = 0.5 \times \frac{1.96}{1.2} + 4.9 = 5.72 \,\text{N to 2 d.p.}.$$

Q14. As the person and the elevator car are in contact and have no motion relative to one another, they can be modelled as a single particle of mass 375 kg. The car is moving at constant velocity, therefore, it is in equilibrium and the resultant force will be $F = 0 \,\text{N}$.

The forces acting on the car are the combined weight of the car and the person, acting vertically downwards, and the tension in the cable above the car, acting vertically upwards. Therefore, the resultant force on the car is given by

$$F = T - W = 0. \tag{6.9}$$

We can calculate W:

$$W = mg = 375 \times 9.8 = 3675 \,\text{N}.$$

Therefore, from equation (6.9) we have

$$T = W = 3675 \,\text{N}.$$

Worked Solutions — Exercise 29.1

Q1. 0.68 or 0.85 should be selected. Based upon the spring season in England, and the history of rain during the month of April, it is reasonable to suggest that there is a high probability that it will rain during April again.

Q2. (a) Three fair coins each have two outcomes, heads or tails. Thus the combinations would be: HHH, HHT, HTH, THH, HTT, THT, TTH, TTT.
(b) Given that three of the possibilities from (a) contained two heads, and that the probability of an event is defined to be the number of outcomes divided by the total possible outcomes (Definition 29.2), then the probability of getting exactly two heads is $\frac{3}{8}$.

Q3. (a) Since all six sides of the die are equally likely, and the number four only occurs on one of these, the probability of rolling a four will be $\frac{1}{6}$.

(b) All of sides of the die do *not* have a four, and therefore the probability of not rolling a four must be $\frac{5}{6}$.

Q4. (a) In a regular pack of cards there are 52 cards divided into four equal suits (diamonds, hearts, spades and clubs). Therefore the probability of drawing a spade at random from a shuffled deck must be equivalent to $\frac{1}{4}$.

(b) Since the probability of an event not happening is one minus the probability of the event happening (Definition 29.3), this means not drawing a spade must have probability $\frac{3}{4}$.

(c) Each suit contains a single seven, so there are four sevens in the full pack of cards. Therefore the probability of randomly selecting one will be equivalent to $\frac{1}{13}$.

(d) Only one of these sevens will be a spade, so the probability of drawing a seven which is not a spade is 3 cards out of 52. Thus the probability will be $\frac{3}{52}$.

Q5. (a) Assuming that the order of the scoops is irrelevant then there are six combinations of two scoop ice creams: Vanilla-Vanilla, Vanilla-Chocolate, Vanilla-Strawberry, Chocolate-Chocolate, Chocolate-Strawberry, Strawberry-Strawberry.

(b) Of the above six combinations, three has at least one chocolate scoop of ice cream so the probability of this event is equivalent to $\frac{1}{2}$.

(c) There are three flavours, and so three possibilities of repeated flavour ice creams (also demonstrated with the combinations in (a)). Thus the probability of an ice cream having two scoops of the same flavour is equivalent to $\frac{1}{2}$.

Q6. It can be found that there are ten possible withdrawals from the box: BB, BY (×6), YY (×3).

Of these possibilities only one contains two blue counters, therefore the probability that two blue counters are removed must be $\frac{1}{10}$.

Q7. (a) Since only one section of the spinner is blue, then the probability of the spinner *not* landing on blue must be $\frac{3}{4}$.

(b) There are two sections which are red and one section green, thus three sections in total of the spinner that we are interested in. This means that the probability the spinner will land on red or green will also be $\frac{3}{4}$.

Q8. (a) Since in the word 'PROBABILITY' there are two B's, and there are eleven letters in total, the probability that a B is randomly selected is $\frac{2}{11}$.

(b) Additionally, there are also two I's and thus the probability that a B or an I is randomly chosen must be $\frac{4}{11}$.

(c) It follows then, from Definition, 29.3 that the probability of the letter **not** being a B or an I must be $\frac{7}{11}$.

Worked Solutions — Exercise 29.2

Q1. (a) Since there were 100 people served during the hour and 41 bought tea, the probability of the randomly selected customer being one of these people is $\frac{41}{100}$.

(b) As in part (i), since there were 100 people served and 15 bought both tea and coffee, then the probability of the randomly selected customer being one of these people is $\frac{15}{100}$ (or equivalent).

(c) Since we know 72 people ordered coffee, and that 15 people ordered both tea and coffee, we can deduct that 57 of the customers bought only coffee. As such, the probability that a randomly selected customer bought only coffee is $\frac{57}{100}$.

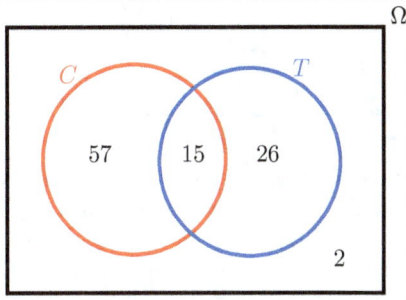

Q2. (a) Since 5 students do not study either language, this means that 25 students study French and/or Spanish. We can, with some logical thinking, deduce that there should in fact be 7 students who study both languages. This means that the probability a randomly selected student studies French and Spanish is $\frac{7}{30}$.

(b) This means that, since 17 students study French, there must only be 10 students whom study only French and not Spanish. Therefore the probability of a selected student studying French but not Spanish is $\frac{10}{30}$ (or equivalent).

(c) Likewise to (ii), since there are 15 students studying Spanish, there must be only 8 students who study just Spanish. Therefore the probability that a randomly chosen student studies Spanish but not French is $\frac{8}{30}$ (or equivalent).

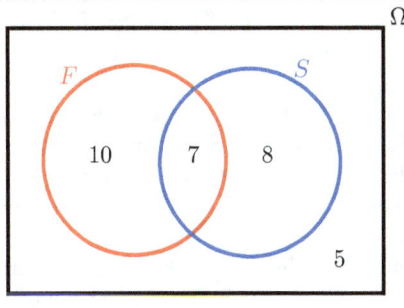

Q3. (a) The appropriate Venn diagram is shown below.

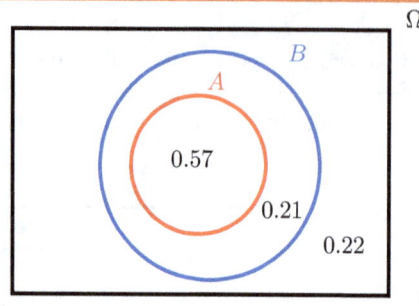

(b) If Amy is to miss the target then she either hits the board (but not the target) or misses the board entirely. As such, using (a) and Definition 29.3 to help us, it is clear that the probability that Amy will not hit the target is 0.43.

Q4. (a) The completed Venn diagram is shown below.

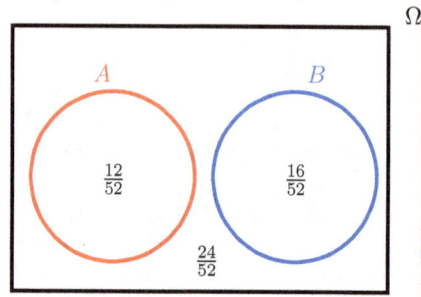

(b) i. Given that there are three picture cards in each suit of a pack of cards (Jack, Queen and King), this means there are twelve picture cards in the whole pack. So the probability of not selecting a picture card (i.e. event A') is clearly $\frac{40}{52}$ (or equivalent).

ii. As can be seen in (a) there are 12 picture cards and also 16 prime number cards. Therefore the probability of the union of the two events is given as $P(A \cup B) = \frac{28}{52}$ (or equivalent).

iii. Clearly, a picture card cannot also be a prime number card (see the missing intersection in the Venn diagram in (a)) so therefore $A \cap B = \emptyset$ and thus $P(A \cap B) = 0$.

iv. The probability of not drawing a picture and drawing a prime number card is clearly equivalent to the probability of simply drawing a prime number card. Therefore $P(A' \cap B) = P(B)$ and thus $P(A' \cap B) = \frac{16}{52}$ (or equivalent).

Q5. (a) The completed Venn diagram is shown below.

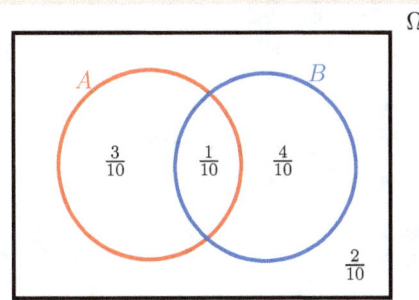

(b) i. Since 2 is the only prime number which is also even then $P(P \cap E) = \frac{1}{10}$.
   ii. The probability that a randomly select number is not even is clearly equivalent to $P(E') = \frac{1}{2}$.
   iii. $P(P \cup E')$ is the probability that a randomly selected number is either prime or not even. Since there are five numbers which are odd and only one even number which is prime this indicates that $P(P \cup E') = \frac{6}{10}$.
   iv. Here we are looking at the probability that the chosen number is not a prime, nor even. This leaves only two numbers between 1 and 10, the number 1 and the number 9. Thus $P(P' \cap E') = \frac{1}{5}$ (or equivalent).

Q6. (a) Since we are given the probability that a chosen person did not partake in football or swimming is 0.14, we can deduce that $P(F \cup S) = 0.86$.
(b) We can, with some logical thinking, then deduce that the probability that a randomly selected person does both swimming and football is 0.59.
(c) The probability that someone does not engage in football is, using the Venn diagram drawn, clearly 0.24.
(d) $P(F' \cup S)$ is the probability that the chosen person swims or does not do football. This, again from using the Venn diagram, is easily found to be 0.83.

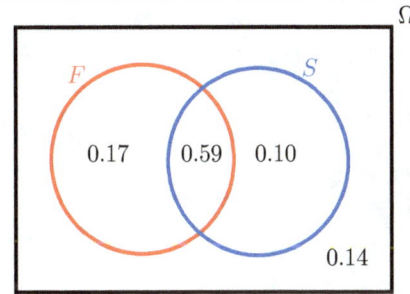

Worked Solutions — Exercise 29.3

Q1. (a) Using Formulae 29.1

$$P(A \cup B) = P(A) + P(B) - P(A \cap B)$$
$$= 0.4 + 0.5 - 0.2$$
$$= 0.7$$

(b) We are looking for all sections not in A which intersect with B. Using the Venn diagram it is clear that $P(A' \cap B) = 0.3$

(c) In this case we want the sections which are in A or not in B. Therefore $P(A \cup B') = 0.7$.

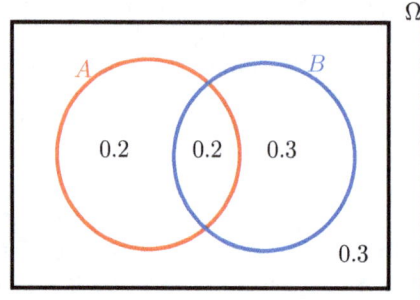

Q2. (a) Using Formulae 29.1

$$P(M \cap N) = P(M) + P(N) - P(M \cup N)$$
$$= 0.3 + 0.5 - 0.6$$
$$= 0.2$$

(b) $P(M \cap N')$ indicates the probability of M intersection with not N. Using a Venn diagram it becomes apparent that $P(M \cap N') = 0.1$

(c) This is the probability of not M. We can use Definition 29.3 to find that $P(M') = 0.7$.

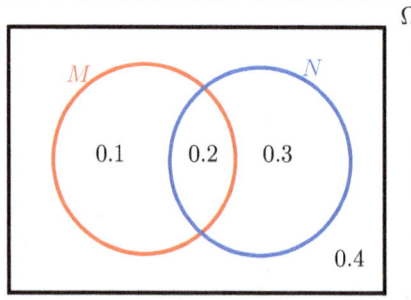

Q3. (a) Given that P(X') = 0.6, using Definition 29.3 we can deduce that P(X) = 0.4.

(b) We are looking for all of the event X which intersects with event not Y. Using a Venn diagram we can see that P($X \cap Y'$) = 0.3.

(c) P($X' \cup Y$) is the probability of something not being in X or being in Y. From the Venn diagram we can determine that P($X' \cup Y$) = 0.7.

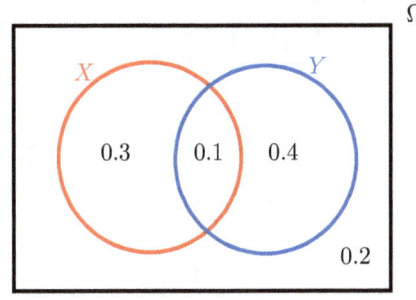

Q4. (a) Making use of Formulae 29.1 we can determine that

$$\begin{aligned} P(R \cap C) &= P(R) + P(C) - P(R \cup C) \\ &= 0.58 + 0.77 - 1 \\ &= 0.35 \end{aligned}$$

(b) Since we are told that every app user at least either cycles or runs then we know that the probability of a randomly select user doing neither must be equal to 0.

(c) Since the probability that someone runs is 0.58 and the probability that someone runs and cycles is 0.35, it follows that the probability that someone who runs but does not cycle is 0.23.

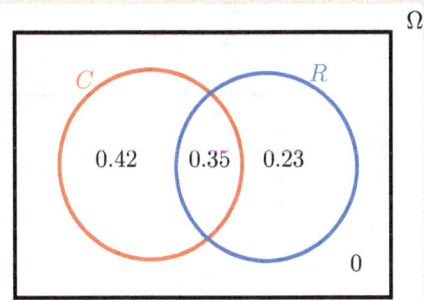

Q5. (a) Using Formulae 29.1 we find that

$$P(A \cap E) = P(A) + P(E) - P(A \cup E)$$
$$= 0.53 + 0.46 - 0.76$$
$$= 0.23.$$

(b) Neither three eyes nor three arms indicates to the section outside of the union (i.e. $1 - P(A \cup E)$). Therefore $P(A' \cap E') = P([A \cup E]') = 0.24$.

(c) In considering the probability that a given Necromorph will have three eyes but not three arms we consider $P(E) - P(A \cap E)$, which indicates that $P(A' \cap E) = 0.23$.

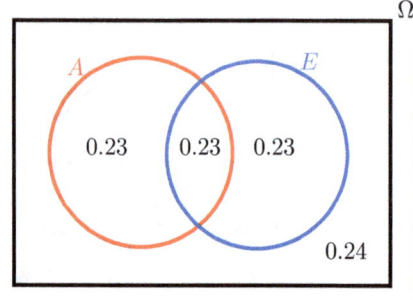

Q6. (a) From Formulae 29.1

$$P(S \cup T) = P(S) + P(T) - P(S \cap T)$$
$$= 0.62 + 0.44 - 0.28$$
$$= 0.78.$$

(b) A silver car which has two passenger doors, using our Venn diagram or otherwise, clearly gives the probability of 0.34.

(c) The probability that the car chosen is not silver is equivalent to $1 - P(S)$. Therefore $P(S') = 0.38$.

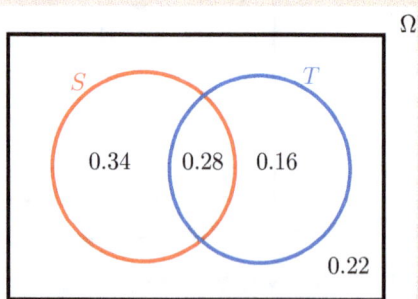

Worked Solutions — Exercise 29.4

Q1. As a result of Formulae 29.3 0 should be selected.

Q2. (a)

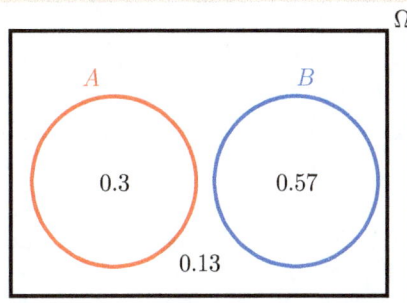

(b)(i) Since the probability of B' is 0.43 the from Definition 29.3 it follows that $P(B) = 0.57$.
(ii) Likewise, the probability of A is 0.3, thus from Definition 29.3 then $P(A') = 0.7$.

Q3. If the events A and B are mutually exclusive then they contain the sample space. However, if the events A and B have the same outcomes then A could be contained in B or vice versa meaning that $A \cap B = A = B$, and thus $P(A \cap B) \neq 0$. Therefore A and B could be mutually exclusive, though we need further information to be certain of the relationship between the events A and B.

Q4. (a) We are asked to find the probability that Dan does not have either poached or scrambled eggs for breakfast. Since the sample space has probability 1 and we know the probability that Dan has poached eggs is 0.47 and the probability Dan has scrambled eggs is 0.25, then we can suggest that

$$P(P' \cap S') = P(\Omega) - P(P) - P(S)$$
$$= 1 - 0.47 - 0.25$$
$$= 0.28$$

(b) Using Definition 29.3 we can determine that, since the probability of Dan having scrambled eggs in 0.25, then $P(S') = 0.75$.

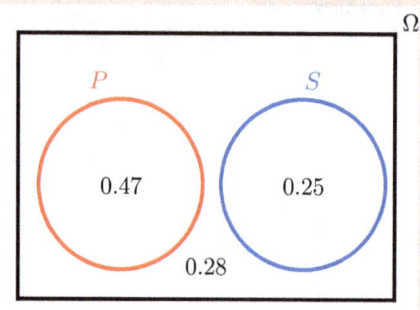

Q5. (a) Since the probability that the baby has blue eyes is 0.06, using Definition 29.3 we can determine that the probability the baby does not have blue eyes is 0.94.
(b) Since the sample space has probability 1 (i.e. the baby will have eyes), then we can find the probability that the baby does not have blue or brown eyes as

$$P(B' \cap Br') = P(\Omega) - P(B) - P(Br)$$
$$= 1 - 0.75 - 0.06$$
$$= 0.19.$$

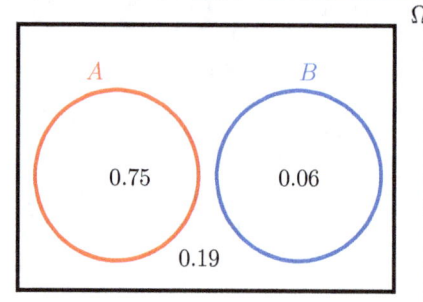

Q6. See the Venn diagram below.

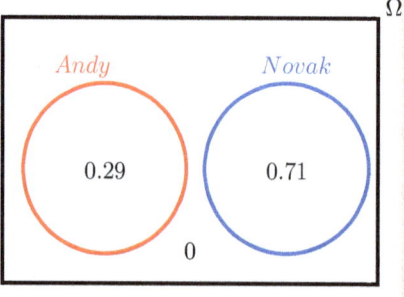

Q7. (a)

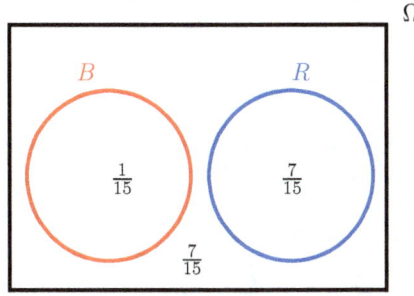

(b)(i) Since the probability that a black ball being chosen is $\frac{1}{15}$ and the sample space has probability 1, using Definition 29.3 $P(B') = \frac{14}{15}$.

(b)(ii) The probability that a yellow ball is not chosen indicates that either a red ball or a black ball is chosen. Thus we consider $P(B \cup R)$ which is clearly equivalent to $\frac{8}{15}$ using Formulae 29.3.

Q8. (a) Given that these events are mutually exclusive then the probability that neither team win is

$$P(\Omega) - P(S) - P(W)$$
$$= 1 - 0.37 - 0.59$$
$$= 0.04.$$

(b) Since the probability that the London Wasps do win is 0.59, using Definition 29.3 the probability that the Wasps do not win is 0.41.

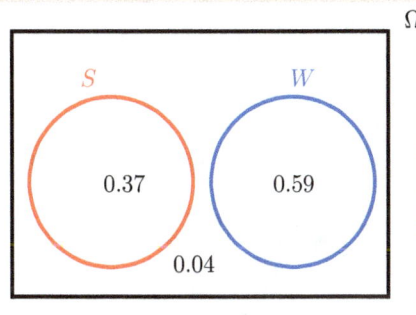

Worked Solutions — Exercise 29.5

Q1. If the events A and B are independent then, from Formulae 29.4, $P(A \cap B) = P(A) \times P(B)$.

(a)
$$P(A) \times P(B) = 0.4 \times 0.3$$
$$= 0.12$$
$$= P(A \cap B).$$

Therefore the events A and B are independent.

(b)
$$P(A) \times P(B) = 0.1 \times 0.1$$
$$= 0.01$$
$$\neq P(A \cap B).$$

Therefore the events A and B are not independent.

(c)
$$P(A) \times P(B) = 0.5 \times 0.49$$
$$= 0.245$$
$$\neq P(A \cap B).$$

Therefore the events A and B are not independent.

(d)
$$P(A) \times P(B) = 0.44 \times 0.8$$
$$= 0.352$$
$$= P(A \cap B).$$

Therefore the events A and B are independent.

(e)
$$P(A) \times P(B) = 0.17 \times 0.62$$
$$= 0.1054$$
$$= P(A \cap B).$$

Therefore the events A and B are independent.

(f)
$$P(A) \times P(B) = 0.78 \times 0.22$$
$$= 0.1716$$
$$\neq P(A \cap B).$$

Therefore the events A and B are not independent.

Q2. (a) Since independent
   i.
   $$P(A \cap B) = P(A) \times P(B)$$
   $$= 0.4 \times 0.2$$
   $$= 0.2$$

   ii. Thus, using Formulae 29.1,
   $$P(A \cup B) = P(A) + P(B) - P(A \cap B)$$
   $$= 0.4 + 0.5 - 0.2$$
   $$= 0.7.$$

(b) Since independent
   i.
   $$P(A \cap B) = P(A) \times P(B)$$
   $$= 0.72 \times 0.4$$
   $$= 0.288$$

   ii. Thus, using Formulae 29.1,
   $$P(A \cup B) = P(A) + P(B) - P(A \cap B)$$
   $$= 0.72 + 0.4 - 0.288$$
   $$= 0.832.$$

(c) i. Since independent
   $$P(A \cap B) = P(A) \times P(B)$$
   $$= 0.57 \times 0.68$$
   $$= 0.3876$$

   ii. Thus, using Formulae 29.1,
   $$P(A \cup B) = P(A) + P(B) - P(A \cap B)$$
   $$= 0.57 + 0.68 - 0.3876$$
   $$= 0.8624.$$

Worked Solutions — Exercise 29.6

Q1. (a) The events A and B are independent since the probability of Kate drawing any coloured counter from the first bag **cannot** influence the outcome of which coloured counter she draws from the second bag.
   (b) Due to (a) and Formulae 29.4 $P(A \cap B) = P(A) \times P(B)$. Thus $P(A \cap B) = \frac{16}{121}$.
   (c) This is the event that Kate selects a green counter from the first bag and a blue counter from the second bag. Thus $P(A' \cup B) = \frac{28}{121}$.

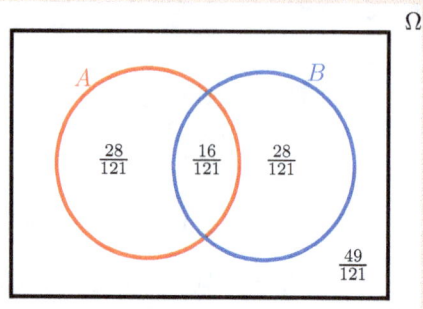

Q2. (a) It could be argued that someone who visits a library does so to withdraw a fiction or non-fiction book, and thus each event should not have any influence over the other's probability and therefore the events should be statistically independent. It could, however, be argued that someone who withdraws a non-fiction book might be more likely to withdraw a non-fiction book (similarly for fiction books). Therefore the probabilities would be influenced in this case and so the events would *not* be statistically independent.

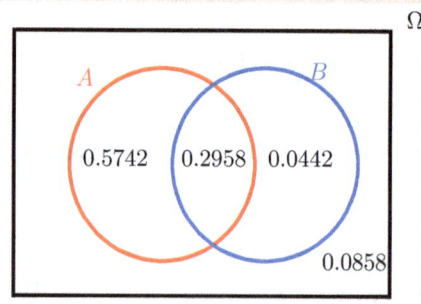

(b) i. Since independent

$$P(A \cap B) = P(A) \times P(B)$$
$$= 0.87 \times 0.34$$
$$= 0.2958.$$

ii. The probability of not drawing a fiction book and it being non-fiction is, from the Venn diagram, clearly 0.0442.

iii. The probability of not drawing a fiction book, or the book being non-fiction is, again from the Venn diagram, clearly 0.4258.

Q3. This question revisits a similar one seen in Exercise 29.1. In that case we identified that we three coins there were eight possible combinations (HHH, HHT, HTH, THH, HTT, THT, TTH, TTT).

(a) Therefore, given there are eight combinations, only one combination has both a head on the first and second coin so $P(H \cap I) = \frac{1}{8}$.

(b) Additionally, there is only one outcome where all three coins will display a head, so therefore $P(H \cap I \cap J) = \frac{1}{8}$.

(c) P($I \cup J'$) asks us to find the probability that the second coin shows a head or the third coin does not. This indicates us to the possible combinations HHH, HHT, THH, THT, HTT and TTT. Therefore P($I \cup J'$) = $\frac{6}{8}$ = $\frac{3}{4}$

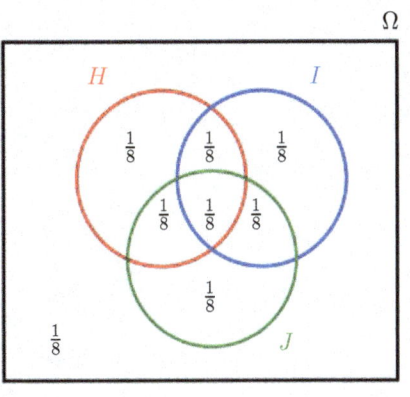

Worked Solutions — Exercise 29.7

Q1. For this question we define the event of choosing a spade as S and choosing something else as O (other).

(a) Constructing a tree diagram we have

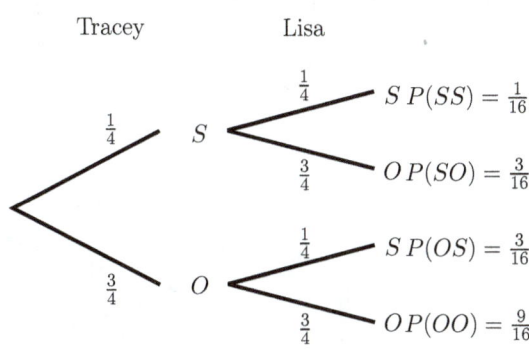

(b) For exactly one card to be spade then either Tracey draws a spade OR Lisa draws a spade - two of the possible outcomes. Since probabilities are found by multiplying branches the probability of exactly one spade occurring must be ($\frac{1}{4} \times \frac{3}{4}$) + ($\frac{3}{4} \times \frac{1}{4}$) (the probability of each event added together). This gives a final probability of $\frac{6}{16}$ which simplifies to $\frac{3}{8}$.

(c) If neither card is a spade then we must follow the lower branch for both Tracey and Lisa's draw from the pack of cards. This will result in the only possible outcome that produces no spades which has a probability $\frac{3}{4} \times \frac{3}{4} = \frac{9}{16}$.

Q2. For this question we define the two events as W and L for winning and losing respectively.

(a) Constructing a tree diagram we have

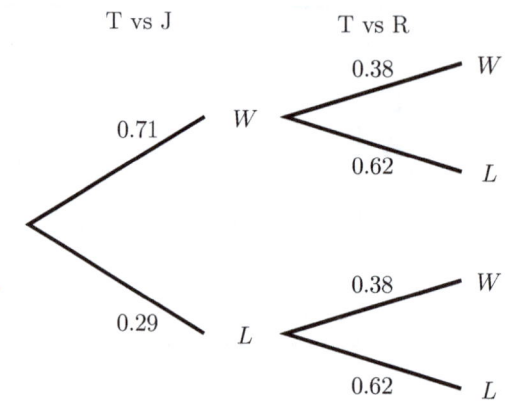

(b) If Tim wins both games we must follow the upper branch for his game against Jack and Richard which will result in the only possible outcome where Tim can win both games. This will have probability $0.71 \times 0.38 = 0.2698$.

(c) There are three outcomes whereby Tim wins at least one game, and thus two possible ways of calculating the solution as seen in Example **??**. Here we will consider the first way only: Calculate the probability that Tim loses both games, 0.29×0.62, which gives 0.1798. This can then be subtracted from the sample space ($\Omega = 1$) to find that the probability of Tim winning at least one game is 0.8202.

Q3. For this question the events are G for green light and R for red light (i.e. stopping).

(a) Constructing a tree diagram we have,

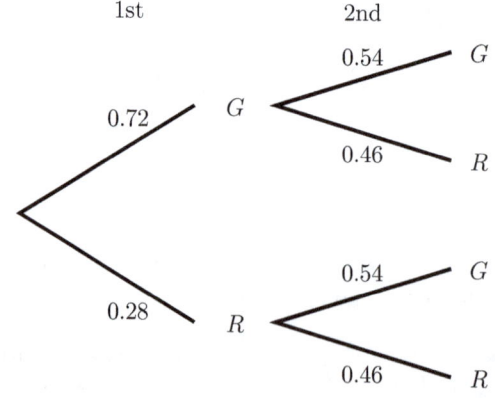

(b) If Tom does not stop then he passes through both sets of lights whilst they are green. Therefore we can calculate the probability to be $0.72 \times 0.54 = 0.3888$.

(c) There are only two outcomes where Tom will stop exactly once on his journey, either he stops at the first set of lights or he stops at the second set. This gives us the calculation $(0.72 \times 0.46) + (0.28 \times 0.54)$ which gives the probability 0.4824.

Worked Solutions — Exercise 29.8

Q1. (a) Making use of the addition rule (Formulae 29.1) we determine that

$$P(A \cup B) = P(A) + P(B) - P(A \cap B)$$
$$= 0.27 + 0.41 - 0.15$$
$$= 0.53.$$

(b) Given that from Definition 29.3 we can determine that $P(A') = 0.73$, and that we are looking for the probability of the union of events A' and B we can deduce that

$$P(A' \cup B) = P(A') + P(A \cap B)$$
$$= 0.73 + 0.15$$
$$= 0.88.$$

See also the Venn diagram in part (d).

(c) Since events A and C are independent

$$P(A \cap C) = P(A) \times P(C)$$
$$= 0.27 \times 0.21$$
$$= 0.0567.$$

(d) Constructing the Venn diagram, we have,

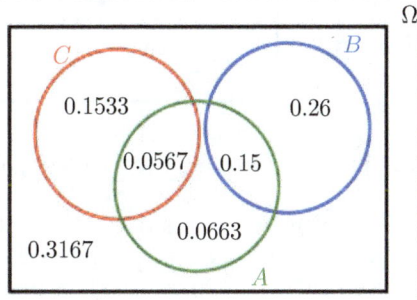

(e) i. Since events B and C are mutually exclusive the Formulae 29.3 applies

and
$$P(B \cup C) = P(B) + P(C)$$
$$= 0.41 + 0.21$$
$$= 0.62.$$

ii. Clearly, considering the Venn diagram in part (d), we can see that since B and C are mutually exclusive, then $P(B' \cap C) = P(C)$. Thus $P(B' \cap C) = 0.21$.

Q2. (a) i. Given that 98 people took part in a field events out of a possible 200 students, this equates to a probability of 0.49 that a randomly selected student was a field competitor.

ii. There were 43 year 8 students who competed in a track event, so the probability is equivalent to 0.215.

(b) Let the event 'in year 7' be S and 'completed a track event' be T. If independent $P(S \cap T) = P(S) \times P(T)$. Since $P(S) = 0.39$ and $P(T) = 0.51$ then

$$P(S) \times P(T) = 0.39 \times 0.51$$
$$= 0.1989.$$

However, there were 37 out of 200 pupils who were year 7 track competitors - therefore $P(S \cap T) = 0.185$. Thus $P(S \cap T) \neq P(S) \times P(T)$ and the events S and T are not statistically independent.

Q3. (a) Constructing the Venn diagram, we have,

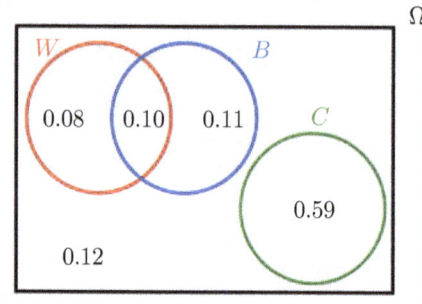

(b) From the Venn diagram formed in part (a) this can be easily identified as 0.11.

(c) Here we are looking for the probability that someone used a car or a bus (i.e. $P(B \cup C)$). Since we should have identified (in part (a) and later in part (e)) that the events B and C are mutually exclusive then

$$P(B \cup C) = P(B) + P(C)$$
$$= 0.21 + 0.59$$
$$= 0.8.$$

(d) If these events (B and W) are statistically independent then $P(B \cap W) =$

$P(B) \times P(W)$. Since $P(B) = 0.21$ and $P(W) = 0.18$ then

$$P(B) \times P(W) = 0.21 \times 0.18$$
$$= 0.0378.$$

However, the probability that a randomly selected person used the bus **and** walked was 0.10. Thus $P(B \cap W) \neq P(B) \times P(W)$ and the events B and W are not statistically independent.

(e) Using part (a) and the information provided it is evident that no-one used a car and another form of transport. Therefore the events B and C are mutually exclusive and W and C are also mutually exclusive.

Q4. (a) Since the sample space must equal one

$$b + w = 1 - (0.22 + 0.17 + 0.06 + 0.33)$$
$$= 0.22.$$

Therefore, since b and w are equal probabilities $b = w = 0.11$.

(b) Using the information provided in the Venn diagram, W and B will be mutually exclusive if

$$P(W) + P(B) + 0.22 + 0.06 = 1$$

Using the given information

$$P(W) + P(B) = 0.28 + 0.44$$
$$= 0.72.$$

Therefore, since $0.72 + 0.22 + 0.06 = 1$, the events W and B are mutually exclusive.

(c) If the events P and B are statistically independent then $P(P \cap B) = P(P) \times P(B)$. Since $P(P) = 0.56$ and $P(B) = 0.44$ then

$$P(P) \times P(B) = 0.56 \times 0.44$$
$$= 0.2464.$$

However, the probability that a randomly select player can play both the piano **and** a brass instrument is 0.33. Thus $P(P \cap B) \neq P(P) \times P(B)$ and the events P and B are not statistically independent.

(d) The probability that a randomly selected player could only play piano was 0.06, so from a group of 18 players we would expect on 1 player to be able to play only the piano (since $0.06 \times 18 = 1.08$).

Q5. (a) Since the customer must have bought a meal, drink or snack then the probability that they did not buy any of these is 0 and therefore $a = 0$.

(b) Since M and S are independent events $P(M \cap S) = P(M) \times P(S)$. Therefore

$$P(M) \times P(S) = 0.51$$
$$(b + 0.10 + 0.51) \times (0.51 + 0.13) = 0.51$$
$$0.64b + 0.3904 = 0.51$$
$$b = 0.1868\ldots$$

Therefore, rounding to two decimal places, $b = 0.19$.

(c) As a result, since the sample space must equal one, the final missing value can be determined, $c = 0.08$.

(d) i. To find the probability of the complement of $M \cup S$ we must take $P(M \cup S)$ away from 1. Therefore

$$P([M \cup S]') = 1 - (0.18 + 0.1 + 0.51 + 0.13)$$
$$= 0.08.$$

ii. Given that, from the Venn diagram, $P(D \cap S') = P(D) - P(S)$ then $P(D \cap S') = 0.18$.
Therefore $P([D \cap S']') = 0.82$.

Worked Solutions — Exercise 30.1

Q1. (a) We must write down every possible combination of heads and tails for four tosses of a coin. Since every flip of the coin has two possible outcomes, and each one is independent, we should have $2^4 = 16$ different outcomes.
One systematic approach is to build up the set of outcomes one flip at a time. For example, the outcomes for one flip are $\{H\}$ and $\{T\}$. Then the outcomes for two flips can be generated first by adding an H to these, to get $\{H, H\}$ and $\{H, T\}$, and then adding a T, to get $\{T, H\}$ and $\{T, T\}$. At each step, we double the number of outcomes by adding H and then T to the current list.

(b) There are 16 possible outcomes. Since the coin is fair, we expect to see each outcome roughly an equal number of times. Therefore, the probability of each outcome is $\frac{1}{16}$. We can count which outcomes have at least two heads in a row and see that there are eight such outcomes:
$\{HHHH\}, \{HHHT\}, \{HHTH\}, \{HHTT\},$
$\{HTHH\}, \{THHH\}, \{THHT\}, \{TTHH\}.$
By summing the probabilities of these outcomes, we calculate that the probability of seeing any of them is equal to $8 \times \frac{1}{16} = \frac{1}{2}$.

(c) Let Y be the maximum number of heads in a row. It takes values in the set $\{0, 1, 2, 3, 4\}$. We can work out the probability of each possible value by counting the number of outcomes which give that value and multiplying by $\frac{1}{16}$.
4 heads: $\{HHHH\}$
3 heads: $\{HHHT\}, \{THHH\}$
2 heads: $\{HHTH\}, \{HHTT\}, \{HTHH\}, \{THHT\}, \{TTHH\}$

1 head: $\{HTHT\}$, $\{HTTH\}$, $\{HTTT\}$, $\{THTH\}$, $\{THTT\}$, $\{TTHT\}$, $\{TTTH\}$

0 heads: $\{TTTT\}$

Q2 (a) There are $6^2 = 36$ possible outcomes. We can list the outcomes by choosing every possible pair from the set of outcomes of a single roll: $\{1, 2, 3, 4, 5, 6\}$. Since the dice are fair, the outcomes all have the same probability.

(b) There are 36 possible outcomes of equal probability. Therefore the probability of each outcome is $\frac{1}{36}$. There are 20 outcomes with at least one 5 or 6.

$\{1,5\}, \{1,6\}, \{2,5\}, \{2,6\}, \{3,5\},$
$\{3,6\}, \{4,5\}, \{4,6\}, \{5,1\}, \{5,2\},$
$\{5,3\}, \{5,4\}, \{5,5\}, \{5,6\}, \{6,1\},$
$\{6,2\}, \{6,3\}, \{6,4\}, \{6,5\}, \{6,6\}.$

Therefore the probability of seeing any of these outcomes is $20 \times \frac{1}{36} = \frac{5}{9}$.

(c) We categorise the possible outcomes according to the score we are awarded.

1 point: $\{1,1\}, \{2,2\}, \{3,3\}, \{4,4\}, \{5,5\}, \{6,6\}$
2 points: $\{1,2\}, \{2,1\}$
3 points: $\{1,3\}, \{2,3\}, \{3,1\}, \{3,2\}$
4 points: $\{1,4\}, \{2,4\}, \{3,4\}, \{4,1\}, \{4,2\}, \{4,3\}$
5 points: $\{1,5\}, \{2,5\}, \{3,5\}, \{4,5\}, \{5,1\}, \{5,2\}, \{5,3\}, \{5,4\}$
6 points: $\{1,6\}, \{2,6\}, \{3,6\}, \{4,6\}, \{5,6\}, \{6,1\}, \{6,2\}, \{6,3\}, \{6,4\}, \{6,5\}$

The probabilities for each value are then caclulated by multiplying the number of outcomes that give that value by the probability of a single outcome, $\frac{1}{36}$.

Now we have the probability distribution, we can work out the expected value.

$$\sum_{k=1}^{6} k\mathbb{P}(X=k) = 1 \cdot \frac{1}{6} + 2 \cdot \frac{1}{18} + 3 \cdot \frac{1}{9} + 4 \cdot \frac{1}{6} + 5 \cdot \frac{2}{9} + 6 \cdot \frac{5}{18} = \frac{146}{36}$$

This value is just a little over four, slightly higher than the expectation for a throw of a standard die, which is 3.5.

Q3. Let X be the drawer containing the calculator. It takes values from the set $\{t, m, b\}$.

(a) At first, the only knowledge we have about the location of the calculator is that it is in one of the three drawers. We must give equal weight to each possible outcome, and so each outcome has a probability of $\frac{1}{3}$.

(b) Consider $\mathbb{P}(X = m | X \neq t)$, the probability that the calculator is in the middle drawer given that it is not in the top drawer. If $X = m$ then it is certainly true that $X \neq t$. Therefore we use the conditional probability equation to say that

$$\mathbb{P}(X=m|X\neq t) = \frac{\mathbb{P}(\{X=m\} \cap \{X \neq t\})}{\mathbb{P}(X \neq t)} = \frac{\mathbb{P}(X=m)}{\mathbb{P}(X \neq t)} = \frac{1/3}{2/3} = \frac{1}{2}.$$

Similarly, $\mathbb{P}(X = b | X \neq t) = \frac{1}{2}$.

Q4. The random variable X has the distribution

$$\mathbb{P}(X=1) = 4\alpha, \qquad \mathbb{P}(X=2) = 10\alpha, \qquad \mathbb{P}(X=3) = 18\alpha.$$

(a) Since the probabilities must sum to 1,

$$4\alpha + 10\alpha + 18\alpha = 32\alpha = 1,$$

and so $\alpha = \frac{1}{32}$.

(b) We use the result from probability that $\mathbb{P}(A \cap B) = \mathbb{P}(A|B)\mathbb{P}(B)$. Here, A is the event that $X = 1$ and B is the event that X is odd. If $X = 1$ then X is definitely odd, and so $A \cap B = A$. Since $\mathbb{P}(X = 1) = 4\alpha = \frac{1}{8}$ and

$$\mathbb{P}(X \text{ is odd}) = \mathbb{P}(X=1) + \mathbb{P}(X=3) = 22\alpha = \frac{11}{16},$$

the solution is given by $\mathbb{P}(X=1|X \text{ is odd}) = \mathbb{P}(X \text{ is odd})/\mathbb{P}(X=1) = \frac{1}{8} \cdot \frac{16}{11} = \frac{2}{11}$.

(c) Using the same technique as the previous question, we can say that $\mathbb{P}(Y=3) = 3\beta$, $\mathbb{P}(Y=4) = 4\beta$ and $\mathbb{P}(Y=5) = 5\beta$ for some constant β. We must select a value of β such that the probabilities sum to 1. Therefore, $\beta = \frac{1}{12}$ and the distribution is given by $\mathbb{P}(Y=3) = \frac{1}{4}$, $\mathbb{P}(Y=4) = \frac{1}{3}$ and $\mathbb{P}(Y=5) = \frac{5}{12}$.

(d) To obtain $Y - X = 3$ we must either have $(X=1, Y=4)$ or $(X=2, Y=5)$. The two variables are independent and the two events are mutually exclusive and so the probability is given by

$$\mathbb{P}(Y=4) \cdot \mathbb{P}(X=1) + \mathbb{P}(Y=5) \cdot \mathbb{P}(X=2) =$$
$$\frac{1}{3} \cdot \frac{1}{8} + \frac{5}{12} \cdot \frac{5}{16} = \frac{1}{24} + \frac{25}{192} = \frac{33}{192}.$$

Q5. Let X be the colour of the first ball, and Y the colour of the second.

(a) The observation for X is made by placing all the balls in the bag, and selecting one at random. Over time, we would expect each ball to be drawn a similar number of times, so $\mathbb{P}(X = \text{red}) = \frac{8}{12} = \frac{2}{3}$ and $\mathbb{P}(X = \text{green}) = \frac{4}{12} = \frac{1}{3}$.

(b) If the first ball was red, then we are left with 7 red balls and 4 green balls in the bag. Therefore the conditional distribution for the colour of the second ball is $\mathbb{P}(Y = \text{red}|X = \text{red}) = \frac{7}{11}$ and $\mathbb{P}(Y = \text{green}|X = \text{red}) = \frac{4}{11}$.

(c) We have the distribution for the colour of the second ball if the first ball is red. Similarly, we can write down the distribution if the first ball is green: $\mathbb{P}(Y = \text{red}|X = \text{green}) = \frac{8}{11}$ and $\mathbb{P}(Y = \text{green}|X = \text{green}) = \frac{3}{11}$. The probability that $(Y = \text{red})$ is equal to the probability that $(Y = \text{red}, X = \text{red})$ plus the probability that $(Y = \text{red}, X = \text{green})$. Then we can use the identity $\mathbb{P}(A \cap B) = \mathbb{P}(A|B)\mathbb{P}(B)$ to show that

$$\mathbb{P}(Y = \text{red}) = \mathbb{P}(\{Y = \text{red}\} \cap \{X = \text{red}\}) + \mathbb{P}(\{Y = \text{red}\} \cap \{X = \text{green}\})$$
$$= \mathbb{P}(Y = \text{red}|X = \text{red}) \cdot \mathbb{P}(X = \text{red}) +$$
$$\mathbb{P}(Y = \text{red}|X = \text{green}) \cdot \mathbb{P}(X = \text{green})$$
$$= \frac{7}{11} \cdot \frac{2}{3} + \frac{8}{11} \cdot \frac{1}{3} = \frac{2}{3}$$

and

$$\mathbb{P}(Y = \text{green}) = \mathbb{P}(Y = \text{green}|X = \text{red}) \cdot \mathbb{P}(X = \text{red}) +$$
$$\mathbb{P}(Y = \text{green}|X = \text{green}) \cdot \mathbb{P}(X = \text{green})$$
$$= \frac{4}{11} \cdot \frac{2}{3} + \frac{3}{11} \cdot \frac{1}{3} = \frac{1}{3}$$

In fact, X and Y *must* have the same distribution, since all we are really doing is selecting two balls and randomly calling one X and the other one Y. We would get the same distribution of results if we called the first one Y and the second one X.

Worked Solutions — Exercise 30.2

Q1. Every sequence of heads and tails has the same probability:

$$\frac{1}{2} \times \frac{1}{2} \times \frac{1}{2} = \frac{1}{8}.$$

To calculate the probability of an event, we count up the number of different sequences for which the event occurs, and multiply that by the probability of a single sequence. For the first three parts of the question, there is a single sequence for which the event occurs, and the probability is $\frac{1}{8}$. For the final part, there are three separate sequences, so the probability is $\frac{3}{8}$.

Q2. The experiment is to throw four dice and count the number of fives and sixes. The chance of rolling a 5 or a 6 is $p = \frac{1}{3}$.

(a) The probability of not throwing a five or six on the first throw is $1 - p = \frac{2}{3}$. The probability of this happening four times, for four independent throws, is $(1-p)^4 = 0.198$.

(b) The probability that every throw is a five or a six is $p^4 = 0.012$.

(c) Imagine that we throw the dice one at a time, since this does not change the probabilities. There are four different ways in which we could throw a five or six exactly once: we could throw it on the first throw, the second, the third or the fourth. The probability of throwing it on the first throw is

$$\mathbb{P}(5 \text{ or } 6) \times (\mathbb{P}(\text{not a } 5 \text{ or } 6))^3 = p(1-p)^3 = 0.099.$$

Each of the four possible ways of throwing exactly one five or six has the same probability, the events are mutually exclusive and so the total probability is found by summing the probabilities, to obtain $4p(1-p)^3 = 0.395$.

Worked Solutions — Exercise 30.3

Q1. (a) To three decimal places,

$$\mathbb{P}(X=0) = \binom{8}{0} \times (0.3)^0 \times (0.7)^8 = (0.7)^8 = 0.058.$$

(b)

$$\mathbb{P}(X=4) = \binom{8}{4} \times (0.3)^4 \times (0.7)^4 = \frac{8!}{4!4!} \times (0.3)^4 \times (0.7)^4$$

$$= \frac{8.7.6.5}{4.3.2.1} \times (0.3)^4 \times (0.7)^4 = 70 \times (0.3)^4 \times (0.7)^4 = 0.136.$$

(c) We use

$$\mathbb{P}(X \geq 2) = 1 - [\mathbb{P}(X=0) + \mathbb{P}(X=1)].$$

We can calculate $\mathbb{P}(X=1)$ in the same way that we found $\mathbb{P}(X=0)$.

$$\mathbb{P}(X=1) = \binom{8}{1} \times (0.3)^1 \times (0.7)^7 = 0.198$$

Therefore $\mathbb{P}(X \geq 2) = 1 - (0.058 + 0.198) = 0.745.$

(d) We can use the binomial formula to find

$$\mathbb{P}(X=2) = \binom{8}{2} \times (0.3)^2 \times (0.7)^6 = \frac{8!}{6!2!} \times (0.3)^2 \times (0.7)^6$$

$$= \frac{8.7}{2.1} \times (0.3)^2 \times (0.7)^6 = 28 \times (0.3)^2 \times (0.7)^6 = 0.296$$

and

$$\mathbb{P}(X=3) = \binom{8}{3} \times (0.3)^3 \times (0.7)^5 = \frac{8!}{5!3!} \times (0.3)^3 \times (0.7)^5$$

$$= \frac{8.7.6}{3.2.1} \times (0.3)^3 \times (0.7)^5 = 56 \times (0.3)^3 \times (0.7)^5 = 0.254.$$

Using these, together with the values for $\mathbb{P}(X=0)$ and $\mathbb{P}(X=1)$ that we have already found, we calculate

$$\mathbb{P}(X < 4) = \sum_{k=0}^{3} \mathbb{P}(X=k) = 0.058 + 0.198 + 0.296 + 0.254 = 0.806$$

The probability that X is both odd and less than four is given by

$$\mathbb{P}(X=1) + \mathbb{P}(X=3) = 0.198 + 0.254 = 0.452.$$

And then we use the properties of conditional probability to calculate

$$\mathbb{P}(X \text{ is odd}|X < 4) = \frac{\mathbb{P}(X < 4 \text{ and is odd})}{\mathbb{P}(X < 4)} = \frac{0.452}{0.806} = .561.$$

Q2. We know that $X \sim B(7, 0.5)$, that is, the probability of a head is 0.5. Therefore, the probability of a tail is also 0.5, since the two probabilities must sum to one. Therefore $Y \sim B(7, 0.5)$. Note that X and Y are *not* independent, since for any given observation $X + Y = 7$.
 (a) We can find $\mathbb{P}(X = 1)$ directly from the binomial formula:

$$\mathbb{P}(X = 1) = \binom{7}{1} \times (0.5)^1 \times (0.5)^6 = 0.055.$$

 (b) Similarly for $\mathbb{P}(X = 2)$

$$\mathbb{P}(X = 2) = \binom{7}{2} \times (0.5)^2 \times (0.5)^5 = \frac{7.6}{2.1} \times (0.5)^2 \times (0.5)^5 = 0.164.$$

 (c) If $Y = 5$ then there are five tails and two heads, and so $X = 2$. Therefore $\mathbb{P}(Y = 5) = \mathbb{P}(X = 2) = 0.164$.
 (d) We can calculate this directly using the binomial distribution. Alternatively, if $Y \leq 3$ then there are more heads than tails. If $Y > 3$ then there are more tails than heads. So the question is asking "What is the probability that there are more heads than tails?" Since the coin is fair the probability that $X > Y$ must equal the probability that $X < Y$. Since, for any observation, X and Y cannot be equal we have $\mathbb{P}(X < Y) = \mathbb{P}(X > Y) = 0.5$.

Q3. (a) Let $X_n \sim B(6n, \frac{1}{6})$. Use the definition of the binomial distribution to prove that $\mathbb{P}(X_1 \geq 1) > \mathbb{P}(X_2 \geq 2) > \mathbb{P}(X_3 \geq 3)$.
 (b) Let $Y_n \sim B(6n, 0.25)$. Now prove that $\mathbb{P}(Y_1 \geq 1) < \mathbb{P}(Y_2 \geq 2) < \mathbb{P}(Y_3 \geq 3)$.

Q4. (a) Let X be the number of defective widgets in a box, so $X \sim (10, 0.05)$. The probability of exactly one defective widget in a box is $\mathbb{P}(X = 1) = 0.315$.
 (b) The probability that a box contains at least one defective widget is

$$\mathbb{P}(X \geq 1) = 1 - \mathbb{P}(X = 0) = 1 - 0.599 = 0.401.$$

 (c) All ten widgets have been checked and you have been told that at least one is defective. That is, you have been told $X \geq 1$. Therefore,

$$\mathbb{P}(X \geq 2|X \geq 1) = \frac{\mathbb{P}(X \geq 2)}{\mathbb{P}(X \geq 1)} = \frac{0.086}{0.401} = 0.215$$

 (d) Only one widget has been checked, and it is defective. The other nine widgets have not been inspected. Let Y be the number of defective widgets remaining in the box. Then Y has the distribution $B(9, 0.05)$ and

$$\mathbb{P}(Y \geq 1) = 1 - \mathbb{P}(Y = 0) = 1 - 0.630 = 0.370.$$

Worked Solutions — Exercise 30.4

Q1. (a) Setting $k = 0$ in the given probability distribution formula gives, to three decimal places, $\mathbb{P}(X = 0) = e^{-3} = 0.050$.

(b)
$$\begin{aligned}\mathbb{P}(X \geq 2) &= 1 - [\mathbb{P}(X = 1) + \mathbb{P}(X = 0)] \\ &= 1 - (3e^{-3} + e^{-3}) = 0.801.\end{aligned}$$

(c) We already have the values of the probability distribution for $k = 0$ and $k = 1$. We can also calculate that

$$\mathbb{P}(X = 3) = \frac{3^3}{3!}e^{-3} = 0.224$$

and

$$\mathbb{P}(X \geq 3) = 1 - \left(\frac{9}{2}e^{-3} + 3e^{-3} + e^{-3}\right) = 0.577.$$

Putting these together, we have

$$\mathbb{P}(X = 3 | X \geq 3) = \frac{\mathbb{P}(X = 3)}{\mathbb{P}(X \geq 3)} = 0.388.$$

Q2. (a) Let X be the number of drives that fail in an hour. Then X has a Poisson distribution with parameter 2 and

$$\begin{aligned}\mathbb{P}(X > 2) &= 1 - (\mathbb{P}(X = 0) + \mathbb{P}(X = 1) + \mathbb{P}(X = 2)) \\ &= 1 - (0.135 + 0.271 + 0.271) = 0.323.\end{aligned}$$

(b) If the mean number of failures per hour is 2 then the mean number of failures per day is 48.

(c) Failures occur independently and randomly at a constant rate, and so the distribution is Poisson. Therefore the distribution is a Poisson distribution with mean 48.

(d) The distribution for Y, the number of failures in the next two hours has a Poisson distribution with $\lambda = 4$. Therefore $\mathbb{P}(Y > 3)$ is

$$1 - \sum_{k=0}^{3} \mathbb{P}(Y = k) = 1 - (0.018 + 0.073 + 0.147 + 0.195) = 0.567.$$

Q3. There are an average of 32 pieces of mushroom on a pizza, and so there are an average of 4 pieces of mushroom on a single slice. The mushroom pieces are distributed randomly, so the number of pieces on a single slice can be modelled with the Poisson distribution with $\lambda = 4$.

Therefore, the probability that any given slice has no pieces of mushroom on it is equal to 0.018.

Since the whole process is random, each slice in a pizza has the same probability of having no mushroom pieces, and these events are independent. Therefore the number of mushroom-free slices can be modelled as a binomial distribution with $n = 8$ and $p = 0.018$. The probability that a value with this distribution is zero is 0.863. Therefore, the probability of at least one slice with no mushrooms is approximately equal to 0.137.

Q4. The expected number of colour blind men in a sample of 100 is eight, so we may approximate this with a Poisson distribution with mean 8. Let X be the number of colour blind men in the sample. To three decimal places,

$$\mathbb{P}(X = 0) = \frac{8^0 e^{-8}}{0!} = 0.000$$

$$\mathbb{P}(X = 1) = \frac{8^1 e^{-8}}{1!} = 0.003$$

$$\mathbb{P}(X = 2) = \frac{8^2 e^{-8}}{2!} = 0.011$$

$$\mathbb{P}(X = 3) = \frac{8^3 e^{-8}}{3!} = 0.029$$

and so

$$\mathbb{P}(X < 4) = \sum_{k=0}^{3} \mathbb{P}(X = k) = 0.042.$$

Q5. We start with the definition of expectation and substitute in the Poisson probability distribution.

$$\mathbb{E}(X) = \sum_{k=0}^{\infty} k \mathbb{P}(X = k) = \sum_{k=0}^{\infty} \frac{k \lambda^k e^{-\lambda}}{k!}$$

Then we can take a constant term of $\lambda e^{-\lambda}$ out of the terms being summed.

$$\mathbb{E}(X) = \lambda e^{-\lambda} \sum_{k=0}^{\infty} \frac{k \lambda^{k-1}}{k!}$$

The $k = 0$ term is equal to zero, so we can remove this term, and then cancel down by k.

$$\mathbb{E}(X) = \lambda e^{-\lambda} \sum_{k=1}^{\infty} \frac{k \lambda^{k-1}}{k.(k-1)!} = \lambda e^{-\lambda} \sum_{k=1}^{\infty} \frac{\lambda^{k-1}}{(k-1)!} = \lambda e^{-\lambda} \sum_{k=0}^{\infty} \frac{\lambda^k}{k!}$$

By the expansion of the exponential function given in the question, this gives us the solution:

$$\mathbb{E}(X) = \lambda e^{-\lambda} e^{\lambda} = \lambda.$$

Worked Solutions — Exercise 30.5

Q1. (a) Substituting $k = 0$ into the given distribution, we calculate that
$$\mathbb{P}(X = 0) = \frac{2}{5} = 0.4.$$

(b) We can calculate the answer directly using $\mathbb{P}(X \geq 2) = 1 - [\mathbb{P}(X = 0) + \mathbb{P}(X = 1)]$.
Alternatively, we can say that there are at least two failures if and only if both of the first two attempts are failures. The probability of this is given by
$$\mathbb{P}(X \geq 2) = \left(\frac{3}{5}\right)^2 = 0.36.$$

(c) Using the same technique, $\mathbb{P}(X \geq 4)$ is the probability that the first four events are all failures, and this is given by
$$\mathbb{P}(X \geq 4) = \left(\frac{3}{5}\right)^4 = 0.1296.$$

(d) The answer can be found using the properties of conditional probability:
$$\mathbb{P}(X \geq 4 | X \geq 2) = \frac{\mathbb{P}(X \geq 4)}{\mathbb{P}(X \geq 2)} = \frac{0.1296}{0.36} = 0.36.$$

Alternatively, once we have seen two failures the probability that we see at least two more is given by $\left(\frac{3}{5}\right)^2 = 0.36$.

Q2. Let X be the number of strawberries scanned before the first small one is found.
(a) The observations are all independent, and so the probability that we see k large strawberries and then a small one is $\mathbb{P}(X = k) = \frac{1}{10}(\frac{9}{10})^k$.
(b) After diverting a small strawberry, two strawberries pass through the scanner without being scanned. Both of these could be small, one could be small or none could be small. The probability that the scanner misses a small strawberry is therefore,
$$\mathbb{P}(X = 0) + \mathbb{P}(X = 1) + \mathbb{P}(X = 2) = 0.1 + 0.09 + 0.081 = 0.271.$$

(c) From our probability distribution we have $\mathbb{P}(X = 1) = 0.09$.
(d) The chance of seeing exactly one more large strawberry given we have already seen three is equal to
$$\mathbb{P}(X = 4 | X \geq 3) = \frac{\mathbb{P}(X = 4)}{\mathbb{P}(X \geq 3)}.$$

We calculate $\mathbb{P}(X = 4) = 0.06561$ and
$$\mathbb{P}(X \geq 3) = 1 - \mathbb{P}(X \leq 2) = 1 - \mathbb{P}(X = 0) - \mathbb{P}(X = 1) - \mathbb{P}(X = 2)$$
$$= 1 - 0.1 - 0.09 - 0.081 = 0.729.$$

Therefore $\mathbb{P}(X = 4 | X \geq 3) = 0.06561/0.729 = 0.09.$

Worked Solutions — Exercise 31.1

Q1. (a) If $H_1 : p < 0.2$ and the critical value is 10, the critical region is $X \leq 10$ and the acceptance region is $X \geq 11$.

Since $7 < 10$, we have sufficient evidence to reject H_0 in favour of H_1.

(b) If $H_1 : p \neq 0.6$ and the critical values are 6 and 14, the critical region is $X \leq 6$, $X \geq 14$ and the acceptance region is $7 \leq X \leq 13$.

Since $7 < 12 < 13$, we have insufficient evidence to reject H_0.

(c) If $H_1 : p > 0.5$ and the critical value is 35, the critical region is $X \geq 35$ and the acceptance region is $X \leq 34$.

Since $45 > 35$, we have sufficient evidence to reject H_0 in favour of H_1.

Q2. (a) $H_0 : p = 0.1$, $H_1 : p > 0.1$. We choose a one-tailed test, since we are specifically interested in testing whether the company has *underestimated* the proportion of their customers that make complaints.

(b) $H_0 : p = 0.2$. There are 5 flavours in each back, so if each of the flavours are represented equally, the probability of picking a sweet of each flavour (e.g. raspberry) is $1/5 = 0.2$. $H_1 : p \neq 0.2$. We simply wish to test whether the claim is true, so we use a two-tailed test.

(c) $H_0 : p = 0.7$, $H_1 : p > 0.7$. We use a one-tailed test, since the gardener's purchase is justified if the success rate *improves*.

Q3. (a) In Q2(a), $n = 50$, $p_0 = 0.1$. We find that:
$P(X \geq 11) = 0.0094 < 0.01$, $P(X \geq 10) = 0.0245 > 0.01$ so the 1% critical region is $X \geq 11$,
$P(X \geq 9) = 0.0579 > 0.05$, so the 5% critical region is $X \geq 10$,
$P(X \geq 8) = 0.1221 > 0.1$, so the 10% critical region is $X \geq 9$.

(b) In Q2(b), $n = 20$, $p_0 = 0.2$. We find that:
$P(X = 0) = 0.0115 > 0.005$, so there is no lower limit for the 1% critical region. $P(X \geq 9) = 0.0100 > 0.005$ and $P(X \geq 10) = 0.0026 < 0.005$, so the 1% critical region is $X \geq 10$.
$P(X \leq 1) = 0.0692 > 0.025$, so the lower part of the 5% critical region is $X = 0$. Given the earlier calculations, and $P(X \geq 8) = 0.0321 > 0.025$, the upper part of the 5% critical region is $X \geq 9$. Hence, the 5% critical region is $X = 0$, $X \geq 9$.
$P(X \geq 7) = 0.0867 > 0.05$, so the 10% critical region is $X = 0$, $X \geq 8$.

(c) In Q2(c), $n = 80$, $p = 0.7$. We find that:
$P(X \geq 65) = 0.0161 > 0.01$, $P(X \geq 66) = 0.0079 < 0.01$, so the 1% critical region is $X \geq 66$.
$P(X \geq 63) = 0.0531 > 0.05$, $P(X \geq 64) = 0.0302 < 0.05$, so the 5% critical region is $X \geq 64$.
$P(X \geq 62) = 0.0873 > 0.1$, $P(X \geq 61) = 0.1352 > 0.1$, so the 10% critical region is $X \geq 62$.

Q4. For this test, we have $n = 30$, $p_0 = 0.3$

(a) The probability of incorrectly rejecting H_0 is the probability that we reject H_0 given that H_0 is true. This is given by $P(X \leq 4 | p_0 = 0.3) = 0.0302$. We obtain a value less than 0.05, the significance level of the test due to the fact that the binomial distribution is discrete. Hence, it is rarely possible to obtain a critical value of X such that the probability of making a type I error is precisely the significance level. Instead, we find the least integer x such that $P(X \leq x | p = p_0) \leq 0.05$.

(b) If we increase the significance level of the test, we increase the size of the critical region. Hence, the new critical value is greater than 4.

(c) Since $3 < 4$ and the critical value for the test at the 10% level is greater than 4, we reject H_0 at both the 5% and 10% levels.

Q5. For this test, $n = 100$, $p_0 = 0.85$.

(a) Since there is only a problem if the amount of defect-free glassware is significantly less than 85%, we use a one-tailed test with
$H_0 : p = 0.85$, $H_1 : p < 0.85$.
Since $P(X \leq 78) = 0.0393$, $P(X \leq 79) = 0.0663$, the critical value of X is 78. Hence, the critical region is $X \leq 78$. The critical region is illustrated below.

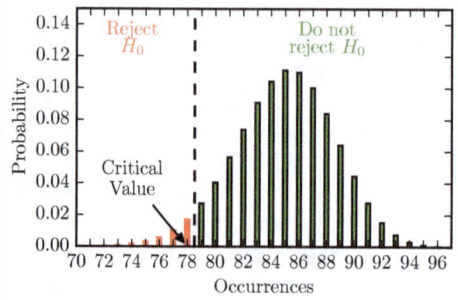

(b) (i) If the test statistic is $X = 79 > 78$, then we have insufficient evidence to reject H_0 at the 5% level. Thus, there is insufficient evidence that the factory is not meeting its quality requirement.

(ii) If the test statistic is $X = 75 < 78$, then we have sufficient evidence to reject H_0 at the 5% level in favour of H_1. Thus, there is sufficient evidence to suggest that the factory is working below the required rate of quality.

Q6. The information in the question gives $n = 1235$, $p_0 = 0.45$ and $X = 495$. Carrying out the five steps for conducting a hypothesis test, we obtain the following.

1) We state the null and alternative hypotheses:

$H_0 : \quad p = 0.45,$
$H_1 : \quad p \neq 0.45.$

We choose a two-tailed test since we simply wish to test whether the true proportion is 0.45.

2) Since each individual in the sample makes a binary choice whether to support the Government or not, we can assume that we are sampling from an underlying binomial population. Since we are testing the proportion in the binomial distribution, the appropriate test statistic is X, where $X \sim \text{Bin}(1235, 0.45)$.

3) As instructed, we choose a significance level of $\alpha = 0.01$. Using a calculator, we find the $P(x \leq 510) = 0.0047$, and $P(x \leq 511) = 0.0056$, so $X_1^{\text{crit}} = 510$.

Also, $P(x \geq 601) = 0.0053$, and $P(x \geq 602) = 0.0045$, so $X_2^{\text{crit}} = 602$. Hence, the critical region is $510 \leq X \leq 602$ and illustrated below.

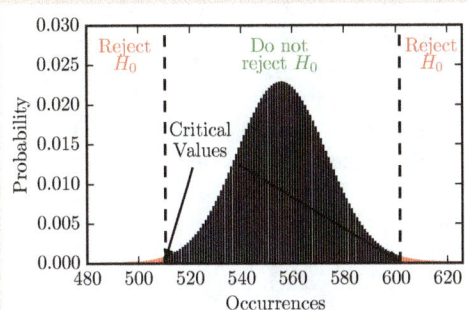

4) We are given that $X = 495$.
5) Since $495 < 521$, the test statistic lies in the *critical region*. Hence, we have sufficient evidence to reject H_0 in favour of H_1. The interpretation is that there is sufficient evidence that the true proportion of people that support the government is *not* 0.45.

Worked Solutions — Exercise 31.2

Q1. Since this is a two-tailed test, we need $np_0 = 150$ to determine whether each value of the test statistic is less than or greater than the most likely value given that $p = p_0$.
  (a) If $X = 145 < 150$, then the p-value is given by $P(X \leq 145) = 0.2293$.
  (b) If $X = 160 > 150$, then the p-value is given by $P(X \geq 160) = 1 - P(X \leq 159) = 0.0579$.
  (c) If $X = 151 > 150$, then the p-value is given by $P(X \geq 151) = 1 - P(X \leq 150) = 0.4729$.
  (d) If $X = 130 < 151$, then the p-value is given by $P(X \leq 130) = 0.0010$.

Q2. (a) If $X = 5$, then the p-value is given by $P(X \geq 5) = 1 - P(X \leq 4) = 0.1036$. Insufficient evidence to reject H_0 at the 10% level.
  (b) If $X = 8$, then the p-value is given by $P(X \geq 8) = 1 - P(X \leq 7) = 0.0032$. Sufficient evidence to reject H_0 in favour of H_1 at the 10% level. In fact, we would even reject at the 1% level.
  (c) If $X = 10$, then the p-value is given by $P(X \geq 10) = 1 - P(X \leq 10) = 0.0002$. Very strong evidence to reject H_0 in favour of H_1 at the 10% level.

Q3. (a) Here, the null and alternative hypotheses are
$H_0 : p = 1/6$, $H_1 : p < 1/6$, where p is the probability of throwing a six. The test statistic is X, the number of sixes thrown, where $X \sim \text{Bin}(24, 1/6)$. The observed value of X is $x = 1$, so the p-value is given by $P(X = 0) + P(X = 1) = 0.0729$.
  (b) Since the test in **(a)** is a one-tailed test and the p-value is $0.0729 > 0.05$, we have insufficient evidence to reject H_0 at the 5% level. In terms of the original problem, we conclude that there is insufficient evidence that the probability of throwing a six is less than $1/6$, and so the die is fair.

(c) If no sixes were thrown in 24 throws, the test statistic is still X, where $X \sim \text{Bin}(24, 1/6)$. The p-value is now given by $P(X = 0) = 0.0126 < 0.05$, so we now have sufficient evidence to reject H_0 at the 5% level. Hence, we have sufficient evidence that the probability of rolling a six is less than $1/6$, so the die is unfair.

(d) If one six is thrown in 50 throws, the sample size has changed. The test statistic is now $X \sim \text{Bin}(50, 1/6)$. The p-value is given by $P(X = 0) + P(X = 1) = 0.0011$. Since $0.0011 < 0.05$, we have substantial evidence against to reject H_0 at the 5% level. Note that we also reject H_0 at the 1% level in this case. Hence, there is substantial evidence that the die is unfair.

Q4. (a) The women must be chosen randomly so that a binomial probability model can be used. The women must also be independent of each other.

(b) Each woman sampled either did or did not wait for more than 20 minutes for their scan. We can consider one of the two outcomes as a "success" and the other as a "failure", so assuming an underlying binomial distribution is appropriate here.

(c) The null hypothesis is $H_0 : p = 0.25$, where p is the probability that the waiting time is more than 20 minutes. Since the midwife is investigating whether the true proportion of women waiting for more than 20 minutes is more than $\frac{1}{4}$, the alternative hypothesis is $H_1 : p > 0.25$.

(d) Since the sample size is 30, the test statistic is X, the number of women who wait for more than 20 minutes, where $X \sim \text{Bin}(30, 0.25)$. Since the test is one-tailed and the observed value of X is $x = 15$, the p-value is $P(X \geq 15) = 0.0002$. Since 0.0002 is very small, we have substantial evidence to reject H_0, even if we choose a significance level as small as 0.1%. Hence, the midwife has substantial evidence that the proportion of women that wait for more than 20 minutes for their scan is higher than 1 in 4.

Q5. (a) Since the customer believes that the proportion of winning cereal boxes *decreases* over time, the null and alternative hypotheses are
$H_0 : p = 0.1$, $H_1 : p < 0.1$, where p is the proportion of cereal boxes containing a prize.

(b) If value of the test statistic $X = k$ leads the customer to reject H_0 in favour of H_1, then k must satisfy $P(X < k) < 0.05$, assuming $X \sim \text{Bin}(60, 0.1)$. Furthermore, if $X = k+1$ causes the customer to not reject H_0, then k must also satisfy $P(X < k+1) > 0.05$. We find that $P(X \leq 1) = 0.0138 < 0.05$ and $P(X \leq 2) = 0.0530 > 0.05$. Hence, $k = 1$.

Q6. In this case, the null hypothesis is $H_0 : p = 0.6$, where p is the proportion of customers that visit the website and make a purchase. Since the member of the sales team believes that the proportion is less than 0.6, the alternative hypothesis is $H_1 : p < 0.6$. Since the sample size is 40, the test statistic is X, the number of customers who visit the website and make a purchase, where $X \sim \text{Bin}(40, 0.6)$. Since the test is one-tailed, the p-value is $P(X \leq 21) = 0.2089$. Since $0.2089 > 0.1$, there is insufficient evidence to reject H_0, even at the 10% level. Hence, the member of the sales team has insufficient evidence to dispute the marketing manager's claim.

Q7. (a) The null hypothesis is $H_0 : p = 0.85$, where p is the proportion of patients for whom the drug is successful. The junior doctor believes that the true proportion is less than 0.85, so the alternative hypothesis is $H_1: p < 0.85$. We assume an underlying binomial distribution. Since the sample size is 50, the test statistic is X, the number of patients for whom the drug is successful, where $X \sim \text{Bin}(50, 0.85)$. Since the test is one-tailed, and the observed value of X is $x = 38$, the p-value is given by $P(X \leq 38) = 0.0628$. Since $0.0628 > 0.05$, there is insufficient evidence to reject H_0 at the 5% significance level. Hence, the junior doctor has insufficient evidence to dispute the pharmaceutical company's claim.

(b) The null hypothesis is again $H_0: p = 0.85$, where p has the same definition as in (a). Since the rival company desires to show that their drug has a higher success rate than the first company, the alternative hypothesis is $H_1: p > 0.85$. Since the sample size is 25, the test statistic is X, the number of patients for whom the drug is successful, where $X \sim \text{Bin}(25, 0.85)$. Since the test is one-tailed, and the observed value of X is $x = 24$, the p-value is given by $P(X \geq 24) = 0.0931$. Since $0.0931 < 0.1$, we have sufficient evidence to reject H_0 at the 10% level. Hence, the rival company has sufficient evidence to conclude that their drug has a higher success rate than that of the first company.

(c) The test in (a) is reliable, since a large sample size was used, with a low enough significance level that we are unlikely to incorrectly reject H_0.

The test in (b) is unreliable, since the sample size is relatively small. Furthermore, the significance level is high, so it is likely that we could incorrectly reject H_0. Even at the 10% level, there is very weak evidence to reject H_0, since 0.0931 is very close in value to 0.1. We should also note that, were we to conduct a two-tailed test at the 10% level, we would conclude that there is insufficient evidence that the true success rate is not 0.85 (since $0.0931 > 0.05$). Thus, in reality there is little evidence that the rival company's drug is more effective than the original drug.

Q8. The fact that the company has 300 buses in its fleet is not relevant when conducting the hypothesis test. The null hypothesis is $H_0: p = 0.2$, where p is the proportion of buses that fail to meet the pollution control guidelines. Since the company is interested in whether there is evidence that the true proportion of non-compliant buses is more than 0.2, the alternative hypothesis is $p > 0.2$. Since the sample size is 22, the test statistic is X, the number of non-compliant buses, where $X \sim \text{Bin}(22, 0.2)$. Since the test is one-tailed, and the observed value of X is $x = 7$, the p-value is 0.1330. Since $0.1330 > 0.1$, we have insufficient evidence to reject H_0, even at the 10% level. Thus, there is insufficient evidence that more than 20% of the bus company's fleet is not compliant with pollution guidelines.

Q9. Since we just want to test whether the claim is accurate or not, the null and alternative hypotheses are
$H_0: p = 0.6$, $H_1: p \neq 0.6$, where p is the proportion of branded products that are cheaper in the supermarket than their competitors.
According to the null hypothesis the test statistic is sampled from a binomial distribution such that, $X \sim \text{Bin}(65, 0.6)$. The most likely value of X is $np = 39$. The p-value for the observed value of $X = 44 > 39$ is given by $P(X \geq 44) = 0.1266$. Since $0.1266 < 0.1$, we have insufficient evidence to reject H_0, so conclude that there is little reason to doubt the supermarket's claim based on this data.

Q10. The null and alternative hypotheses are
$H_0: p = 0.5$, $H_1: p > 0.5$, where p is the proportion of coin tosses that land on heads.

(a) (i) If the coin is tossed a total of 9 times and lands on heads *more than twice* as often as tails, it lands on heads at least 7 times. According to the null hypothesis, the test statistic is $X \sim \text{Bin}(9, 0.5)$. The largest possible p-value is given by the p-value for $X = 7$, which is given by $P(x \geq 7) = 1 - P(X \leq 6) = 0.0898$. Since $0.0898 > 0.05$, there is insufficient evidence to reject H_0 at the 5% level, and there is insufficient evidence that the coin is biased towards heads.

(ii) If the coin is tossed a total of 21 times, following the same reasoning as in (i), the coin lands on heads at least 15 times. This time, the null hypothesis gives $X \sim \text{Bin}(21, 0.5)$. The largest possible p-value is $P(X \geq 15) = 1 - P(x \leq 14) = 0.0392$. Since $0.0392 < 0.05$, there is sufficient evidence to reject H_0 at the 5% level in favour of H_1, and there is sufficient evidence that the coin is biased towards heads.

(b) Since the total number of coin tosses, n, is discrete, and the number of times it lands on heads, H is twice the amount of time it lands on tails, T, n must be a multiple of 3 in order to be minimal. If n is known, then

$$H = \frac{2}{3}n + 1, \quad T = n - H = \frac{1}{3}n - 1.$$

We know that we no not reject H_0 for $n = 9$ and reject for $n = 21$. Checking the multiples of 3 between $n = 9$ and $n = 21$ gives:
$n = 12$, $H = 9$, $P(X \geq 9) = 0.0730 > 0.05$,
$n = 15$, $H = 11$, $P(X \geq 11) = 0.0592 > 0.05$,
$n = 18$, $H = 13$, $P(X \geq 13) = 0.04813 < 0.05$. Hence, the minimum number of coin tosses is 18.

www.ingramcontent.com/pod-product-compliance
Lightning Source LLC
Chambersburg PA
CBHW082314230426
43667CB00034B/2721